John Adams

A New Collection of Voyages, Discoveries and Travels

Containing whatever is worthy of notice, in Europe, Asia, Africa and America: in respect to the situation and extent of empires, kingdoms, and provinces; their climates, soil, produce

John Adams

A New Collection of Voyages, Discoveries and Travels
Containing whatever is worthy of notice, in Europe, Asia, Africa and America: in respect to the situation and extent of empires, kingdoms, and provinces; their climates, soil, produce

ISBN/EAN: 9783744794176

Printed in Europe, USA, Canada, Australia, Japan

Cover: Foto ©Andreas Hilbeck / pixelio.de

More available books at **www.hansebooks.com**

A NEW
COLLECTION
OF
VOYAGES,
DISCOVERIES and TRAVELS:

CONTAINING

Whatever is worthy of Notice, in

EUROPE, ASIA,

AFRICA and AMERICA:

IN RESPECT TO

The Situation and Extent of Empires, Kingdoms, and Provinces; their Climates, Soil, Produce, &c.

WITH

The Manners and Cuſtoms of the ſeveral Inhabitants; their Government, Religion, Arts, Sciences, Manufactures, and Commerce.

The whole conſiſting of ſuch ENGLISH and FOREIGN Authors as are in moſt Eſteem; including the Deſcriptions and Remarks of ſome celebrated late Travellers, not to be found in any other Collection.

Illuſtrated with a Variety of accurate

MAPS, PLANS, and elegant ENGRAVINGS.

VOL. IV.

LONDON:

Printed for J. KNOX, near Southampton-Street, in the Strand. MDCCLXVII.

CONTENTS

OF THE

FOURTH VOLUME.

A com-

CONTENTS.

TRA-

A
COLLECTION
OF
VOYAGES AND TRAVELS.

HAVING gone through the preceding Collection of Voyages in as ample a manner as our limits would admit, in which we hope our selection and method will meet the approbation of our readers; we here enter on our second department, which is to consist of the most modern and authentic travels. The objects now before us for description, are Europe, Africa, and Asia; which all together compose a continent so amazingly extensive in a collective view, and so full of materials for observation on a separate one, that there is no small degree of embarrassment in the consideration where to begin. The most natural method, to avoid confusion, appears to be to commence with the northern extremity of Europe, and from thence to proceed southward and eastward. According to this plan, though we are to enter first on very unhospitable tracks; yet will the descriptions they furnish, and the rude manners of the chilled inhabitants, not be altogether void of entertainment to the speculative reader. However, there will at least be this satisfaction resulting, that our scenes will improve upon us; as we shall soon arrive at milder climates, inhabited by more populous and civilized nations.

TRAVELS

THROUGH THE

Moſt NORTHERN Parts of EUROPE,

Particularly NORWAY; DANISH, SWEDISH, and MUSCOVITE LAPLAND; BORANDIA; SAMOJEDIA; ZEMBLA; and ICELAND.

Extracted from the JOURNAL of a Gentleman employed by the NORTH SEA COMPANY of COPENHAGEN to make DISCOVERIES.

FREDERIC III. king of Denmark, being deſirous of advancing the trade of his kingdom, eſtabliſhed two companies of merchants at Copenhagen, his capital; the one an Iceland company, and the other a company of traders to the north. The latter having obſerved that the trade to Norway was very beneficial, preſented a petition to his Daniſh majeſty, in February 1653, repreſenting that great profit would ariſe to his ſubjects by making farther diſcoveries to the north, whence ſeveral valuable merchandizes might be imported; his majeſty readily granted their requeſt, and allowed them to extend their commerce as far northward as they thought proper; upon which they fitted out ſeveral ſhips for that purpoſe.

A French gentleman, who happened to be at Copenhagen when one of the northern fleets was outward-bound, and being informed that the king had commanded thoſe concerned in this enterprize, to make

make all poſſible diſcoveries of the countries to which they came, he procured himſelf to be recommended to go ſurgeon of one of the ſhips. Having given this introduction, we ſhall proceed as near as poſſible in the gentleman's own words.

We embarked, ſays our author, in the beginning of April, 1653, weighed anchor, and ſet ſail from Copenhagen with two ſhips in our company. We ſoon arrived at Kat-gat, a ſtreight which divides the German from the Baltic Sea. This is a dangerous paſſage, full of rocks, extending about forty leagues from Elſinore to Schagerhort.

When we arrived a-breaſt of Mailſtrand, a ſmall ſea-port town thirty leagues from Copenhagen, the wind drove us back ten leagues, and forced us into a creek called Schalot, where we caſt anchor, and rode ſafe under the caſtle, which looked rather like a heap of ruins than a place inhabited, and is only famous for its promontory, which is well known to all the mariners who uſe the Baltic. Here we ſtaid three days, when the wind ſhifting again to the eaſtward, we proceeded on our voyage; and after a few days ſailing had ſight of Chriſtianſand in Norway, a promontory that takes its name from a ſmall village at its foot, where there is a commodious port. Our ſtay here was very ſhort: for the next day we proceeded to Chriſtiana or Obſlo, the capital of one of the five governments of that kingdom.

As ſoon as we were got into port, we went aſhore to deliver our letters to the company's agents, who gave us a very cordial reception. One of them hearing I was a ſtranger, and had been recommended by one of their ſociety, behaved to me with great civility; ſhewed me every thing worth ſeeing, and commanded one of his ſervants, who ſpoke French, to attend me in a ſhort excurſion, three or four miles up into the country. Early the next morning we took horſe, and rode to a large village named

Wiſby, the capital of Gothland, where the famous marine laws were made, nine miles from Chriſtiana. The houſes are here built of wood, and covered with turf; they are very low, without either iron-work or windows, except a lattice on the top to admit the light.

The peaſants of Norway are remarkable for their ſimplicity and hoſpitality. The women, who are very handſome, though red-haired, are fond of ſtrangers, and look after the cattle, of which there is here great plenty: they are alſo excellent houſe-wives, and in general make their own family-cloth. The country affords excellent game.

When we were returning towards Chriſtiana, we met one of the neighbouring gentlemen, followed by two ſervants and a pack of dogs going to hunt the elk; who, knowing the man that was with me, invited us both to partake of his diverſion. After we had rode about a mile we met his huntſman with more of his ſervants, and ten or twelve of the peaſants, who led us three miles farther to a wood full of buſhes, at the entrance of which we diſmounted, and gave our horſes to one of his domeſtics. Preparations had been made for the chace the day before by the gentleman's vaſſals. We were ſcarce forty yards within the wood before we perceived an elk, who inſtantly dropped, being ſeized, as they told me, with the falling ſickneſs, whence they derive the name of elk, which ſignifies a miſerable creature; and it ſeems that they often fall in this manner at the beginning of the chace. Had not this accident happened, I believe it would have been hard for us to have brought him down, as I perceived ſoon after, when we had rouſed another, which we chaced above two hours, and ſhould never have been able to have taken him, had he not alſo dropped down dead. He killed three of the beſt dogs with his fore-feet, and the gentleman being extremely ſorry for their loſs, would

would hunt no more; but ſent to a farm of his a mile off, for a cart to carry the game we had caught to his caſtle, and inſiſted on our going home with him, where he treated us in a very ſplendid manner. This Caſtle was an odd ſort of building, and like the reſt in that country, void of elegance or taſte.

The elk is as big as a large horſe, and his body like a ſtag's, but larger and longer; his legs are alſo long, his feet broad and cloven, his antlers large, hairy, and broad like a fallow deer's, but he is not ſo well furniſhed with horns as a ſtag.

At my departure, the lord of the caſtle made me a preſent of the two left ſhanks of the elks we had killed, or rather ſeen die of themſelves, letting me know that this was no ſmall favour, they being an excellent cure for the falling ſickneſs. To which I replied by my interpreter, that I wondered, ſince the foot of an elk had ſuch virtue in it, why the animal, that always carried it about with him, did not cure himſelf. The gentleman reflecting on what I had ſaid, laughed out aloud, and told me I was in the right, for he had given it to ſeveral perſons afflicted with the ſame diſeaſe, without its producing a cure; upon which he had long ſuſpected that the pretended virtue of the elk's foot was a vulgar miſtake, of which he no more doubted, than that the eating of the fleſh of the beaſt infected people with their diſtempers. He then gave me many inſtances of the ill effects produced on human bodies by eating the fleſh of elks.

The gentleman obliged us to ſpend the night with him, and having entertained us in a plentiful and agreeable manner, we took our leaves of him early the next morning, and returned to Chriſtiana, where we ſtaid four or five days, and then weighing anchor, ſailed for Berghen; but being becalmed in our paſſage for five days, we employed ourſelves in catching fiſh, of which we caught ſuch a quantity, that we kept Lent a long while after.

Berghen, the capital of the province of the same name in Norway, has one of the finest ports in Europe. It is a large trading town full of merchants, and was formerly an archbishoprick; but it has not been acknowleged such since the reformation. The archbishop's palace was given to the Hans towns, for their ancient merchants to live in, and the greatest part of the houses were turned into warehouses, which still bear the name of cloisters, and the merchants are called monks, though they do not wear a cowl, nor observe the rules of any order. The king has, however, obliged them so far, to keep up the form of a religious house, that none of the merchants who live in it are allowed to marry without removing. The principal branch of trade carried on at Berghen, are herrings, cod, and stock-fish, for which there is a great vent in Muscovy, Sweden, Poland, Denmark, Germany, Holland, and other parts of Europe.

As soon as we had discharged the cargo we had to deliver at Berghen, we set sail with a south-west wind for Drontheim, half our lading being consigned to the surveyor of the copper and silver mines, for the use of the miners and other workmen; it consisting principally of bread and beer: but being several days becalmed, we again caught a great quantity of klip-fish, a great part of which we salted and barrelled. They are a kind of cod, bigger than those of Newfoundland, and obtain the name of klip-fish from their never leaving the rocks; klippe, in the German tongue, signifying a rock.

On our arrival at Drontheim, we applied to the surveyor to unlade our ships as fast as possible, that we might pursue our voyage; but he told us, he could not begin till the officer, who was to receive their provisions, came back from the mines, and offered to send a messenger for him, whom I got leave to accompany. Early the next morning the surveyor's man and I mounted on horseback, and began this journey; but the roads were ſo very rugged that we could reach only eighteen miles from Drontheim: for the night came on, and we had a long wood to paſs through, in which were wolves, lynxes and boars in great numbers, that render travelling in the dark very dangerous. The next night we arrived at our journey's end, and lodged at the forges; where, according to the cuſtom of the country, we were entertained by the people who have the care of the mines, with tobacco, beer, and brandy: and our hoſt believing that we would not think ourſelves welcome unleſs we were made drunk, plied us ſo faſt with bumpers, that there was no avoiding a debauch. I here became acquainted with one of the officers of the mines who ſpoke French, and promiſed, on my expreſſing a deſire to go down into one of them, to gratify my curioſity.

Having breakfaſted with the perſon who ſpoke French, and the maſter miner, they went with me fifty or ſixty paces from the forges, which are upon an high mountain, to the mouth of one of the mines, over which was erected a machine reſembling a crane, turned by two men in two great wheels to draw up the ore; and the maſter and I being fixed in a wooden bucket, were let down above fifty fathoms. Never did I ſee a more horrid proſpect, or what appeared a truer picture of the infernal regions. Nothing was to be ſeen all around but rugged caverns, flames of fire, and creatures that appeared to have a nearer reſemblance to fiends than to men. They were dreſſed in black leathern jackets, with leathern mufflers about their heads, juſt under their eyes, reaching down to the breaſt, and had leathern aprons These miners have all different employments. Some uſe the chiſſel and ſome the hatchet, to knock out the copper ſtones: others ſearch for new veins of metal, and others try to diſcover caverns filled with water, which ſometimes unexpectedly burſt forth, and drown thoſe in the mines. The maſter miner who deſcended with me, perceiving I was afraid, and that I was taken with a cold fit, rung a bell, which being a ſignal for the people above to draw us up, we ſoon aſcended with the ſame eaſe with which we had gone down.

We went to the houſe of the officer who ſpoke French, and were entertained in a very handſome manner: after dinner that gentleman ordered horſes to be got ready to take me to the ſilver mines, and the maſter miner accompanied us. Having introduced me to the ſurveyor, we were each of us preſented with a large glaſs of brandy, and then treated with beer and tobacco. When we had ſmoaked and drank as much as the ſurveyor thought fit, he conducted us to the forges, which were about a mile from his houſe. Theſe mines turn to a very good account, and are not the leaſt part of his Daniſh majeſty's revenue. We ſoon after reached the mouth of a mine, down which we went in the ſame manner as at the copper mine. Theſe miners are cloathed like the others, and their work and habitatations are much the ſame. The miners both in the one and the other never work in winter. In ſpring and autumn they only labour three hours in the forenoon, and three after dinner; but in ſummer they work four hours in the morning, and five in the afternoon. The reſt of their time they ſpend in mirth and feaſting. They delight much in dancing, and have their hautboys, violins, and other inſtruments for that purpoſe. This merry life they are able to ſupport, being paid a crown a day all the year round. On my return to the copper forges, I found the people at their ſports, and was not a little pleaſed to ſee the variety of their humours and paſtimes.

Having ſeen every thing worth notice at the mines, the ſurveyor took us home with him, and treated us with the uſual collation of brandy, beer, and tobacco: we afterward partook of a good ſupper, and when we had ſufficiently refreſhed ourſelves, went to bed.

In

In the morning the maſter miner and I, after a plentiful breakfaſt, took leave of the ſurveyor, and rode back to the copper mines, where having thanked the officer who ſpoke French for his civilities, the maſter miner and I ſet out for Drontheim.

In two days after my return, the ſhip having taken in her ſtock of proviſions and other neceſſaries, ſet ſail with a fair wind, to continue our voyage to the north; but after a few days we were becalmed under the arctic circle, and ſome of our crew being ſo ſuperſtitious as to give credit to the opinion, that the inhabitants of the neighbouring coaſt, like thoſe of Finland, could rule the elements, and diſpoſe of the winds at their pleaſure, our captain ſent his boat aſhore with the mate to purchaſe a wind of them, that being the commodity he moſt ſtood in need of, and though I believed nothing of the matter, I had the curioſity to accompany thoſe employed in this ridiculous commiſſion.

We landed at the firſt village we came to, and as the mate could ſpeak enough of the language to make himſelf underſtood, he ſoon found out the chief necromancer, told him what he wanted, and aſked if he could furniſh us with a wind that would laſt till we arrived at Mourmanſkeimore: to this the necromancer gravely replied, that he could not, for that his power extended no farther than the promontory of Rouxella. The mate conſidering it was a great way thither, and that if we reached ſo far, we might eaſily make the north cape, deſired him to go on board with us, and drive a bargain with the captain: to this the wizard conſenting, took three of his comrades with him, and leaping into a ſmall fiſhing-boat, went aboard our ſhip, where the captain and he ſoon agreed upon the price, and he was paid ten kroners, which is about five or ſix and thirty ſhillings ſterling, and a pound of tobacco. When the bargain was concluded and the money paid, the wizard tied a woollen rag, about half a yard long and a

nail

nail broad, to the fore-maſt. This rag, which had three knots, was all the captain had for his money; and the necromancer immediately returned in the fiſhing-boat to the village with his companions.

He had not been gone long when the captain, according to the inſtructions he had received, untied the firſt knot in the rag, and ſoon after a briſk gale ſprung up from the weſt ſouth-weſt, which drove us and the other ſhips in our company thirty leagues beyond Maelſtroom, a whirlpool in the Norwegian ſea, that has proved fatal to many veſſels. For this reaſon ſuch as are acquainted with thoſe coaſts, keep eight or ten leagues out to ſea, to avoid both that and ſeveral other eddies, as well as the rocks that lie off Oſtraford.

The wind beginning now to ſhift a little to the northward, the captain untied the ſecond knot, and the wind continued till we reached the cape of Rouxella. After we had paſſed that promontory, the needle of our compaſs turned back half an inch, from which ſome fancied that there was a loadſtone in the mountain. However, if we had not had a very expert pilot we ſhould certainly have loſt our courſe. He ſhut up the compaſs, and knowing that the other ſhips in our company were in the ſame trouble as ourſelves, hung out a flag on the fore-top-maſt head, as a ſignal for the ſhips to follow us. We were two days and nights in this dangerous ſituation, having nothing to depend upon but the pilot's experience; but on the third day, when we were at a conſiderable diſtance from the mountains of Rouxella, the needle again pointed to the north, whence we concluded that we drew near the north cape.

By this time the wind failing us, our captain untied the third knot, and ſoon after a moſt dreadful tempeſt blew from the north north eaſt, upon which we were obliged to take in all our ſails and drive before the wind under our bare poles, expecting every minute to go to the bottom; dreading leſt

this

this ſhould be a judgment inflicted upon us for our infernal commerce. However, on the 4th day the ſtorm ceaſed, when we were under great concern at our having loſt ſight of the other veſſels, which we feared were by this time loſt: but having a favourable gale, we continued our courſe, reſolving to make the firſt port in order to refit.

With reſpect to the ſale of winds, for which theſe northern people are very famous, it is neceſſary to obſerve, that like all other ſpecies of witchcraft and necromancy, it is no more than mere fraud and impoſture. Thoſe who deal in it ſtudy the weather, and from conſtant obſervation, are liable to judge of the variation of winds for ſeveral days to come, and take care to ſtart ſo many difficulties in making their bargains, that they are ſure never to come to a concluſion, till the ſigns appear by which they are morally certain that thoſe winds will blow, which they pretend to ſell. When our ſuppoſed conjuror affirmed that his power reached no farther than Rouxella, it ought to be underſtood, that he well knew by experience that cape to be the limit of his obſervations, and that he ſhould riſk his credit, if he preſumed to exceed his bounds. This account we have received from ſome intelligent perſons who reſided a while in Iceland, where the people are the moſt famous for this kind of traffic, and they ſell them with leſs limitation, becauſe living in an iſland, they are more able to judge of the variation of winds in all the ſeas round about them. This ſpecies of knowlege is confined among a few people, who by this means keep their neighbours in ſubjection, and put foreigners under tribute: nor are theſe ſtrange notions much to be wondered at in a barbarous country, where religion is at a very low ebb, and learning has not improved the mind.

The coaſts of the ſea all over the north are ſo full of rocks, that the ports and creeks are almoſt inacceſſible, and we were obliged to ſail two days longer before

before we could make a proper port. However, we at length reached the coast of Wardhuys, the chief town of Danish Lapland, where there is a castle, with a garrison of two companies of soldiers, belonging to the king of Denmark, and a collector to receive the duties imposed on foreigners trading to or from Archangel. We then sailed to Varanger, and cast anchor half a league from the town, when the captain being impatient till he found a place where we might refit, and being desirous of obtaining some information in relation to trade, ordered out the long-boat, and taking with him eight men well armed, rowed toward the town, where he arrived in about half an hour. Varanger is a populous town and a convenient port, but so little frequented, that the inhabitants, amazed at seeing them, gave them small encouragement for trade, but offered their assistance to refit the ship.

The captain having observed the commodiousness of the harbour, returned with the boat, upon which we weighed anchor, and entered the port; when we unladed the cargo, which consisted of bales of cloth, and rolls of tobacco, with which we designed to have traded. These goods were locked up in a house near the shore, and a watch set to guard them. To some of the principal inhabitants we presented bits of roll tobacco, which they valuing more than gold, it secured their friendship, and in return, they treated us with the best they had, particularly with dry fish, which serves them instead of bread; the flesh of rain-deer, which I did not think very palatable; bear's flesh, and that of other wild beasts, of which we had no knowlege. They also treated us with fresh fish, boiled without salt, and served up either with the oil of other fish, or a sour liquor that is highly esteemed by them. We could not, however, bear them company in their repasts, and their dainties not suiting our taste, we sent for provisions from the ship, the chief of which was salt

beef

beef and biſcuits; but when we offered ſome of it to the Laplanders, we found that our food was as diſagreeable to them as theirs was to us.

The religion of Lapland is Lutheraniſm; but they are ſo ſuperſtitious, that if in the morning they meet a beaſt in their way whoſe appearance is eſteemed ominous, they return home and do not ſtir out again all that day; and when they go a fiſhing, if they take but one fiſh in the firſt draught, they think it an ill omen, pack up their nets, and leave work for that time.

Both the men and women are of a low ſtature, but are ſtrong and active. Their faces are broad and flat, and particularly their noſes. Their eyes are ſmall like a hog's, and their eye-lids in general make them look as if they were blear-eyed. There are of a ſwarthy complexion, and are of a rude uncivilized and laſcivious diſpoſition; eſpecially the women, who readily proſtitute themſelves to all comers, if they can do it without the knowlege of their huſbands.

The men are cloathed in rain-deer ſkins, with the hair outward; their coats are ſhort and reach down to the middle of their thighs: but their breeches and ſtockings are of the ſame materials, with their hair outward; but over theſe ſome of them wear a kind of boots made of fiſh ſkin, which, though rough and coarſe, are ſtitched ſo neatly, that the ſeams are hardly to be ſeen. Their bonnets are alſo made of rein-deer ſkins, with the hair outward, but are edged with a ſtrip of either grey or white fox ſkin. Their caps are like thoſe of the Norwegian women, and are made of coarſe canvas, and their hair is twiſted up in two rolls, that hang down on each ſhoulder. Some of them wear a ſort of ruff eight fingers broad, which they tie behind. Their ſhoes are of fiſh ſkins with the ſcales on, and ſomewhat reſemble the wooden ſhoes worn by the peaſants in France.

Their houſes reſemble thoſe of the boors about Chriſtiana. They have no light but what enters by

a hole

a hole at the top of the hut, and do not make uſe of beds any more than the other Laplanders. The whole family, as the maſter, miſtreſs, children, and men and maid ſervants, lie down together promiſcuouſly, upon bear ſkins ſpread in the middle of the room, which, when they riſe in the morning, are taken up and laid by, till they are wanted again at night. In every houſe there is a great black cat which they highly value. The Laplanders talk to it as if it was a reaſonable creature: and in parties of fiſhing or hunting it follows the people like a dog.

We unladed the ſhip the day after our arrival, and the inhabitants helped us to haul her aſhore, when the captain finding that ſhe was more damaged than he expected, deſired the Laplanders to provide him timber to refit her, to which they readily agreed, and the crew went to a neighbouring mountain to fell it.

As we found that the ſhip would be ſome time in refitting, our ſupercargo thought it would not be improper to take a journey into the country, to try whether any trade could be carried on with the peaſants there; and for this purpoſe took me with two more of the ſhip's company, to attend him.

Early the next morning, which was the 12th of May, we ſet out, taking with us ſome cloth and tobacco to trade with, and ſalt beef and pork for proviſions; having engaged three of the inhabitants of Varanger to attend us, both to ſhew us the way, and to help to carry our goods and proviſions to the next village. We followed them through the woods, mountains, and valleys without meeting any living creature, till about four o'clock in the afternoon, when we perceived two white bears of a prodigious ſize approach; but they ſoon fled away ſo faſt, that they were preſently out of ſight.

As we were deſcending a mountain an hour before night, we perceived at the foot of it a dozen houſes at a conſiderable diſtance from each other, and a little

beyond

beyond them a herd of beaſts like ſtags, which our guides told us were rein-deer. On our arrival at the village, our guides conducted us to a hut, when being very weary, we were glad to reſt ourſelves, for we had made a long journey in a very bad way, with our luggage at our backs, which tired and encumbered us. We preſented our hoſt with a piece of roll tobacco, and he received it with extraordinary joy; aſſuring us, he had not had ſo valuable a preſent in nine months before: in return he brought out his brandy bottle, ſome rein-deer's fleſh dreſſed without ſalting, and ſome dried fiſh, which we gave to our guides, and ſupped ourſelves upon the proviſions we had brought with us; after which we went to ſleep upon bear's ſkins, after the faſhion of the country.

In the morning we aſked our hoſt if he had nothing to barter with us for cloth and tobacco, to which he anſwered that he had ſome wolf, fox, and white ſquirrel ſkins, and that his neighbours had ſome of the ſame commodities, and would gladly exchange with us. We bid him, by our interpreters, bring out his ſkins, and if he had any cloaths made of rein deer ſkins, we would deal with him for four ſuits, which we wanted to keep us warm; according he brought forth his merchandize, which we bought, and paid him part in tobacco and part in cloth. We alſo trucked with his neighbours as long as they had any thing worth buying, and then deſired our hoſt to lend us ſome rein-deer to carry us further up the country, to which he readily conſented; and taking-down a horn that hung up in his cottage, went out and blew it, upon which fourteen or fifteen of thoſe animals came running toward the hut, ſix of whom he immediately yoked to ſix ſledges. In one of them we put our merchandize and proviſions, another we aſſigned to one of our guides, who underſtood the language of the Muſcovite Laplanders, and that of the Kilops, diſmiſſing the two other inhabitants of Varanger, after having firſt paid them in tobacco for their trouble. We then put on our Lapland cloaths, and each of us lying down in his ſledge, was covered with a bear's ſkin. At the back of the ſledge were two girths made of rein-deer's ſkin leather, in which we thruſt our arms up to the ſhoulders to keep ourſelves ſteady, and we had each a ſtick with a ſtrong ferrel to it to ſupport the ſledge, if it ſhould be in danger of overturning againſt the ſtumps of trees, or ſtones lying in the way. We were no ſooner ready to ſet out, than our hoſt muttered ſome words in the ear of the rein-deer; and when I afterward enquired of our guide what he meant by it, he gravely replied with the utmoſt ſimplicity, that it was to tell them whither they ſhould carry us. However, cuſtom had made this muttering ſo familiar to them, that when our hoſt had gone to all the ſix, they ſet off with an amazing ſwiftneſs, and continued their pace over hills and dales without keeping any beaten path, till ſeven o'clock in the evening; when they brought us up to a large village ſituated between two mountains, on the borders of a great lake. Stopping at the fourth houſe in the place, and beating the ground with their feet, the maſter of the houſe came with ſome of his ſervants to take us out of the ſledges, and unharneſs our cattle: one of them brought out ſome brandy, of which he gave each of us a brimmer; our guide having informed him, that we were frightened at being drawn ſo ſwiftly by theſe animals, not being uſed to that way of travelling.

The rein-deer is of the colour of the ſtag, and is not much bigger. The horns of this animal are ſomewhat higher than thoſe of the ſtag, but more crooked, hairy, and not ſo well furniſhed with branches. They have cloven feet like theirs, but they are as big as the hoofs of oxen. Of the milk of the females the Laplanders make good butter and cheese.

When we got out of our ſledges, our hoſt conducted us into his hut, which, like the beſt of the cottages in the place, was very little, low, and covered with the bark of trees, the light entering into it at a hole in the top. We gave our hoſt a piece of our roll tobacco about two inches long, with which he was highly pleaſed, and in the moſt hearty manner returned us his thanks. We alſo gave a piece not quite ſo long to each of the inhabitants of the place to make them our friends, and the better to ſecure ourſelves againſt their attempts; for they ſeemed more uncivilized than thoſe we laſt dealt with. After ſupper we lay down on bear ſkins, to take our reſt, having firſt exchanged with our hoſt, our Lapland habits, for thoſe that were longer; and a parcel of tobacco, for the ſkins of one hundred grey ſquirrels, a furr much eſteemed in Denmark and other parts of Europe.

The next day our hoſt, at our deſire, provided us with ſledges to go farther into the country, and the other inhabitants of the village came to ſee us depart; bringing brandy with them to drink to us at our taking leave of them: when our hoſt having performed the ſame ceremony of muttering in the ears of the ſix rein-deer, they ſet off, and we were drawn with the ſame ſwiftneſs as before. We came to no place that was inhabited till about three in the afternoon, when we arrived at a village, in which were eight cottages built on a high mountain by a wood ſide; where our cattle ſtopped, by which we gueſſed that there were ſome inhabitants: but finding that nobody came to us, we baited our rein-deer with moſs, which grew there very plentifully, and refreſhed ourſelves with ſalt beef and biſcuit; while our interpreter regaled himſelf upon ſome rein-deer veniſon and dried fiſh; all of us making merry with the brandy we had given us in the laſt village.

We ſtaid in this place near an hour, and this being the uſual ſtage, the rein-deer had no inclination to quit it; in order to induce them to move, our guide uſed many ridiculous and ſuperſtitious ceremonies. He went alone into the wood, and coming out again, muttered ſome words in the ears of theſe animals, which, whether they underſtood or not, had but little effect on them, till he had played this farce over four or five times, when they began to proceed, though not ſo ſwiftly as before. We then aſked him why we ſaw nobody in the village; to which he replied, that it was a very common thing in that country, theſe dwellings belonging to the Kilops, a nation of Laplanders who often change their habitations, fly from ſtrangers, and ſubſiſt only upon what they get by hunting. We now deſcended the mountain, and about nine o'clock diſcovered four Kilops at a ſmall diſtance, returning from hunting in ſledges drawn by rein-deer, but they turned aſide, and took another way to avoid us. In leſs than half an hour after we entered a long wood, in which we heard terrible howlings, but ſaw no beaſt of prey. When we had paſſed the wood we had another mountain to deſcend, at the bottom of which we obſerved a village. Thither our cattle carried us, and ſtopping, beat their feet before a cottage, at which the maſter made his appearance, and we having ſollicited his friendſhip with a piece of tobacco, he made us welcome: we ſupped on our proviſion, and then laid down to reſt on our bear ſkins, being ſufficiently tired with our journey.

The next morning we aſked the interpreter how many leagues we had travelled the preceding day, to which he replied, at leaſt forty; but he muſt certainly have been miſtaken, or elſe the leagues muſt not be ſo long as they are generally calculated, for forty of their leagues make one hundred and ſixty of thoſe of France, each Lapland league being as long as a German. Our guide alſo informed us, that we were

were in Muſcovite Lapland; and we bid him aſk the inhabitants of the village, whom we had preſented with tobacco, and been treated by them with brandy, whether they had any commodities to exchange with us for tobacco and cloth. We had ſome rolls of the former left, and moſt of our bales of the latter. The Laplanders replied, that they had ſome furrs, and on our deſiring to ſee them, brought us white, black and grey fox ſkins, grey ſquirrels and ſables. Theſe were what we wanted; we therefore ſoon agreed with them, and paid them in cloth and tobacco. When we had finiſhed our buſineſs, we ſat down to drink with them, and though they were not quite ſo brutal as ſome other of the Laplanders, their converſation was extremely rude and indecent. It now grew late, and we deſigning to proceed yet farther to diſpoſe of the few rolls of tobacco we had left, deſired our hoſt to furniſh us with ſledges and freſh rein-deer.

He harneſſed and prepared as many ſledges as we had occaſion for, upon which we departed at one o'clock, and ran with our former ſpeed, through different and unbeaten waſtes, till paſt ſix, without meeting with one habitation; when deſcending a hill, we obſerved two huts under a rock a little out of the way. Our guide told us, that they belonged to two Kilops, who no ſooner ſaw us, than they fled with their wives and families. We travelled two hours longer, but came to no houſe, till we at laſt diſcovered a large village at the foot of a hill by a river ſide, where we arrived at eleven o'clock at night, and went to a cottage in the middle of the place, whither our cattle were pleaſed to conduct us. The maſter of the houſe gave us a very kind reception, made us a fire in the middle of his hut, and treated us with brandy, dried fiſh, and ſalted veniſon, with ſalt butter and milk. We were ſurpriſed at this change, for we had not before met with any ſalt proviſions in our journey: we had already eat up our bread, and ſhould have been very much put to it had we not met with ſuch good entertainment here. Our guide, however, would not taſte a bit of ſalt meat, and was therefore obliged to live on the freſh veniſon he brought with him. In the morning we found they had nothing to trade with, and that they could not ſupply us with ſledges: upon which we croſſed the river, and ſoon reaching another village, went to the moſt likely houſe, to hire ſledges and rein-deer, to carry us to Kola, where having furniſhed ourſelves, we arrived there about noon. Kola is a large town ſituated on the ſide of a river near ten leagues from the North Sea, having large foreſts and deſerts to the eaſt, Mourmanſkeimore to the weſt, and prodigious high mountains to the ſouth. It conſiſts of one indifferent ſtreet, the houſes of which are built of wood, and very low; but are handſomely covered with fiſh-bones on the top, where the light enters at a hole, as in other parts of Lapland. The inhabitants, like the other Muſcovites, are ſo jealous of their wives, that they lock them up to prevent their being ſeen by ſtrangers. Our landlord took all our cloth off our hands, giving us ſkins in exchange; and engaging to ſupply us with proviſions for our journey both to Varanger, and to help us to ſledges as far as the river we had lately paſſed. He treated us as well as he was able, and we ſupped and ſlept as we had done in other places.

The next morning when we were preparing to depart, ſome of the town's people enquired whether we had any rolls of tobacco left, and whether we would exchange them for ſkins. We replied, with all our hearts. Upon which they fetched ſome, for which we gave them the remainder of our cargo of tobacco, except ſeven or eight rolls, which we reſerved for our own uſe, and to pay for the hire of our rein-deer and ſledges in our way back. For tobacco is more neceſſary than money to thoſe who travel in this wild and unfrequented country; the Laplanders valuing a piece of tobacco of the length of one's finger, at above a crown piece. The kings of Denmark

and

and Sweden have taxed it ſeverely, and there are collectors ſettled in every frontier town to gather the impoſts upon it.

When we had diſpatched our buſineſs, we were obliged, according to the cuſtom of the place, to drink with our chapmen. Our entertainment every where was brandy, and it laſted till two in the afternoon, when we deſired our hoſt to get the ſledges ready, which he did in a minute, packed up our furrs for us, furniſhed us with biſcuit, gingerbread, and ſalted rein-deer veniſon, beſide a rundlet of brandy. Every thing being thus ready, we ſtored our merchandize in one of the ſledges, got into the others ourſelves, drank a full glaſs at parting with our friendly chapmen, and ſet out on our return for the village on the other ſide of the river, which we had paſſed the day before.

We arrived at the firſt village by ſeven o'clock, ſoon croſſed the river, and went directly to our old quarters, where our landlord, in hopes of getting more tobacco, received us very joyfully. He immediately preſented us a cup of brandy, and aſked us if we would have the rein-deer put to the ſledges; to which we replied, that we choſe to reſt ourſelves till morning, there being no village for ſeveral leagues from his habitation. Upon this he filled us another cup, and when we had drank it, offered to take us with him to the funeral of one of his neighbours who had been dead about four hours.

We were glad of this opportunity of ſeeing their funeral ceremonies, and therefore accompanied him to the houſe of the deceaſed, when we ſaw the corpſe taken from the bears ſkins on which it lay, and removed into a wooden coffin, by ſix of his moſt intimate friends; the body being firſt wrapped in linen, and the face and hands only left bare. In one hand they put a purſe with money in it, to pay the fee of the porter of the gate of paradiſe, and in the other a certificate, ſigned by a prieſt, directed to

St. Peter, to certify that he was a good chriſtian, and ought to be admitted into heaven: and at the head of the coffin was placed a picture of St. Nicholas, who was one of the ſeven deacons mentioned in the Acts of the Apoſtles, a ſaint greatly reverenced in all parts of Muſcovy, where he is ſuppoſed to be a particular friend of the dead. They alſo put into the coffin a rundlet of brandy, ſome dried fiſh, and rein-deer veniſon for him to eat and drink on the road. They then lighted ſome fir-tree roots, piled up at a convenient diſtance from the coffin, wept, howled, and made a variety of ſtrange geſtures, aſſuming a thouſand different attitudes to ſhew the extravagancies of their ſorrow. When this noiſe and theſe geſticulations were over, they marched round the corpſe ſeveral times in proceſſion, aſking the deceaſed, why he died? whether he was angry with his wife? whether he ſtood in need of meat, drink or cloaths? if he had not ſucceeded when fiſhing, or had loſt his game when hunting? they then reſumed their howling, and ſtamped with all the ſigns of diſtraction. One of the prieſts who aſſiſted at the ſolemnity frequently ſprinkled holy water upon the corpſe, as alſo did the mourners. Being now almoſt deafened with noiſe, and wearied with looking on theſe barbarous rites, we left our landlord behind us, and returned to his cottage, where we found his wife at home. She had made a ſally from the place in which her huſband had confined her, on our arrival, and no ſooner ſaw us, than ſuppoſing he was in our company, would have retired to her corner; but our interpreter letting her know that the good man was at the funeral, and would not return for ſome time, ſhe ſtaid and viewed us all round, one after another, drew her ſeat near us, and ſhewed us a bonnet of her own embroidering, very curiouſly performed with tinſel thread. The wives of the Muſcovite Laplanders make cloaths for themſelves, their huſbands, and their children, and at the edges they are all embroidered with that thread. She was pretty handſome,

ſome, well ſhaped, and appeared to be good humoured, and well pleaſed with us. While our hoſt was buſied about the funeral, we pulled out ſome of our proviſions, and gave our landlady ſome of every ſort to taſte. She liked them all, eſpecially the gingerbread; but having drank two or three glaſſes of brandy, withdrew to her place of confinement, for fear of her huſband's return; for he would have certainly reſented her having taken ſuch liberty, which would have raiſed his jealouſy, had he found her among us. When he came home, he obliged us to take a cup or two more, to ſmoke a pipe, and to ſup with him; for he brought ſuch proviſions as he thought would be moſt grateful to our palates, particularly ſalt butter, which we eat with bread.

All the cottages in this village were, like thoſe we had obſerved in other places, built of wood and covered with turf, but they were handſomer than any we had yet ſeen, being both within and without adorned with fiſh bones, curiouſly inlaid. We, according to cuſtom, laid down with the family on bears ſkins, our landlady alone being obliged to conceal herſelf till we were gone.

Early the next morning our hoſt got ready our rein-deer and ſledges, when having ſtowed our bales, our cattle ſet off, and in two hours carried us ſix leagues. As we were paſſing between two hills, we ſaw a Laplander going a hunting, who came up to us ſkating on the ſnow, as faſt as we rode in our ſledges, for the ſnow ſeldom melts there till midſummer. His ſkates, which were made of the bark of a tree, were ſeven feet and a half long, four fingers broad, and flat at the bottom. He was dreſſed like the other Laplanders, in a garment made of the ſkin of a rein-deer, had an arrow in one hand, a bow in the other, and a large quiver hanging at his back, and was followed by a black cat. He kept company with us about half a league, and we parted at the foot of the next mountain.

We continued our rout three days, ſtopping at the ſame places where we lay before, and meeting with nothing extraordinary; our entertainment, our way of travelling, and every thing elſe being the ſame as before: and on the 21ſt of May, about nine o'clock at night, we arrived ſafe at Varanger, having every where been received with great civility, and ſuffering no injury in our whole journey.

[All that country which lies above the gulph of Bothnia along the coaſt of the North Sea, even to the White Sea, and is ſomewhat in the ſhape of a horſe-ſhoe, is known by the general name of Lapland; it lies between 65° and 72° north latitude. It is divided into Daniſh, Swediſh, and Muſcovite; of which, on account of the extreme coldneſs of the climate, the Swediſh Lapland is the only one that is tolerably peopled. This latter is bounded on the north by the Daniſh Lapland, on the eaſt by Muſcovite Lapland, on the ſouth eaſt and ſouth, by Bothnia, Angermania, and Jempterland; and on the weſt, it is parted from Norway by a ridge of mountains called the Dofrine mountains.

Lapland lies ſo near the pole, that the ſun does not ſet in ſummer, nor riſe in winter: in the latter ſeaſon the cold is ſo intenſe, that none but the natives can endure it; and the rapid rivers are then frozen up: in ſummer the heat is as ſultry. This country is full of rocks and mountains; thoſe called the Dofrine mountains are of a frightful height, and the prodigious winds that blow there prevent all trees from taking root: at the foot of theſe mountains are large marſhes and vaſt foreſts; and at the bottoms of the hills are charming vallies, watered with an infinite number of ſprings and brooks, which run into the rivers and lakes, and from thence into the Bothnic gulph.]

From obſerving the manners and diſpoſitions of the Laplanders, I am enabled to affirm, that notwith-

ſtanding

ſtanding their ignorance and ſuperſtition, they are remarkable for their honeſty, and are unacquainted with theft or fraud. They throw the dart with ſuch dexterity, as eaſily to hit a mark of the ſize of a crown piece, at the diſtance of thirty paces; and are ſo expert in the uſe of the bow and arrow, that they can ſhoot their game in what part they pleaſe, and yet are ſo averſe to war, that whenever the king of Denmark or Sweden, or the czar of Muſcovy, have occaſion for ſoldiers, they leave their dwellings and fly to the woods, for fear of being preſſed into the ſervice.

They have plenty of fowl, which they feed with the grain of which they make their drink, and when that is ſcarce, give them dried fiſh. Moſt of the beaſts of Lapland are white, as the wolves, bears, foxes, and hares; even their crows may be compared to the ſwan for whiteneſs, and have nothing black about them but their bills and feet. The fiſh, which when dried, ſerves them for bread, is called raff, and is firm, ſubſtantial, and excepting the fat, has a very good taſte. They have plenty of other ſorts of fiſh, and though they have an antipathy to ſalt, yet they boil all their meat in ſalt water, if they are near enough to the ſea to get it conveniently.

Within two or three days after our return to Varanger, the captain had repaired the ſhip, and taken in his lading and ballaſt; in the mean time our crew treated the inhabitants with brandy and tobacco, to keep them in good humour; for fear leſt if they were not bribed to be our friends, they ſhould, in revenge, plague us with contrary winds. We ſet ſail from Varanger on the 26th of May, with a gale as much in our favour as we could poſſibly deſire, which the ſailors ignorantly attributed to the friendſhip of the Laplanders: but this breeze ſoon ſhifting, we were obliged to caſt anchor under the ſhore oppoſite the iſland of Wardhuys. The next day the wind ſettling, we proceeded again to ſea, and held our courſe north north eaſt. On the 31ſt day of May, we ſaw the mountains of Greenland, at which time a north wind blew with ſuch violence, that we could not keep to ſea, and were obliged to ſteer to the eaſt ſouth-eaſt, in order to make the ſhore, that we might be ſheltered from the weather. We continued our courſe for ſeveral days, and at length caſt anchor in a good harbour on the coaſt of Borandia.

We had ſcarce entered this harbour, before we eſpied two ſhips that were at anchor about a muſket-ſhot from us, which we found were the two ſhips in our company that had been ſeparated from us in the ſtorm that drove us into Varanger. But though we wiſhed for an opportunity of ſending our long-boat to them, to learn the particulars of their eſcape, the wind blew ſo ſtiff, that we durſt not attempt it till twenty-four hours after. They were no leſs impatient to know how we eſcaped, and as ſoon as the wind ſlackened, a boat came off from each of them on board us, when we embraced each other with extraordinary joy and affection, as people who had found friends whom they thought buried in the deep. A council being held, it was reſolved, that a captain, a ſupercargo, two accountants, who underſtood both the language of the north and the Ruſſian, with twenty ſeamen, and myſelf, well armed, ſhould land, and take with us ſeveral days proviſions, and ſome goods for traffic.

Purſuant to this reſolution, two long-boats were got ready, and having landed, we aſcended a hill, to ſee if we could diſcover my habitations; but perceiving none, we marched to a neighbouring mountain at half a league's diſtance, where we obſerved five or ſix perſons among ſome buſhes of thorns and briars, who came toward us, till they perceived us advancing; and then turned their back and fled away ſo faſt, that we loſt ſight of them in an inſtant. However, imagining that their track would lead us to ſome village, we followed it, and after a march of

two

two hours, as we deſcended a mountain, we obſerved ſome huts in a valley below; and advancing toward them, perceived thirty or forty men armed with darts and arrows, prepared to give us battle; for ſeeing ſo ſtrong a body of us, they took us for enemies. We halted for ſome time, in order to conſult whether we ſhould retreat to our ſhips or attack them; when one of our accountants offered to go to them by himſelf, and to let them know that we were friends and merchants, who were come with a view of trading with them, if they had any thing to exchange with us.

This propoſal being approved, he approached them, carrying two rolls of tobacco, and a ſmall keg of brandy. When he came within hearing, one of them, who ſeemed to be their chief, called to him in the Muſcovite language, aſking who we were, and what we would have; and on being anſwered that we were merchants come to trade with them, they ſeemed ſatisfied, and made ſigns to him to come nearer, when giving us the ſame ſignal, we, to our mutual ſatisfaction, joined companies.

On our coming up to them, I was ſurprized to ſee them much ſhorter than the Laplanders, their eyes are ſmall like ferrets, and what is uſually called the white, is of a reddiſh yellow; their heads are large, their faces flat and broad, with flat noſes, and ſwarthy complexions; and their legs are ſhort and thick. The Borandian women are not at all handſomer than the men; they dreſs like them, and alſo, like them, ſpend the time in fiſhing and hunting. Their cloaths are a cap, a jacket that reaches down to their knees, a ſtrait pair of breeches, and ſtockings, all made of white bears ſkin, with the hairy ſide outward; but their ſhoes are made of the bark of a tree. They roaſt all the meat they obtain by hunting, eat it without ſalt, and uſe fiſh inſtead of bread. Their common drink is water, in which juniper-berries are ſteeped till they rot, which gives the water an agreeable taſte, at leaſt in a country where nothing

nothing better is to be had. Their huts are low and oval, covered with fiſh bones, and have no light, but what comes in at the door, which reſembles the mouth of an oven. They drink immoderately when they can get brandy, and the moſt acceptable preſent that can be made them, is either ſome of that liquor or tobacco: but they ſeem to have little or no notion of religion.

They ſoon purchaſed all the brandy and tobacco we had brought aſhore with us, for fox ſkins, wolves ſkins, and a few ermines. When finding that they had a great quantity remaining, we perſuaded them to take them to the beach, to which they readily agreed, and having carried them to the ſhore, ſtood admiring our ſhips. We then made a ſignal for the boats to be ſent off to fetch our chapmen, upon which each ſhip ſent two; in one of which went the ſupercargo, the accountant who treated with the Borandians, and myſelf, with ſeveral of the Borandians; while others ſtaid on the ſea-ſhore. On our going on board, the captain being informed of their fondneſs for brandy and tobacco, filled out a brimmer for each of them, and alſo made a preſent to each of a bit of roll tobacco of about an inch long, at which they were tranſported with joy.

Having purchaſed all the furrs they brought with them, we aſked if there was any conveniency for travelling in order to trade with the inhabitants; to which they anſwered in the affirmative, but that we muſt expect nothing but furrs. This we let them know was the commodity we wanted, and they aſſured us that we might have what we would of that kind, for tobacco, brandy and money; and if we pleaſed, might trade as far as Siberia, whither they would conduct us. We accordingly agreed with them to be our guides thither and back again, and to furniſh us with what conveniences the country afforded in our journey, for two rolls of tobacco, and two quarts of brandy; promiſing them farther rewards, in caſe the trade turned to account, and they contributed to it by their aſſiſtance. The bargain being concluded, our captain gave them another brimmer of brandy, and ſent them aſhore to prepare what was proper for our journey. They ſoon got every thing ready, and made ſuch a report of our kindneſs to them, while they were on board, that their countrymen expreſſed great friendſhip for us; and two boats were ſent aſhore with our ſupercargo to purchaſe for us. They were, however, at firſt unwilling to come aboard our ſhips; but we ſoon became better acquainted, and they came freely whenever they had an opportunity. We bought their furrs, treated them with brandy, and, in return, they invited us to their habitations.

In ſeven or eight hours we had provided every thing ready for our journey, and our two Borandian guides had brought ſix ſledges drawn by ſix rein-deer to the water ſide, which were all that were to be had in thoſe parts. The rein-deer, however, being larger than thoſe of Lapland, were able to draw two men, and the Borandian ſledges were contrived to hold them. The captain now called a council of all the officers, and it was agreed that our ſupercargo, the two accountants, who could ſpeak the Ruſſian language, myſelf, and a ſeaman out of each ſhip, ſhould go with the two Borandians. One of the ſledges we loaded with tobacco, brandy, gold, ſilver, and copper, to the value of three or four thouſand pounds: our ſupercargo and myſelf rode together in another of theſe ſledges; one accountant and a Borandian, in a third; the other accountant and the other Borandian, in the fourth; two ſeamen in the fifth; and the other ſeaman in the ſixth: and as he rode by himſelf, we ſtowed ſome barrels of brandy and tobacco in his ſledge. We ſat one at one end of the ſledge, and the other at the other, facing each other. The rein-deer in eight hours time drew us twenty leagues over hills and dales, and through ſeveral woods; yet in all

this

this great extent of country we met nobody in our way. We then ſtopped at a village, and baited our rein-deer with moſs, while we ourſelves ate ſome biſcuit and beef, and our Borandians refreſhed themſelves with dried fiſh dipped in fiſh oil; for they would not touch our ſalt meat, and did not like our biſcuit. Both they and we drank at a neighbouring ſpring, and then cheared ourſelves with a glaſs of brandy. Being thus refreſhed, we again mounted our ſledges, and travelled three hours longer; when we perceived a large village at the foot of a mountain, the huts of which were better built, and cloſer together than thoſe of Lapland, thither we haſtened to take up our lodging. We met with the ſame reception from our landlords as in Lapland, and gratified them with a piece of roll tobacco and a cup of brandy; our guides took care of our rein-deer, and we laid down to reſt on bears ſkins.

I diſtinguiſhed one part of the day from the other, by day and night, though there was really no night at all; but having ſlept ſix or ſeven hours we aroſe, in order to trade with the inhabitants of the village, who being informed of our buſineſs by our guides, ſoon produced ſome ſkins: but they were neither ſo fond of tobacco nor brandy as the Laplanders or the Borandians dwelling on the coaſt. Hunting is their only diverſion and employment. In the ſummer, they eat their meat either boiled or broiled on the coals, and during that ſeaſon provide enough to ſerve them in winter, preſerving it by drying it in the ſun, cutting it in pieces, and ſpreading it on the tops of the houſes, which is the only dreſſing they beſtow upon it. They change their dwellings like the Kilops, are extremely ſtupid, and have very diſagreeable features. The only difference obſervable between the women, who are dexterous hunters, and the men, is that their hair is twiſted, and hangs down on their ſhoulders, and their carrying only a ſtick in their hand, which is ſharp at one end, and

being

being of a tough wood, ſerves them for a defenſive weapon. The men carry at their backs a quiver, and the ſtrings of their bows are made of the rind of a tree.

We bought the furrs the inhabitants had to ſell, for money, and copper; ordered our rein-deer to be put to the ſledges; mounted them, and having each of us drank a glaſs of brandy, proceeded on our journey. We now rode eight or nine hours before we came to any habitation; but at laſt our guides perceiving three or four huts, turned our rein-deer up to them; but finding nobody there, we regaled ourſelves on our own proviſions, while our cattle fed on the moſs which grew there in abundance, and having refreſhed ourſelves and our beaſts for three hours, proceeded on our journey.

We were now fifteen hours without ſeeing any human creature, or ſo much as a hut, when we overtook three hunters at the foot of a hill, one of whom was dreſſed after the Muſcovite faſhion in a long robe, tied round his waiſt with a girdle four inches broad. It was made of a white bear's ſkin, with the hair outward, and edged with a fine black. His cap was made of a black fox's ſkin, and his breeches and ſtockings of the ſkin of a rein-deer; his ſhoes were made of fiſh ſkin, and were not unlike thoſe worn at Varanger. The two other perſons were dreſſed like us, in white bear ſkins with the hair outwards, and carried at their backs bear ſkins, wolve ſkins, white fox ſkins, ſome ermines, and very fine ſables. The former carried only twelve white crows, and ſeven ſables, which hung at his girdle. On our coming near them, one of our guides ſtopt to talk with them, and to our great ſurprize got out of the ſledge, and the other went into it. Neither the ſupercargo who rode with me, nor I, could tell how to account for this complaiſance. We however purſued our journey, with the hunter in our company, for above an hour longer through this deſolate

desolate country, without meeting any other person; or the least sign of an habitation: but at last drawing near the brow of a high mountain, we perceived at the foot of it several houses built close together, and had a distant view of the sea. When we arrived at the village, we stopped at the door of the person who had taken our guide's place, and soon found that he was a man of authority, and he desired the inhabitants to serve us as his friends.

The name of this village is Vitzora. The inhabitants no sooner saw this person in our company, than they ran to help us out of the sledges, and to unharness our rein-deer. He bartered all his skins with us for brandy and tobacco, except his bear skins, which we did not chuse to buy, and his sables, which he durst not sell: for the czar reserving that commodity for himself, those in any part of his dominions who sell it without a licence from him are severely punished.

Having dealt with the Borandian gentleman for all the furrs he had to sell, he sent two of his servants about the village to tell the inhabitants, that if they would bring their skins to his house, they might have brandy and tobacco for them, as their master had already had for his. The Borandians of Vitzora were glad to hear of so good a market; they immediately brought us all their furrs, and we bought in this place above 1500 skins of all sorts, excepting sables; when our cargo becoming too bulky to be carried in a sledge, we desired our landlord to do us the favour to lend us his bark, and some of his servants to go in it with one of our seamen, who was a good sailor, to carry the furrs aboard our ship, which lay at above 100 leagues distance: for the sailor and the Borandian servants who were used to the coasts might easily manage that small vessel and convey our merchandize to our companions. He readily agreed to this request, and we paid him for the use of his bark in tobacco and brandy.

This bark was built in the form of a gondola, it being broad in the middle and ſharp at each end. It was entirely of wood, joined with pegs, without ſo much as a nail in it, or the leaſt bit of iron. When they were about to put to ſea, he privately ſhewed us thirty pair of ſable ſkins, which we bought with ready money, ſlipt them on board, and the veſſel put off immediately. This, however, was running a dangerous riſk, for had there been any ſearchers at hand, he would not only have been corporally puniſhed, but alſo he and his whole family ſent as ſlaves into Siberia.

The bark being out of ſight, our ſupercargo and accountants ſat down to drink with the Borandian gentleman, while the two ſeamen and I walked out to take a view of the place, the ſituation of which was very pleaſant, having two mountains one each ſide of it, almoſt a league in height. All the houſes were built and artfully covered with fiſh bones, and the crannies every where ſtopped up with moſs, as cloſe as the caulking of a ſhip, and in ſome places that were moſt expoſed to the wind, were covered with turf very neatly laid. The doors, like thoſe we had ſeen in other parts of the country, were built like the mouths of ovens, and at the top of the houſes were a kind of lattices to admit the light. The inhabitants were very ſhort, and ſwarthy, with flat noſes and diſagreeable perſons. All the women and children appeared induſtrious, for we found them buſily employed; ſome making fiſhing nets of the rind of trees, others ſails, which looked like fine mats, with needles formed of fiſh bones. Others were employed with knives, and others again with hatchets, in different kinds of buſineſs.

As we had not yet diſpoſed of half our commodities, and were in a country abounding with furrs, we, at our return to our lodgings, conſulted with our ſupercargo and accountants; when it was agreed, that as our commiſſion for traffic and diſcovery was very extenſive, we would proceed as long as we found the trade good, and our caſh, brandy, and tobacco held out. Having taken this reſolution, we ſent our guides back with three rein-deer and ſledges, and with letters to our captains to inform them of our ſucceſs and reſolution; and then, by the aſſiſtance of our hoſt at Vitzora, hired a bark to carry us to Petzora, the capital of a principality of the ſame name, on the north coaſt of the Muſcovite ſea: our landlord was ſo kind as to embark with us, and by the help of an eaſterly wind, we coaſted along the ſhore, and in fifteen hours reached Petzora.

On our arrival at Petzora, we waited upon the collector of the cuſtoms, who there aſſumes the title of governor, and lives at the caſtle. He was dreſſed after the manner of his country, in a robe of violet coloured cloth, with a mixture of red, and entertained us with ſome excellent metheglin, which was as racy as ſack; after which we had brandy and gingerbread, the common collation all over Muſcovy. As we knew that he had the care of the czar's ſables, we aſked him to ſell us ſome, and on his deſiring to know how many we wanted, we told him we would take all he had, if he would let us have them a pennyworth. Upon this he conducted us to the warehouſe, where there were five zimmers, each zimmer being fifty pair, among which there were two zimmers as black as jet, and the fineſt I ever ſaw, for which we paid him five hundred ducats, and the other three zimmers were purchaſed for eight hundred crowns or four hundred ducats. Having paid him his money, he gave us a noble entertainment of roaſted wild fowl, young rein-deer veniſon, which is very good meat, and freſh fiſh; two boats having at our firſt arrival been ordered out to catch ſome for our entertainment. After this meal, we ſat eight hours drinking brandy and metheglin, the fumes of which would much ſooner have got into my head, had I not every now and then eat a Muſcovite biſcuit, which is moſt excellent

cellent bread. At length, however, becoming intoxicated, the governor and his guests all laid down on white bear ſkins, for he had no beds; when having ſlept ſix or ſeven hours, we aroſe, and the governor immediately preſented us with a bumper of brandy.

After breakfaſt being deſirous of going through the town, in order to try whether we could carry on any trade with the inhabitants, the governor ordered one of his officers to accompany us, and we ſoon bought of ſeveral people 2000 grey ſquirrels, 4 dozen of ermines, 500 fox ſkins, the greateſt part of which were as white as ſnow, 120 white wolf ſkins, and 200 martens of a greyiſh colour: all which we purchaſed for 400 ducats; half of which we obliged them to take in copper money, becauſe it incumbered us, and the other half in gold and ſilver. We then returned to the caſtle, whither we ſent our merchandize, and there packed it up in bales, covered with the ſame ſort of ſtuff as the ſails of the bark. Having thus taken care of our goods, it was reſolved that one of our accountants ſhould return with them to the ſhips, for which purpoſe we deſired the governor to furniſh us with a bark, to which he agreed. We alſo hired three Borandians to aſſiſt the accountant in his voyage, the governor paſſing his word for them, that they ſhould be truſty.

This veſſel having ſet ſail, we fell to drinking again, when the quantity drank by the gentlemen of Vitzora was quite ſurpriſing; but having continued drinking four hours together, we compoſed ourſelves to reſt on bears ſkins, as before.

The next morning our ſupercargo deſired the governor to let us have ſome rein-deer to carry us into Siberia, which he furniſhed us with. He alſo ſupplied us with proviſions, that were to laſt till our arrival at Papinowgorod, a city in the province of Petzora, on the borders of Siberia; but he would not let us go without our drinking five or ſix glaſſes at parting.

Having returned our hearty thanks to the governor and the gentleman of Vitzora, for their many civilities, we got into our ſledges, and travelled four hours through intricate unbeaten ways, without ſeeing any living creature; till at laſt we met four white bears of an enormous ſize, which croſſed our way, and ſeeing us fled into a wood. In about two hours after we arrived at a village, conſiſting of ſeven or eight cottages; but the inhabitants being all gone to hunt, we alighted to refreſh ourſelves on the proviſions we had brought with us. In the mean time, five or ſix men with their wives and children returned from hunting, having ſkins with them. They were ſurprized to ſee us there, and would have fled, had not the governor of Petzora's ſervant aſſured them that we were friends and merchants bound for Papinowgorod; when coming up to us, they viewed us narrowly, being amazed at ſeeing ſo many ſtrangers in ſo unfrequented a place. However, by the aſſiſtance of our interpreter, we bought all the ſkins they dared to ſell us, and they lent us rein-deer and ſledges to carry us to the mouth of the river Papinowgorod.

We now left the river Petzora, the coaſt of which we had followed ſome time, and proceeded toward that of Papinowgorod, through almoſt impaſſable ways, over high mountains, and through woods and foreſts for three hours: but at length, on our approaching a thick wood, we obſerved five men in white bear's ſkin long coats, made after the Muſcovite faſhion; each of whom had a gun on his ſhoulder, a pouch on one ſide, and a knife and ſheath on the other. As they made up toward us, our guides ſtopped their rein-deer, when the five men being near enough to be heard, one of them perceiving that we were ſtrangers, bad us good-morrow in the German tongue, wiſhing that they were as free as we were. Our ſupercargo being a native of Lower Saxony, was attracted by the ſound of his own language, and aſked him what countryman he was, when entering into conver-

conversation, several things were started, by which they understood that they had been formerly acquainted. Upon which the supercargo alighted out of his sledge, embraced him, and asked how he came there; to which he replied, that he had been banished for hunting sables, a very capital offence, for which some are sent into exile for ten years, some for six, and some for three.

While they were discoursing, I had time to look at the other four, when I imagined that I had some knowlege of one of them, but could not recollect who he was; and the more I looked at him, the more firmly was I persuaded that I had seen him before, and therefore could not forbear getting out of the sledge to satisfy my curiosity: but I no sooner set my foot on the ground, than the man who remembered me, better than I did him, ran to me and embraced me, asking in French, whence I came, and where I was going. Finding that I could not recollect him, he told me his name, and that he had often drank with me at Stockholm. Upon this I immediately recollected, that he was a person to whom I had been very much obliged, and had received many civilities from, in Sweden. He was born in Lorrain, was a gentleman by birth, and lieutenant-colonel of a regiment of Muscovite horse. He had endeavoured to persuade me to go with him to Moscow, by offering to procure me an honourable and profitable post; but I declined accepting his proposal. When I compared the fine appearance he made at that time, the respect with which he was treated, as well on account of his estate, as the place he enjoyed, and his bearing the character of a man of honour and bravery; with the miserable condition to which I now saw him reduced, I could not help being afflicted: I embraced him with extraordinary affection and tenderness, and asking the cause of his disgrace, he replied, that the czar suspecting that he had not been so zealous in his service as he ought to have been, had banished him to Siberia for three years, where he endured miseries that are not to be expressed; he being exposed to the greatest dangers in hunting wild beasts for his subsistance, to the miseries of hunger, and the rigour of the seasons, which he and his companions were forced to endure, no body daring to afford them any relief. He added, that they were almost every day attacked by wild beasts, which they met in herds seeking for prey, and that they frequently found great difficulty in defending themselves; that beside, they were condemned to supply the czar's officers with a certain number of sables, under the penalty of being severely lashed with a whip of leathern thongs, on their naked backs, till they were covered with blood. One of the other had been receiver-general of the czar's revenues in one of the provinces, another had been a major-general, and the fifth a man of note. They all joined in deploring their misfortunes, exclaimed loudly against the czar, and declared, that when once their time of exile was expired, they would get far enough out of his power.

We now sat down with them on the moss, took out the best provisions we had, and desired them to partake with us; we even offered them our assistance to facilitate their escape; but they told us it was impracticable, they being known to all the governors of the forts, and places through which they and we must necessarily pass; and in case they should be taken, both they and we should be put to a most cruel death. This increased our concern for these unfortunate gentlemen, and we all shed tears at the sight of what they suffered, and the ideas of what they were still to endure. We could not think of parting immediately with persons in such a disconsolate state, some of whom we had known in better days; we therefore told them, our trade was not in such haste as to prevent our spending a day or two with men in their unhappy circumstances, whom we equally loved and esteemed. They received this proposal

poſal with great joy, told us they had five little huts, which they had built in the neighbouring wood, and if we would be ſo kind as to go thither with them, they ſhould be infinitely obliged to us, and all the ſkins they had ſhould be at our ſervice, except the ſables, which they were forced to reſerve for the czar: they added, that the remembrance of the happy hours they ſhould ſpend with us in their ſolitude, would make many future months glide on the more ſweetly. We therefore ordered our guide to unharneſs their rein deer, and to convey our goods into the huts the gentlemen had erected to defend themſelves from the weather.

We found, on approaching theſe huts, that neceſſity had rendered theſe unhappy men ingenious. They were built of fir, higher than any we had ſeen in our travels; there were two or three rooms in each of them, and lattices to let in the light at the ſides. They were each ſhaded by trees, and ſo artfully paved with fiſh-bones, that the floors looked as if they were inlaid with ivory. To ſecure themſelves from the wild beaſts, they had dug a trench round theſe buildings, and palliſaded the inſide with ſtrong poſts, and pieces of wood nailed acroſs them, on the top of which were ſpikes of fiſh-bones. Thus when their gate was ſhut, they were as ſecure as in a fortified place. They had within all ſorts of hunting and fiſhing tackle, beſide a good ſtore of ſalted rein-deer veniſon, biſcuit, and metheglin.

While the reſt of the company ſat down to drinking, my friend and I withdrew to his hut to converſe together. We entered into diſcourſe on his adventures; he told me, he intended to return home after his time of exile ſhould be expired, and gave me his direction in Lorrain. Our converſation turned partly on our former acquaintance, and partly on the wildneſs of the country, and the barbarity of its inhabitants.

When my friend and I had tired ourſelves with talking, we laid down upon bear-ſkins, as our companions alſo did when wearied with drinking, and ſlept ſound till the next morning.

We aroſe early, and at the deſire of the five baniſhed gentlemen, took each of us a gun, and went with them into the woods to examine their ſnares, to ſee what prey was caught in thoſe they had laid the night before. We killed among us ten or twelve white foxes, and half a dozen grey martens, but met with none of the larger game; and as we reſolved to purſue our journey in the afternoon, we did not chuſe to loſe our time in hunting; we therefore ſoon returned to the huts, and both we and our hoſts furniſhing proviſions, refreſhed ourſelves as well as could be expected in ſo wretched a place. After we had drank plentifully, the gentlemen forced us to take ſeven bear ſkins, ten white fox ſkins, two pair of ermines, and eight wolf ſkins, for which they would take no money. However, we with difficulty prevailed on them to accept ſome brandy, tobacco, and cloth, which we took care ſhould exceed in value the commodities they had given us. We wept reciprocally at parting, wiſhing them patience to endure their ſufferings, and a happy deliverance out of them; and having mounted our ſledges, continued our travels with the uſual expedition.

Having now proceeded three hours without meeting with any habitation, we diſcovered five or ſix huts together, in which were about a dozen perſons, from whom we bought all their ſkins. We now following the courſe of the river Petzora, frequently met with ſmall villages, in ſome of which we found inhabitants, and in others none; but whenever we met with any body to trade with us, we bought their furrs either with money or brandy.

We now reached a large ridge of mountains, that are almoſt always covered with ſnow, and ſo barren, that neither man nor beaſt can live upon them. On both

both ſides of theſe mountains were vaſt numbers of white bears and wolves, which put us in fear of our lives; we being under continual apprehenſions of their falling upon us, though perhaps theſe animals were as much terrified at us as we at them; for they fled before us, ſome on the one hand and ſome on the other, frightened perhaps at the glittering of our arms. We were twelve hours in croſſing the mountains, over which our cattle had much ado to draw us; but we at laſt reached the deſcent, and arrived at a village in Siberia, where the people had linen ſhirts, cloſe buſkins, and garments of bear ſkins, with the hair outward; but they appeared to be leſs barbarous than thoſe with whom we had lately converſed. They received us very civilly, aſked whence we came, and whither we were going: having reſolved their queſtions, we bought all their ſkins for ready money, feaſted with them on dried bear's and wolf's fleſh, rice-cakes, and brandy; and then ſlept upon bears ſkins, in houſes built after the manner of the Laplanders.

[Siberia comprehends a vaſt extent of country, and with Samojedia, compoſes the moſt northern part of the Ruſſian empire in Aſia as well as in Europe. It is bounded on the weſt by Ruſſia, from which it is parted by a ridge of mountains, reaching from mount Caucaſus to the Northern Ocean, on the north by Samojedia, on the eaſt by the Japanic Ocean, and part of Great Tartary; and on the ſouth by the ſame Tartary. It extends from 50° to 68° north latitude; and, according to its preſent limits, may be computed to be about 400 German leagues from north to ſouth, and about 900 from eaſt to weſt; including all the provinces appertaining to it, which extend themſelves ſouth-eaſt, as far as the river Argun, which is within a few days journey of the famous wall of China.

This country is chiefly inhabited by people of Tartarean race, and was called Siberia only ſince its conqueſt

queſt by the Ruſſians, from a Sclavonic word ſignifying a priſon. For, on account of its extreme barrenneſs and coldneſs, it is made uſe of as ſuch for priſoners of ſtate, who are baniſhed hither either for life, or for a term of years, according to their crimes, and the pleaſure of the czars. Here they have a very ſmall or no allowance, ſo that they are obliged to ſhoot for their living, or ſtarve; and moreover, to bring weekly a tribute of furs for the czar: and as theſe furs muſt neither be ſtained with blood, nor have any holes in them, this makes them very dextrous in ſhooting the animals only in the head, and with a ſingle ball.

This country is moſtly covered with impenetrable woods, high frozen mountains, lakes, and fenny grounds; ſo that it is quite barren and thinly inhabited, except by thoſe who are forced thither from Muſcovy againſt their wills.]

We no ſooner awaked than we mounted our ſledges, and ſet forward for Papinowgorod, which we reached in about twenty hours. The governor hearing of our arrival, ſent for us to come to his caſtle, to enquire into our country and buſineſs. Upon which we immediately waited on him; and our accountant, who underſtood the Muſcovite language, anſwered all his queſtions to his ſatisfaction. Being informed that we were Daniſh merchants, who travelled ſo far to buy furrs, he treated us in a very friendly manner; and, as a mark of reſpect, ſent for his wife to entertain us: upon which ſhe came with a bottle of brandy in one hand, and a ſilver cup in the other, followed by a maid ſervant with a plate of gingerbread. We ſaluted her according to the cuſtom of the country, by bowing our heads, when untying the knot of her ſhift-ſleeve, ſhe let it fall to the ground, and the ſupercargo taking it up, we each of us kiſſed it. She then furled it up again with her left-hand, and taking the bottle and cup, which ſhe had ſet down to perform this ceremony, gave each of us a

bumper

bumper of brandy and a piece of ginger-bread, ſtanding all the while near her huſband, at the end of the table. She then withdrew, and the governor regaled us with an excellent ſupper.

This entertainment being over, we were conducted to lodgings prepared for us, in the caſtle; and, conſidering the country, lay in very good beds. Having ſlept about ſeven hours, we aroſe; of which the governour being informed by one of his ſervants, got up and came to ſee us, bringing a bottle of brandy with him, and one of his domeſtics having another, filled a large cup for a morning's draught. We each of us drank one, and then the governor aſking if we would buy his ſkins, our ſupercargo ſaid he would if he liked them, and could agree on the price. His furrs were extremely well choſen, and though they were valued much higher than any we had met with in all our travels, they were the beſt worth our money. Theſe being bought and paid for, he ordered one of his men to call ſome of the inhabitants who had a quantity to ſell; and while our ſupercargo was dealing with the governor and his neighbours, I took a turn about the town.

Papinowgorod is commodiouſly ſituated in a ſmall plain, in the midſt of a fruitful country, ſurrounded with high mountains; and near it runs a large river, well ſtocked with fiſh. The houſes are low, and meanly built of wood, with the chinks ſtopped with moſs, and the ſtreets are paved with timber laid cloſe together. The people of faſhion wear a long cloth coat, which reaches down to their toes, with very cloſe ſleeves of another colour, under which they have breeches and ſtockings of the ſame cloth. Their ſhoes, or rather boots, are of blue, red or yellow leather, buttoned on the top; and upon their heads they wear cloth caps lined, and bordered with ermine, ſable or black fox ſkins. The women are fair, beautiful, and ſomewhat fat; their hair is of a light cheſnut colour, hanging down to their waiſt, and their head-

head-drefs is an oval-cap: their upper garment, like the men's, hangs down to the feet, and is made of a red, blue, or violet coloured cloth, and is lined with white fox ſkin or ſable. They have round their waiſts a broad girdle adorned with pearls, and their ſhifts are made of fine callico, with ſleeves all ruffled up from the wriſt to the ſhoulders, ſome of which are five ells long; and this bundle prevents their uſing the arms of their robes, which therefore hang uſeleſs, and are only pinned on. On their feet they have ſhoes made of Ruſſia leather.

The people of Siberia are grave, robuſt, ſwift, and very dexterous at ſhooting with the croſs-bow; but they are ignorant, churliſh, and jealous of their wives, whom they generally lock up; and even if they do not, none of them dare quit their rooms, without their huſband's leave. The religion of this province is called Nicholation. Their judicial proceedings are terminated with great expedition; for all their courts of juſtice are courts of equity. There are no petty-foggers either here or in Ruſſia, who, under the pretence of relieving the innocent, and ſuccouring the diſtreſſed, rob the poor, and inrich themſelves with the ſpoils of the widow and the fatherleſs.

When we had bought up all the furs we liked at Papinowgorod, we found we had enough to load a ſledge and a half; and having ſtill ſome tobacco, and about 5000 ducats left, our ſupercargo reſolved to proceed farther, in order to purchaſe more, and then to return to our ſhips through Samojedia. As our brandy fell ſhort, we bought a ſupply of the beſt the governor had; we agreed with him for proviſions ſufficient to laſt us twelve days, and for rein-deer to carry us to the end of our journey. When we had concluded all our dealings with him, and paid our money, we were forced to have a drunken bout at parting, without which there is no getting away.

We proceeded ſeventeen hours, all the way buying up what furs we could find of the Siberians;

and

and having in ſix hours more croſſed the Riphean mountains, we entered Samojedia, a deſolate mountainous country, full of juniper-trees, pines, and firs. It abounds in moſs, as well as ſnow; and we, every moment, to our no ſmall terror, met with white bears, wolves, and foxes.

[The province of Samojedia lies to the north of Siberia, extending itſelf quite to the North or Frozen Ocean: the people are called Samojedes, which, in the Ruſſian tongue, ſignifies men-eaters. They have no towns, but live in tents or caverns, according to the ſeaſon. They are excellent archers, and very nimble after their game, which with fiſh being their only food, they are expert in catching them from their childhood: when winter comes they retire to their dens under ground, living by lamp-light, on their dried ſtock of fiſh and game; their ſauce being ſtinking fiſh oil.

Though theſe people are for eight or nine months in the year confined to their ſubterranean habitations in ſtench and ſmoak, yet are they ſo far from being diſcontented with this wretched way of life, that Olearius tells us of two of their deputies, ſent to the court of Moſcow, who told the czar, that if he knew the charms of their country and climate, he would doubtleſs chuſe to go and live among them. They are by all writers repreſented as the moſt ſtupid and diſagreeable people in the world.]

On our aſcending mount Stolphen, whence ariſes the river Borſagatz, we came to eight or nine houſes, where we ſtopped, in order to reſt ourſelves and our cattle, and exchanged with the inhabitants brandy for white and black wolf and fox ſkins, caſtor and otter ſkins. They had ſeveral dozen of ſables, which they would not ſell upon any terms, though they were aſſured by our Borandian guide, that there was no manner of danger, we being traders who were going to our ſhips, and could not be diſcovered before we reached the coaſt, becauſe we were not to paſs through any

any place where there were officers impowered to ſearch for prohibited goods. All our arguments had, however, no effect, till we had drank them down; when our brandy rendering them courageous, they brought out their ſables, and ſold us the beſt and the greateſt quantity we had picked up in our whole journey.

We ſtaid to reſt ourſelves in one of the chief huts of the village. The maſter of the houſe, with his wife and children, and we his viſitors lying all together on bear ſkins. Having ſlept four or five hours, I was awakened by the noiſe made by our hoſt to raiſe his family, all of whom went out; when having the curioſity to follow them at a little diſtance, I obſerved them fall down on their knees behind the cottage, lifting up their hands and eyes to adore the ſun.

The people of Samojedia are ſhorter and thicker than either the Laplanders or the Borandians. They have large heads, their faces and noſes are flat, they are of a ſwarthy complexion, and have ſcarcely any hair. They wear a round fur cap, and a white bear's ſkin coat that reaches down to their knees, and is faſtened round the waiſt with a girdle four inches broad; they alſo wear breeches, ſhoes and ſtockings, made of the ſame ſkin with the hair outwards; and inſtead of a cloak, they hang a black bear's ſkin over their ſhoulders, the feet dangling at the four corners: this ſkin is placed more on the left ſide than on the right, to leave the right arm at liberty in the management of their bows and arrows, and upon this ſkin they tie their quiver. They alſo wear upon their feet a kind of ſkates two feet long, with which they ſlide with prodigious ſwiftneſs over the ſnow, that almoſt always lies on the mountains.

The Samojedian women have more diſagreeable perſons than thoſe of the men. They are capable of enduring great hardſhips, and take care to breed up their children in uſing their bows with great dexterity.

terity. They are dreſſed like the men, only their upper garment is a little longer, and all the difference in their head-dreſs is, that the women have a lock of twiſted hair hanging down on their ſhoulders, at the end of which is a knot, formed of a long ſlip taken from the bark of a tree, which hangs down as low as their heels, and this is all their finery. They hunt as well as the men, and are in the ſame manner armed with bows and arrows. The huſbands are true to their wives, and the wives to their huſbands, and if either man or woman is found guilty of adultery, the criminal is immediately ſtoned to death.

Having traverſed Samojedia, and exchanged away our money and goods for ſkins, we returned; and in twelve days after our departure from Papinowgorod, reached the coaſt of Borandia, without meeting with any adventure worth notice. Upon that coaſt our ſhips had waited for us at an appointed place, where we put all our merchandize on board, paid off our Borandian guide, and embarked.

Having weighed anchor, we ſailed from the coaſt of Borandia with a fair wind, and the next day in the afternoon caſt anchor near the coaſt of Zembla, when we obſerved upon the ſhore, about thirty perſons with quivers on their backs, worſhipping on their knees the ſetting ſun. Our maſter and ſupercargo immediately conſulted what courſe it would be proper for us to take to come at the ſpeech of them. They thought them more wild than any ſavages they had yet ſeen, and thinking it would be difficult to perſuade them to deal with us, it was reſolved to ſend out three long boats, with ten men well armed in each, that they might be able to defend themſelves in caſe they ſhould be attacked. I was one of the number diſpatched upon this ſervice; but when we were about a quarter of a mile from the land, the ſavages aroſe from their knees, diſcharged their arrows at us, and then fled with ſurpriſing ſwiftneſs;

but

but being at a great diſtance when they let fly at us, they did not do us the leaſt harm.

We no ſooner reached the ſhore than we landed, and purſued them to the place whither we thought they had fled, in hopes of making ſome of them our priſoners; but we found it impoſſible, though we followed them till we approached ſome mountains covered with ſnow. However, we continued to advance farther into the country, till we came to a riſing ground, upon which was erected a piece of wood, very wretchedly cut into the figure of a man, and before it two Zemblians on their knees, with their arms lying by them. They were worſhipping this idol, who was called Fetizo, as the others on aſhore had been adoring the ſun; but the moment they beheld us they fled into an adjoining wood of firs, and as night approached, we thought it would be in vain to purſue them.

[Nova Zembla, called by the Dutch the Iſland of Weygats, is ſituated in the Frozen Ocean, between 70° north latitude and the pole, and between 50° and 80° eaſt longitude. It is ſeparated from Samojedia by the ſtreights of Weygats; but whether it be an iſland, or part of ſome great continent, is uncertain, no ſhips having paſſed to the northward of it. It is repreſented as the moſt forlorn ſpot that can be imagined; the greateſt part of which is hid under ſnow and ice; and where there are neither of theſe, nothing is met with but diſmal quagmires covered with moſs. Upon digging two or three feet into the earth, it was found as hard as marble; ſo that all attempts to winter in caves under ground there would be vain.]

From thence we ſteered toward the ſtreights of Weygats, to catch ſea-horſes; and having proceeded about ſix leagues, kept near the ſhore, and put out our long-boat with eight harpooners in each, beſide the rowers. We were three days without catching any thing; but at laſt obſerved two great fiſh approach-

ing

ing us, one of which had a large horn in his forehead, when the boats coming near, the harpoons were thrown at him on all ſides; and the ropes to which they were faſtened let looſe, after which the men haſtily retired, to be out of his reach while he was ſtruggling. At laſt the fiſh ſwimming above the water, which was a proof of his weakneſs, the men in the boats drew him to them by the ropes faſtened to the harpoons, and then cutting off his head, threw the body into the ſea; it being neither fit for food nor oil. This was a ſea-horſe, which is taken only for the ſake of his teeth and horn, the former being more valuable than thoſe of the elephant, becauſe they are whiter, and not ſo apt to turn yellow. The horn of this ſea-horſe was ten feet long, and very heavy; from the root, which was as thick as a man's ſhoulder, it gradually decreaſed, wreathing handſomely, till it ended in a ſharp point. One of the boats coming too cloſe to the other fiſh, in order to make ſure of it, and not retreating with ſufficient ſpeed, was unhappily overturned by his tail, with which he laſhed the boat with prodigious fury, on his feeling the harpoon; by this means two of the men were drowned, notwithſtanding which the fiſh was taken: but though this was no recompence for the loſs of our ſailors, yet it was a good prize, the teeth being larger and whiter than the former.

We were four days cruiſing about before we met with any more, and were preparing to change our ſtation, when we perceived four of the ſame fiſh, that ſeemed larger than thoſe we had caught; three of them we took, but none of them had any horn. Twelve hours after we diſcovered five more, but three of them eſcaped, one of which had a horn. Two hours after we eſpied three more, one of which we took, each of whoſe great teeth weighed twenty-nine pounds. Two days after we caught five more, among which was one with a horn, like that of the firſt we caught, but it was neither ſo heavy nor ſo large, it being ſcarce ſeven feet long.

We ſtaid there five days longer; and perceiving no more fiſh, took the advantage of a north north-eaſt wind to ſail towards Weygats, in hopes of paſſing thoſe ſtreights, which, if practicable, would ſhorten the paſſage to the Eaſt Indies, by three-fourths. We purſued our courſe pretty well for thirty-ſix leagues; but were unable to proceed any farther on account of the large pieces of ice that oppoſed our paſſage, and thoſe mountains covered with ſnow which lie at the mouth of the Frozen Sea, and are known by the name of the Pater noſters. Hence theſe ſtreights have received the name of Weygats, which ſignifies impaſſable.

We now came to an anchor on the eaſtern coaſt of Zembla, when one of the ſeamen landing, a bear came behind him and ſtruck him down with his paw; and had we not happily ſeen it, and ſhot the bear dead, he would certainly have been devoured. This accident deterred the reſt of the mariners from venturing on land.

Shortly after, three bears ſwam to the ſides of the ſhips, and ſtrove to come on board; but though we cut off the paws of one of them with our hatchets, and ſhot the other with a muſket, the third, while we were diſpatching theſe, mounted the ſide of the ſhip, and got upon deck, when a ſailor who was near cried out, for the bear was juſt at his heels. We all took up the firſt offenſive weapons that came to hand, as oars and pieces of timber, with which we knocked him down and diſpatched him; while others ſhot at and killed two more that were ſwimming toward us. This ſlaughter, we thought, would have hindered any more attempting to board us, but we were miſtaken; for about four or five hours afterwards, ten or twelve came as far toward us on the ice as they could, and then took to the water, making directly for the ſhips; when we uſed our arms ſo

ſucceſs-

ſucceſsfully that not one of them eſcaped. However, many others ſtill approaching from the high mountains, and being unwilling to continue expoſed to ſuch hourly attacks, we weighed and ſtood over to the weſt coaſt of Zembla, where we firſt anchored, and got clear of the ſtreights of Weygats, but not without great danger of running upon the rocks of ice that lay in our way.

There is an iſland at the mouth of this ſtreight which appeared very green, and is covered with fir and juniper-trees. Some of the ſailors going on ſhore, ſaw a bird ſo large as to be ſcarcely able to fly; and giving at their return an account of what they had ſeen, I deſired leave to land with about forty men to hunt theſe birds, and make diſcoveries; which being granted, we killed about ſixty of them, ſome of which we ſhot, and others we knocked down with clubs, and afterward carried them on board. Theſe birds, which are not much taller than ſwans, though a great deal larger, are called penguins. They have a ſharp beak, under which begins a gullet that reaches down to their breaſt, in the form of an urinal, only it is larger; and in this bag they ſtore their proviſions, which they take out to eat as they have occaſion. They are of a brown colour, and have webbed feet like a gooſe. Their fleſh is extremely palatable, and taſtes like that of a wild-duck, only it is fatter. We eat heartily of it, and had not ſuch a feaſt in all our voyage; but before we dreſſed them, we were obliged to take off the ſkin, which is very tough.

Having ſtaid at this iſland two days, we ſailed with a ſouth-eaſt wind; and in about thirty hours arrived at a cape, near which we again found the Zemblians worſhipping the ſun.

As his Daniſh majeſty was very deſirous of having a perfect account of the riches and nature of Zembla, and for the more eaſy acquiring of that knowledge, had ordered our officers to bring off ſome of the natives, we resolved, if possible, to put this order in execution; and thirty persons, of which I was one, were ordered to land in the long-boat: but we had scarcely got over the ship's side before we discovered a *Zemblian* in his boat, about half a league off land, who seeing us make toward him, he rowed so fast that it was impossible to get up with him; and as soon as he set his foot on shore, throwing his boat upon his shoulder, ran so swiftly, that we perceived we should find it very difficult to overtake him, nor did he seem encumbered either with his boat or a dart he had in his hand. We however landed, and pursued him toward a hill, which we saw him mount, and he was quickly out of sight. We therefore gave over all thoughts of taking him; but as we were rowing back to our ships, we perceived two Zemblians further out at sea; and they observing us at the same time, rowed toward the promontories and rocks on the coast to hide themselves; but we plied our oars so briskly, that we surrounded them in four boats, as they were rowing with all their strength toward a rock; when finding no possibility of making their escape, they set up a howling that was the most hideous I had ever heard. They were a man and woman dressed in cloaths made of the skin of the sea-calf, with the hair outward, and their waistcoats were formed of two skins joined together, the tails dangling, the one before and the other behind, almost as low as their knees. Their drawers were very strait. The man seemed to be about fifty years of age, and though he had no hair on his head, he had a round beard of a chesnut colour. The woman, who seemed to be about thirty, had her ears and nose bored, and pendants of blue stones hanging at them; her hair was twisted, and dangled on her shoulders. Their features were extremely disagreeable, and they here both of them shorter and squatter than either the Laplanders, Samojedians, Borandians, or Siberians. They had squeaking voices and stink-

ſtinking breaths; the latter was probably cauſed by their eating of fleſh without ſalt, or fiſh with train-oil.

We ſoon took them into one of the boats, and towed that in which we found them, by faſtening it to one of our own boats. It was made of the rib-bones of fiſh, very artfully joined, and neatly covered with fiſh-ſkins ſewed together. It was ſixteen feet in length, and two feet and a half broad. They were ſhut up in it as high as their waiſts, by having a fiſh ſkin drawn over it, with two holes that fitted their waiſts; ſo that a drop of water could not get into it. They therefore expoſe themſelves in the fouleſt weather to all the dangers of the ſea, without the leaſt fear of foundering. But though we made all the friendly ſigns we could to them, in order to induce them to let us know their habitations, it was impoſſible for us to learn any thing from them *.

We now reſolved to try whether we could not get ſome other of theſe people into our power, who were leſs ſtupid and more communicative. Upon which thirty of us landed again, taking ſeveral days proviſions with us, and went in two companies well armed, about a hundred yards diſtance from each other, and having hid ourſelves in caverns under the rocks, poſted centinels in proper places, to diſcover if any ſavages approached, whom we intended to ſeize, and to force them to ſhew us their habitations. We were two days without ſeeing any of the natives; but at laſt one of our centinels gave us notice that two of them were deſcending a hill toward the ſea-ſide. On this we divided ourſelves into companies, at proper diſtances, and the poor Zemblians ſoon entered the ſnare, without ſuſpecting any treachery, till one of our companions diſcharging his fuzee, we all made our appearance; and the ſavages finding it impoſ-

* Theſe people appear to be of the ſame race with the Eſkimaux of Hudſon's Bay. See Ellis's Voyage to Hudſon's Bay, in vol. 3.

ſible to fly, were eaſily taken. Their garments were of penguins ſkins with the feathers outward. They had each a pair of ſtrait breeches which reached to their knees, a kind of waiſtcoat, the ſleeves of which reached only to their elbows, the reſt of their arms being naked. The feathers were picked from their waiſtcoats before and behind. They had caps in the form of a ſugar-loaf, and ſtockings made of the ſkin of a ſea-calf, with the hair outward. Though their dreſſes were the ſame, yet we ſoon perceived that one of them was a man and the other a woman. The man ſeemed to be abou twenty four years of age; his face was very broad, his noſe flat, and his complexion ſwarthy. He had neither beard on his chin, nor hair on his head; at his back hung a quiver filled with arrows; on his ſhoulder he carried an ax, and in his other hand he held a bow. The woman ſeemed to be about twenty, and held a dart in her hand; her hair hung down in two twiſted locks on each ſhoulder; ſhe had blue ſtreaks on her forehead and chin, and her ears and noſtrils had holes bored in them, in which were faſtened blue ſtones, thoſe in her ears being as large as filberts, and thoſe in her noſe no bigger than peas.

We tried all the ways we could think of to oblige them to ſhew us where they dwelt, but without effect. They were as reſolute and ſullen as thoſe we had taken in the boat, and we carried them on board without making any further diſcoveries. When we brought them to their fellow-priſoners we found, that notwithſtanding their being ſo differently dreſſed, they knew each other. Theſe four *Zemblians* ſeemed the moſt deſpicable part of the human ſpecies I had ever ſeen. Their features were extremely diſagreeable; and when they walked they waddled like ducks. We could never make them eat any bread, ſalt-meat, or fiſh, nor drink any beer; they being uſed to drink nothing but water; they ſometimes taſted our brandy, but had a great averſion to the ſmell of tobacco. The

wood-

wood-work of their bows and darts was very heavy, and of a red-brown colour, but that of the arrows was much lighter and paler. Their needles, the points of their darts, arrows, and all their other ſharp inſtruments were made of fiſh-bones.

The ſummer was now far advanced, it being the latter end of Auguſt, and the cold increaſing, we began to think of returning home; and therefore weighing, held on a ſouth-weſt courſe, but the wind ſhifting to the ſouthward, obliged us to make the coaſt of Greenland, where we dropped anchor near a French and Dutch fleet employed in the whale-fiſhery. The ſhips ſeldom lie far from the ſhore; for the whales, which are caught in the ſame manner as we took the ſea-horſes, are like them commonly found near the land. When they are caught they are cut to pieces, and the blubber being taken out, is put into large kettles, and melted to oil in huts erected for that purpoſe along the ſea-ſhore. During our ſtay here, I ſaw one whale that yielded 350 pounds weight of good bone, which together with its oil, muſt have afforded a conſiderable profit. Our arrival in this place proved very fortunate for our Zemblian priſoners, who had for ſome time pined away for want of whale oil, they being able to eat nothing unleſs it was ſoaked in it, and our ſtore was entirely exhauſted: but for their ſakes we here took in a freſh ſupply.

[Greenland or Spitzbergen, as it is called by the Dutch, lies nearer to the pole than any country yet known; it is as yet undiſcovered on the north: on the weſt it has the Northern Ocean; on the ſouth, the ſame ocean between it and Lapland, and the moſt northern part of Norway, over againſt which i tlies; on the eaſt it has an undiſcovered country, to which it is joined by an iſthmus, which country is by ſome called Eaſt or New Greenland. It lies from 76° to 82° north latitude, and perhaps much farther.

This country is not known to have any inhabitants except white bears of an enormous ſize, deer, and foxes. There is plenty of fowls, especially water-fowl, which harbour on the sunny sides of the mountains, and in the cliffs of the rocks. The dung of these birds, with moss, washed down by the melted snow, make a rich kind of mould in some places near the shore, where it produces several of the anti-scorbutic plants: and notwithstanding the inconceivable coldness of its situation, in June and July, the sun shines so hot as to melt the tar in the seams of a ship.]

Having staid two days on this coast, we took the advantage of a north-east wind, and proceeded on our voyage: but being overtaken by a storm, we steered to the coast of Iceland. On our approaching that island we heard a dreadful noise at land, like the firing of several pieces of ordnance; after which we saw flames issue in abundance from mount Hecla. We found so many rocks on the coast, and the sea was so extremely rough, that we were afraid of venturing within a league of the land; but we steered to cape Heri, under which we anchored in safety.

[Iceland, so called from its excessive coldness, is a large island in the Northern Ocean, subject to Denmark, about 480 miles distant from the coast of Norway to the west, and 400 from Scotland to the north. It extends from 63° 45′ to 67° north latitude; so that the arctic polar circle passes through the northern part of this island; and it lies between 11° and 27° west longitude.

Agriculture is not practised in this island, though Mr. Horrebow, whose account of this island is rather a favourable one, says that wheat may be produced in it; and that, from some old laws they have relating to ploughed lands, and from the appearance of some tracks of land, which bear all the marks of having been tilled, it is evident that agriculture was antiently attended to by the inhabitants.

The country is mountainous and stony; but the pastures are excellent. They make great quantities

of

of butter, which they lay up in caſks; or for want of them pile up in their huts like heaps of mortar: and they have tolerable good horſes, which in the winter when hay fails them, they feed with dried fiſh, as they alſo do their other cattle. The Icelanders dwell generally near the ſea-ſhore or rivers, for the conveniency of fiſhing and paſture, ſo that the inland country is almoſt deſart.

Their language is a dialect of the antient Runic tongue; and, according to Wormius, is the pureſt now ſpoke any where.]

Soon after, a ſtrong party of us landed at the village of Heri, whence we proceeded to Kirkebar, a large town, where we met with eight or nine Daniſh merchants, who were much ſurprized at ſeeing us there, and entertained us very cordially with diſhes of freſh meat, good bread, and excellent wine. From them we learned, that the day before the iſland had ſo terrible an earthquake, that they expected to be ſwallowed up alive.

Our captain, ſupercargo, and others of our company, intimating to the chief merchant at Kirkebar, that they were deſirous of ſeeing whatever was worth notice in the iſland; he very obligingly ordered horſes to be got ready for all of us that were willing to go into the country; and I ſaying that I would make one of them, eight of us mounted, while the reſt, having leſs curioſity, choſe to ſtay and drink at this merchant's houſe. This gentleman gave us one of his ſervants and two Icelanders to be our guides, and alſo furniſhed us with a horſeload of proviſions. We travelled two days in rugged and unfrequented roads; when we found ourſelves about five miles from mount Hecla, and perceived the ground ſtrewed with aſhes and pumice-ſtones, over which we paſſed to the foot of the mountain. The weather being now very ſerene and calm, and ſeeing no flames iſſue out of the volcano, we reſolved to go up to the top; but we being informed by our guides, that if we went farther we ſhould be in danger of falling into pits, where we might be ſuffocated with the fumes cauſed by the fire in the bowels of the earth, and that it would be impoſſible to pull us out; all our company except myſelf declared againſt proceeding: but I told them, that if they would ſtay for me I would go up alone; and they promiſing that they would, I alighted and prepared to aſcend the mountain, when one of the Daniſh merchants whom we met at Kirkebar, and who accompanied us out of curioſity, ſaid he would go along with me.

Having given our horſes to our guides, who ſtaid behind with the reſt of our company, we boldly ventured forward, reſolving to reach the top of Hecla, and in a ſhort time we ſaw a large flight of crows and vultures, that had their neſts in the top of the mountain. When we had aſcended about half a league, we felt the ground ſhake under us, and heard a terrible noiſe in the bowels of the earth, which ſeemed ready to burſt open. At the ſame time there appeared on all ſides chinks, out of which iſſued bluiſh flames, that had a ſtrong ſuffocating ſmell of burning brimſtone. This made us turn back, for fear of being burnt to aſhes. But we had ſcarce proceeded thirty yards back, before a black cloud of ſmoke aſcended out of the mountain, obſcured the light of the ſun, and covered us ſo thick that we could not ſee each other. Our fears encreaſed every ſtep we took; for behind us came flames of fire, ſhowers of aſhes, and pumice-ſtones, that fell as thick as hail, and this dreadful ſtorm was attended with horrible noiſes. We beſide every moment expected that the earth would open and ſwallow us up, which added wings to our flight, and we ran as faſt as we were able, to eſcape the danger to which we had expoſed ourſelves by our idle curioſity; and indeed our fears made us ſo nimble, that in a quarter of an hour we got to the bottom of the mountain.

Our

Our companions, on ſeeing us come down ſo faſt, burſt into a fit of laughter, which was ſoon increaſed by their obſerving us to be as black as if we had been covered with ſoot; their mirth, however, ſoon abated; for on our approaching them, we both dropt down ſpeechleſs.... They immediately came to our aſſiſtance, and by rubbing our temples, noſtrils, and hands with vinegar, brought us to ourſelves, and then revived us with a cup of canary; upon which recovering our ſtrength and ſpirits, we related what had happened, and they rejoiced at our eſcape.

We now left the foot of the mountain in order to ſee two ſprings at ten or twelve miles diſtance from the mountain, one of which is always boiling, and the other ſo cold, that it is ſaid to turn every thing put into it into iron. When we had proceeded about 100 yards from the foot of mount Hecla, we found a pumice-ſtone as large as a hogſhead, which had been lately thrown out of the volcano; when our guides ſeeing us aſtoniſhed at its prodigious ſize, ſaid they had ſeen ſeveral much bigger, which ten men could not ſtir.

After three hours riding we drew near to the ſprings, which are thirty yards diſtance from each other. We came firſt to the cold one, when putting in a ſmall cane I had in my hand, I was ſurprized on taking it out again to ſee the end which touched the bottom metamorphoſed into iron *. From thence we went to the boiling fountain, from which we ſaw a number of what appeared to be fowls, of a red colour, and about the ſize of ducks, playing in the water; when being pleaſed with the novelty of the ſight, we ſtood for ſome time looking at them, but on our approaching nearer, they dived to the bottom; but we had ho ſooner left it than they appeared again.

From this ſpring we travelled to the ſea-ſide, within half a league of which we heard diſagreeable ſounds,

* The author's miſtake probably aroſe from the cane being incruſted with a ſtony concretion reſembling iron ruſt.

that

that were not unlike the cries of perſons complaining. Our ignorant guides, who were natives of the country, would fain have perſuaded us that they were the lamentations of the damned, who, when the devil had roaſted them in the flames of Hecla, cooled them by plunging them amongſt the ice on the coaſt; and that they were thus alternately tormented, by making them feel the extremes of heat and cold. On our arrival at the coaſt we found that theſe imaginary complaints were only occaſioned by the agitation of the ice and water driven violently againſt the rocks by the wind.

Having ſeen all that was worth obſervation, we returned to Kirkebar, where we arrived on the 16th of September; and having ſtaid a few hours in the town, went on board, when we found the governor of the iſland, accompanied by the biſhop of Sceltholt, who, hearing that we had been at Zembla, came to ſee our ſhips, and to diſcourſe with us.

As Iceland abounds in rich paſtures, it produces great plenty of all ſorts of cattle, and the beaſts that feed in theſe paſtures are ſo fond of an herb called caitophe, that the inhabitants are forced to prevent their eating too much of it, for fear they ſhould burſt themſelves; but though the fields look green and pleaſant, yet the north eaſt wind, which blows here with great violence, is ſo very cold, that no wheat, or any other grain fit to make bread will grow there.

The Icelanders, for the moſt part, dwell in caverns hewn out of the rocks, and the reſt live in huts built after the manner of thoſe in Lapland, ſome with wood, and others with fiſh-bones, covered with turf; and both they and their cattle lie under the ſame roof. Their beds are compoſed of hay or ſtraw, upon which they lie in their cloaths, with ſkins upon them, and make but one bed for the whole family. Both the men and women have very diſagreeable perſons; they are ſwarthy, and dreſſed like the Norwegians,

wegians, in coats made of the ſkins of the ſea-calf with the hair outward, with no other linen than ſack-cloth. They live by fiſhing, and are very naſty. [The food of the poor is very coarſe, it conſiſting of a ſort of ſtock-fiſh pounded with a ſtone, very bad butter and cheeſe, and no other drink but water, milk, or whey; yet on this hard fare many of them are ſaid to live without the help of a phyſician to a hundred and fifty years of age.] Moſt of them pretend to witchcraft, and are ſaid to worſhip the devil under the name of Kobald, who, it is pretended, frequently appears to them under a human ſhape. They have alſo a kind of houſhold god cut out of a piece of wood with a knife, who is extremely hideous; this idol they adore privately, and hide it for fear of the Lutheran miniſters, who endeavour to inſtruct them in the principles of Chriſtianity.

Three days after our coming on board, we took the opportunity of a north wind, and ſet ſail. We continued our courſe to the ſouth ſouth-eaſt, and at length happily arrived at Copenhagen, where having ſaluted the caſtle, we dropt anchor, and went aſhore.

His majeſty being informed, on our entering the city, that we had brought ſome Zemblians with us, commanded us to bring them to court, which we immediately did, every body gazing at them as if they had been born in another world. The king himſelf admired the oddneſs of their dreſs, and the ſtrangeneſs of their figures. He ordered the ſteward of his houſhold to give directions for their being kept with care, well provided for, and taught the Daniſh language, hoping he might then get ſomething out of them relating to their country, that would be beneficial to his own. He commanded us to give him an account of the ſeveral places we had viſited, the manners of the people, and their way of living: and having given his majeſty full ſatisfaction with reſpect to all he deſired to know, we went to wait upon our owners, in order to inform them of the markets we had met with, and what returns we had brought home, which proved highly to their advantage.

TRAVELS

OF

Monſieur MAUPERTUIS,

And his ASSOCIATES of the ROYAL ACADEMY of SCIENCES.

Made by Order of the FRENCH KING, to determine the Figure of the EARTH at the POLAR CIRCLE.

IN order to give a clear idea of this undertaking, it is neceſſary to obſerve, that the great Sir Iſaac Newton and Mr. Huygens had from different obſervations concluded that the earth was flatted at the poles; but upon meaſuring the whole area of the meridian that paſſes through France, and from other operations, it was concluded by ſeveral of the members of the Academy of Sciences at Paris, that the terraqueous globe was prominent at the poles. Hence the members became divided in their ſentiments, and perplexed by their own enquiries, upon ſo important a ſubject, that was juſtly conſidered as having a real influence upon aſtronomy and navigation. To put an end to this diſpute, the French king reſolved that it ſhould be finally decided, and to the great joy of the academy, an order was diſpatched from court for a certain number of the members to go and meaſure the firſt degree of the meridian at the

equator.

equator*. These, says Monf. Maupertuis, fet out a whole year before us. The reft were commiffioned northward to meafure the remoteft degree they could reach: and the fame alacrity, the fame zeal to ferve their country appeared in thofe who were to endure the rage of the equator funs, and thofe who were to freeze beneath the polar circle. The travels in the north were wrote by Monf. Maupertuis, and we fhall give them in his manner.

The company deftined for the north, fays he, was compofed of four academicians, Meffrs. Clairaut, Camus, Le Monnier, and myfelf; the abbe Outhier, and M. Celfius, the celebrated profeffor of aftronomy at Upfal, alfo affifted at all our operations, and their abilities and advice were of fingular ufe to us.

No fooner was the veffel that carried us arrived at Stockholm, than we refolved without lofs of time to fet out for the bottom of the gulph of Bothnia, where we might judge which fide of the gulph was proper for our operations, better than we could do by trufting to our charts.

We arrived at Tornea time enough to fee the fun perform his courfe for feveral days together without fetting; a fight which ftrikes with wonder an inhabitant of the temperate zones, even though he knows it is what muft neceffarily happen in that climate.

We had flattered ourfelves with the hopes of performing our operations upon the coafts of the gulph of Bothnia, where we fhould have the convenience of tranfporting ourfelves and our inftruments to the different ftations by fea, and where the many advantageous points of view, from the iflands in all our charts, feemed to promife us fuccefs. But when we went with great impatience to view them, all our labour ferved only to convince us, that this defign was impracticable. The iflands that line the coafts of the gulph, and the coafts themfelves, which we

* See Ulloa's voyage in vol. i. of this collection.

had fancied to be ſo many promontories, that might furniſh us with diſtant points of view from one to another, lay all of them ſo low upon the ſurface of the water, that at a ſmall diſtance, the convexity of the earth muſt ariſe between them and us. So that after ſeveral voyages in purſuance of our firſt deſign of making uſe of theſe iſlands, we were at laſt obliged to give it up.

We now reſolved to endeavour to perform our operations upon the tops of the mountains to the northward of Tornea, though it appeared next to impoſſible. In the deſarts of a country ſcarcely habitable, in that immenſe foreſt which extends from Tornea to Cape Nord, we muſt go through operations that are not eaſy, even where no convenience is wanting. There were but two ways of penetrating into theſe deſarts, both of which we muſt prove; one the ſailing up a river full of cataracts, the other croſſing thick woods and deep marſhes on foot; and if we ſhould be able to make our way into the country, we muſt, after the moſt painful marches, be obliged to clamber up ſteep rocks, and to clear the tops of mountains of the wood that would intercept our ſight. In theſe deſarts we ſhould be forced to take up with the moſt wretched diet, be expoſed to the flies, which in this ſeaſon are ſo inſufferable as to drive the Laplanders and their rain-deer from their habitations, to ſeek ſhelter on the coaſts of the ocean. We were, in fine, to undertake this work without knowing, or being able to inform ourſelves, whether it was practicable; whether the want of one mountain might not, after all our toils, interrupt the ſeries of our triangles; or whether it would be poſſible to find upon the river a baſe by which they might be connected. But if we ſhould ſurmount all theſe obſtacles, we ſhould ſtill have the labour of building obſervatories on the moſt northerly of the mountains; the trouble of carrying thither as numerous a collection of inſtruments as is perhaps to be be ſeen in Europe, and of making there the niceſt aſtronomical obſervations: but we were ſo far from being deterred by theſe difficulties, that the proſpect of conquering them filled us with pleaſure.

We ſet out from Tornea on Friday the 6th of July 1736, with a company of Finland ſoldiers, and a good number of boats laden with inſtruments and proviſions. We began our journey by sailing up the great river, which, riſing in the inmoſt parts of Lapland, purſues its courſe till it falls into the gulph of Bothnia; having firſt divided itſelf into two branches that form the iſle of Swertzar, where is built a town of the ſame name in the latitude of 65° 51′. From this day forward, our only habitation was the deſarts, and our time was ſpent on the ſummits of thoſe mountains which we were to connect by our triangles.

After a voyage of twelve hours, we landed in the evening at Korpikyla, an hamlet by the river-ſide, inhabited by Finlanders; and having for ſome time travelled on foot acroſs the foreſt, arrived at the bottom of a ſteep mountain called Niva, whoſe ſummit, which is a bare rock, we choſe for our firſt ſtation. Upon the river we had been tormented by great flies with green heads, that fetched blood wherever they fixed: but on the top of this mountain we were peſtered with ſeveral other kinds that were ſtill more intolerable. By good luck we found two Lapland girls tending a ſmall herd of rein-deer, but almoſt hid in the ſmoke of a great fire they had kindled: and being told, on enquiry, that they thus defended themſelves from the flies, we had immediately recourſe to the ſame method.

On the 8th of July, at one in the morning, Mr. Camus and I left our company upon Niwa, to reconnoitre the mountains to the northward. We travelled up the river to a high mountain called Avaſaxa, where having cleared its top of the trees, we cauſed a ſignal to be built. Our ſignals were hollow cones, compoſed of a great many large trees,

 ſtripped

ſtripped of the bark, by which means they were white enough to be viſible at ten or twelve leagues diſtance.

This being finiſhed, we came down from Avaſaxa, and embarking on the little river of Tenglio, which falls into the great river at the foot of this mountain; we directed our courſe upward to the neareſt place we could find, to a mountain that ſeemed to ſuit our purpoſe; and from thence a march of three hours, over a moraſs, brought us to the foot of Horrilakero. Though extremely fatigued, we got to the top of it, and ſpent the night in cutting down the wood that covered it. Moſt part of this mountain is a reddiſh ſtone, interſperſed with a kind of white cryſtal. Here the flies, more mercileſs than thoſe at Niwa, were not to be driven off by ſmoke, and we were obliged, notwithſtanding the exceſſive heats, to wrap our heads in our cappmudes, a ſort of gown made of rein-deer ſkins, and to cover ourſelves with branches of fir, and even whole trees, which rather ſtifled than defended us from theſe troubleſome inſects.

Having cut down all the wood on the top of Horrilakero, and built a ſignal, we returned by the ſame road to our boats, which we had drawn upon the bank. It is indeed no hard matter to drag along, or even to carry the boats uſed in the rivers of Lapland. A few thin fir boards compoſe the whole veſſel, which is ſo extremely light and flexible, that its beating, with all the forces of the ſtream, againſt the ſtones, which theſe rivers are full of, does it no manner of harm. It is terrible to thoſe not accuſtomed to it, and aſtoniſhing even to thoſe who are, to ſee one of theſe weak veſſels drive down a cataract, in a torrent of foam and ſtones, ſometimes raiſed aloft in the air, and the next moment loſt in the deep. A bold Finlander ſteers it with a long oar, while his two companions row hard to ſave it from the purſuing waves that threaten every moment

ment to overwhelm it. You may then ſee the whole keel by turns raiſed above water, and leaning only with one extremity on the top of a yielding billow. With ſuch courage and addreſs do theſe Finlanders paſs the cataracts; but their art and ſkill in the management of their boats upon other occaſions, is no leſs remarkable: a tree, branches and all, commonly ſerves them both for maſt and ſail.

We now embarked again on the Tenglio, which brought us down into the river of Tornea on our return to Korpikyla. At four leagues from Avaſaxa we left our boats, and after an hour's walk over the foreſt, reached the foot of Cuitaperi, a ſteep mountain; its ſummit is a rock covered with moſs, affording an extenſive proſpect all round, and to the ſouth taking in the gulph of Bothnia: here we erected a ſignal, whence we could diſcover all the others we had raiſed, and then continued our courſe down the river. Between Cuitaperi and Korpikyla we found ſome frightful cataracts, where the Finlanders always ſet their paſſengers aſhore; but our exceſſive fatigue made us chuſe rather to riſk the paſſage in the boat than to walk only an hundred yards. At laſt, on the evening of the 11th, we joined our friends on the top of Niwa, who had deſcried our ſignals, but from the continual fogs, were unable to make any obſervations.

The fogs being at length diſperſed by the cold north wind, we had ſuch a view of our ſeveral ſignals, as to take their angles; and having finiſhed our obſervations there, we ſet up ſignals at Kakama and Pullingi, where having alſo made our obſervations, we all ſet out for Avaſaxa.

This mountain is ſeated on the bank of the river, fifteen leagues from Tornea. Its aſcent is difficult, lying through a wood that reaches half way up, where it is interrupted by ſteep ſlippery rocks; and afterward continued to the very top of the mountain before we cut down ſo much of it as was neceſſary to open our proſpect. The north-eaſt ſide is a moſt frightful rocky precipice, where the falcons build their neſts. At its foot runs the Tenglio, by which it is encircled. From its ſummit the proſpect is the moſt beautiful that can be imagined; to the ſouth it is unbounded, and diſcovers the courſe of the river to a vaſt extent: toward the eaſt the Tenglio may be traced in its paſſage through ſeveral lakes; and the view is terminated on the north, at twelve or fifteen leagues diſtance, by a prodigious number of hills heaped one upon another. Upon this mountain we ſpent ten days, during which curioſity prompted the inhabitants to pay us frequent viſits, bringing us fiſh and ſheep, and ſuch bad fruits as are produced in the woods.

The day we left Avaſaxa we croſſed the polar circle, and at three the next morning, which was the 31ſt of July, arrived at Turtula, a hamlet where they were cutting their little crop of barley and hay. After having travelled for ſome time in the woods, we embarked on a lake that brought us to the foot of Pullingi, the higheſt of all our mountains, and of exceeding difficult acceſs; as well on account of its ſteepneſs, as the depth of the moſs wherein we were obliged to fix our ſteps. Our ſtay here, which was till the 6th of Auguſt, was no leſs diſagreeable than the aſcent had been painful. We had a whole wood of the largeſt trees to fell, and the flies attacked us with ſuch fury, that our ſoldiers of the regiment of Weſtro-Bothnia, a body diſtinguiſhed for their bravery even in Sweden, and hardened by the greateſt fatigues, were obliged to wrap up their faces, or to ſmear them all over with tar. Theſe inſects alſo poiſoned our victuals; no ſooner was a diſh ſerved, but it was quite covered over with them, while another ſwarm, with all the rapaciouſneſs of birds of prey, was fluttering round, to carry off ſome pieces of a ſheep that was dreſſing for us.

On

On the 6th of Auguſt we left this mountain to go to Pello, where we arrived the ſame day, after having forced our way up four cataracts. Pello is a village inhabited by a few Finlanders; in its neighbourhood is Kittis, the loweſt of all our mountains, where was one of our ſignals. As we were going up, we diſcovered a copious ſpring of pure water, that reſiſts the keeneſt froſts; for when we returned to Pello about the end of winter, while the ſea at the bottom of the gulph, and all the rivers were frozen as hard as marble, we found this ſpring running as in ſummer. We had the good fortune to make our obſervations ſoon after our arrival, and the next day went to Turtula.

For a month paſt we had been inhabitants of the deſarts, or rather of the mountain tops; the earth or rocks ſpread with the ſkins of rein-deer had been our beds; and our food was chiefly fiſh, brought us by the Finlanders, or which we ourſelves had caught; and berries or wild fruit that grew in the woods.

I left Turtula, in company with Meſſrs. Outhier and Celſus, to croſs the foreſt and find the ſignal erected at Niemi; and a frightful journey it was. We ſet out on foot, and walked till we got to a brook, where we embarked in three little boats: but they paſſed with ſuch difficulty between the ſtones, that we were obliged every inſtant to get out of them and leap from one rock to another. The brook brought us to a lake ſo full of little yellowiſh grains of the bigneſs of millet, that the whole water was diſcoloured with them. I took them to be the chryſalis of ſome inſect, and was tempted to fancy, that this inſect muſt be ſome kind of thoſe flies that ſo tormented us, for I could think of no other ſpecies of animals whoſe numbers correſponded to the quantity of grains that covered this large body of water. From the extremity of this lake we had to walk to another of very clear water. Here we found a boat, and putting our quadrant on board, reſolved to follow it along the side of the lake on foot; but the wood was so thick, that we were forced to cut our way through it, and were intangled at every step by the depth of the moss, and the fallen fir-trees that lay across our way.

In all these woods there are almost as many trees fallen as standing; for the soil, after it has reared them to a certain height, can no longer furnish the proper nourishment, nor is it deep enough to allow them to take firm root: whence the least blast of wind oversets them; and in all these woods nothing is to be seen but firs and birches blown down. Time reduces the wood of the latter to dust, without affecting the bark; and one is surprized to find pretty large trees that crumble upon the slightest touch. This probably gave the Swedes the hint of covering their houses with this bark, and indeed nothing could be imagined fitter for the purpose. In some provinces they cover the bark with earth, and form upon the roof a kind of garden, such as are to be seen upon the houses of Upsal. In Westro-Bothnia the bark is bound with fir poles that hang down on either side of the roof.

Having at length reached a third lake, which was very large, and the finest water imaginable; we put our instruments and baggage on board two boats we found there, and waited their return upon the coast; when we were ferried over to the foot of Niemi.

The fine lakes that surround this mountain, and the many difficulties we encountered in getting thither, gave it the air of an inchanted island in romance. On one hand you see a grove of trees rise from a plain, smooth and level as the walks of a garden; and at such easy distances, as neither to embarrass the walks, nor the prospect of the lake that washes the foot of the mountain. On the other, you have apartments of different sizes that seem cut by art in the rocks, and to want only a regular roof to complete them. The rocks themselves are so perpendicular, so high,

and

and ſo ſmooth, that you would take them for the walls of an unfiniſhed palace, rather than for the work of nature. From this height we ſaw thoſe vapours riſe from the lake which the people of the country call Haltios, and deem the guardian ſpirits of the mountains. We had been frightened with ſtories of bears haunting this place, but ſaw none. Indeed it ſeemed rather a place of reſort for fairies and genii, than for thoſe ſavage animals.

Having compleated our obſervations, we left Niemi, repaſſed the three lakes, and got back to Turtula. We afterward departed from thence, and ſet out for Horrilakero, entering the Tenglio with four boats. Its cataracts are troubleſome, rather from the lowneſs of the water, and the great number of ſtones, than the rapidity of the ſtream. As we ſailed along, I was ſurprized to ſee upon the banks of this river, roſes of as lively a red as any in our gardens. We compleated our obſervations at Horrilakero on the 17th of Auguſt, and the next day went to Oſwer-Tornea, where our whole company was now aſſembled.

But afterwards going up to Avaſaxa to take the angles that muſt connect the baſe, which we had fixed on the bank of the river with our triangles, we ſaw Horrilakero all in flames. This is an accident not uncommon in theſe woods, where there is no living during the ſummer, without ſmoak, and where the moſs and firs are ſo combuſtible, that a fire once kindled will ſpread over ſome thouſand acres; and the ſmoke of theſe fires have ſometimes retarded our obſervations as much as the thickneſs of the air. As this fire on Horrilakero had been doubtleſs occaſioned by our not taking ſufficient care to extinguiſh thoſe we had kindled there, we diſpatched thirty men to cut off its communication with the neighbouring woods. But three days after, when we had finiſhed our obſervations at Avaſaxa, Horrilakero was ſtill burning; we ſaw it involved in a cloud of ſmoak. and the flames, which had made their way downward were ravaging all the foreſt below.

By the 9th of September, when we had paſſed ſixty-three days in theſe deſerts, we had finiſhed as compleat a ſet of triangles as we could have wiſhed for: and an undertaking begun in a manner at random, without knowing whether it was at all practicable, had turned out ſo much better than expectation, that it looked as if the placing of theſe mountains had been at our diſpoſal. We had built two obſervatories upon Kittis in the one was a quadrant of two foot radius, a clock of Mr. Graham's, and an inſtrument which we owed to the ſame gentleman, conſiſting of a teleſcope, moveable about an horizontal axis, which was to determine the direction of our triangles with reſpect to the meridian. The other obſervatory, which was much larger, was built ſo near the firſt, that the voice of him who counted the pendulum's vibrations, could be diſtinctly heard from one to the other. An admirable ſector alſo made by Mr. Graham took up almoſt the whole room. What difficulty we had in carrying up ſo many inſtruments to the top of the mountain, I ſhall not mention; it is ſufficient that we carried them up.

We had ſome ice on the 19th of September, and ſnow on the 21ſt; ſome parts of the river were alſo frozen. On the firſt of November it began to freeze harder, and on the morrow the river was quite frozen up. The ice, which thawed no more, was preſently covered over with ſnow; and this vaſt body of water, but a few days before full of ſwans and other water-fowl, was now one immenſe plain of ice and ſnow. Our work was now in a manner compleated, we had only to meaſure our baſe, which was no more than ſurveying the diſtance between the two ſignals we had erected laſt ſummer; but this was to be done upon the ice of a river in Lapland, at the diſtance of above three leagues, in a country where the cold was growing every day more intenſe. On the 21ſt of December

cember this work was begun. In this ſeaſon the ſun but juſt ſhewed itſelf above the horizon toward noon; but the long twilights, the whiteneſs of the ſnow, and the meteors continually blazing in the ſky, furniſhed us light enough to work four or five hours every day. We lodged at the houſe of the curate of Oſwer-Tornea, and at eleven in the forenoon began our ſurvey, attended by ſo great an equipage, that the Laplanders, drawn by the novelty of the ſight, came down from the neighbouring mountains. We ſeparated into two bands, each of which carried four rods of fir, each thirty feet long. I ſhall ſay nothing of the fatigues and dangers of this operation Judge what it muſt be to walk in ſnow two feet deep, with heavy poles in our hands, which we were obliged to be continually laying on the ſnow, and lifting again, in a cold ſo extreme, that whenever we would taſte a little brandy, the only thing that could be kept liquid, our tongues and lips froze to the cup, and came away bloody: in a cold that congealed the fingers of ſome of us, and threatened us with ſtill more diſmal accidents. While the extremities of our bodies were thus freezing, the reſt, through exceſſive toil, was bathed in ſweat. Brandy did not quench our thirſt; we muſt have recourſe to deep wells dug through the ice, which were ſhut almoſt as ſoon as opened, and from which the water could ſcarcely be conveyed unfrozen to our lips; thus were we forced to run the hazard of the dangerous contraſt which ice-water might produce in our heated bodies.

Our work, however, advanced apace; for ſix days labour brought it to within five hundred toiſes, where we had not been able to plant our ſtakes ſoon enough: three of the gentlemen therefore undertook this office, while the abbé Outhier and I went upon a pretty extraordinary adventure. We had laſt ſummer omitted an obſervation of ſmall moment; this was taking the height of an object that we made uſe of in meaſur-

ing

ing on the top of Avaſaxa; and to perform this, I undertook to go with a quadrant to the top of the mountain, ſo ſcrupulouſly careful were we that nothing ſhould be wanting to the perfection of the work. Imagine a very high mountain full of rocks, that lie hid in a prodigious quantity of ſnow, as well as their cavities, wherein you may ſink through a cruſt of ſnow as into an abyſs, and the undertaking will ſcarce appear poſſible: yet there are two ways of performing it, one by walking, or rather ſliding along upon two ſtrait boards eight feet in length, which the Finlanders and Laplanders uſe to keep them from ſinking into the ſnow: but this way of walking requires long practice. The other is by truſting yourſelf to a rein-deer uſed to ſuch journies.

The machine drawn by theſe animals is here a kind of boat ſcarcely large enough to hold the half of one's body. As this travelling in the ſnow is a kind of navigation, that the veſſel may ſuffer the leſs reſiſtance in its courſe, it has a ſharp head, and a narrow keel, like an ordinary boat; and on this keel it tumbles ſo from ſide to ſide, that if a man does not take good care to balance himſelf, it will be every moment in danger of overſetting. It is fixed by thongs to the collar of the rein-deer, who, as ſoon as he finds himſelf on a firm beaten road, runs with incredible fury. If you would ſtop him, it is to little purpoſe to pull a ſort of rein that is tied to his horns: wild and unmanageable, it will only make him change his track, or perhaps turn upon you, and revenge himſelf by kicking. If this happens to a Laplander, he turns the boat over him, and uſes it as a buckler againſt the attacks of the rein-deer: but as we were ſtrangers to this addreſs, we might have been killed before we could put ourſelves in ſuch a poſture of defence. We had nothing to defend us with but a little ſtick each of us held in his hand, by way of rudder to ſteer our courſe, and keep clear of the trunks of trees. In this manner was I to climb Avaſaxa, accompanied by the abbé Outhier; but we were attended by two men and a woman of the country, and Mr. Brunnius their curate.

The firſt part of our journey was performed in a moment; for our flight over the plain beaten road from the curate's houſe to the foot of the mountain can be compared only to that of birds. And though the mountain where there was no track greatly abated the ſpeed of our rein-deer, they got at length to the top of it; where we immediately made the obſervation for which we came. In the mean while, our rein-deer had dug deep holes in the ſnow, where they browzed on the moſs that covers the rocks; and the Laplanders had lighted a great fire, and we preſently joined them to warm ourſelves. The cold was ſo extreme, that the heat of the fire could reach only to a very ſmall diſtance. As the ſnow juſt by it melted, it was immediately froze again, forming a hearth of ice all round.

Our journey up hill had been painful; but now our concern was leſt our return ſhould be too rapid. We were to proceed down the ſteep in conveyances, which, though partly ſunk in the ſnow, ſlid on notwithſtanding, drawn by animals, whoſe fury in the plain we had already tried, and who, though ſinking to their bellies in the ſnow, would endeavour to free themſelves by the ſwiftneſs of their flight. We very ſoon found ourſelves at the bottom of a hill; a moment after this a great river was croſſed, and we were returned back to the curate's houſe.

The next day we finiſhed our ſurvey, and made all poſſible haſte back to Tornea to ſecure ourſelves in the beſt manner we were able from the increaſing ſeverity of the ſeaſon. The town of Tornea, at our arrival on the 30th of December, had really a moſt frightful aſpect. Its little houſes were buried to the tops in ſnow, which, had there been any day light, muſt have effectually ſhut it out.

But

But the ſnow continually falling, or ready to fall, for the moſt part hid the ſun the few moments he might have appeared at mid-day. In the month of January the cold was increaſed to that extremity, that Mr. Reaumur's mercurial thermometers, which at Paris, in the great froſt of 1709, it was thought ſtrange to ſee fall to fourteen degrees below the freezing point, were now got down to thirty-ſeven. The ſpirit of wine in the others was frozen. If we opened the door of a warm room, the external air inſtantly converted all the vapour in it into ſnow, whirling it round in white vortexes. If we went abroad, we felt as if the air was tearing our breaſts in pieces; and the crackling of the wood of which the houſes are built, as it ſplit by the violence of the froſt, continually alarming us with an encreaſe of cold. The ſolitude of the ſtreets was as great as if the people had been all dead: and in this country you may often ſee people who have loſt an arm or leg by the froſt. The cold, which is always very great, ſometimes increaſes by ſuch violent and ſudden fits, as are almoſt infallibly fatal to thoſe who are ſo unhappy as to be expoſed to it; and ſometimes there riſe ſudden tempeſts of ſnow that are ſtill more dangerous. The winds ſeem to blow from all quarters at once, and drive about the ſnow with ſuch fury, that all the roads are in a moment rendered inviſible. Dreadful is the ſituation of a perſon ſurpriſed in the fields by ſuch a ſtorm; his knowlege of the country, and even the mark, he may have taken by the trees, cannot avail him; he is blinded by the ſnow, and if he attempts to find his way home is generally loſt. In ſhort, during the whole winter the cold was ſo exceſſive, that on the 7th of April, at five in the morning, the thermometer was fallen to twenty diviſions below the point of freezing, though every afternoon it roſe two or three diviſions above it: a difference in the height not much leſs than that which the greateſt heat and cold felt at Paris uſually produce

produce in that inſtrument. Thus in the ſpace of twenty-four hours, we had all the variety felt in the temperate zones in the compaſs of a whole year.

But though in this climate the earth is thus horrible, the heavens preſent the moſt beautiful proſpects. The ſhort days are no ſooner cloſed, than fires of a thouſand colours and figures light up the ſky, as if deſigned to compenſate for the abſence of the ſun in this ſeaſon. Theſe fires have not here, as in the more ſoutherly climates, any conſtant ſituation. Though a luminous arch is often ſeen fixed toward the north, they ſeem more frequently to poſſeſs the whole extent of the hemiſphere. It would be endleſs to mention all the different figures theſe meteors aſſume, and the various motions with which they are agitated. Their motion is moſt commonly like that of a pair of colours waved in the air, and the different tints of their light gives them the appearance of ſo many vaſt ſtreamers of changeable taffeta. On the 18th of December I ſaw a phænomenon of this kind, that in the midſt of all the wonders to which I was now every day accuſtomed, raiſed my admiration. To the ſouth a great ſpace of the ſky appeared tinged with ſo lively a red, that the whole conſtellation of Orion looked as if it had been dipped in blood. This light, which was at firſt fixed, ſoon moved, and changing into other colours, violet and blue, ſettled into a dome, whoſe top ſtood a little to the ſouth-weſt of the zenith. The moon ſhone bright, but did not in the leaſt efface it. In this country, where there are lights of ſo many different colours, I never ſaw but two that were red; and ſuch are taken for preſages of ſome great misfortune. After all, when people gaze at theſe phænomena with an unphiloſophic eye, it is not ſurpriſing if they diſcover in them armies engaged, fiery chariots, and a thouſand other prodigies.

During

During the winter we repeated many of our obſervations and calculations, and found the moſt evident proofs of the earth's being conſiderably flatted at the poles. Mean time, the ſun came nearer, or rather no more quitted us. It was now May, when it was curious enough to ſee that great luminary enlighten for ſo long a time a whole horizon of ice; and to ſee ſummer in the heavens, while winter ſtill kept poſſeſſion of the earth. We were in the morning of that long day of ſeveral months; yet the ſun with all his power wrought no change either upon the ice or ſnows.

On the 6th of May it began to rain, and ſome water appeared on the ice of the river. At noon a little ſnow melted; but in the evening, winter reſumed his rights. At length, on the 10th, the earth which had been ſo long hid began to appear; ſome high points that were expoſed to the ſun ſhewed themſelves, as the tops of the mountains did after the deluge, and all the fowls of the country returned. At the beginning of June, winter yielding up the earth and ſea, we prepared for our departure back to Stockholm, and on the 9th ſome of us ſet out by land and others by ſea.

THE NATURAL HISTORY OF NORWAY,

BY ERICH PONTOPPIDON,

Bishop of BERGEN, and Member of the Royal Academy of Sciences at COPENHAGEN.

[NORWAY is, next to Lapland, the most northern country of Europe; it is bounded on the south by the entrance into the Baltic called the Schager Rack or Categate; on the west and north by the northern ocean; and on the east it is parted from Sweden by a long ridge of mountains called by different names, but commonly stiled the Dofrine mountains. This country lies between 57° and 71° 30′ north latitude, and between 5° and 31° east longitude; so that it extends about 5° 30′ beyond the polar circle.]

Norway, which is subject to the crown of Denmark, affords many curious particulars for observation: as, though we are yet in the cold regions of the north, yet we come now among inhabitants not quite such strangers to the arts of civil society, as the Nova Zemblians and Laplanders. Of this country the latest and most authentic account is that of bishop Pontoppidon; whose character, added to his being bishop of Bergen in Norway, gave him the best opportunities of being well informed concerning what he writes. The substance of his relation is as follows.

To

To the weſt the ſea forms innumerable little iſlands and rocks about the coaſt of Norway; ſome indeed are nine leagues over, but the greater part are ſo ſmall, as to be inhabited only by fiſhermen and pilots: ſo that Norway is defended by a rampart which conſiſts perhaps of more than a million of ſtone columns that have their baſes at the bottom of the ſea, and their capitals a few fathoms only above the ſurface. There are among theſe rocks good harbours, but they are difficult and dangerous of acceſs; eſpecially to large ſhips without oars; but to prevent accidents, as much as poſſible, the government has cauſed many hundreds of large iron rings to be fixed to theſe rocks, as moorings for ſhips where there is not room for anchoring.

The ſhore is almoſt every where ſteep, angular, and impendent; ſo that the ſea cloſe to the rocks is three hundred fathoms deep, and in ſome places no bottom can be found: even creeks which run ten leagues up the country, have been found four hundred fathoms deep.

Beſide the ebb and flood, there is a current or eddy in the Norway ſea, called Maleſtrom, or Moſkoeſtrom. The iſland Moſkoe, from whence this ſtream derives its name, lies between the mountain Heſleggen in Lofoden, and the iſland Ver, which are about one league diſtant; and between the iſland and coaſt on each ſide the ſtream makes its way. Between Moſkoe and Lofoden, it is near four hundred fathoms deep; but between Moſkee and Ver, it is ſo ſhallow, as not to afford paſſage for a ſmall ſhip. When it is flood, the ſtream runs up the country between Lofoden and Moſkoe with a boiſtrous rapidity; and when it is ebb, returns to the ſea with a violence and noiſe, unequalled by the loudeſt cataracts. It is heard at the diſtance of many leagues, and forms a vortex or whirlpool of great depth and extent; ſo violent, that if a ſhip comes near it, it is immediately drawn irreſiſtibly into the whirl and there disappears; being absorbed and carried down to the bottom in a moment, where it is dashed to pieces against the rocks: and just at the turn of ebb and flood, when the water becomes still for about a quarter of an hour, it rises again in scattered fragments, scarcely to be known for the parts of a ship. When it is agitated by a storm, it has reached vessels at the distance of more than a Norway mile, where the crews have thought themselves in perfect security. Perhaps it is hardly in the power of fancy to conceive a situation of more horror, than of being thus driven forward by the sudden violence of an impetuous torrent to the vortex of a whirlpool, of which the noise and turbulence still increasing as it is approached, are an earnest of quick and inevitable destruction; while the wretched victims in an agony of despair and terror, cry out for that help which they know to be impossible, and see before them the dreadful abyss in which they are about to be plunged and dashed among the rocks at the bottom.

Even animals which have come too near the vortex, have expressed the utmost terror, when they find the stream irresistible. Whales are frequently carried away, and the moment they feel the force of the water, they struggle against it with all their might, howling and bellowing in a frightful manner. The like happens frequently to bears, who attempt to swim to the island to prey upon the sheep.

It is the opinion of Kircher, that the Malestrom is a sea vortex, which attracts the flood under the shore of Norway, and discharges it again in the gulph of Bothnia: but this opinion is now known to be erroneous, by the return of the shattered fragments of whatever happens to be sucked down by it. The large stems of firs and pines rise again so shivered and splintered, that the pieces look as if covered with bristles. The whole phænomena are the effects of the violence of the daily ebb and flood,

 occasioned

occaſioned by the contraction of the ſtream in its courſe between the rocks.

The climate of Norway is much more various than in moſt other European countries, it extending three hundred Norway miles * from Cape Lindeſnaes in the ſouth, to the north cape on the borders of Ruſſia. In the ſummer nights the horizon, when unclouded, is ſo clear and luminous, that at midnight one may do all kinds of work as in the day; and in the extremity of this country toward the iſlands of Finmark, the ſun is continually in view in the midſt of ſummer, and is obſerved to circulate day and night round the north pole. On the other hand, in the depth of winter the ſun is inviſible for ſome weeks; all the light perceived at noon being a faint glimmering of about an hour and a half's continuance; which, as the ſun never appears above the horizon, chiefly proceeds from the reflexion of the rays on the higheſt mountains, whoſe ſummits are ſeen more clearly than any other objects. But beſide the moon-ſhine, which by reflexion from the mountains is exceeding bright in the valleys, the people receive conſiderable relief from the Aurora Borealis, or northern lights, which often afford them all the light neceſſary to their ordinary labours.

On the eaſt ſide of Norway, the cold of winter generally ſets in about the middle of October, and laſts till the middle of April. The waters are congealed to a thick ice, and the mountains and valleys covered with ſnow. However, this is of ſuch importance to the welfare of the country, that in a mild winter, the peaſants who live among the mountains, are conſiderable ſufferers: for without ſevere froſt and ſnow, they can neither convey the timber they

* The common miles of Norway are computed to be about one fourth larger than a German mile, or nearly equal to five or ſix Engliſh miles.

have felled to the rivers, nor carry their corn, butter, furs, and other commodities, in their ſledges, to the market-towns; and after the ſale of them carry back the neceſſaries they are there ſupplied with. For the largeſt rivers, with their roaring cataracts, are arreſted in their courſe by the froſt; and the very ſpittle is no ſooner out of the mouth, than it is congealed, and rolls along the ground like hail. But the wiſe Creator has given the inhabitants of this cold climate a greater variety of preſervatives againſt the weather, than moſt countries afford. Extenſive foreſts ſupply them with plenty of timber for building, and for fuel: the wool of the ſheep, and the furs and ſkins of wild beaſts, furniſh them with warm lining for their cloaths, and covering for their beds: innumerable flights of wild fowl ſupply them with down and feathers: the mountains themſelves ſerve them for fences againſt the north and eaſt winds, and their caverns afford them ſhelter.

But while the winter rages thus in the eaſt of Norway, the lakes and bays on the weſt ſide are kept open by the warm exhalations of the ocean, though lying in a direct line with theſe frozen eaſtern parts; and the froſts are ſeldom known to laſt above a fortnight or three weeks. Even in the centre of Germany, which is two hundred leagues nearer the line, the winters are generally more ſevere, and the froſts ſharper than in the dioceſe of Bergen: for here the inhabitants often wonder to read in the public papers, of froſt and ſnow in Poland and Germany, when they feel no ſuch weather. The harbours of Amſterdam, Hamburgh, Copenhagen, and Lubeck, are frozen ten times oftener than ours; for with us this ſeldom happens above two or three times in a whole century. Thus our winter at Bergen is ſo moderate that the ſeas are always open to the fiſhermen and mariners, and here the north ſea continues navigable during the whole winter as far as the 80th or 82d degree.

In the ſummer months the weather is not only warm but very hot. Theſe violent heats, which are, however, of ſhort duration, may be partly derived from the valleys incloſed within high mountains, where the reverberation of the rays of the ſun on all ſides heat the air; and as there is almoſt no night, neither the atmoſphere nor the mountains have time to cool. Indeed there cannot be a more deciſive proof of the ſummer's heat in Norway, than that ſeveral vegetables (and particularly barley) grow up and ripen within ſix weeks or two months.

The air is pure and ſalubrious, eſpecially in the middle of the country about the mountains, where the inhabitants know little of ſickneſs. Phyſicians are only to be found in the chief towns, where they are eſtabliſhed with a public ſalary; but have generally very little employment. However, Bergen and all the eaſtern coaſt, is ſo ſubject to frequent rains, that the women, when they go abroad, in all weathers wear a woollen or ſilken black veil over their heads, while the men ſecure themſelves by wearing rain-hats, made like umbrellas.

Norway contains a vaſt number of mountains, ſome of which extend themſelves in a long chain from north to ſouth, while others are ſcattered about, and ſurrounded by, a level country. The chain already mentioned is ſaid to equal at leaſt the Alps in height; and abounds with frightful caverns of an amazing extent. Hearing at the parſonage of Oerſkoug, that from the ſide of a neighbouring mountain called Limer, iſſued a ſtream, over which was a cavern, I reſolved to take a view of it, and furniſhed myſelf with a tinder-box, candles, a lanthorn, and a long line to ſerve me as a clue to find the way out. The aſcent to it being extremely ſteep, we were obliged to climb with our hands as well as feet, and ſometimes were hard put to it to clear our way through the buſhes. After getting through the thicket which almoſt hides the mouth of the cavern, I beheld a

vaulted

vaulted paſſage of pure marble without the leaſt flaw, but with ſeveral angles and protuberances ſo bright as to reſemble a paſte moulding into ſmooth globular forms. The paſſage continues about one hundred paces in a ſtraight direction; then winds to the right with aſcents and deſcents; in ſome places growing narrower, and in others widening to double its former breadth, which was about four or five ells: thus two perſons might go abreaſt, only we were now and then obliged to ſtoop and even creep, when we felt a damp vapour, which prevented my going ſo far as I intended. Another thing remarkable was the terrible roaring of the waters under us, the courſe of which was what moſt excited my wonder, as over it lies a pavement of ſmooth ſtone, inclining a little on each ſide, but flat in the middle, and not above three fingers thick, with ſome crevices, through which the water may be ſeen.

The inhabitants of a mountainous country may be ſaid to labour under more inconveniencies than others. Thus the arable ground is here but little in compariſon with the waſtes and deſarts, which obliges the inhabitants to procure half of their ſubſiſtence from the ſea: the villages are ſmall, and the houſes ſcattered among the valleys. But in ſome places the peaſants houſes ſtand ſo high, and on the edge of ſteep precipices, that ladders are fixed to climb up to them: ſo that when a clergyman is ſent for, who is unpractiſed in the road, he riſks his life in aſcending them, eſpecially in winter, when the ways are ſlippery. In ſuch places the bodies of the dead muſt be let down with ropes, or be brought on men's backs before they are laid in a coffin, and, at ſome diſtance from Bergen, the mail muſt likewiſe in winter be drawn over the ſteepeſt mountains.

One of the principal inconveniences, eſpecially to travellers, ariſes from the roads: they cannot without terror paſs ſeveral places, even in the king's road over the ſides of ſteep and craggy mountains; on ways that are either ſhored up, or ſuſpended by iron bolts fixed in the mountains, and though not above the breadth of a foot path, have no rails on the ſide. If two travellers were to meet there in the night, and not ſee each other ſoon enough to ſtop where the road will ſuffer them to paſs, it appears to me, as it does to others whom I have aſked, that they muſt ſtop ſhort, without being able to paſs by each other, or to find a turning for their horſes, or even to alight. The only reſource I can imagine in this difficulty is, that one muſt endeavour to cling to ſome cliff of this ſteep mountain, or if help be at hand, be drawn up by a rope, and then throw his horſe headlong down a tremendous precipice, in order to make room for the other traveller to paſs.

Another evil reſulting from the mountains, is the ſhelter they afford in their caverns and clefts to the wild beaſts, which render it difficult to extirpate them. It is not eaſy to deſcribe the havock made by the lynxes, foxes, bears, and eſpecially wolves, among the cattle, and other uſeful animals. It often happens, that the cows, ſheep, and goats belonging to the peaſants fall down the precipices and are deſtroyed. Sometimes they make a falſe ſtep into a projection called a mountain-hammer, where they can neither aſcend nor deſcend: on this occaſion a peaſant chearfully ventures his life for a ſheep or a goat; and deſcending from the top of a mountain by a rope of ſome hundred fathoms in length, he flings his body on a croſs ſtick, till he can ſet his foot on the place where his goat is; when he faſtens it to the rope to be drawn up along with himſelf. But the moſt amazing circumſtance is, he runs this riſk with the help of only a ſingle perſon, who holds the end of the rope, or faſtens it to a ſtone, if there be one at hand. There are inſtances of the aſſiſtant himſelf having been dragged down, and ſacrificing his life from fidelity to his friend, on which both have periſhed,

riſhed. On theſe melancholy accidents, when man or beaſt falls ſome hundred fathoms down the precipices, it is obſerved that the air preſſes with ſuch force againſt their bodies thus falling, that they are not only deprived of life long before they reach the ground, but their bellies burſt, and their entrails guſh out; which is plainly the caſe when they fall into deep water.

On the other hand, a great chain of theſe mountains ſerve as a barrier between Norway and Sweden, and are excellent natural fortreſſes for the defence of thoſe ſtates. Beſide, theſe mountains exhibit the moſt delightful proſpects: nature has here been moſt profuſely favourable in adding greater beauties to the ſituation of cottages and farm-houſes, than can be enjoyed by royal palaces in other countries, though aſſiſted with all the varieties of groves, terraſſes, canals, and caſcades. A predeceſſor of mine is ſaid to have given the name of the Northern Italy to the diſtrict of Waas, which lies ſome leagues to the eaſtward of Bergen; and certainly there cannot be a more inchanting proſpect. All the buildings in it are the church, the parſonage, and a few farm-houſes ſcattered on different eminences. The beauty of the place is much heightened by two uniform mountains gradually riſing to a vaſt height, betwixt which runs a valley near half a league in breadth, and a river which ſometimes precipitates itſelf down the rocks in foaming cataracts, and at others ſpreads itſelf into ſmall lakes. On both ſides it is bordered with the fineſt meadows, intermingled with little thickets, and by the eaſy declivities of the verdant mountains covered with fruitful fields and farm-houſes, ſtanding above each other in a ſucceſſion of natural terraſſes. Between theſe a ſtately foreſt preſents itſelf to the view, and beyond that, the ſummits of mountains covered with perpetual ſnow; and ſtill beyond theſe ten or twelve ſtreams iſſuing from the ſnow mountain, form an agreeable contraſt in their meanders along the blooming ſides of the hill, till they loſe themſelves in the rivers beneath.

From the many ſprings iſſuing from the mountains, and the vaſt maſſes of ſnow accumulated on their ſummits, whence in ſummer they gently diſſolve, are formed many conſiderable rivers, the largeſt of which is the Glaamen or Glommen; but none of them are navigable far up the country, the paſſage being every where interrupted by rocks and cataracts. The bridges over them are no where, that I remember, walled, but merely formed of timber caſes filled with ſtones, which ſerve for the piers, on which the timbers are laid. The largeſt bridge of this kind is a thouſand paces in length, and has forty-three ſtone caſes. In many places, where the narrowneſs and rapidity of the current will not admit of ſinking ſtone caſes, thick maſts are laid on each ſide on the ſhore, with the thickeſt end faſtened to the rocks; one maſt being thus laid in the water, another is placed upon it, reaching a fathom beyond it, and then a third or fourth, in the like manner, to the middle of the ſtream, where it is joined by other connected maſts from the oppoſite ſide. Thus in paſſing over the bridge, eſpecially in the middle, it ſeems to ſwing, which to thoſe who are not uſed to theſe bridges appears ſo dangerous, that they alight from their horſes, till they imagine themſelves ſafe.

Within the bowels of ſome of the mountains are the moſt beautiful kinds of marble. The mountains alſo contain that ſurpriſing ſubſtance called the magnet or loadſtone, in ſuch quantities that ſome tons of it have been exported. They likewiſe yield the amianthus or aſbeſtos, of which incombuſtible linen or paper have been made.

Having heard of ſome wood petrified by a certain ſpring, I wrote for ſome ſamples, and a large parcel of it was ſent me. At firſt I thought it reſembled

6 hazle

hazle that had lain a long time in the water; but upon a narrower inſpection, and drawing out ſome of the filaments, I found it to be amianthus, much finer than the Greenland ſtone-flax, which the rev. Mr. Egede ſays, is uſed there as wicks in the lamps, without being in the leaſt waſted, while ſupplied with oil or fat. This amianthus, from the ſoftneſs and fineneſs of its fibres, deſerves to be called ſtone-ſilk, rather than ſtone-flax: I alſo made a wick for a lamp of it, but its light being much dimmer than that produced by cotton, I laid it aſide. I have alſo in my poſſeſſion a piece of paper of this aſbeſtos, which when thrown into a fierce fire is not in the leaſt waſted, but what was written on it totally diſappears.

The manner of preparing this ſtone-ſilk or ſtone-flax, is this; after its being ſoftened in water, it is beaten with a moderate force, till the fibres, or long threads, ſeparate from each other: afterward they are carefully and repeatedly waſhed till clear of all terrene particles; when the flax is dried in a ſieve. All that remains now is to ſpin theſe fine filaments, wherein great care is required: beſides which, the fingers muſt be ſoftened with oil, that the thread may be the more ſupple and pliant.

It is remarkable, that though this country thus abounds in ſtones, no flints have been yet found there, ſo that thoſe for fire-arms are imported from Denmark or Germany: but though there are no flints, there are amathiſts, garnets, chalcedonies, agate, jaſper, and cryſtals.

This country formerly produced gold, but the expence of working the mines, and ſeparating the gold from the ore being greater than the profit, they have been neglected. There are, however, ſilver mines of great value, which give employment to ſeveral thouſand perſons. The copper mines are likewiſe extremely rich, and employ vaſt numbers. Iron is alſo one of the moſt profitable products of Norway; here are however ſome lead mines, but none of either tin or quickſilver.

The

The country produces wheat, rye, barley, white, grey and green peas; vetches, used as provender for horses; hops, flax, and hemp; many kinds of roots and greens for the kitchen, with a considerable number of hardy flowers. Several sorts of plums attain to a tolerable ripeness, which can very seldom be said of peaches, apricots, or grapes. However, apples and pears of several kinds are found all over the country; but the greatest part of these are summer fruits, which ripen early, for the winter fruit seldom comes to perfection, unless the summer proves hotter, and the winter sets in later than usual.

But though with respect to fruit-trees Norway must be acknowleged inferior to most countries in Europe, yet this deficiency is liberally compensated in the blessings of inexhaustible forests: so that in most provinces immense sums are received from foreigners for masts, beams, planks, boards, &c. Not to mention the home consumption for houses built entirely of wood, ships, and bridges: and the infinite number of foundaries, require an immense quantity of charcoal, in the fusion of metals, beside the demands for fuel and other domestic uses. To which must be added, that in many places the woods are felled only to clear the ground and be burnt; the ashes serving for manure.

Among the animals, we shall begin with the horses, which are better for riding than drawing; their walk is easy; they are full of spirit, and are very surefooted: when they mount or descend a steep cliff, on stones like steps, they first tread gently with one foot, to try if the stone they touch be fast; and in this they must be left to themselves, or the best rider will run the risk of his neck. But when they are to go down a very steep and slippery place, they, in a surprising manner, draw their hind-legs together under them, and slide down *. They shew a great deal of

* See a like method practised by the mules of Peru, in Ulloa's voyage in vol. i. of this collection.

cou-

courage in fighting with the wolves or bears, which they are often obliged to do; for when the horſe perceives any of them near him, and has a mare or gelding with him, he places them behind him; attacks his antagoniſt by ſtriking at him with his fore-legs, and uſually comes off conqueror. If he turns about to kick with his hind legs he is ruined: for the bear, who has double his ſtrength, inſtantly leaps on his back, while the poor horſe gallops on, until he drops down for the loſs of blood.

The Norway cows are generally of a yellow colour, as are alſo the horſes; they are ſmall; but their fleſh is fine grained, juicy, and well taſted.

The ſheep here are ſmall, and reſemble thoſe of Denmark. The goats, in many places, run wild in winter and ſummer in the fields, till they are ten or twelve years old; and when the peaſant who owns them, is to catch them, he muſt either do it by ſome ſnare, or ſhoot them. They are ſo bold, that if a wolf approaches them, they ſtay to receive him, and if they have dogs with them, they will reſiſt a whole herd. They frequently attack the ſnakes, and when they are bit by them, not only kill their antagoniſts but eat them, after which they are never known to die of the bite, though they are ill for ſeveral days. The owner warms their own milk, and waſhes the ſore with it.

Near Roſtad, is a flat and naked field, on which no vegetable will grow; the ſoil is almoſt white with grey ſtripes, and has ſomewhat of ſo peculiarly poiſonous a nature, that though all other animals may ſafely paſs over it, a goat or a kid no ſooner ſets its foot upon it, than it drops down, ſtretches out its legs, its tongue hangs out of its mouth, and it expires if it has not inſtant help.

There are few hogs in Norway, and not many of the common deer; but the hares, which in the cold ſeaſon change from brown or grey to a ſnow white, are very cheap in winter. Here are alſo in ſome parts of this country elks, but they are not numerous. The rein-deer, however, run wild in herds, and are ſhot for food by the inhabitants. Theſe animals conſtitute the greateſt, and almoſt the only riches of the Finlaplanders, who live upon the milk, the cheeſe they make of it, and on their fleſh. They make their cloathing, tents, and bed-covering of their ſkins; and of the tendons they make their ſewing thread. In Finmark, there are vaſt numbers of them both wild and tame, and many a man has there from ſix or eight hundred to a thouſand of theſe uſeful creatures which never come under cover: they follow him wherever he is pleaſed to ramble, and when they are put to a ſledge, tranſport his goods from one place to another. They provide for themſelves, and live chiefly on moſs, and on the buds and leaves of trees. They ſupport themſelves on very little nouriſhment, and are neat, clean, and entertaining creatures.

It is remarkable, that when the rein-deer ſheds his horns, and others riſe in their ſtead, they appear at firſt covered with a ſkin; and till they are of a finger's length, are ſo ſoft, that they may be cut with a knife like a ſauſage, and are delicate eating even raw: therefore the huntſmen, when far out in the country, and pinched for want of food, eat them, and find that they ſatisfy both their hunger and thirſt. When the horn grows bigger, there breeds within the ſkin a worm which eats away the root. The rein-deer has over his eye-lids a kind of ſkin, through which he peeps, when otherwiſe, in the hard ſnows, he would be obliged to ſhut his eye entirely.

The hurtful beaſts are the bears and wolves already mentioned; the lynx; vaſt numbers of white, red, and black foxes; and the glutton, a creature which few other countries know any otherwiſe than by report. This animal receives its name from its voracious appetite; it in ſize and ſhape has ſome reſemblance

blance to a long-bodied dog, with thick legs, ſharp claws and teeth; his colour is black, variegated with brown and yellowiſh ſtreaks. He has the boldneſs to attack every beaſt he can poſſibly conquer, and if he finds a carcaſe ſix times as big as himſelf, he does not leave off eating as long as there is a mouthful left: when thus gorged, he preſſes and ſqueezes himſelf between two trees that ſtand near together, and thus empties himſelf of what he has not time to digeſt. As his ſkin ſhines like damaſk, and is covered with ſoft hair, it is very precious; it is therefore well worth the huntſman's while to kill him without wounding the ſkin, which is done by ſhooting him with a bow, and blunt arrows.

The marten is alſo hunted on account of its ſkin, as is likewiſe the ſquirrel and the ermine, both of which are therefore ſhot with blunt arrows: I am in doubt whether the ermine be different in kind from the Daniſh weaſel: its valuable ſkin is of a beautiful white, and it has a black ſpot on the tail. The ermines run after mice like cats, and drag away what they catch, particularly eggs, which are their niceſt delicacy. Here alſo are caſtors, badgers, otters, and hedgehogs.

Among the mice, ſome are thought poiſonous, and others are remarkable for their being white, and their having red eyes. But the moſt pernicious vermin is a little animal, called the læmus or lemming, which is between the ſize of a rat and a mouſe; the tail is ſhort, and turned up at the end, and the legs are alſo ſo ſhort that they ſcarce keep the belly from the ground. They have very ſhort hair, and are of different colours, particularly black, with yellow and brown in ſtreaks, and ſome in ſpots. About once or twice in every twenty years, they aſſemble from their ſecret abodes in prodigious numbers, like the meſſengers of heaven to puniſh the neighbouring inhabitants. They proceed from Kolens rock, which divides the Nordland manor from Sweden, and is held

held to be their peculiar and native place; marching in vaſt multitudes through Nordland and Finmark to the weſtern ocean; and other bodies of them through Swediſh Lapmark to the Sinus Bothnicus, devouring all the graſs and vegetables in their way. They do this in a direct line, and going ſtraight forward proceed into the rivers of the ſea; thus if they meet with a boat on any freſh water river, they run in at one end or ſide, and out again at the other, in order to keep their courſe. They carry their young with them on their backs, or in their mouths; and if they meet with peaſants who come to oppoſe them, they will ſtand undaunted, and bark at them like dogs. This evil is, however, of no long duration; for on entering the ſea, they ſwim as long as they are able, and then are drowned; if they are ſtopped in their courſe, ſo that they cannot reach the ſea, they are killed by the froſts of winter, and if they eſcape, moſt of them die as ſoon as they eat the new graſs.

As to the reptiles, there are neither land ſnakes nor toads beyond the temperate zone; and even thoſe ſnakes on the extremities of the temperate climate, are leſs poiſonous than in more ſouthern countries: lizards are here of various colours, as brown, green, and ſtriped. Thoſe that are green are found in the fields, and the others in the cracks and holes of rocks.

Among the fowls are moſt of thoſe ſeen in the reſt of Europe, and ſome of them peculiar to this country: of thoſe that are in a manner peculiar to this country is the francolin, an excellent land bird, which ſerves the Norwegians inſtead of the pheaſant; its fleſh being white, firm, and of a delicious taſte. The black cap is almoſt as ſmall as the wren; the body is black and yellow, it is white under the belly, and the top of the head is black. Theſe birds keep near the houſes, and are ſuch lovers of meat, that the farmers can hardly keep them from it, and therefore catch them like mice in a trap.

In

In ſhort, there are here ſuch incredible numbers of ſea and land fowl near the rocks on the ſea-ſhore, that they ſometimes obſcure the ſight of the heavens for many miles out at ſea, ſo that one would imagine all the fowl in the univerſe were gathered together in one flock.

Norway is alſo as plentifully ſupplied with fiſh as any country in the world.———

Hitherto the biſhop has deſcribed only ſuch animals as we may eaſily credit the exiſtence of; but he now proceeds to the mention of ſome which will perhaps appear rather apocryphal: however, the relation will not be unentertaining; and the biſhop does not deliver the deſcriptions from his own knowlege.—

The hav-manden and hav-fruen, the mer-man and mer-maid, are ſaid to be often ſeen in the North Sea. In the dioceſe of Bergen, and manor of Nordland, are ſeveral hundred perſons of credit and reputation, who affirm, with the ſtrongeſt aſſurance, that they have ſeen this creature ſometimes at a diſtance, and at other times cloſe to their boats erect, and formed like a human creature down to the middle; the reſt they could not ſee. Our author has examined ſeveral of the witneſſes with all poſſible precaution, and found them agree invariably with the deſcription publiſhed by Jablonſky and Kircher. He brings an evidence who had ſeen one out of the water, and handled it, viz. the reverend Mr. Peter Angel, miniſter at Sundmoer, living when this hiſtory was wrote, and who declares, that in 1719, being then twenty years old, himſelf and ſeveral other inhabitants ſaw a mer-man, dead, on a point of land, with ſeveral ſea-animals. Its length was three fathoms, its colour grey, the lower part like a fiſh, with a porpoiſe's tail. The face reſembled a man's; the noſe flat and preſſed down to the face, in which the noſtrils were very viſible. The breaſt was near the head; the arms, which ſeemed to hang by the ſide, were joined by a thin membrane; and the hands, to appearance, were like

like the paws of a ſea-calf. Mr. Strom, another clergyman, relates that a mer-man and a ſea-calf were both found dead on a rock, all bloody; from whence it was conjectured they had killed each other. Mr. Randulf, rector of the place, endeavoured to preſerve the mer-man; but the peaſants had unluckily cut both to pieces for the fat. In regard to ſize they differ remarkably, according to the fiſhermen, from that called mar-male, or mar-mœte, (the different ſexes) which our author calls a well known ſea-animal, and thinks it may be a dwarf of the ſame ſpecies. This is often caught on hooks, of different ſizes, from that of a child of one year old to three; and the biſhop thinks, till it is further enquired into, it may be ſuppoſed, though he does not affirm it to be, the infant of the former. But the ſtrongeſt and lateſt proof of the mer-man's exiſtence happened in Denmark. On September 20, 1723, three ferrymen, viz. Peter Gunnerſen, Nicholas Jenſen, and Jappe Jenſen, were, by his majeſty's orders, examined upon oath before Fred. Van Gram, privy-counſellor, and depoſed in ſubſtance, that two months before, being towing a ſhip arrived from the Baltic, at the diſtance of a quarter of a Norway mile, they rowed up to ſomething floating like a dead body. When they came within ſeven or eight fathoms, it appeared as at firſt; for it had not ſtirred, but ſunk at that inſtanr, and came up again immediately almoſt at the ſame place. Frighted at this, they lay ſtill, and letting the boat float, the monſter, by the help of the current, came ſtill nearer to them. He turned his face, and ſtared at the men, which gave them a good opportunity of examining him narrowly. He remained in the ſame place for half a quarter of an hour, and was ſeen above the water down to his breaſt. At laſt, apprehending ſome danger, they began to retire; on which he blew up his cheeks, made a kind of roaring noiſe, and dived without riſing any more. He appeared to them like a ſtrong-limbed,

limbed, broad-ſhouldered old man, his head ſmall in proportion, with ſhort curled black hair, with a black beard; his eyes deep in his head, his ſkin coarſe, and very hairy. Gunnerſen added, (which the others did not obſerve) that about the body downward he was quite pointed like a fiſh; and depoſed, at the ſame time, that about twenty years before, he had ſeen near Culleor, a mer-maid with long hair and large breaſts. The weather was fine and calm. That this examination was taken in the moſt regular and exact manner, is atteſted by Andrew Buſſæus.

The ſoe-ormen, or ſea-ſnake, is indeed an amazing and terrible ſea-monſter; to procure credit to which, our author gives many general teſtimonies of its exiſtence, previous to the deſcription which muſt ſuppoſe it. He acknowleges it is ſeldom ſeen, even on the coaſt of Norway, though he ſuppoſes that the only place in Europe, or indeed in the known world, where this great peculiar ſea-ſnake is ſeen at all. He adds, that in all his enquiry about them, he has hardly ſpoke with any intelligent perſon, born in the manor of Norland, who was not able to give a pertinent anſwer concerning, and ſtrong aſſurances of, the exiſtence of this fiſh; and ſome of thoſe traders, coming yearly to Bergen, think it as ridiculous to queſtion its exiſtence, as that of an eel or cod. To give a ſtill more recent and authentic teſtimony of this monſter, which, at the ſame time, exhibits ſome deſcription of it, we have that of captain Laurence de Ferry, a commander in the navy, who doubted of it, till he was convinced by ocular demonſtration. His letter follows at length, and contains in ſubſtance, that in a very calm, hot day in Auguſt, 1746, being in his boat with eight rowers at Julé-neſs, and reading, he heard a noiſe among the men, and obſerved the helms-man keep off from the land. On enquiring the occaſion, he was informed a ſea-ſnake was before them. He ordered them to come up with it, which they did, though afraid. The ſnake passed by them, and they tacked to get nearer to it. As it swam faster than they could row, the captain discharged a gun at it, on which the snake immediately sunk without rising; and as the water about it appeared thick and red, and the distance was small, the captain thinks it might be wounded. The head, which it held more than two feet above water, resembled a horse's; it was grey, with a quite black, and very large mouth; had black eyes, and a long white mane, hanging from the neck to the surface of the water. Beside the head and neck, they saw seven or eight folds of the snake, which were very thick, and, as far as they could guess, there was the distance of a fathom between each fold. To witness the truth of this, two of the rowers, Nicholas Pedersen Kopper, and Nicholas Nicholson Anglewigen, inhabitants of Bergen deposed in court, in due form, before the king's chief advocate in Bergen, the recorder, and nine sworn burghers, on the 22d of February, 1751. A copy of the attestation, under their hands and seals, being granted by the recorder to Mr. Reutz, the procurator for capt. de Ferry, from whom the letter had been addressed to him.

'Though one, the bishop proceeds, cannot have an opportunity of taking the exact dimensions of this creature, yet all that have seen him are unanimous in affirming, as well as they can judge at a distance, it appears to be 600 English feet long; that it lies on the surface of the water (when it is very calm) in many folds, and that there are, in a line with the head, some small parts of the back to be seen above the water, when he moves or bends. These at a distance appear like so many hogsheads floating, with a considerable distance between each. Five and twenty folds are the greatest number which are well attested. The forehead is broad and high. The whole animal is of a dark-brown colour, but variegated with light streaks or spots, that shine like tortoise-shell. The eyes are said to be very large, bluish, and to resemble a couple a couple of bright pewter-plates. The ſpecies in the Norwegian ſea does not ſpout up the water like a whale, but puts it by its motion, into a great agitation, and makes it run like the current of a mill. The ſkin of it is as ſmooth as glaſs, without the leaſt wrinkle, except about the neck, from whence the mane ariſes.' That there is another monſtrous kind of ſea-ſnake, and particularly about Greenland, appears in ſome paſſages cited by the biſhop; but particularly by an extract from the reverend Mr. Egede's journal, who was appointed to the miſſion there, and who affirms, 'That on the 6th of July, 1734, there appeared a very large and frightful ſea-monſter, which raiſed itſelf ſo high out of the water, that its head reached above the main-top. It had a long ſharp ſnout, ſpouted water like a whale, and had very broad paws. The body ſeemed to be covered with ſcales, the ſkin was uneven and wrinkled, and the lower part was formed like a ſnake. After ſome time it plunged backward into the water, and then turned its tail up above the ſurface, a whole ſhip-length from the head.' A drawing of this monſter is annexed, with a three-maſted veſſel near it, doubtleſs to give ſome idea of its amazing proportion. Mr. Egede adds, that the body was as thick and big as the ſhip he ſailed in, whoſe tonnage, however, he does not ſpecify: but Mr. Bing, another miſſionary, who took the drawing, affirmed the eyes were red, and like burning fire. The reader will find a conſiderable diverſity between this and the former ſea-ſerpent. The biſhop mentions the opinion of Bernſen, in his Account of Norway, and the accounts of ſome traders informing that it ſnapped a ſingle man out of a boat, and has ſunk even a veſſel of ſome hundred tons burthen, by throwing itſelf acroſs it. The fiſhermen, when they cannot row away into ſhallow water from him, row againſt ſome of the folds above water, or throw any ſcuttle ſo as to touch him, on which he generally dives, or takes another courſe. If they imagine themſelves purſued by it, they tack their boat ſo, that the ſnake muſt face the ſun in his purſuit, which his eyes cannot bear; beſide, the leaſt wind is ſaid to drive him to the bottom. July and Auguſt are the only months in which he riſes to the ſurface; at which time his excrements (the ſtench of which is thought poiſonous) have been ſeen floating on the water like a fat ſlime.

But a much greater, and indeed the moſt enormous animal that has ever been mentioned, with expectation of gaining a ſerious aſſent, is the KRAKEN, as we are told it is named by way of eminence; whence it probably ſignifies the Creature. By others it is called Crabben, from its ſuppoſed reſemblance to a crab, being round, flat, and full of arms or branches. As this immane monſter is likely to exerciſe the reader's faith and imagination ſtill more than the ſea-ſerpent, we could wiſh the evidence of it had been at leaſt as particular and cogent, which is not altogether the caſe. Now as a full grown Kraken has never been ſeen in all its parts and dimenſions, an accurate ſurvey of which muſt employ ſome time, and not a little motion, it is impoſſible to give a compleat deſcription of one. Nevertheleſs we ſhall ſubmit the probability of its exiſtence on the beſt information our author could collect, which ſeems to have fixed his own belief of it.

'Our fiſhermen,' ſays the author, 'unanimouſly and invariably affirm, that when they are ſeveral miles from the land, particularly in the hot ſummer days, and by their diſtance, and the bearings of ſome points of land, expect from eighty to a hundred fathoms depth, and do not find but from twenty to thirty; and more eſpecially if they find a more than uſual plenty of cod and ling, they judge that the Kraken is at the bottom: but if they find by their lines, that the water in the ſame place ſtill ſhallows on them, they know he is riſing to the ſurface, and row off with the greateſt expedition, till they come into the uſual ſoundfoundings of the place; when, lying on their oars, in a few minutes the monfter emerges, and fhews himfelf manifeftly, though his whole body does not appear. Its back, or upper part, which feems an Englifh mile and an half in circumference, (fome have affirmed more) looks at firft like a number of fmall iflands, furrounded with fomething that floats like fea-weeds. At laft feveral bright points or horns appear, which grow thicker the higher they emerge, and fometimes ftand up as high and large as the mafts of middle-fized veffels. In a fhort time it flowly finks, which is thought as dangerous as its rifing, as it caufes fuch a fwell and whirlpool as draws every thing down with it, like that of Maleftrom'. The bifhop juftly regrets the omiffion of, probably, the only opportunity that ever has, or may be prefented, of furveying it alive, or feeing it entire when dead. This, he informs us, once did prefent, on the credit of the reverend Mr. Friis, minifter at Nordland, and vicar of the college for promoting Chriftian knowlege; who informed him, that in 1680, a Kraken came into the waters that run between the rocks and cliffs near Alftahoug; where, in turning about, fome of its long horns caught hold of fome adjoining trees, which it might have eafily torn up; but that it was alfo entangled in fome clifts of the rocks, whence it could not extricate itfelf, but putrified on the fpot. Our author has heard of no perfon deftroyed by this monfter, but relates a report of the danger of two fifhermen, who came upon a part of the water full of the creature's thick flimy excrements which he voids for fome months, as he feeds for fome other: they immediately ftrove to row off, but were not quick enough in turning to fave the boat from one of the Kraken's horns, which fo crufhed the head of it, that it was with difficulty they faved their lives on the wreck, though the weather was perfectly calm, the monfter never appearing at other times. His excrement is faid to be attractive of other fish, on which he feeds; which property was probably necessary, by reason of his slow unwieldy motion, to his subsistence: as this slow motion again may be necessary to the security of ships of the greatest force and burthen, who must be overwhelmed on rencountering such an immense animal, if his velocity was equal to his weight: the Norwegians supposing, that if his arms, (on which he moves, and with which he takes his food) were to lay hold of the largest man of war, they would pull it down to the bottom.

In confirmation of the reality of this animal, the bishop cites Debes's description of Faroe, for the existence of certain islands, which suddenly appear, and as suddenly vanish. 'Many sea-faring people, he adds, give accounts of such, particularly in the North Sea, which their superstition has either attributed to the delusion of the devil, or considered as inhabited by evil spirits.' But the bishop supposes such mistaken islands to be nothing but the Kraken, called by some the Soe trolden, or sea mischief: in which opinion he was greatly confirmed by the following quotation of Dr. Hierne, a learned Swede, from baron Grippenhielm; and which is certainly a very remarkable passage: viz. "Among the rocks about Stockholm there is sometimes seen a track of land, which at other times disappears and is seen again in another place. Buræus has placed it as an island in his map. The peasants, who call it Gummars-ore, say that it is not always seen, and that it lies out in the open sea, but I could never find it. On Sunday when I was out amongst the rocks, sounding the coasts, it happened that, in one place, I saw something like three points of land in the sea, which surprised me a little, and I thought I had inadvertently passed them over before. Upon this I called to a peasant, to enquire for Gummars-ore; but when he came we could see nothing of it: upon which the peasant said, all was well, and that this prognosticated a storm, or a great quantity

quantity of fish."——To which our author subjoins, 'Who cannot discover that this Gummars-ore, with its points, and prognostications of fish, was the Kraken, mistaken by Buræus for an island, who may keep himself about that spot where he rises.' He closes with affirming, he could add much more concerning this and other Norwegian monsters, whose existence he does not take upon him to deny; but that he does not chuse, by a mixture of uncertain relations, to make such accounts appear doubtful, as he believes to be true and well attested.

It must be confessed, indeed, that our natural propensity to the marvellous, and the frequent profusion of writers in gratifying this propensity, does often render a certain regulation and continence of assent both prudent and delicate. This delicacy, however, is not without its proper limitations; and a competent enquirer will determine of every surprising relation, by the force and consistence of the evidence; by the harmony or discordance of the various circumstances respecting it; and by the analogy of the object related with less rare and astonishing appearances in nature. In the present instances, and particularly in that of the Kraken (not the most digestible of them) after paying but a just respect to the moral character, the reverend function, and diligent investigations of our author, we must admit the possibility of its existence, as it implies no contradiction: though it seems to encounter a general prepossession of the whale's being the largest animal on our globe; and the eradication of any long prepossession is attended with something irksome to us. But were we to suppose a salmon, or a sturgeon, the largest fish any number of persons had seen or heard of, and the whale had discovered himself as seldom, and but in part, as the Kraken; it is easy to conceive, that the existence of the whale had been as indigestible to such persons then, as that of the Kraken may be to others now. Some may incline to think, such an extenſive monſter would encroach on the ſymmetry of nature, and be over-proportionate to the ſize of the globe itſelf: as a little retroſpection will inform us, that the breadth of what is ſeen of him, ſuppoſing him nearly round, muſt be full 2600 feet, (if more oval or crab-like, full 2000) and his thickneſs, which may rather be called altitude, at leaſt 300; our author declaring, he has choſen the leaſt circumference mentioned of the animal, for the greater certainty. Theſe dimenſions, nevertheleſs, we apprehend, will not argue concluſively againſt the exiſtence of the animal, though conſiderably againſt a numerous increaſe or propagation of it. In fact, the great ſcarcity of the Kraken, his confinement to the North Sea, and perhaps to equal latitudes in the South; the ſmall number propagated by the whale, who is viviparous; and by the largeſt land animals, of whom the elephant is ſaid to go near two years with young, all induce us to conclude from analogy, that this creature is not numerous. This coincides with a paſſage in a manuſcript aſcribed to Svere, king of Norway, as it is cited by Ol. Wormius in his Muſæum, p. 280, in Latin, which we ſhall exactly tranſlate.——' There remains one kind, which they call ' Hafgufe, whoſe magnitude is unknown, as it is ' ſeldom ſeen. Thoſe who affirm they have ſeen its ' body, declare it is more like an iſland than a beaſt, ' and that its carcaſe was never found; whence ſome ' imagine, there are but two of the kind in nature.' Whether the vaniſhing iſland Lemair, of which captain Rodney went in ſearch, was a Kraken, we ſubmit to the fancy of our readers. In fine, if the exiſtence of the creature is admitted, it will ſeem a fair inference, that he is the ſcarceſt as well as largeſt in our world. But to return to our author,

The inhabitants of the mountains, in Norway, do the work of horſes, for nine ſucceſſive hours, ſinging all the time; and throw themſelves every half hour on the ſnow, though in a profuſe ſweat, ſucking it

to

to ſlake their thirſt, and without the leaſt apprehenſion of a cold or fever. All the peaſants are, in general, handy and ingenious, having no tradeſmen among them, nor buying any things made up in the towns; as the farmers ſay, no boy can ever make a good man without being his own taylor, ſhoemaker, weaver, ſmith, carpenter, &c. &c. though without derogating from their ingenuity, it is moſt probable that neceſſity is, in a great meaſure, the parent of it; as the produce of their ſoil would be unequal to the employment of ſuch a number of tradeſmen. They ſeem, however, to excel in carving with their toll-knive (a broad ſhort one) ſome of the greateſt artificial curioſities in the royal muſæum, conſiſting of their carvings in wood. They do not fall ſhort of the French in politeneſs, whom he thinks them to reſemble moſt of any people; their peaſants being politer than the Daniſh burghers. Their character for valour appears not ill founded, on the ſettlement their progenitors forced in France, from whence many of their poſterity came over into England with William, ſtiled the Conqueror: but the mountaineers, from the difficulties and dangers of their country, and from the cuſtom of bearing arms very early, to defend themſelves againſt beaſts of prey, have ſome advantage on this point. Quarrelſomeneſs and brutality, however, reſult from this quality among them; the peaſants have buckled themſelves together by the belts, and fought with their ſhort knives till one was mortally wounded: ſo that, till the middle of the laſt century, ſays our author, when a peaſant's family was invited to a wedding, the wife generally took her huſband's ſhroud with her.

The farmers do not uſe rye in their bread but at weddings and entertainments, oats being their general corn; and in a ſcarcity of grain they add a little oatmeal to a greater quantity of the bark of fir powdered, which makes a bitteriſh and leſs nutritive bread; but which, however, they accuſtom themſelves to in

plentiful

plentiful ſeaſons, to be prepared againſt a time of ſcarcity. Indeed, in 1743, and 1744, they improved their bread by ſubſtituting elm bark, which was better taſted. In parts where there were great fiſheries, they attempted to mix cod-roes with oatmeal; but this gave ſome the bloody-flux. It ſeems odd, that they chuſe to let their fiſh ſour before they ſalt it. They make a ſtock of ſtrong ale againſt Chriſtmas, chriſtenings, &c. but at other times regale on Mungat, a very bad ſmall beer, milk, and water, or water and ſour whey. They are great lovers of tobacco, expending annually ſeveral thouſand dollars in it, which makes our author, as a patriot, wiſh for its perfect production there; ſnuff they properly enough call Næſe-meel.

Their houſes are commonly built of whole trunks of pine and fir-trees, chopped ſo as to make them lie cloſe, and joined by mortiſes. They are covered firſt with birch-bark, and over that three or four inches thick with turf, wherein ſervice-trees and good graſs grows, whence many a farmer mows a pretty load of hay from the top of his houſe. They are often let to three, four, or five families; and have a Staubaret for all their proviſions at a diſtance, for fear of fire. Even the rich farmers have ſeldom any windows, but a ſky-light, called Liur, at top of the houſe, over which they place the midriff of ſome animal, in a frame, to keep out the rain. The membrane is ſtrong and tranſparent as a bladder; it is called Siaa, and lifted on or off with a pole; which pole, every perſon coming on important buſineſs, and eſpecially on courtſhip, muſt touch before they utter a word. The ſmoak paſſes through the Liur; and kings, till the eleventh century, lived in ſuch houſes. The maſter of the houſe, with all his politeneſs, always ſits at the upper end of the table on the Hoy-Sædet, [high ſeat] where he has a little cupboard to lock up his valuable things. They burn the roots of thoſe fir-trees that have been cut down

ſeveral

ſeveral years, for tar. As a great part of their livelihood is obtained from the water, many ſpend half their time on that element, and die in it; and though their bodies are ſeldom found, they have a funeral ceremony and ſermon, called Gravfæſtelſe. A miniſter at Karſund affirmed, that during fifty years of his reſidence, there had not died above ten grown men on ſhore; and at Chriſtianſand, they ſay, moſt of the women have had five or ſix huſbands.

The lakes and rivers furniſh the people with plenty of freſh water fiſh, and the mountains with game. For their winter ſtock they kill cows, ſheep, and goats; part of which they pickle and ſmoak, and ſome of it they cut in thin ſlices, ſprinkle it with ſalt, and then dry it in the wind, and eat it like hung beef. They are fond of brandy, and of ſmoaking and chewing tobacco.

The Norwegians who live in towns have nothing remarkable in their dreſs; but the peaſants do not trouble themſelves about faſhions. Thoſe called ſtrile-farmers have their breeches and ſtockings of one piece. They have a wide looſe jacket, made of a coarſe woollen cloth; as are alſo their waiſtcoats; and thoſe who would appear fine, have the ſeams covered with cloth of a different colour. The peaſants of one pariſh are remarkable for wearing black cloaths edged with red; another for wearing all black; the dreſs of another pariſh is white edged with black; others wear black and yellow; and thus the inhabitants of almoſt every pariſh vary in the colour of their cloaths. They wear a flapped hat, or a little brown, grey, or black cap, made quite round, and the ſeams ornamented with black ribbons. They have ſhoes of a peculiar conſtruction, without heels, conſiſting of two pieces; the upper leather fits cloſe to the foot, to which the ſole is joined by a great many plaits and folds. When they travel, and in the winter, they wear a ſort of half-boots which reach up to the calf of the leg, and are laced on one ſide; and when they

go

go on the rocks in the ſnow, they put on ſnow-ſhoes. But as theſe are troubleſome when they go a great way to travel, they put on ſkates as broad as the foot, but ſix or eight feet long, and pointed before; they are covered underneath with ſeal-ſkin, ſo that the ſmooth grain of the hair turns backward to the heel. With theſe ſnow ſkates they ſlide about on the ſnow as well as they can upon the ice, and faſter than any horſe.

The peaſant never wears a neckcloth, or any thing of that kind, except when he is dreſſed; for his neck and breaſt are always open, and he lets the ſnow beat into his boſom. On the contrary, he covers his veins, binding a woollen fillet round his wriſts. About their body they wear a broad leather belt, ornamented with convex braſs plates; to this hangs a braſs chain, which holds their large knife, gimblet, and other tackle.

The women at church, and in genteel aſſemblies, dreſs themſelves in jackets laced cloſe, and have leather girdles, with ſilver ornaments about them. They alſo wear a ſilver chain three or four times round the neck, with a gilt medal hanging at the end of it. Their handkerchiefs and caps are almoſt covered with ſmall ſilver, braſs, and tin plates, buttons, and large rings, ſuch as they wear on their fingers, to which they hang again a parcel of ſmall ones, which make a gingling noiſe when they move. A maiden-bride has her hair platted, and hung as full as poſſible with ſuch kind of trinkets, as alſo her cloaths.

The peaſants are buſied in cutting wood, felling and floating of timber, burning charcoal, and extracting of tar. Great numbers are employed in the mines, and at the furnaces and ſtamping mills; and alſo in navigation and fiſhing, beſide hunting and ſhooting; for every body is at liberty to purſue the game, eſpecially in the mountains, and on the heaths and commons, where every peaſant may make uſe of what arms he pleaſes.

The

The catching of birds afford ſome of the inhabitants a very good maintenance: but it is impoſſible to give a juſt idea of the fatigue and danger with which the people ſearch for the birds in the high and ſteep rocks, many of which are above 200 fathoms perpendicular. Theſe people, who are called birdmen, have two methods of catching them: they either climb up theſe perpendicular rocks, or are let down from the top by a ſtrong and thick rope: when they climb up they have a large pole of eleven or twelve ells in length, with an iron hook at the end. They who are underneath in a boat, or ſtand on a cliff, faſten this hook to the waiſtband of the man's breeches who climbs, by which means they help him up to the higheſt projection he can reach, and fix his feet upon. They then help up another to the ſame place, and when they are both up, give each his bird-pole, and a long rope which they tie at each end round their waiſts. The one then climbs up as high as he can, and where it is difficult, the other, by putting his pole under his breech, puſhes him up till he gets to a good ſtanding-place: the uppermoſt of the two then helps the other up to him with the rope; and thus they proceed till they get to the part where the birds build, and there they ſearch for them. As they have many dangerous places yet to climb, one always ſeeks a convenient place to ſtand ſure, and be able to hold himſelf faſt, while the other is climbing about. If the latter ſhould happen to ſlip, he is held up by the other who ſtands firm; and when he has got ſafe by thoſe dangerous places, he fixes himſelf in the ſame manner, that he may aſſiſt the other to come ſafe to him: and then they clamber about after birds where they pleaſe. But accidents ſometimes happen; for if the one does not ſtand firm, or is not ſtrong enough to ſupport the other when he ſlips, they both fall and are killed; and thus ſome periſh every year.

When they thus reach the places that are ſeldom viſited, they find the birds ſo tame that they may

take

take them with their hands; for they are loth to leave their young; but where they are wild, they either throw a net over them in the rock, or entangle those that are flying with a net fixed to the end of their poles. Thus they catch vast numbers of fowls, and the boat keeping underneath them, they throw the dead birds into it, and soon fill the vessel. When the weather is tolerably good, and there is a great deal of game, the birdmen will continue eight days together on the rocks; for there are here and there holes in which they can securely take their repose: they draw up provisions with lines, and boats are kept coming and going to take away the game.

On the other hand, many rocks being so steep, and dangerous that they cannot possibly climb up them, they are then let down from above; when they have a strong rope eighty or an hundred fathoms long. One end of it the birdman fastens about his waist, and then drawing it between his legs, so that he can sit on it, he is let down with his bird pole in his hand, by six men at the top, who let the rope sink by degrees, but lay a piece of timber on the edge of the rock for it to slide on, to prevent its being torn to pieces by the sharp edge of the stones. Another line is fastened round the man's waist, which he pulls to give signs when he would have them pull him up, let him lower, or keep him where he is. He is in great danger of the stones loosening by the rope, and falling upon him; he therefore wears a thick furred cap well lined, which secures him from the blows he may receive from small stones; but if large ones fall, he is in the greatest hazard of losing his life. Thus do these poor men often expose themselves to the most imminent danger, merely to get a subsistence for their families. There are some indeed who say there is no great hazard in it, after they are accustomed to it; but at first the rope turns round with them, till their heads are giddy, and they can do nothing to save themselves. Those who have learnt the art make a

play

play of it; they put their feet againſt the rock, throw themſelves ſeveral fathoms out, and puſh themſelves into what place they pleaſe. They even keep themſelves out on the line in the air, and catch with their poles numbers of birds flying out and into their holes. The greateſt art is required in throwing themſelves out, ſo as to ſwing under the projection of a rock where the birds gather together: here they fix their feet, looſen themſelves from the rope, which they faſten to a ſtone, to prevent its ſwinging out of their reach, and then the man climbs about and catches the birds, either with his hands or his pole; and when he has killed as many as he thinks proper, he ties them together, faſtens them to the ſmall line, and by a pull gives a ſign for thoſe above to draw them up. In this manner he works all day, and when he wants to go up, he gives a ſign to be drawn up, or elſe works himſelf up with his belt full of birds.

When there are not people enough to hold the rope, the birdman fixes a poſt in the ground, faſtens his rope to it, and ſlides down without any help, to work as before. There are in ſome places ſteep cliffs, of a prodigious ſize, lying under the land, and yet more than a hundred fathoms above the water, which are likewiſe very difficult to be got at. Down theſe cliffs they help one another in the above manner, and taking a ſtrong rope with them, faſten it here and there in the cliff, where they can, and leave it all the ſummer: upon this they will run up and down, and take the birds at pleaſure. It is impoſſible to deſcribe how frightful and dangerous this bird-catching appears to the beholders, from the vaſt height and exceſſive ſteepneſs of the rocks, many of which hang over the ſea: it ſeems impoſſible for men to enter the holes under theſe projections, or to walk 200 yards high on crags of rock where they can but juſt fix their toes.

The birds being brought home, they eat ſome of them freſh, and ſome are hung up to dry for the winter

ſaſon.

season. These birds afford the inhabitants a very good maintenance, partly from their feathers and down, which are gathered and sent to foreign parts, and partly from their flesh and eggs.

A SUCCINCT ACCOUNT OF THE KINGDOM OF SWEDEN,

With respect to its Climate, Produce, Inhabitants, and Government.

Collected from the Writings of an English Minister residing there.

THE following remarks on Sweden were made by a minister who resided there on the part of king William, in the reign of Charles XI. a man in all respects qualified for his ministry in that country; as having a solid understanding, great uprightness of heart, and a hearty desire to serve both nations. The account furnished by a writer of such character must, in every respect, be worthy perusal; we shall give it therefore nearly in his own words.

The kingdom of Sweden and dukedom of Findland have the Baltic Sea on the south, the unpassable mountains of Norway on the west, Lapland on the north, and Muscovy on the east; being extended from 56° to 69° of northern latitude and from 32° to 55° in longitude. It is consequently more than twice as big as the kingdom of France; but the abatements to be made for seas and lakes, some whereof are above eighty English miles long and twenty broad, as also for rocks, woods, heaths, and morasses, will reduce

reduce the habitable part to a very ſmall portion of the whole. The ſoil, in places capable of cultivating, is tolerably fruitful; though ſeldom above half a foot deep, and therefore more eaſily ploughed, as it frequently is by one maid and an ox, and is generally beſt where there is leaſt of it; that is, in the little ſpaces betwixt the rocks.

If the inhabitants were induſtrious above what neceſſity forces them to, they might at leaſt have corn ſufficient of their own; but as things are managed, they cannot ſubſiſt without great importations of all ſorts of grain from other parts of Germany adjacent to the Baltic Sea. And notwithſtanding theſe ſupplies, the poorer ſort, in many places remote from traffic, are forced to grind the bark of trees to mix with their corn, and make bread, of which they have not always plenty. The cattle, as in all other northern countries, are generally of a very ſmall ſize; neither can the breed be bettered by bringing in larger from abroad, which ſoon degenerate; becauſe in ſummer the graſs is leſs nouriſhing than in the places from whence they come, and in winter they are half ſtarved for want of fodder of all kinds, which often falls ſo very ſhort, that they are forced to unthatch their houſes, to keep a part of their cattle alive. Their ſheep bear a very coarſe wool, only fit to make cloathing for the peaſants. The horſes, eſpecially the fineſt, though ſmall, are hardy, vigorous, ſtrong, ſure-footed, and nimble trotters: which is of great uſe to them, becauſe of the length of their winters, and their fitneſs for ſleds.

The chief lakes in Sweden are the Vetter, the Wenner, and Waſter; the firſt in Oſtrogothia, remarkable for its foretelling of ſtorms, by a continual thundering noiſe the day before, in that quarter whence they ariſe; as alſo for ſudden breaking of the ice on it, which ſometimes ſurpriſes travellers, and in half an hour becomes navigable; for its great depth, in ſome places above 300 fathom, though no part of the Baltic Sea exceeds fifty. The second is in Westrogothia, from which issues the river Elve, that falling down a rock near sixty feet, passes by Gottenburgh. The third empties itself near Stockholm, furnishing one side of the town with fresh water, as the sea does the other with salt. There are abundance of other lakes, whereof many, like ponds, have no vents, and are called in-seas; and not ill stored with variety of fish.

The north bottom or bay that separates Sweden and Finland abounds with seals, of which a considerable quantity of train-oil is made and exported; and in the lakes in Finland are vast quantities of pike, which being taken are salted, dried, and sold at very cheap rates. These lakes are of great use for the conveyance of carriages, both in summer by boats, and by sleds in winter; and among them, and on the sea-coasts, are almost innumerable islands of different sizes; whereof there are, in Sweden, above six thousand that are inhabited: the rest are either bare rocks, or covered with wood. Gotland, Oland, and Aland, are isles of large extent, one being sixty miles long, and the other two little less: their woods and vast forests overspread much of the country, and are, for the most part, of pines, fir, beech, birch, alder, juniper, and some oak, especially in the province of Bleaking.

Of mines in Sweden: there is one of silver, into which workmen are let down in baskets to the first floor, which is one hundred and fifty fathoms under ground. The roof there is as high as a church, supported by vast arches of ore. The next descent is by ladders and baskets to the lowest mine, above forty fathoms, where they now work. They have no records so antient as the first discovery either of this or the copper mines, which must needs have been the work of many ages. The ore seldom yields above four per cent. and requires great pains to refine it. They are also at the charge of a water mill

to

to drain the mine, and have the benefit of another that draws up the ore. It yearly produces about twenty thousand crowns of fine silver, of which the king has the pre-emption, paying only one fourth less than the real value.

The copper mine is about eighty fathom deep, of great extent, but subject to damage by the falling in of the roof; the occasion of which falls is attributed to the throwing the earth and stones brought out upon the ground over the mine, by which the pillars become overcharged, and give way.

The copper yearly made out of this mine amounts to the value of about two hundred thousand pounds, of which the king has a fourth part, not by way of pre-emption, but in kind; beside that, upon the remainder, he has a custom of twenty five per cent. when it is exported unwrought. Lately a gentleman of Italy came to Sweden, with proposals to make copper a shorter and cheaper way than has hitherto been practised, as to make that in four days which before required three weeks, and with one fifth part of the charge, and with fewer hands. The bargain was made, and his reward agreed to be a hundred thousand crowns; and the first proof he made succeeded to admiration: but when he came to work in earnest, and had got his new-invented ovens made to his mind; the miners, as he complained, picked out the very worst ore, and were otherwise so envious and untractable that he failed of success, and lost his reward, and not without difficulty obtained leave to buy ore, and practise his invention at his own charge, as he now does. Iron mines and forges are in great numbers, especially toward the mountainous parts, where they have the convenience of water-falls to turn their mills. From these, beside supplying the country, there is yearly exported iron, to the value of near three hundred thousand pounds; but of late years the number of those forges has been so much increased, that each endeavouring to undersell others,

 the

the price has been much lowered: and ſince the prohibition of foreign manufactures, in exchanging of which iron was plentifully taken off, it is grown ſo cheap, that it is found neceſſary to leſſen the number of forges.

The ſeaſons of the year, though regular in themſelves, do not altogether anſwer thoſe of other climates. As a French ambaſſador obſerved, who in raillery ſaid, there were in Sweden only nine months winter, and all the reſt was ſummer; for as winter commonly begins very ſoon, ſo ſummer immediately ſucceeds it, and leaves little or no ſpace to be called ſpring. The productions of the earth therefore ought to be, as they are, more ſpeedy in their growth than in other parts; the reaſon of which ſeems to be, that the oil and ſulphur in the earth (as it appears by the trees and minerals it produces) being bound up all the winter, are then of a ſudden actuated by the heat of a warm ſun, which almoſt continually ſhines, and thereby makes amends for its ſhort ſtay, and brings to maturity the fruits proper for the climate: yet withal, its heat is ſo intenſe, that it often ſets the woods on fire, which ſometimes ſpreads itſelf many leagues, and can ſcarce be ſtopt till it comes to ſome lake or very large plain.

The ſun at higheſt is above the horizon of Stockholm eighteen hours and an half, and for ſome weeks makes a continual day. In winter the days are proportionably ſhorter, the ſun being up five hours and an half; which defect is ſo well ſupplied by the moon, the whiteneſs of the ſnow, and the clearneſs of the ſky, that travelling by night is as uſual as by day; and journies begun in the evening are as frequent as in the morning. The want of the ſun's heat is repaired by ſtoves within doors, and warm furrs abroad; inſtead of which the meaner ſort uſe ſheepſkins, and other the like defences, and are generally better provided with cloathing befitting their condition,

tion, and the climate they live in, than the common people of any part of Europe.

This country is divided into twenty-five provinces, each of which is governed by an officer called Landſhofding, whoſe authority comprehends that of lord lieutenant and ſheriff together, except where there is a general governor, as in Finland, or upon the borders of Denmark and Norway, to whom the governor of each province is ſubordinate, and has thereby a more reſtrained authority. Theſe officers are placed by the king, and take an oath to keep the province for his majeſty and his heirs, to govern according to the laws of Sweden, and ſuch inſtructions as they ſhall receive from his majeſty, and to quit the province whenever he ſhall call them thence. To them and their ſubordinate officers (who are all of the king's chuſing) the execution of judicial ſentences, the collection of the king's revenues, the care of foreſts, parks, and other crown lands, &c. is committed.

Of cities, thoſe of Stockholm, Gottenburgh, Calmar, and two or three more, may deſerve that name; the other corporations, which in all make not an hundred, ſcarce exceed ſome villages in England. They are all governed by burgomaſters and counſellors, choſen by the king out of their own body, or at leaſt ſuch as are of the quality of burghers; no gentleman accepting of theſe employments. Their offices and ſalaries are for life, or rather during their good behaviour. The privilege of cities are derived from the king, and for the moſt part are owing to the wiſdom of Guſtavus Adolphus, the author of their beſt, and moſt regular conſtitutions at home, as well as of their glory abroad.

The city of Stockholm lies in 59° 20′ north latitude, and about 41° longitude. About three hundred years ago it was only a bare iſland, with two or three cottages for fiſhers; but upon the building of a caſtle there, to ſtop the inroads of the Ruſſians, and the tranſlation of the court thither, it grew by degrees to ſurpaſs the other more antient cities: it is at preſent the metropolis of this kingdom, and is ſuppoſed to be as populous as Briſtol. The caſtle here, which is covered with copper, is a place of no ſtrength or beauty, but of great uſe, being a ſpacious building; that beſide entertaining the court, furniſhes room for moſt of the great offices. It lodges very few of the inferior officers and ſervants of the court; they, together with the foot guards, being quartered upon the burghers at their landlord's charge, for lodging, fire, and candle. The palace of the nobility, which is the place of their aſſembly at the convention of eſtates, and the depoſitory of their privileges, titles, and ſuch other records as concern their body, is a very ſtately pile; as is alſo the bank, built at the city's charge; which, together with ſeveral magnificent houſes of the nobility, are covered with copper, and make a handſome proſpect. Moſt of the burghers houſes are built of brick, except in the ſuburbs, where they are of wood, and therefore expoſed to the danger of fire; which commonly, when it gets to a head, deſtroys all before it in the quarter where it happens: to repair which misfortune, they ſometimes ſend the dimenſions of their houſes to Finland; where the walls and ſeveral ſeparations are built of pieces of timber laid one upon another, and joined at the corners, and afterwards marked, taken down, and ſent by water to Stockholm, there to be ſet up and finiſhed. Theſe when they are kept in good repair, will laſt thirty or forty years, and are warmer, cleaner, and more healthful than thoſe of either brick or ſtone.

This city is in a manner the ſtaple of Sweden, to which moſt of the goods of their own growth, viz. iron, copper, wire, pitch, tar, maſts, deals, &c. are brought to be exported. The greateſt part of the commodities imported from abroad come into this port,

port, where there is a haven capable of receiving a thousand ships, and a bridge or key near an English mile long, to which the greater vessels may lie with their broadsides. The only inconvenience is, that it is ten miles from the sea, and the river very crooked, and no tides.

The laws of Sweden were antiently as various as the provinces were numerous; each of which had statutes and customs peculiar to itself, enacted, as occasion required, by the Laghman or governor of the province; who was chosen by the people, and invested with great authority, especially while the king was elective; his suffrage concluding the province he governed. This variety was necessarily attended with great confusion; for remedy whereof, about fourscore years ago, one body of laws was compiled for the direction of the whole kingdom: yet this collection is but an imperfect piece, and the laws so few, and conceived in such general terms, that in most cases they need the assistance of the civil law. After all, the final determination depends much upon the inclinations of the bench, which in a poor country, where salaries are small, is often filled with such as are of weak parts, and subject to corruption on very small temptations.

The ordinary charges of law suits are no where more moderate than in Sweden; the greatest burthen arising from a late constitution, that all declarations, acts and sentences must be written upon sealed paper. This is of different prices, from two-pence to seven shillings a sheet, according to the quality of the cause; the benefit of which accrues to the king, and is computed to bring in 3000 l. a year. Other charges are very few, every man being permitted (in criminal actions compelled) to plead his own cause. Accordingly the practice of the law is below a gentleman, and rather the refuge than the choice of meaner persons, who are very few in number, and for the most part very poor. The custom of a jury of twelve men is ſo antient in Sweden, that their writers pretend it had its original among them, and was thence derived to other nations: but at preſent it is diſuſed every where, except only in the lower courts in the country, and there the jurymen are for life, and have ſalaries. Titles to eſtates are rendered more ſecure, and leſs ſubject to conteſts, by the regiſters that are kept of all ſales and alienations, as well as of other engagements of them; the purchaſer running the hazard of having an after-bargain take place of a former. If he omit the recording of his tranſaction in the proper court in criminal matters where the fact is not very evident, or where the judges are not very favourable, the defendant is admitted to purge himſelf by oath; to which is oftentimes added the oath of ſix or twelve men, who are all vouchers of his integrity*. Treaſon, murder, double adulteries, burning of houſes, witchcraft, and the like heinous crimes, a e puniſhed with death, which is executed by hanging of men and beheading of women. To which burning alive or dead, quartering and hanging in chains is ſometimes added, according to the nature of the crime. Criminals of the nobility and gentry are generally ſhot to death.

The puniſhment of ſtealing is of late, inſtead of death, changed into a perpetual ſlavery; the guilty party being condemned to work all his life for the king, in making fortifications or other drudgery: and always has a collar of iron about his neck, with a bow coming over his head, to which a bell is faſtened that rings as he goes along. Duels between gentlemen, if the one party be killed, are puniſhed by the ſurvivor's death, and a note of infamy upon the memory of both: if neither be killed, they are both condemned to a priſon with bread and water for two

* A method like this is admitted in caſes of debt by our Engliſh law; as may be ſeen in our books, under the name of *waging of law*.

years;

years; to which is added, a fine of one thousand crowns, or one year's imprisonment, and two thousand crowns. Reparation of honour, in case of an affront, is referred to the respective national courts, where recantation and public begging of pardon is usually inflicted. Estates, as well acquired as inherited, descend to the children in equal portions, of which a son has two and a daughter one; nor is it in the power of the parents to alter this proportion, without the intervention of a judicial sentence. In case of their children's disobedience only, they may bequeath a tenth of their acquired possessions to such child or other person as they will favour: where an estate descends incumbered with debts, the heir usually takes two or three months time, as the law allows, to search into the condition of the deceased's estate, and then either accepts the inheritance, or leaves it to the law, which in that case administers.

The nature of the climate, which is very healthful and dry, as well as sharp, disposes the natives to a very vigorous constitution; and that confirmed by a hardy education, coarse fare, and hard lodging, qualifies them to endure whatever uneasy circumstance befals them, better than those who are born in a milder climate, and more indulgently bred. But, on the other side, it seems as if the severity of the clime does, in a manner, cramp the faculties of their mind, which seldom are found endued with any eminent pregnancy of wit.

These dispositions of body and mind qualify them more for a life of labour and fatigue than of art and curiosity; and the effect of it is visible in all orders of men amongst them.

In point of learning, they, like their neighbours the Germans, are more given to transcribe and make collections, than to digest their own thoughts; and commonly proportion their studies to their occasions. In matters of trade they rather undergo the drudgery, than dive into the mystery either of commerce or manufactures,

nufactures, in which they generally ſet up for maſters before half-taught; ſo that in all ſuch things as require ingenuity, neatneſs, or dexterity, they are forced to be ſerved by ſtrangers. Their common ſoldiers are allowed to endure cold and hunger, long marches, and hard labour, to admiration: but they learn their duty very ſlowly, and are ſerviceable more by obedience to command, and ſtanding their ground, than by any great forwardneſs to attack their enemy; or addreſs, in executing their orders. Their peaſants alſo are tolerably laborious when need compels them, but have little regard to neatneſs in their work, and are hardly brought to quit their old ſlow methods for ſuch new inventions as are more dextrous and eaſy.

The clergy are but moderately learned, and little acquainted with diſputes about religion, as having no adverſaries to oppoſe. They affect gravity, and wear long beards, are eſteemed for their hoſpitality, and have great authority among the common people. The peaſants, when ſober, are obſequious and reſpectful; but drink makes them mad and ungovernable: moſt of them live in a very poor condition, are taught by neceſſity to practiſe ſeveral arts in a rude manner, as the making their ſhoes, cloaths, &c. and the ſeveral inſtruments of huſbandry, and other neceſſaries they cannot ſpare money to buy. And to keep them to this, as alſo to favour the cities, it is not permitted for more than one taylor, or other artiſan, to dwell in the ſame pariſh, though it be ever ſo large; as many of them are above twenty miles in compaſs. In general, it may be ſaid of the whole nation, that they are a people very religious in their way, and frequenters of the church, eminently loyal and affected to monarchy; grave even to formality; ſober more out of neceſſity than temperance; apt to entertain ſuſpicions, and envy each other as well as ſtrangers; more inclined to pilfering, and ſuch ſecret frauds, than to open violence, or or robbing on highways; crimes as rarely committed in this, as in any country whatever.

The reformation there, as in Denmark and Norway, began soon after the neighbouring parts of Germany had embraced Luther's tenets, and was established according to his platform. The tyranny of king Christiern the Second, gave an opportunity to Gustavus, the founder of the present royal family, to alter religion, and advance himself to the regal dignity; which till that time was elective, but was made hereditary to his family, in which it has since continued.

The church is governed by an archbishop, and ten bishops, whose studies are confined to their own employments; being never called to council but at the assembly of the states, nor troubled with the administration of secular affairs. Their revenues are very moderate. The archbishopric of Upsal is not worth four hundred pounds a year, and their bishops are in proportion. Under them are seven or eight superintendants, who have all the power of bishops, and over each ten churches is a provost, or rural dean, with some authority over the inferior clergy. They are all the sons of peasants or burghers, and can therefore content themselves with their small income, which, beside more inconsiderable dues, arise from glebe lands, and one third of the tithes; of which the other two thirds are annexed to the crown, to be employed in pious uses: however, the clergy have generally wherewithal to exercise hospitality, and are the constant refuge of poor travellers, especially strangers, who go from priest to priest, as elsewhere from constable to constable.

The government and revenue of Sweden are like those of other places, subject to so many and so great changes, that one would imagine our author's account should, at this distance of time, be almost out of date: but there is one advantage attends whatever has the appearance of a parliament, which

is,

is, that how much ſoever it may ſink and be depreſſed by fraud or force, under certain conjunctures, it has nevertheleſs ſtrength to riſe again in more favourable ſeaſons, and even to recover all that it has loſt. In our author's time the ſtates of Sweden were but inſtruments of the king's authority; and only met to ſanctify ſuch acts of power as the crown did not care to take upon itſelf. At this day things have quite changed their face; the kings of Sweden have wholly loſt their abſolute power, which remains where it ought to remain, in the repreſentatives of the nobility, clergy, and the people of the kingdom. The uſual time of aſſembling the ſtates is once in three years, or oftener, if affairs require it. The body of the nobility and gentry are repreſented by one in each family, of which there are about a thouſand in Sweden, and with them the colonel, lieutenant-colonel, major, and one captain of each regiment ſit and vote. For the clergy, beſide the biſhops and ſuperintendants in each rural deanry, or ten pariſhes, one is choſen and maintained at the charge of his electors. Theſe make a body of about five hundred. The repreſentatives of the burghers are choſen by the magiſtrates and common council of each corporation, of which Stockholm ſends four, others two, and ſome one; who make about one hundred and fifty. The peaſants of each diſtrict chuſe one of their own quality to appear for them, whoſe charges they bear; and give him inſtructions in ſuch matters as they think need redreſs: they are about two hundred and fifty.

The ſtanding revenues of Sweden ariſe from crown lands, cuſtoms, poll-money, tithes, copper and ſilver mines, proceedings at law, and other leſs conſiderable particulars, which are calculated in all to near a million a year; of which the lands make above one third, and the cuſtoms almoſt a fourth. The poll-money is paid only by the peaſants, each of which above ſixteen, and under ſixty, pays above

twelve

twelve pounds a year. In the treafury-chamber a prefident, with four chancellors, and other officers, fit and act as a court of juftice, in fuch matters as relate to the king's revenue, or rather that of the ftate.

The conquefts made by Sweden in the laft age, were not fo much owing to its native ftrength, as to the affiftance of Germans, French, Englifh, and efpecially Scots; of whom they have ufed great numbers in all their wars with Mufcovy, Poland, Germany, and Denmark: and by them the art of war and military difcipline has been, by degrees, introduced into this nation, that in former times had only the advantage of courage and numbers. For though the original conftitution of the country, and its divifion into hundreds and other large portions that ftill retain military names, feems to have been the work of armies, and the frequent expeditions of the Goths, and other inhabitants of thofe parts, fhew that in all ages they were addicted to war and violence; yet it was in a tumultuous manner, their infantry always confifting of unexperienced peafants raifed for the occafion, and difbanded as foon as it was over.

The feudal laws indeed provided for a competent number of cavalry; all eftates of the nobility and gentry being held by knights fervice: and while the kingdom was elective, the kings were bound to maintain fome horfe out of the revenue of the crown. But this eftablifhment had been in a great meafure corrupted, and the kingdom fo fhattered by domeftic broils, that it made a very inconfiderable figure, and was little known in Europe till the crown became hereditary, and the intereft of the royal family confifted in the ftrength and profperity of the nation. Since that time the ftanding forces of the kingdom have been augmented, yet not fo effectually eftablifhed as its neceffities required; for it generally happened that the nobility and gentry were fo backward in fitting out their horfe, and the levies of foot not being to be made without the conſent of the peaſants in the aſſembly of the ſtates, it was ſo hardly obtained, that the regiments were very thin, and recruits extreme difficult: nor were the officers ſalaries ſo punctually paid as to enable them to be in readineſs on all occaſions.

To remedy theſe inconveniencies, Charles XI. on whom the ſtates had conferred an abſolute power to put the militia into ſuch a method as he ſhould think fit, made ſuch regulations in all the particulars relating to this matter, as were required to bring it to perfection.

In times of peace, all treſpaſſes committed by the ſoldiery fall ordinarily under the cognizance of a civil magiſtrate; who has the ſame authority over them as over the reſt of the king's ſubjects, except when they are incamped, or in garriſon, or in any way under flying colours: in all which caſes, as alſo in matters that relate ſolely to their profeſſion, their officers have juriſdiction over them; without whoſe leave a private ſoldier is not permitted to lodge out of his quarters, or be out a day from the pariſh he belongs to.

The inferior officers cannot be abſent from their charge but by the colonel's permiſſion; nor captains, nor thoſe above them, without the king's leave: and the good effect of the officers conſtant reſidence upon their reſpective charges, appears in the quiet and peaceable behaviour of the ſoldiers, who have not hitherto broke out into any enormities, nor given the common people any great occaſion of complaint. To keep them in diſcipline, each company meets, and is exerciſed once a month, and every regiment once or twice a year; at which time only they wear the king's cloaths, which, at their return, are carefully laid up in the churches. For their government in time of war, the king hath lately cauſed the articles of war to be reviewed and printed, together with a new eſtabliſhment of courts martial, and inſtructions for the auditors, governors, and other officers concerned in the miniſtration of juſtice: and for his majeſty's informa-

4 tion

tion on all occaſions, a book hath been lately made, ſpecifying the names of every military officer in the king's army, the time when they firſt came into the ſervice, and by what ſteps they have riſen; by which means, at one view, his majeſty knows the merit and ſervice of any officer. The whole body of the king of Sweden's forces, according to the beſt and moſt exact accounts, are as follow:

The eſtabliſhed militia in SWEDEN, FINLAND, and LIEFLAND, or LIVONIA, are

	Men
Cavalry, fifteen regiments, is - -	17,000
Infantry, twenty-eight regiments, is - -	35,000
Foot-guards, one regiment, is - - - -	2,000
Forces in Pomoren and Bremen, 6 reg. (now loſt)	6,000
In all fifty regiments, - - -	60,000

Sweden has, in all times, furniſhed Europe with thoſe commodities it abounds with: yet either the warlike temper, idleneſs, or ignorance of the inhabitants formerly, kept them from being much concerned in trade, and gave ſtrangers the management and advantage of it. This for a long time the Hanſe towns ſituate on the Baltic Sea monopolized; till the ſeven provinces of the Netherlands were erected into a republic, and became ſharers with them. Before that time very little iron was made in Sweden; but the ore being run into pigs, was carried into Dantzick, and other parts of Pruſſia, and there forged into bars; for which reaſon the country ſmiths in England call foreign iron Dantzick or Spruce iron. This nation owes the greateſt improvements it has made in trade, to the art and induſtry of ſome ingenious mechanics that the cruelty of the duke of Alva drove into theſe parts. Their ſucceſs invited great numbers of reformed Walloons to tranſplant themſelves thither, whoſe language and religion remain in the places they ſettled in. They erected

erected forges and other conveniencies for making of iron guns, wire, and all other manufactures of copper, braſs, and iron; which, for the moſt part, are ſtill carried on by their poſterity.

The Swediſh navigation was very inconſiderable till Queen Chriſtina, at the concluſion of the wars in 1644, obtained from Denmark a freedom from cuſtoms for all ſhips and goods belonging to Swediſh ſubjects in their paſſage through the Sound: and eſtabliſhed in her own dominions that difference in cuſtoms that ſtill ſubſiſts between Swediſh and foreign ſhips. This is in proportion of four, five, ſix; the firſt called whole free; the ſecond, half; and the laſt, unfree: ſo that where a whole free Swediſh ſhip pays four hundred crowns, half free pays five hundred, and a foreign veſſel ſix. But as great as this advantage was, it had but little effect, till the Engliſh act of navigation bridled the Hollanders, and opened the intercourſe between England and Sweden. Since that time, their commerce has been much augmented as well as ours that way; and goods tranſported by both, or either party, according to the various junctures of affairs.

The general direction of their trade belongs to the college of commerce; which conſiſts of the preſident of the treaſury, and four counſellors, who hear cauſes of that nature, and redreſs any diſorders that happen. The bank at Stockholm is of great benefit to trade, as well in regard that the king's cuſtoms for that city are paid in there, as alſo that the merchants ordinarily make payments to each other by bills drawn upon it: this eaſes them of a great deal of trouble in tranſporting their money from place to place, that would otherwiſe be very difficult and chargeable. The management of the trade of Sweden has always been in the hands of ſtrangers, moſt of the natives wanting either capacity or application, and all of them ſtocks to drive it: for without credit from abroad, they are not able to keep their iron works going; and therefore at the beginning of winter they usually made contracts with the English, and other foreigners, who then advance considerable sums, and receive iron in summer.

Were it not for this necessity, foreign merchants would have but little encouragement, or scarce permission to live and trade amongst them; and even, as the case stands, the treatment of them is as rigorous as in any country, occasioned chiefly by the burghers, who cannot, with any patience, see a stranger live among them. This is the less sensible to the Dutch and others, who some become burghers, and the rest, by their near way of living, are less subject to envy; but is more especially the case of the English merchants, who find it not their interest to become burghers, and usually live somewhat too high. The interest of England in the trade of Sweden, may be computed by the necessaries sent to us, and the vent of ours there: their copper, iron, tar, pitch, masts, &c. cannot be had elsewhere, except from America, whence it has been supposed such supplies were furnished; and, if so, this consideration ought in reason to have an influence on the Swedish councils, and engage them to make the English trade with them as easy as possible, that the merchants be not driven upon new designs. As to our importations thither, they scarcely amount to one third of what we export from thence, and consist chiefly of cloth, stuffs, and other woollen manufactures, of which there have been formerly vended yearly there, to the value of about fifty thousand pounds: beside those, tobacco, Newcastle coals, pewter, lead, tin, fruit, and sugar, with several other of our commodities, are sold at the market; as also good quantities of herrings from Scotland, with other of their wares: that in all, we are supposed to vend goods to about one hundred thousand pounds a year. If any more than half be paid for, it is looked on as very extraordinary.

These observations and remarks upon the kingdom of Sweden were written about fifty years ago, and yet it is not eaſy to obtain any thing relating thereto more perfect in its kind. It muſt be allowed that great alterations have happened in Sweden ſince that time. Upon the death of the late king Charles XII. the Swediſh nation very wiſely laid hold of that opportunity to recover their antient conſtitution; to reſtrain the power of the crown within juſt bounds, to reſtore that of the ſtates, and of the ſenate: and they have made the beſt uſe that could be of this alteration, by electing a prince of the royal family to be the ſucceſſor of the preſent king, and making the crown hereditary in his family; but in ſuch a manner as is conſiſtent with their freedom. They have likewiſe taken very juſt and prudent precautions for preſerving, increaſing, and extending the commerce of their country; which, though at preſent leſs conſiderable than it formerly was, is, however, in ſuch circumſtances as ſeem to promiſe the recovery of its former interior ſtrength. This muſt be attended, ſooner or later, with the reſtoration of its ancient grandeur; ſince both reaſon and experience teach us, that when due care is taken for ſecuring the peace, the freedom, and proſperity of any people at home, they certainly become reſpected by their neighbours, and conſequently conſiderable abroad.

THE PRESENT STATE OF THE Dominions of DENMARK, and of its SUBJECTS:

With occaſional OBSERVATIONS and REMARKS.

Collected from the writings of Lord MOLESWORTH, and other authors of credit.

CONSIDERING that the Danes were once maſters of a great part of this iſland, that our princes have ſince frequently intermarried with the families

families of the Daniſh kings, the late and preſent queens of Denmark being daughters of the royal family of Great Britain; and that we have as great connection with this kingdom and court as with any of the northern powers: from all theſe concurrent circumſtances, there is not a country in Europe, eſpecially in the north, which it behoves us to be better acquainted with than Denmark. But notwithſtanding this, it ſo happens, that we are very far from being generally well informed as to this nation and its concerns. It is true that Mr. Moleſworth, who reſided at Copenhagen in the reign of king William, has written a valuable and much eſteemed treatiſe upon this ſubject; in which he very fully explains the cauſes of, and the manner in which that great revolution happened, whereby the kings of Denmark, from being elective and limited, became hereditary and abſolute in 1660. And by the way it may not be amiſs to obſerve, that this is the only legal abſolute monarchy, perhaps, in the world: the king being declared ſo by the ſtates of the kingdom, who had that power by the conſtitution.

It is indeed true that there was a force put upon the nobility; but it was a force put upon them by the people, who knew that they made a very bad uſe of the authority they enjoyed in virtue of their old conſtitution; and therefore made it their choice to live under an abſolute king, rather than under a tyrannical ariſtocracy. We may learn, from hence, ſeveral things worthy of our obſervation; and, among them, theſe: That when, in a mixed or limited government, any part of it gains ſuch a ſuperiority over the reſt as is deſtructive of the good of the whole, it cannot long ſubſiſt; but muſt infallibly be diſſolved. That as a democracy, or popular ſtate, is, of all others, ſooneſt corrupted; ſo an ariſtocracy, or government by a few, is, when corrupted, the leaſt to be borne, eſpecially in ſtates which have a viſible

 head:

head: and that, in ſuch revolutions, the change is ſeldom, if ever, from a tyrannical to a mixed government; but from one deſpotic power to another. But though the book before-mentioned, ſtates thoſe points very clearly; and, for the time in which it was written, is certainly as good a one as can be wiſhed; yet it is now, in ſome meaſure, out of date: and, therefore, in order to have a tolerable idea of the preſent ſtate of this country, we muſt alſo have recourſe to later obſervations.

The dominions of the crown of Denmark conſiſt of the great kingdom of Norway, of which ſome account has already been given; of the peninſula of Jutland, which, from the frontiers of Germany to its utmoſt northern bounds, is about two hundred and ſeventy miles in length, and of different breadths; of the dutchy of Holſtein, which the king of Denmark holds jointly with the duke of that title; of the Daniſh iſlands, the chief of which are Zealand, Funen, and Iceland; and of ſeveral countries in Germany, ſuch as Oldenbourg, Delmenhorſt, and other places, partly the hereditary dominions of the royal family, and partly obtained by conqueſt. We may eaſily diſcern, from hence, that this crown muſt always have a conſiderable ſhare in the general ſyſtem of Europe, as well as in the particular diſtribution of power in the north: and conſequently, though its dominions lie a little out of the way, and we do not very frequently hear of the effects either of the power or policy of the kings of Denmark; yet the nature of their dominions, and the temper of their ſubjects, are very well worth knowing.

The air of Denmark is not good, eſpecially near Copenhagen, which is ſuppoſed to proceed from its low ſituation, and the frequent fogs there. The air of Sleſwick and Holſtein is better than that in the northern parts, and the country more deſirable upon many accounts, as will appear hereafter. The ſame obſervations are made as to the ſeaſons in Denmark and

and Sweden, viz. that the year is divided into winter and ſummer; that they have no ſpring, and very ſeldom any autumn: but proceed immediately from an extreme cold to an extremity of heat; and from violent hot weather to an extremity of cold. During the months of June, July, and Auguſt, the heat is more intenſe than in England, and the nights not near ſo cool as with us, though they are ſo many degrees more to the northward; nor do they enjoy a clear ſunſhine during thoſe heats, but thick vapours all the time between them and the ſun It is a general obſervation, that the heaven is much brighter and more ſerene far within the continent, than it is near the ſea coaſt; nor is the air leſs clear and pleaſant at ſea, a great diſtance from land, than it is in the middle of the continent. But this obſervation holds more true within the tropics, than it does either in the northern or the ſouthern latitudes. The air of Norway is exceſſive cold; but eſpecially within the polar circle, which is inhabited by the Laplanders. The more ſoutherly part of the country differs but little from Sweden, from which it is ſeparated only by the Dofrine hills.

The ſeas bordering on the Daniſh dominions are the German ocean, the Baltic, in which is that famous ſtreight or paſſage into the Eaſt Sea, called the Ore Sound, or generally the Sound of the Baltic. It is to be obſerved, that being a mediterranean ſea, there are no tides in it, and that its waters are freſher than the ocean; ſuppoſed to be occaſioned by the rivers that run into it. The Sound is about four miles over, having the iſland of Zealand on the weſt, and the continent of Schonen on the eaſt. In the narroweſt part of the ſtreight of Zealand, or Denmark ſide, ſtands the town of Elſenore, and the ſtrong caſtle of Cronenbourg; before which there is a tolerable road for ſhipping. On the ſide of Schonen, in the poſſeſſion of the Swedes, is the town of Helſingbourg, and a ſmall battery of guns, which ſerve only to salute the ships which pass by it. Between those two places sail all the shipping bound to the Baltic. The Danes only, however, receive the toll of all merchantmen who pass by it, though the Swedes are masters of the opposite shore; by virtue of the treaty concluded when they yielded up Schonen to them. But the Swedes themselves were exempted from paying any duties, till the peace in the year 1721, when the affairs of Sweden were in a very desperate condition; and then they condescended to pay a toll to Denmark, as other nations did, on their passing the Sound.

This duty is supposed to have arisen from the mutual consent of the merchants trading to the east country; who at first contributed a small sum toward maintaining of light-houses on the coast for their own security: and thereupon this passage of the Sound came to be more used than that of either Belt to the westward of the isle of Zealand, which, in other respects, seem as commodious as this. From some such beginnings the Danes proceeded to demand large sums, and that as their undoubted right, being masters of both shores. The emperor Charles V. in behalf of his subjects of the seventeen provinces of the Low Countries, came to an agreement with the Danes, that every ship of two hundred tons and under, passing the Sound, should pay two rose nobles going and coming from the Baltic; and every ship above that burden, three nobles: which agreement remained in force until the United Provinces set up for independent states; after which the Danes obliged the Dutch to pay extravagant rates. But the Hollanders and Lubeckers opposing these exactions about the year 1600, obliged the Danes to accept of more moderate duties. The first solemn treaty the Dutch made with the Danes concerning this toll was in the year 1647, wherein they agreed to pay about twenty-five pounds for every ship of two hundred tons passing the streights, for forty years; at the expiration

of

of which, the firſt agreement with the emperor was to be in force: and the Engliſh, in their treaties with Denmark, agreed to pay toll as the Dutch and other nations in friendſhip with them did. As to the free ſtates of England and Holland, they need aſk no permiſſion of the Danes to paſs the Sound; for the caſtles on the ſhores are at too great a diſtance to prevent it; and, if they had not a ſquadron of men of war ready to compel the merchant to pay the toll, he might paſs by unhurt. Beſide, the paſſage called the Great Belt, between the iſlands of Zealand and Funen, is much wider; and that of the Leſſer Belt, between Funen and the continent of Jutland, is not at all impracticable.

The nature of the ſoil, in dominions ſo far extended, and ſo much disjoined, as thoſe of Denmark are, muſt be various. The iſland of Zealand, wherein the capital city of Copenhagen ſtands, produces no corn but rye, of which moſt of their bread is made. Of this they have enough for the ſubſiſtence of the inhabitants, but not to export. There is not much meadow or paſture ground in the iſland; but what they have is ſhort and ſweet. One fourth part of the country is foreſt, and reſerved for the king's game, ſuch as ſtags, wild boars, &c. which no ſubject dares meddle with, though he finds whole herds of them devouring his corn, and the farmers are generally great ſufferers by them. In a wet ſeaſon they have the greateſt plenty of grain in Zealand. Their cattle are ſmall, and lean in the winter, kept within doors for ſeven or eight months of the year, and fed with grains, roots, weeds, and ſuch ſtuff as their owners can provide: but in ſummer, when there is graſs to be had, their beef is pretty good. Near Copenhagen the ſea is not ſtored with fiſh, which is ſuppoſed to proceed from the water not being ſo ſalt as that in other ſeas.

The only city worthy of notice in this iſland, and indeed in all Denmark, is the city of Copenhagen, there being no other in the king's whole dominions much better than our town of St. Alban's. Copenhagen is neither a very ancient, nor a very large place; it approaching nearest to Bristol or any of our English cities: but its excellent port, renders its situation for trade one of the best in the world. It is surrounded with fortifications, and the port is inclosed by the bulwarks of the town, the entrance being so narrow, that but one ship can pass at a time: and this entrance is every night shut up with a strong boom: the citadel on one side, and on the other a good block-house well furnished with cannon, command the mouth. Within this haven rides the royal navy, every ship having her place assigned her: a wooden gallery ranges the whole inclosure where the fleet lies, and extending over the water, the ships may be viewed from it in as easy and commodious a manner as if they lay on dry land. This harbour is capacious enough to hold five hundred sail, out of the reach of storms and tempests. But it has been found that their fortifications cannot protect them from a bombardment at sea, nor are they always secure on that side against the attacks of a land army. For the Baltic has been so hard frozen, that the Swedes have drawn their artillery over the ice, and laid siege to the city. The buildings of Copenhagen were in general very mean, they being formed of a kind of case-work, with the intervals between the timbers filled up with brick. The public edifices, and particularly the palace, formerly made a very indifferent appearance; and several of the noblemen were infinitely better lodged than the royal family. But on the 28th of October 1728, the city was reduced to ashes, and this conflagration has contributed greatly to its beauty; for it rose again in a more magnificent form; the houses were built with brick and free-stone, and the king has erected a very noble palace. The royal museum here contains an admirable collection of curiosities both natural and artificial,

artificial, preſerved in eight chambers over the royal library, which is large and well furniſhed.

The houſes of Copenhagen do not take up above half the ground incloſed by the fortifications. The iſle of Amack, which is ſeparated from the city only by a ſmall channel of the ſea, is united to it by ſeveral bridges, that afford an eaſy communication: and in this iſland is what is called the New Town, which conſiſts of about four or five hundred houſes, and contains the arſenal, the mint, the exchange, and the caſtle. This little iſland, which is only about ſix miles in length, is called the garden of Copenhagen, and is eſteemed the moſt fertile ſpot in Denmark. It was given long ago to ſeveral families who came from North-Holland, to make butter and cheeſe for the court; and their deſcendants ſtill retain the habit, language, and cuſtoms of their predeceſſors, together with their cleanlineſs and induſtry: for they will not mix with the Danes, but intermarry with each other. This iſland, through the induſtry of theſe laborious people, plentifully ſupplies the markets of Copenhagen with all ſorts of roots and herbs; beſide butter, milk, great quantities of corn, and ſome hay.

The iſland of Funen produces corn and wood ſufficient for the natives, and they have cattle for their uſe; but it affords nothing for exportation, excepting a few horſes. Laland is a plentiful iſland, and produces all ſorts of corn in abundance, particularly wheat, with which it ſupplies Copenhagen, and all other parts of Denmark.

The iſlands of Falſtria, Langland, and Mona, are reckoned tolerable fruitful; Arroe and Alſen produce anniſeed, which they mix with their bread, and uſe it in ſeaſoning their meat. Jutland has corn enough for the natives, and abounds in cattle. The horſes and hogs of this country are reckoned very good, and black cattle are tranſported lean from hence to Holland, where they grow fat in a ſhort time; of which

which the Dutch make a considerable profit. The country of Sleswick hath a sufficient quantity of corn, cattle, and horses, with which they furnish their neighbours. Holstein is a pleasant, fruitful country, said to resemble England in its variety of hills, woods, rivers, meadows, and corn fields. Stormar and Ditmarch lie down near the Elb, being a rich soil, compared to Holland for fertility and improvement of its lands, which are sometimes overflowed, however, by the neighbouring ocean. Oldenbourg also is a flat country, much exposed to inundations; but abounds in cattle, and hath a breed of horses esteemed for being of a white or cream colour; though they have generally tender feet, and last but a little while. Delmenhorst is a more hilly country than Oldenbourg, and pretty well wooded. Norway and Lapland having been already described, there is no need of dwelling upon them here.

The islands of Iceland, Fero, and Schetland are almost as barren as Norway; corn will scarcely grow in any of them; but they abound in cattle. The natives of Iceland feed on the flesh of bears, wolves, and foxes, and bread made of dried fish beat to powder. They barter their dried fish, tallow, and sulphur, for such other commodities as they want. There are not, either in the islands of Iceland or Fero, any trees, except juniper-shrubs, birch, and willows: but they have roots, and other garden-stuff, which, with their fish, are their greatest support. They have good pasture, and a tolerable breed of black cattle, small sized horses, and some flocks of sheep, and almost all manner of roots and herbs which grow in other kitchen gardens; and are pretty well stocked with fish and fowl. But the cold is very severe in all these islands, and their winter is dark, as may easily be gathered from their situation.

As to the manufactures of Denmark and Norway, there are none, except of iron; which is not very considerable. Holstein and Sleswick seem to be extreamly

treamly well situated for foreign trade, lying both upon the Baltic and the ocean; but reap little advantage from their situation at present. Hamburgh on one side, and Lubec on the other, which border upon Holstein, are indeed towns of great trade, and the Dane sometimes pretends to the sovereignty of Hamburgh: but, by the countenance of the neighbouring powers, that city hath hitherto nominally preserved her liberties, at the expence of heavy contributions occasionally squeezed out of it, by the armies of Denmark; the last of which was in the year 1762. Jutland and Holstein export nothing but horses and cattle. From Norway, indeed, there are great quantities of fir-timber, for masts, yards, and planks exported, with pitch, tar, stock-fish, oil, and iron, for which they receive ready money chiefly of the English; but of the French, wine, brandy, alamodes, and other articles.

The Danes have some inconsiderable factories in the West Indies, and on the coast of Guinea; and in the East Indies, they are masters of the city and fort of Tranquebar, one of the most considerable towns on the east-side of the continent: and from hence are sent home, some years, two or three ships. The Danes are reckoned to have more shipping than the Swedes, the reason whereof may be, that Norway furnishes a considerable number of hardy seamen, who are used to those boisterous seas. The Dutch also maintain great numbers of Norwegians in their fleets, where they live better than on their own barren coasts, which makes these people apply themselves more to the sea-service than any other subjects of Denmark: and there is always a considerable number of them ready to man the royal navy: which brings us to enquire into the strength and forces of the Danes by sea and land.

We cannot enter upon this head without making the same reflections that lord Molesworth does. It is certain that the levying taxes here is not more grievous

ous to the people, than the reaſon for which they are levied; the maintenance of a great ſtanding army. The people are made contributors to their own miſery, and their purſes drained in order to maintain their ſlavery. The French king has taught the princes of Europe that pernicious ſecret of making one part of the people bridle and ſcourge the other; which, in time, muſt needs end in a general deſolation. The king of Denmark hath even endeavoured to exceed his original, in raiſing more men than his country will maintain: and, at preſent, the northern and German princes eſtimate their wealth not by the fertility or extent of their territory, by the trade or induſtry of the people, but by the numbers of horſe and foot in their ſervice: for the ſubſiſtence of which, after they have eaten up their own ſubjects, they make uſe of an hundred cruel and unjuſt pretences to ruin and encroach on their neighbours. When they cannot accompliſh ſuch projects, they foment quarrels among other princes, that they may have an opportunity of letting out their troops for hire; and have found the art of receiving pay, without intereſting themſelves in the quarrel: which hath been the conſtant practice of the Danes, and ſome neighbouring princes, for many years paſt. Thoſe practices, however, have been very pernicious to Denmark.

It is computed that Denmark, Holſtein, and Oldenbourg maintain five thouſand four hundred and fifty horſe, fifteen hundred dragoons, and ſeventeen thouſand foot. Norway maintains twelve hundred and thirty-ſix horſe and dragoons, and fourteen thouſand three hundred foot, making in all a body of near forty thouſand men. The foot ſoldiers, both officers and private men, are generally foreigners, of all countries, Poles, Germans, Swedes, Scots, &c. There are more reaſons than one for not employing too many of the natives; but the principal, leſt they ſhould ſhew too much affection to their own country, and not ſo readily obey the arbitrary commands of their

princes.

princes. Officers of horſe receive no more pay, in time of peace, than thoſe of the foot. The horſe are uſually natives, and maintained every one by a free-holder or farmer, who is obliged to provide him and his horſe with meat, and ſix ſhillings a month in money, half of which the colonel takes toward his mounting: and in Holſtein they have ſomething better pay than in Denmark. In Norway little money is expended in paying the forces; the private ſoldiers being quartered on the boors, and, which is an heavy burthen, ſubſiſted by them.

For the ſea-ſervice three thouſand mariners are conſtantly maintained at Copenhagen, as well in peace as war; having a weekly allowance of ſalt, fleſh, ſtock-fiſh, or meal, grout, &c. for themſelves and their families, and about eighty rix-dollars a year in money. And there are ſeveral ſtreets of little houſes, or barracks, near the walls, where they live, and where their wives and children reſide while they are at ſea. Their buſineſs, in time of peace, is to work in the king's yards and docks, which are over-againſt the palace of Copenhagen, where they take it by turns to ſerve in all laborious works relating to the ſhipping; and once a year it is uſual to equip a ſmall ſquadron of men of war, and ſail with them two or three months for exerciſing the ſailors. All the officers in the fleet are in conſtant pay, as well in peace as war; and the Danes compute, that they can rig out upward of thirty ſail of men of war at a very ſhort warning.

The king's revenues ariſe from the duties paid by his own ſubjects, the cuſtoms paid by foreigners, the crown lands, fines, and confiſcations. The taxes paid by his ſubjects are either fixed or variable. Of the firſt ſort are the duties of import and export, and the exciſe commonly called conſumption, laid upon every thing that is ate or drank in the kingdom. There are alſo duties paid for marriage licences, duties on ſtamp-paper, on which all bargains, contracts, proceedings at law, &c. are written: ſome of theſe duties amounting to ſeveral rix-dollars per ſheet. Duties are alſo laid upon brewing and malt, and corn that is ground in mills. Theſe duties are certain, or ſeldom altered. The uncertain duties are the taxes on land, which are not aſſeſſed by the acre, but according to the annual value of the farm. Poll-money impoſed upon every one according to the perſonal eſtate he is ſuppoſed to have, which is ſometimes levied twice a year. Money levied for erecting or repairing the fortifications. An occaſional tax, raiſed only when a daughter of Denmark is to be married, whoſe portion is uſually an hundred thouſand crowns. A tax laid upon every tradeſman for the liberty of exerciſing his calling, and the gain he is ſuppoſed to make by it; who is obliged alſo to quarter ſoldiers. The ground-rents, in all cities and towns, which the king taxes, according to the value of the houſe or the ability of the poſſeſſor. In Holſtein the lands are taxed according to the ploughs, each plough paying a certain ſum every month. Not many years ſince an eſtimate was made of all the houſes in the cities and towns in the king's dominions; and all the lands were meaſured, that the crown might the better underſtand their value; and the ground-tax, in the cities and towns, was aſſeſſed at four per cent. of the whole value the ground was rated at, if it was to be purchaſed; and the like proportion was obſerved toward others, in regard to their houſes and profeſſion. The moſt moderate aſſeſſment of their poll-tax is according to the following proportion, viz. a citizen worth eight or ten thouſand rix-dollars pays four rix-dollars for himſelf, four for his wife, two for every child, and one for each ſervant; and for every horſe a rix-dollar. An alehouſe-keeper pays one rix-dollar for himſelf, another for his wife, twenty-four ſtivers for every child, and ſixteen for every ſervant. The fortification tax is uſually high. A merchant worth ſix or eight thouſand rix-dollars, hath ſometimes paid ſixty-

ſixty-eight dollars, an ordinary citizen eight or ten, and others in proportion.

Denmark, as has been hinted, was till lately governed by a king choſen by the people of all ranks; but in their choice, they paid a due regard to the family of the preceding prince, and if they found one of his line qualified for that high honour, they thought it juſt to prefer him before any other, and were pleaſed when they had reaſon to chuſe the eldeſt ſon of their former king: but if thoſe of the royal family were deficient in abilities, or had rendered themſelves unworthy by their vices, they choſe ſome other perſon, and ſometimes a private man for that high dignity.

Frequent meetings of the ſtates was a fundamental part of the conſtitution: in thoſe meetings every thing relating to the government was tranſacted; good laws were enacted, and all affairs relating to peace and war, the diſpoſal of great offices, and contracts of marriage for the royal family, were declared. The impoſing of taxes was purely accidental, no money being levied on the people except to maintain a neceſſary war with the advice and conſent of the nation, or now and then by way of free-gift, to add to a daughter's portion: the king's ordinary revenue conſiſting only in the rents of his lands and demeſnes, in his herds of cattle, his foreſts, ſervices of tenants in cultivating his ground, &c. for cuſtoms on merchandize were not then known in that part of the world; ſo that he lived like one of our modern noblemen, upon the revenues of his eſtate. It was his buſineſs to ſee juſtice impartially adminiſtered; to watch over the welfare of his people, to command their armies in perſon; to encourage induſtry, arts, and learning: and it was equally his duty and intereſt to keep fair with the nobility and gentry, and to be careful of the plenty and proſperity of the commons.

But

But in 1660, the three estates, that is, the nobility, clergy, and commonalty, being assembled in order to pay and disband the troops which had been employed against the Swedes; the nobility endeavoured to lay the whole burthen on the commons, while the latter, who had defended their country, their prince, and the nobility themselves with the utmost bravery, insisted that the nobles, who enjoyed all the lands, should at least pay their share of the taxes, since they had suffered less in the common calamity, and done less to prevent its progress.

At this the nobility were enraged, and many bitter replies passed on both sides. At length the principal senator standing up, told the president of the city that the commons neither understood the privileges of the nobility, nor considered, that they themselves were no other than slaves. The word slaves was followed by a loud murmur from the clergy and burghers: Nanson, the president of the city of Copenhagen, and speaker of the house of commons, perceiving the indignation it occasioned, instantly arose, and swearing that the commons were no slaves, which the nobility should soon prove to their cost; walked out, followed by the clergy and burghers, and proceeding to the brewers-hall, debated there on the most effectual means of humbling the insupportable pride of the nobles.

The next morning the commons and clergy marched in great order to the council-house, where the nobles were again assembled; and the president Nanson made a short speech, observing that they had considered the state of the nation, and found that the only way to remedy the disorders of the state, was to add to the power of the king, and render his crown hereditary, in which if they thought fit to concur they were ready to accompany them to the king, whom they had informed of their resolution, and who expected them in the hall of his palace.

The

The ſuddenneſs of this propoſal, and the reſolution with which it was made, cauſed a general conſternation among the nobles. They now endeavoured to ſooth the commons by fair ſpeeches; and urged that ſo important an affair ſhould be managed with due ſolemnity, and that it ſhould be regulated in ſuch a manner that it might not have the appearance of a tumult. To this the preſident replied, that they only wanted to gain time, in order to fruſtrate the intentions of the commons; who came not thither to conſult, but to act. After farther debate, the commons growing impatient, the clergy and burghers, led on by their biſhop and preſident, proceeded without the nobles to the palace; and were met by the prime miniſter, who conducted them to the hall of audience, whither the king ſoon came to them. The biſhop made a long ſpeech in praiſe of his majeſty, and concluded with offering him an hereditary and abſolute dominion. The king returned them his thanks; but obſerved that the concurrence of the nobles was neceſſary; he aſſured them of his protection, and promiſed to eaſe their grievances. The nobles were all this while in the greateſt diſtraction; they could come to no reſolution, and broke up in order to attend the funeral of a principal ſenator; but while they were at a magnificent dinner, which was uſually provided on ſuch occaſions, they were told that the city gates were ſhut up by the king's orders, and the keys carried to court. They were now filled with the apprehenſions of being all maſſacred, and the dread of loſing their lives took away all thoughts of their liberty: they therefore immediately diſpatched meſſengers both to the court and to the commons, to give notice of their compliance. But the king being reſolved to avail himſelf fully of the preſent popular diſpoſition; which by his emiſſaries he had contributed to ſtimulate; would not ſuffer the gates to be opened till the whole ceremony of his inauguration was concluded. Three days time were neceſſary to prepare matters for the fatal hour in

 which

which they were to make a formal ſurrender of their liberty. Scaffolds covered with tapeſtry were erected in the ſquare before the caſtle: orders were given for the ſoldiers and burghers to appear in arms under their reſpective officers; and on the 27th of October in the morning, the king, queen, and royal family being mounted on a theatre erected for that purpoſe, and placed in chairs of ſtate under canopies of velvet, received publicly the homage of all the ſenators, nobility, clergy, and commons. This was performed on their knees, each taking an oath to promote his majeſty's intereſt in all things, and to ſerve him faithfully as became hereditary ſubjects. Here one Gerdorf, a principal ſenator, was the only man who opened his mouth in behalf of their expiring liberties; ſaying, that he hoped and truſted that his majeſty deſigned nothing but the good of his people, and not to govern them after the Turkiſh manner: but he wiſhed his ſucceſſors might follow the example his majeſty would undoubtedly ſet them, and make uſe of that unlimited power for the good, and not for the prejudice, of his ſubjects. Not one of the reſt ſpoke a word, or ſeemed in the leaſt to murmur at what was done, ſo totally had their former haughty ſpirit ſubſided. Thoſe who had paid their homage now retired to the council-houſe, where the nobles were called over by name, and ordered to ſubſcribe the oath they had taken, which they all did.

Thus in four days time the kingdom of Denmark was changed from a ſtate but little different from that of ariſtocracy to that of an unlimited monarchy. The only comfort the commons had left, was to ſee their former oppreſſors almoſt as much humbled as themſelves; while all that the citizens of Copenhagen have obtained by it is, the inſignificant privilege of wearing ſwords: ſo that now not a cobler nor a barber ſtirs abroad without one by his ſide. The clergy were indeed the only gainers; for they reaped many advantages from this change.

However,

However, no ensigns of majesty appear at the court of Denmark, except such as are military; as horse and foot guards, yeomen, and the sounds of drums and trumpets: but the badges of peace, as heralds, maces, the chancellor's purse, and the sword of state, are here unknown. The king sits down to dinner with his queen, children, relations, and general officers of the army, till the round table be filled. The court-marshal inviting sometimes one and sometimes another to eat with his majesty till all have had their turns in that honour. A page in livery says grace before and after meat; for no chaplain appears here but in the pulpit. The attendants are one or two gentlemen, and the rest livery servants. The kettle drums and trumpets, which are ranged before the palace, proclaim aloud the very minute when the king sits down to table; but the ceremony of the knee is not used to his majesty.

As to the persons of the Danes, they are generally tall, and strong limbed; their complexion good; their hair fair, yellow, or red: and as few of the men wear wigs, they take a great deal of pains in curling their yellow locks. Neither men nor women are ashamed of red hair, or endeavour to change the colour. They have bad shapes, and their mien is not to be admired. When we see the Danish women sitting in a coach or chair, some of them appear exquisitely beautiful; but if they rise and attempt to walk, they spoil all. Both ladies and gentlemen in summer affect to wear the French dress; but in winter wrap themselves up in furs or wool, like the rest of the northern people. They are neat in their linen, changing it often, and affect too much magnificence. It is observed that Denmark seldom produces a great genius; they are not good at invention or imitation, and are neither deeply learned, nor exquisite mechanics. Polite learning they are perfect strangers to, and few books are found amongst them, except those of controversial religion.

Lord Molesworth, in summing up their character, says, he never knew a country where the minds of people were more upon a level. As we find none of extraordinary parts or qualifications, or excellent in particular studies or arts, so we see no enthusiasts, madmen, natural fools, or whimsical people: but a certain mediocrity of understanding reigns among them; every one plods on in the ordinary track of common sense, without deviating to the right or left. The common people, however, in general, write and read; and their clergy usually talk Latin, but not in the greatest purity. The vices the gentry are most addicted to, are gluttony and drunkenness. When they sit down to eat and drink, they never know when to rise, but the debauch sometimes continues whole days and nights. The first thing a friend is presented with at his coming into the house is a dram of brandy; and they are no sooner set down to dinner, but every man and woman hath also a glass set by their plate: and on proposing a health take off their glasses together, and by that means make a quick dispatch. The women indeed retire after dinner, but the men sit it out till they have lost (which is not soon done) their little sense.

The liquors drank by people of condition are Rhenish-wines, cherry-brandy, and all sorts of French-wines. The men are fond of them, and the fair sex do not refuse them. The poor people indulge in bad beer and spirits extracted from malt or barley. Nor do the Norwegians, who can afford it, come behind the Danes; it is the custom of the country; and both among the gentry and common people, lewdness and intemperance pass for wit and ingenious conversation. As to their eating, the tables of people of condition are covered with a variety of dishes; but the flesh, except beef and veal, is generally lean and ill tasted; their tame fowls and wild ducks are scarce eatable. There are no fallow deer, woodcocks, pheasants, or rabbits; and red deer are the king's game, and not to be purchased. Their hares and their bacon are excellent,

cellent, as are their fresh-water fish, particularly the carp, perch, and cray-fish; but sea-fish is scarce and ill tasted: and in general, their cookery is not agreeable to an English palate. The common people in town and country live upon coarse rye bread, lean salt fish, stock-fish, roots, and very bad cheese; seldom tasting fresh fish, and hardly ever flesh. As to the character of the common people, they are poor, and mean-spirited, far from the warlike temper of their ancestors; inclined to cheating, and intolerably jealous and suspicious that others have a design upon them; which may be observed to be the case of most men of limited understandings. In our age, says Puffendorf, the Danes have lost much of their ancient glory, because the present nobility and gentry are rather for enjoying their revenues in ease and luxury, than for undergoing the fatigues of war; and the commonalty have followed their example.

The Norwegians undergo all kinds of hardships with more courage and vigour, to which they are inured by the climate they live in: but the Danes, ever since they have been masters of Norway, have endeavoured to depress and keep that people under, by taking from them all the opportunities of exerting themselves; and there are now very few of the ancient nobility left in Norway. The Danes travel either in waggons, on horseback, or in sledges; and there is an officer who regulates the prices of carriage, and punishes those who extort more than their due. If any gentleman can procure a warrant from the court, when he is about to undertake a journey, the peasants or farmers are obliged to furnish him with horses and carriages, in every country through which he passes, without being allowed any thing, as they do for the king and court whenever they travel. The Danes have their playhouse for their diversion; they take their pleasure also in their sledges upon the ice in winter. But downright drinking is their favourite recreation; the most serious affairs submit to this, the great buſineſs of the day and night. Nor do the Danes indulge more in eating and drinking than in their lodging; for as there is no place where there is greater plenty of good feather-beds, they lay one under, another over them, all the winter ſeaſon. But lodgings for ſtrangers are procured with difficulty in private houſes; and in public-houſes they are obliged to eat and ſleep in common, no man being allowed a room to himſelf, except his quality be very high indeed.

The king of Denmark is the great interpreter of his laws, and can change them at pleaſure. He is the ſupream judge and preſident of the high court of juſtice, when he pleaſes to ſit there, which is not often: however, whether preſent or abſent, the advocates always addreſs themſelves to the king. The princes of the blood, and the nobility and gentry, are commonly tried in this high court; and the ſuperintendants, or biſhops, have the ſame privilege, if charged with hereſy, or any other notorious crime.

A perſon guilty of theft is not only ſentenced to be whipped, and to hard labour in the public works, but to reſtore double the value of the goods ſtolen to the owner. Coining is puniſhed with the loſs of life and honour, and confiſcation of the eſtate of the offender; and the ſame puniſhment is inflicted on him who removes an antient landmark. He who counterfeits the hand and ſeal of another, or forges a writing, is ſentenced to have his head cut off, his goods confiſcated, and declared infamous. The torture is ſeldom uſed in Denmark, but in caſes of high treaſon; and then only upon perſons already convicted of the ſame crime, in order to make them diſcover their accomplices. Duels, and even the challenging another to fight, is puniſhed with the loſs of life and eſtate; and ſeconds, who do not endeavour to prevent it, are puniſhed in like manner. He who is killed in a duel is not ſuffered to be buried in conſecrated ground; whoever reflects upon another for

refuſing

refusing a challenge, is punishable, and declared infamous by a Danish law.

In cases of shipwreck, the Danish subjects are required to give all imaginable assistance to those in distress, and to preserve the goods for the owner's use. The ships which guard the coasts are directed to save what effects they can, for which they have a moderate reward; and the owners are permitted to sell them in the country, or embark them on board other vessels. If a ship or goods be driven on the coast, and nobody appears to claim them, the king's officers, or the lord of the manor, takes care to preserve them: or if they are perishable goods they sell them to the best advantage, for the benefit of the owner: but if they are not reclaimed within a year and a day, they become the property of the king, or the lord of the place. If the master of any ship finds goods floating on the sea, he is to take care of, and deliver them to the next magistrate; who must keep them a year and a day, to see if any one can claim them; and if nobody owns them, they belong to the king; and if any one conceal or embezzle such wrecked goods, he is to be punished as a felon: and the law is much the same where the person finds goods or cattle upon the road; for he is obliged to publish them in the court of the district, and can have no property in the goods till a year and a day be past, where nobody comes in to reclaim them.

There being but one university in Denmark, a divinity reader is appointed to reside in every cathedral, to expound the Scriptures to the people; and these divinity readers, as well as the masters of colleges, are examined by the professors of the royal academy of Copenhagen before they are admitted to officiate: private schools are expressly prohibited by the laws of Denmark, and none allowed but those established by public authority in the cities and great towns; and they have two or three masters belonging to each school, who have taken their degree of masters of arts at least, as well as the rector.

No perſon is at liberty to ſend a tutor to travel with his ſon, who hath not been firſt examined by the ſuperintendant of the dioceſe, and found to be orthodox in religion; and the ſame is required where one takes a tutor into his houſe, who alſo ought to be a ſtudent of the univerſity of Copenhagen. As no other method of teaching is allowed, than that preſcribed by the government; ſo no other books may be read, but ſuch as are approved by authority, which are compoſed by the profeſſors of their univerſity. The importation of books is alſo prohibited, eſpecially thoſe which treat of any other ſort of religion, than that eſtabliſhed amongſt them.

The clergy of this kingdom are divided into three claſſes, viz. ſuperintendants or biſhops, intendants, which ſome compare to our archdeacons, and curates or pariſh prieſts. The ſuperintendant is obliged to viſit his dioceſe once every year, and to lie in the parſon's houſe, when he comes to any place; who is to entertain him, ſervants and four horſes, gratis. The ſuperintendants are conſecrated by the biſhop or ſuperintendant of Zealand, aſſiſted by five or ſix prieſts; but are all nominated by the king.

The ſuperintendant holds a kind of ſynod twice a year, conſiſting of the intendant in his dioceſe, where the governor of the province preſides for the king. The overſeers are choſen by the pariſh prieſts of each county or diſtrict, in conjunction with the ſuperintendant: and he is obliged to viſit all the pariſhes under his inſpection once a year, at leaſt, and hath a power of cenſuring the lives and converſations of the prieſts in their reſpective diviſions. They ſee that the churches are kept in repair, and that their revenues are not alienated or miſapplied. No perſon can be admitted into prieſts orders until he hath a cure provided for him. He muſt have a certificate alſo from the divinity-profeſſor of the univerſity, concerning the progreſs he hath made in his ſtudies, and his qualifications for the pulpit; and if he do not come immediately from the univerſity, he muſt have them from

the

the overseer and parish priest, where he resides: and they are obliged to perform divine service according to the established form or ritual, observed at St. Mary's in Copenhagen.

They are obliged to pray for the king and magistracy, and for the propagation of the gospel; and are prohibited to admit any to the sacrament, who have not first been at confession. But the penitent, it is said, need not give an account of every particular sin. A general confession, according to the order the commands stand in, intitles him to absolution. The priest is also forbid to take any money, which the Lutheran ministers frequently do notwithstanding. The priest may not divulge the confession of any one, where it is particular; unless in cases of high treason, or for the prevention of some great mischief by such discovery, on pain of deprivation; and in this case the name of the penitent ought to be concealed as long as possible. Popish priests are prohibited to enter the Danish dominions, on pain of death; nor is their law less severe against those they denominate heretics. Jews are forbid to come into the kingdom without a royal licence; and whoever discovers a Jew is intitled to a reward of fifty crowns. Their laws also are severe against gypsies and fortune-tellers.

A man is not to sell or alienate his lands before he is five and twenty years of age, without the consent of his nearest relation; and a woman, whether she be maid or widow, can never part with her lands, but must leave them to descend as the law directs. An uninterrupted possession of twenty years is held to make a good title, and they are not permitted to run farther back in trials of property. All obligations also, and personal debts, are held to be void if not renewed within twenty years; for notes, and bills of exchange, are of equal force with an obligation: but the law allows eight days for all kinds of payments to be made beyond the time prefixed, and if that time be elapsed four and twenty hours, the creditor may protest

it,

it, and have proceſſes thereon againſt the original debtor or acceptor. No perſon is obliged to pay any money loſt at gaming.

The tenure of villainage ſtill prevails in many parts of Denmark; and their vaſſals, or tenants, who hold by this baſe tenure, are purchaſed, and deſcend with the lands they live upon, like fiſh in the waters, or deer in a park: nor can theſe peaſants leave the lands they belong to, and retire elſewhere; if they do, the lord of the ſoil may reclaim them, with their goods; nor can any town or place receive them, unleſs they produce a licence from their lord, and a certificate from the miniſter of the pariſh where they laſt inhabited: and if a peaſant of this claſs endeavours to conceal himſelf, his lord may ſeize him, and put him in priſon, or remove him to any other tenement or farm, by way of puniſhment. And if the wife of one of theſe peaſants be brought to-bed on the lands of another lord, the child ſhall, however, belong to the lord where the father lives. Although the lord has a power to infranchize his peaſant, or ſell him with the land, yet he cannot ſell him ſingly or ſeparate from the manor or eſtate. The children of the eccleſiaſtics of the peaſant race are free, and ſo are all ſtudents in the liberal arts.

A peaſant cannot have the freedom of any town till he is firſt infranchiſed by the lord; but if he hath reſided ten years in any city unreclaimed, and becomes a tradeſman, or artificer, or applies himſelf to the ſea, he is free. A peaſant alſo who hath lived twenty years in a foreign village out of the lord's land, thereby procures his freedom; or if he goes into the army and obtains a commiſſion, this gives him his freedom. As to game laws, every freeholder may hunt, and fiſh in his own grounds; and the nobility and gentry have the privilege of hunting in common or waſte grounds within ten miles of their ſeats, except in the king's parks; and they may fiſh in lakes and ponds which are not the king's: but if any lord hunt, ſhoot, or fiſh, in any place belonging to his majeſty, he forfeits for every ſtag one thouſand rix-dollars, for a fallow deer eight hundred, for a hare four hundred; and for every ſwan, gooſe, duck, partridge, or other fowl two hundred. And whoever is convicted of hunting in another's lands, forfeits an hundred ounces of ſilver for every offence.

The great alteration that has happened in Denmark, of the changing the monarchy from elective to hereditary, and from being the moſt limited, into the moſt abſolute of any in Europe, has had a very ſtrong effect upon all ranks and degrees of people in that country; and may be ſaid, in ſome meaſure, to have made a total change in their temper, and in the nation. The nobility of Denmark, who were formerly as remarkable for their military virtues as any in Europe, are now very ſeldom mentioned; and thoſe of Norway are in a manner extinguiſhed.

According to the beſt maxims of policy, we may very fairly conclude, that in caſe the kings of Denmark act with the ſame prudence and caution that they have done for many years paſt, they will be in a condition to preſerve what they at preſent enjoy, and be alſo at liberty to promote and improve their manufactures and commerce; which have been greatly encouraged of late years, and been attended with all the ſucceſs they could reaſonably expect.

By theſe methods the interior ſtrength of the kingdom will be daily augmenting; the ſhipping, and conſequently the naval force, of Denmark continually increaſing, and though theſe advantages may be ſlow in their nature, yet they are at the ſame time ſo very certain, and of ſuch high importance, that they will, if ſteadily proſecuted, change the whole face of affairs in this country: and before the cloſe of the preſent century, reſtore the antient luſtre of the crown of Denmark, and perhaps raiſe its ſovereigns to a higher rank, than hitherto they have ever held amongſt the European powers.

A COMPREHENSIVE
ACCOUNT
OF THE
KINGDOM of POLAND.

Collected chiefly from the Writings of Dr. BERNARD CONNER, who resided in that kingdom in quality of physician to king JOHN SOBIESKI.

WITH respect to the extent, situation, and produce of the country, and the force of the inhabitants, Poland is none of the least considerable, though far from being the best known kingdom in Europe. It is thought to extend in length from east to west, about seven hundred miles; and in breadth, from north to south, about six hundred. On the north it has Livonia and other provinces of the Muscovite empire: on the east it is also bounded by the Russian dominions and Lesser Tartary: on the south by Moldavia, Transylvania, and Hungary; and on the west by Pomerania, Brandenburgh, Silesia, and Moravia. By this description, it appears, that the inhabitants of Poland have for their neighbours, the Russians, Turks, Tartars, Hungarians, and other subjects of the house of Austria, and those of the king of Prussia. The air of this country is in general temperate and healthful, and more settled both in winter and summer, than in those countries which border on the ocean. The only sea which washes any part of Poland is the Baltic, which lies to the northward of it; but it is well watered by lakes and rivers.

Their lakes lie chiefly in the Greater Poland, Cujavia, and the territory of Lublin; and both lakes and rivers abound with fish. Their principal rivers

are

are the Weisel, or Vistula, which rises in the Crapatch or Carpathian mountains, which divide Hungary from Poland; its courses are partly to the eastward, but generally it runs from south to north, watering many great cities, particularly Cracow, Lublin, Warsaw, Thorn, Marienburgh, and Dantzick; after which it discharges itself into the Baltic Sea. The Warta or Varta, which rises in the Lesser Poland, and running toward the north-west, passes by Kalisch, Posnan, and several other great towns, after which it falls into the Oder. The Nieper or Boristhenes, which divides the dominions of Muscovy from those of Poland, in several places, falls at length into the Black Sea near Oczakow. The Neister or Tyra, which rises in Red Russia, and running to the south-east, through Podolia, passes on to Bender in Turkey, and falls into the Black Sea, about sixty miles to the northward of the mouth of the Danube. The Dwina, which divides Livonia from Courland, falls into the Baltic near Riga. The Bog, which rises from a lake in Podolia, and bending its course to the south east, unites its waters with the Nieper, a little before that river falls into the Black Sea. Near the mouth of these two united rivers stands the fortress of Kassicarmen, which the late czar of Muscovy took from the Turks; and by that means, is opened a communication with the Black Sea; but he was obliged to restore this place as well as Asoph to the grand seignior, upon the defeat he met with on the banks of the Pruth. Niemen or Russe rises in the palatinate of Novogrodeck, and taking its course to the north-west, passes by Grodno, and at length falls into the Baltic.

The dominions of Poland are usually divided into eight large provinces, viz. Proper Poland, the great dukedom of Lithuania, Prussia, Samogitia, and Courland, Warsovia or Massovia, Palachia and Polesia, Red or Little Russia, Podolia, Volhinia, and the Ukrain. The soil for the most part is champaign and open; but toward the borders of Hungary mountai-

nous

nous and woody; ſo that the places fartheſt diſtant from Hungary are moſt fruitful. There is only one great mountain in the middle of Leſſer Poland, called Mons Calvus. It has a monaſtery on the top, famous, as they pretend, for the real croſs of Chriſt: what other hills one meets with here, are rather riſing grounds than mountains. The eaſtern parts of the kingdom are full of woods, foreſts, lakes, marſhes, and rivers, which afford a delightful proſpect in that open country. Almoſt all of it, is ſaid to have been overgrown with wood, but now being cultivated by the inhabitants is very fertile, and produces every where all kinds of fruit, corn, and herbs. A great part of the corn made uſe of in Holland comes from this country by way of Denmark.

They have a good breed of horſes, ſo that their cavalry is numerous, and well mounted. Their paſtures are good, and feed a great many cattle, which they export to foreign countries: the foreſts abound with wild beaſts, and alſo with bees, that afford vaſt quantities of honey and wax. They have alſo abundance of flax and hemp, and vines in many places, whoſe grapes are grateful to the taſte, eſpecially if the ſummer and harveſt be favourable; but the wine is generally very ſharp when drawn off. In the mountains there are mines of lead, ſilver, copper, and iron; with other kinds of minerals, as quickſilver at Tuſtan in Red Ruſſia, and vitriol near Biecz in the palatinate of Cracovia: but the moſt conſiderable of all are the ſalt mines at Bochina and Veliſca in Leſſer Poland, which are the chief riches of the country. They work in thoſe mines as we do in our coal-pits; the ſalt is generally of a bluiſh colour, but ſome of it white and tranſparent, like cryſtal: when it is new dug it has a brackiſh taſte, but when expoſed to the air becomes brittle, and more ſweet; they have alſo ſome veins of Sal Gemmæ. The woods are well ſtored with hares, coneys, ſquirrels, deer, foxes, bears, wolves, and boars. The Maſſovian foreſts have plenty of elks, wild aſſes, buffaloes, and biſonets, which in ſhape and horns reſemble an ox; have manes like horſes, beards on their lower jaws, tongues rough like a file, and very hard, a bunch on their backs, and their hair ſmells like muſk. They are incredibly ſtrong; the Poliſh nobility hunt them, and eſteem ther fleſh when powdered a great dainty.

The weſtern parts of this kingdom produce a great deal of corn of all ſorts, which is exported from Dantzick; as alſo honey, wax, amber, hides, tanned leather, Muſcovite and Poliſh furs, oak, wainſcot, maſts, planks, fir, deal, pitch, tallow, ſalt, hops, hemp, flax, ſalt-petre, pot-aſhes, opium, Pruſſian wool, for coarſe manufactures; vitriol, lapis lazuli, vermilion, braſs, lead, iron, copper, glaſs, and earthen-ware, oxen, ſheep, hogs, &c. to different parts of Europe. They import ſtuffs, ſilk, and worſted; Engliſh cloths, tapeſtry, jewels, ſables, ſalt-fiſh, tin, ſteel, martens, &c. iron-ware, Rheniſh, French, Spaniſh, and Hungarian wines, ſpirits, aqua vitæ, brandy, ſpice, of which they make great conſumption. They might be much richer, if they were induſtrious and frugal, and applied themſelves to manufactures; but the Poles are little inclined to either: for the gentry are abſolutely forbid to follow trade, of any kind, on pain of forfeiting their honour; and the commonalty generally want funds, ſo that all the trade there is chiefly carried on by foreign merchants: beſide, ſuch of the Poles as have any fortunes, ſpend too much of their revenues in coſtly habits and luxury, to be able to undertake any conſiderable traffic. Nor have they good ports, except Dantzick, which is not enough to improve the trade of ſo large a country. It is to this want of commerce with other nations, that the Poles owe moſt of the defects in their government; for if they were once convinced of them, there is not a nation in Europe more capable of correcting them, as we may gather from a familiar inſtance. One of their monarchs being in Germany, and not having it in his power to converſe with ſtrangers in Latin; he was ſo ſenſible of the defect, that upon his return to Poland,

Poland, he caused a grammar-school to be erected in every town throughout the kingdom; so that now there is not a country in Europe where Latin is so generally understood as it is here.

From the time of Lechus, the kings of Poland have been elected to the crown in a regular descent, though not by an hereditary title. They have really been absolute, and their will went for law; for they made peace and war when they pleased, levied troops as they thought fit, punished or pardoned at pleasure; and all the administration, either of public or private affairs, was so wholly lodged in the king's hands, that the Poles themselves say, that Sigismund II. the last king of the Jagellon family, was to the full as absolute as either the king of France or Denmark is now. Whilst the kings of Poland thus maintained a supreme power over their subjects, they exceedingly enlarged their dominions, were feared abroad and beloved at home, commanded numerous armies, executed enterprizes speedily, and were always sure of success; and this, because they did not then, as now, depend upon the lingering and tedious conclusions of a turbulent dyet. But the family of Jagellon being once extinct by the death of Sigismund II. who had resigned his kingdom to the senate and Polish gentry, and given them full power and authority to dispose thereof as they thought fit; the crown of Poland was declared once more elective; to the end, that all the princes of Christendom, who had due merits and qualifications, might have a right to aspire thereunto.

This has given occasion to most of the princes of Europe ever since to court the Polish nobility; either to get the election determined in their own favour, or else to have some of their friends advanced to that great dignity. The gentry of Poland therefore observing, that several princes always aspired to their crown; and considering that none of them had more right than the rest, and that it lay altogether in their own power to choose whom they pleased, resolved unanimously to elect none but such as would swear to observe the terms and conditions they proposed. By this means, the Poles have clipped and limited the antient power of their kings, and have reduced it to the bounds we now find it; that is, barely to a third part of the dyet. For the Poles availed themselves of a judicious conclusion, that no prince would be so imprudent as to scruple submitting to any reasonable conditions, to become master of so considerable a kingdom, to which he had no right, either by birth or any other claim.

Thus the Polish gentry, of an absolute monarchical government, have made a perfect republic, consisting of three orders; the king, senate, and nobility. The Polish nation is divided into two sorts of people. The nobility, gentry, or free-born subjects, who are hardly a tenth part of the kingdom; and their vassals, who are no better than slaves; for they have no benefit of the laws, can buy no estates, nor enjoy any property.

The dyet of Poland is composed of two houses; the house of senators, answerable to our house of lords; and the house of nuncios, not unlike our house of commons: the senators are the bishops, palatines, castellans, and the ten great officers of the crown; in all about one hundred and forty-two. In the upper-house the senators sit, not by any writ of summons, or letters patent, as in England; but only by virtue of the great preferments in the king's gift, which they enjoy for life; so that the king constitutes the whole upper-house. The lower, are the representatives of the gentry, elected by them alone in their respective provinces, without the concurrence of the common people, who have no privilege in their election: insomuch that nine parts in ten of the people in Poland are excluded from any share in the government.

The grand dyet of Poland is the king, senators, and deputies, assembled in any part of the kingdom his majesty commands. Without this great assembly of the ſtates, the king can neither make nor repeal laws, declare war, conclude a peace, make alliance with any foreign prince, raiſe troops, impoſe taxes, or coin money: in a word, he can determine no matter of any importance, without the unanimous concurrence of this parliament, which they ſtile the free ſtates of Poland. Several motives have inclined the Poles to eſtabliſh this kind of mixt government; which they take to be a juſt temperament, of whatever is to be found moſt excellent in the ſeveral monarchies, ariſtocracies, and democracies that have been in the world. It has however appeared from experience, that their endeavours in this reſpect have not been very ſucceſsful, ſince there is hardly a conſtitution in the world, or at leaſt in Europe, that anſwers the ends of government worſe than theirs; which is very often the caſe, where people aim at ſuch a degree of perfection as is not to be attained in human affairs.

The republic is divided into two ſtates, the kingdom of Poland, and the great dutchy of Lithuania; both which are but as one body, having the ſame king, the ſame dyet, the ſame laws, the ſame privileges, the ſame religion; and, as the natural reſult of all theſe, the ſame intereſt: theſe two ſtates are ſo well united, that a king cannot be elected, a law made, or any thing of conſequence done, without the mutual conſent of both.

A king of Poland, when he is juſt, liberal, and religious; one, who obſerves the laws and conſtitutions; and, in a word, who has no other intereſt but the good and ſafety of his ſubjects; is as much reſpected, and as faithfully obeyed in times of peace and war, as moſt princes in Europe. As to what relates to war, no monarch has greater advantages; for he is neither at the trouble of raiſing forces, or expence in maintaining them; his buſineſs being only to convene the dyet, and they do all theſe things. After war is declared, he can continue the ſame either by himſelf or his generals, can regulate his troops, and

and ſee his army paid out of the treaſury of the republic: he has great reaſon to hope for ſucceſs in his expeditions, becauſe he not having undertaken them on his own account, thoſe that engaged him will infallibly ſupport him in them, and the rather, by reaſon that what was done, was done with their conſent. This has proved the cauſe of almoſt never-failing ſucceſs to the Poliſh army till of late days, when the king and his ſubjects have not had ſuch good intelligence with each other as formerly.

The king of Poland has great incomes of his own; for the Poles never care to elect a poor prince, for fear his children may come to be a charge to them after his death. He gets beſide vaſt ſums of money for nominations to employments; which have been ſold, though directly contrary to the conſtitutions of the kingdom; nay, the eccleſiaſtical benefices, which are very conſiderable, are alſo put under contribution by ſome cunning artifice or other: thus the promotion of the biſhop of Cracow, whoſe biſhopric is worth eight thouſand pounds ſterling per annum, which will go further than twenty thouſand pounds in England, was, in the reign of king John Sobieſki, procured, by laying a wager with the queen of fifty thouſand crowns, that he did not obtain that preferment; which as ſoon as the king knew, he beſtowed upon him, and ſo the queen won her wager. The crown revenues ariſe from cuſtoms and exciſes, from part of the duties of the port of Dantzick, from the heavy tax laid upon the Jews, and from the ſalt mines; which all together bring in rather more than three hundred thouſand pounds of our money annually. But the king's power in beſtowing preferments does not extend to foreigners; neither can he take away any poſt that he beſtows, or leſſen its revenues or privileges. His eldeſt ſon has the title of prince of Poland while his father lives; but he loſes it upon the acceſſion of a new king, and is ſtiled prince by the name of his family: and ſuch precautions are taken, that it is very difficult for a king of Poland to make the crown hereditary in his own family.

We come now to ſpeak of the nobility of Poland, which comprehends all the gentry in that country, and even all thoſe whom in England we ſtile only freeholders. Of theſe every gentleman or nobleman has his coat of arms granted by the republic; but then he, or ſome of his family, muſt have an eſtate in land. They are capable of the greateſt offices in the kingdom, and may buy lands where they pleaſe, and have a right to be elected king, if their credit and intereſt can procure it. Every gentleman is a ſovereign prince in his own lands, and has power of life and death over his tenants; who have no laws nor privileges to protect them. They dare not leave his lands to go to others, on pain of death, unleſs he ſells them; and if he do, his tenants paſs with his lands. But if their lords raviſh their wives, or daughters, the tenants may leave his ſervice.

If one lord kills another's ſervant he is not puniſhed for it, but only obliged to give him another in his room, or as much money as will buy one; and to maintain the family of him that is killed. If he kills one of his own ſlaves he only pays a fine; nay, if one gentleman kills another, he cannot be apprehended or impriſoned, unleſs convicted by a court of juſtice; which gives him time enough to eſcape: and when condemned he cannot be executed without the king's conſent. No ſoldiers can be quartered upon the gentry; if any officer does it, the dyet either ſentences him to die, or declares him infamous. The houſes of the nobility are ſanctuaries, ſo that no delinquent can be taken there by force, though he has been arreſted. If a nobleman will ſwear that his goods were not bought, but are the product of his lands, he may ſend them any where out of the kingdom, and without cuſtom; and after he has ſworn, his certificate ſuffices to exempt the purchaſer from the

the duty. In Pruſſia the nobles are not only free from cuſtoms, but likewiſe all other inhabitants, by the Magna Charta of Culm. All the gentry of Poland are equal by birth, and therefore they don't value titles of honour; but think that of a noble Pole, or gentleman of Poland, the greateſt they can have. Neither the king nor the republic beſtow the title of prince, which belongs only to the ſons of the royal family; for though ſome are made princes of the empire, and as ſuch enjoy the title of prince, they have no precedency upon that account. Nor have they any dukes, marquiſſes, counts, viſcounts, or barons, but what have foreign titles, which the reſt generally deſpiſe.

Theſe great privileges make the Poliſh gentry powerful; many of them have large territories, with a deſpotic power over their tenants, whom they call their ſubjects: ſome of them have eſtates of five, ſome fifteen, ſome twenty, and ſome thirty leagues in extent. But the poor gentry have their votes in the dyet as well as the richeſt. Some of them are hereditary ſovereigns of cities, with which the king has nothing to do. Lubomirſki poſſeſſes above four thouſand towns and villages; ſome of them can raiſe five, ſix, eight, and ten thouſand men, and maintain them at their own charge. The gentry of note have horſe and foot guards, which keep ſentry night and day at their gates. They make an extraordinary figure when they come to the dyet; as ſome of them have five thouſand guards. They eſteem themſelves, eſpecially the ſenators, above any prince in Germany, and want nothing of ſovereign power but the liberty of coining money, which is reſerved to the republic. Foreign ambaſſadors are obliged to make a great figure here, otherwiſe the gentry deſpiſe them. When great men have ſuits at law, the dyet, or other tribunals decide them; yet the execution of the ſentence muſt be left to the longeſt ſword; for the juſtice of the kingdom is commonly too weak for the Gran-

 dees.

dees. Sometimes they raiſe five or ſix thouſand men of a ſide, plunder and burn one another's cities, and beſiege caſtles and forts: for they think it below them to ſubmit to the ſentence of judges without a field battle.

Nobility is forfeited here three ways: by ſome heinous crime; for inſtance, when a nobleman permits one that is ignoble to uſurp his coat of arms; by exerciſing any trade or merchandize; (ſometimes poſterity are reſtored, when parents have quitted their title through poverty) and by bearing office in any city that is not privileged. All the nobility love to make a ſhew, and to be ſplendidly clad.

They formerly delighted in foreign faſhions; when they had wars againſt the Muſcovites they followed theirs, and when with the Turks they took up their habits. Their preſent garb is a veſt that reaches to the middle of their legs, with a long robe lined with fur, and tied about their middle with a ſaſh; little boots with iron heels, fur caps, and a ſabre by their ſide. When they ride they have a ſhort cloak, like an Iriſh mantle, furred within and without. The better ſort have rich furs from Muſcovy, but the poorer gentry content themſelves with the ſkins of tygers, leopards, panthers, and a kind of grey furs. The fineſt of their fur-ſuits coſt above a thouſand crowns, are worn only at dyets, and deſcend from father to ſon. Some of the Poliſh gentry imitate the French faſhion, and wear linen, lace, perukes, and ſwords. The ordinary ſort of gentry put chaff into their boots. Some of their nobles have fifty ſuits of cloaths, all as rich as poſſible, and they love to have their ſervants as well apparelled almoſt as themſelves.

As to the peaſants, they are born ſlaves, have no notion of liberty; in Courland they are as ſubject to their landlords, as in Poland, and in both countries almoſt adore them. They love their landlords, fight for them, and all they have is abſolutely at their devotion.

votion. When they debauch their wives or daughters, thoſe poor wretches do not think their women the worſe, or that they themſelves are diſhonoured by it. They have ſcarce any religion, but, like brutes, work on Sundays for their own ſubſiſtence, being obliged to work three or four days in a week for their maſters, without meat or wages; each of them earns his maſter, at leaſt, ten pounds per annum. They have no property; nor can they be made free, except they go into ſome convent, and are ordained prieſts; or their maſters raviſh their wives or daughters. When a lord lets any ground to a peaſant, he orders his other peaſants, at their charge, to build him a houſe, to give him a cow, hens, geeſe, and as much rye as will keep him a year.

Doctor Connor informs us, he aſked ſome Poliſh noblemen, why they ſo inhumanly treated and undervalued their boors; who anſwered, that formerly all the boors revolted from their landlords, and conſpired to extirpate them; and murdered ſo many, that the reſt were obliged to hide themſelves, or to leave the kingdom. But at laſt, the gentry getting together from all parts, and being aſſiſted by their neighbours, quelled the peaſants, who intended to have ſet up a commonwealth of their own, and brought them to ſuch extremities, that ever ſince they have been contented to live like ſlaves. In winter they wear a ſheep-ſkin with the wool inward, and in ſummer a cloſe-bodied coat of coarſe ſtuff, of a colour much like our chimney-ſweepers, with ſorry caps: their boots are the rinds of trees wrapped about their legs, with the thicker parts to guard the ſoles of their feet againſt the ſtones. They cut their hair cloſe like monks, and ſhave all from their faces but a large whiſker. They walk gravely with a pole-axe in their hand, and a ſabre by their ſide, which they never put off till they go to bed; it hangs by a ſtrap of leather, to which there is faſtened a handkerchief, knife, and ſheath, and a ſmall ſtone to whet their knives.

In Lithuania the boors ſhoes are of the barks of trees, and their ſtockings of thinner bark, which they wrap about the calves of their legs. Before they enter any town, they always take care to put on freſh ſhoes; they alſo wear a ſort of aſh-coloured habit, with ſleeves woven all of a piece. The boors here are more miſerable than in Poland; for gentlemen commonly go into boors houſes, though not their own, take all they have, and beat and wound them, becauſe they are not able to bribe ſuch as have power to do them juſtice. The Pruſſian gentry are not ſo gaudy in their habits, as thoſe of the more ſouthern parts of Poland; their peaſants differ alſo in habits from thoſe of Poland, and wear ſometimes long ſtrait coats of leather.

The Poles never live above ſtairs, and their apartments are not united; the kitchen is on one ſide, the ſtable on another, the dwelling-houſe on the third, and the gate in the front. Their houſes are for the moſt part of wood, but they have ſome of brick and ſtone. Their rooms are generally hung with tapeſtry or arras; but toward Tartary they keep no extraordinary furniture, becauſe of the incurſions of that barbarous people. They content themſelves with a few ſmall beds, with taffaty curtains; and if any lodge at their houſes, they muſt carry their bedding with them. The moveables of the peaſants are a few earthen and wooden diſhes, a hard bed, and a wretched coverlid; their children are not allowed beds till they marry, but lie upon boards by the fire: they have no chimnies, but little holes in the tops of their houſes. The peaſants children go naked till they are four or five years old, and frequently eat in the ſame trough with the pigs. They crawl on their hands and feet till they are ſtrong enough to walk, and when they are dirty, the mother waſhes them in cold water, which makes them exceeding hardy.

The

The peaſants of Lithuania and Samogitia build their houſes round, narrow, and open at top to let out the ſmoke and ſtink; they are generally covered with boards, ſtraws, bark of trees, and live with the family and cattle under the ſame roof. The Poliſh gentry have ſeldom any gardens or orchards, though their country be very proper for it, and might, by making cyder and perry, ſave a great deal of corn which they conſume in beer. Their ordinary meat is beef and veal; for they leave the mutton to their ſervants. The Baltic ſea has ſcarcely any fiſh, but that defect is ſupplied by great plenty of freſh-water fiſh from lakes and rivers.

Their uſual drink is beer, which in Pruſſia is made only of malt; but in the reſt of Poland, of wheat ground ſmall and boiled with hops. Sometimes they mix it with oats and ſpelt, a kind of wheat which grows in Italy and Flanders; in Lithuania, Ruſſia, and Ukrain, they make mead; at Warſaw they mix it with ſpice, and juice of cherries and blackberries. The Lithuanians and Poles have wine from Hungary, Italy, France, and Germany; that of Hungary exceeds Spaniſh wine in ſtrength, is brought to Cracow over the Carpathian mountains, in large caſks drawn by oxen, and ſold at twenty ſhillings the Poliſh pot, which is about three quarts: the Italian wine is alſo brought over land, and on that account is dearer than the other. In the morning, both men and women generally drink ginger, yolk of eggs, and ſugar boiled in beer; they are immoderate lovers of ruſty bacon and peaſe; they eat all manner of muſhrooms, and preſerve them for pickles. They eat great quantities of poppy-ſeed, drink the milk of them, and make it into ſeveral diſhes and ſauces; they make likewiſe abundance of oil of the ſeeds of hemp and flax, which they eat on faſt-days; and uſe ſpice to exceſs.

They generally eat a great deal of meat to a little bread, though they have plenty of corn, eſpecially rye, which is much better than in other countries.

They

They are great admirers of roots; have a dish called crakat, made of coarse flour of wheat, barley, millet, or oats; and sometimes, of a small grain they call manna. on flesh-days they eat it with milk and butter, and on fast-days they eat it with oil. When the boors want bread, they make it of acorns dried and ground. The Poles have a peculiar way of preserving cabbage; they chop it small, put it into a tub between lays of salt, press it very hard, and afterward pour warm water upon it, which makes it ferment, and serves them for pickle: this they preserve all winter, and sometimes the whole year; though it smells strong even at a distance, yet they think it a great rarity. Near the mountains of Hungary there are wild goats, which they admire as very good meat: they also make a dish of beavers-tails; bears-paws pickled, they reckon a great dainty. When they kill elks they do not gut them for fourteen or fifteen days, and in the winter, not in a month. When the grandees come to the dyet, they bring them in their skins and guts, and hang them at their windows by five or six at a time, till they grow rank, then they roast some, and dress others like beef a la-mode; and none but great men have this dish at their tables. The Poles are generally courteous and hospitable to strangers, invite them to their houses, converse with them freely, and endeavour to imitate them; and the slavery of their boors is so much the more tolerable to them, because they seldom want victuals and drink.

They have abundance of flesh, fish, and fowl, and are good marks men; maintaining their families, in a great measure, by fowling. Every house has four or five hand-mills to grind their corn. The peasants of Samogitia are not so laborious as those of Lithuania, and consequently have not such plenty; instead of bread, they eat a sort of turnips as big as one's head, which grow without cultivation. They quench many red-hot stones one after another, in their beer,

beer, metheglin, and mead, after they have boiled it a whole night, in order to make their bellies soluble: this liquor they put into vessels made of the bark of trees. They reward the stoutest drinkers at feasts with a shirt, handkerchief, frock, or the like. They are content with spare diet, and more addicted to sloth than gluttony; yet, like the Poles and Lithuanians, they drink hard, especially at feasts.

When the gentry make a feast, they never supply their guests with spoons, knives, or forks; they must bring them with them. They have a broad piece of starched linen sewed round the table-cloth for napkins; the reason they give for it is, to prevent their servants stealing. Their servants have their meat reached them by their masters, which they eat behind their backs: they bring twice as much wine as their masters need, and drink the remainder themselves; they seize on what is left after dinner, and their ladies each of them carry a napkin for dried sweet-meats or fruits. Their feasts are made by friends and neighbours by turns; brimmers are much in use among the Poles; they will scarce excuse a man except he pledges them. This vice reigns equally at feasts and taverns; and saints-days are not excepted out of their drunkard's calendar.

The inns of this country are long stables built up with boards, and covered with straw, without furniture or windows; there is a chamber at one end, but none can lodge there; because of flies, fleas, and noisome smells: so that strangers chuse rather to lodge among the horses, where there is also an intolerable smell of rotten cabbages, which these people keep always by them. Travellers are obliged to carry provisions with them; and when foreigners want, they apply themselves to the lord of the village, who forthwith supplies them. Poland being for most part a champaign country, a calash and two horses will rid a good deal of ground there in a day. Travellers ought to take more than ordinary care as they

they paſs bridges in this country, becauſe they are generally very bad, and ſeldom repaired. When they go a hunting for bears, they catch thoſe of the biggeſt ſize with nets, and when they have hampered one, all the hunters ride about him; and having pinned down his head and his feet with great wooden forks, they bind him ſo about with ſtrong hempen cords that he is not able to ſtir: then they roll him into a great wooden cheſt; and the knots of the cords are ſo contrived, that with one pull they may be untied. The bear is kept thus, till they have a mind to hunt him, and then they let him out at a trap door made on purpoſe.

They ſurround wild bulls with a great number of horſemen, when each of them rides up and darts an arrow at him; upon this the ox purſues his enemy; then another darts him behind, and as he turns about to purſue him, they dart him ſo by turns, till the beaſt being tired with purſuing ſo many aſſailants, falls down, and is eaſily taken or killed. They have another way of hunting, by making the boors fell a great number of trees; each hunter ſecures his poſt aſſigned him, and throws darts at the bull; and as the beaſt runs toward his enemy, the hunters from behind give him his death's wound: but if he breaks through the incloſure, the next hunter holds out a piece of red cloth, againſt which the beaſt having an antipathy, he immediately leaves that perſon and runs at another, who being provided for him, commonly kills him.

The Poliſh ladies are generally very modeſt, and not very apt to abuſe the great liberty allowed them. They ſeldom ſtir out of doors without a coach and ſix to church, or to viſit a near neighbour, and are always attended by a great number of ſervants. When they go abroad at night, they have twenty-four or more flambeaux carried before their coach. Their train is born up by he or ſhe-dwarfs; and they have always an old woman to attend them, whom they call

governante,

governante, and an old gentleman for their uſher. Notwithſtanding all theſe honours, they are entirely managed by their huſbands, and diſpoſe of no money without his leave. When they want any thing they muſt aſk him for it, kneeling, embrace his knees, and call him their benefactor. The faſhion of the womens cloaths comes nearer to that of the men than in moſt other countries. They formerly wore garlands on their heads, compoſed of gold, jewels, flowers, ſilk, and the like; but now they wear ſilk caps, lined with fur, like the men: in king John III's time they imitated the French mode, becauſe the queen was of that nation.

The peaſants daughters are ſo extremely reſerved, that they will draw a knife at any man who offers to kiſs them; beſide, their mothers have a watchful eye over them, and make them wear little bells before and behind, to give notice where they are, and what they are doing; but theſe precautions do not always ſecure them. The country women are habited as in other countries; but their petticoats are very ſhort: thoſe in Red Ruſſia go generally in ſummer with an apron before them that reaches lower than ordinary. The wedding feaſts of the gentry laſt commonly three days. If a lady marry any of her waiting-maids, ſhe coſts her almoſt as much as one of her daughters. On the ſecond day all the gueſts preſent the bride with ſomething new, which makes a good part of her portion. The princeſs of Poland, when married to the elector of Bavaria, had above an hundred thouſand crowns preſented her.

Among the boors a maid never marries till ſhe be twenty-four or thirty years of age, and has wrought, with her own hands, ſeveral baſkets full of cloaths, of different ſorts: which, at the time of her eſpouſals, ſhe is to diſtribute among the gueſts that her huſband brings with him. She muſt alſo have ſerved her mother for a certain time. The ſame rite is obſerved with reſpect to their ſons: it is alſo obſervable,

able, that thoſe employed to make up the match, always enquire more ſtrictly into the manners and behaviour of the perſons, than as to their ſtock of corn and cattle. Their godfathers and godmothers are always accounted relations, though they be nothing a-kin, and they cannot marry ſuch kindred without a diſpenſation from the biſhop.

The burials of thoſe of quality are celebrated with ſuch pomp and magnificence, that they are more like triumphs. The corpſe is carried in a hearſe or chariot with ſix horſes, all covered with black; the coffin has a large black velvet pall over it, with a croſs of red ſattin in the middle; and has ſix long black ſilk taſſels, ſupported by as many of the deceaſed's domeſtic ſervants in cloſe mourning: ſeveral prieſts, monks, and others, march before the hearſe; each of which carries a white wax torch in his hand. Immediately before the hearſe come three men on horſeback, who carry the arms of the deceaſed; one his ſword, another his lance, and a third his dart: after the burial ſervice is over, thoſe who carry the armour enter the church on horſeback, and riding furiouſly to the coffin, break the arms of the deceaſed upon it; after which the body is interred. Then there is a feaſt, where the lay gueſts not only drink to exceſs, but likewiſe force the clergy to follow their example. When the king dies he is laid on a bed of ſtate; and a certain number of ſenators, eccleſiaſtical and temporal, are appointed to attend his corpſe. The Republic defrays the expences out of the revenues of the crown. The deceaſed queen has the ſame ceremonies and honours allowed her. When women of quality mourn, they wear a coarſe black ſtuff, and their linen is not much finer than canvas; and the greater their quality, their mourning weeds are the coarſer. All ſenators, deputies, and others, that appear at the dyet for electing the new king, muſt be in black.

The language of the Poles is the Sclavonian; but there are ſo many different dialects of it ſpoken in the

the ſeveral parts of this kingdom, that one part of the people ſcarcely underſtand the other; they all agree, however, in multiplying conſonants: and if they did not ſound more vowels when they ſpeak, than are contained in the words they write, it would be impoſſible to utter them. The Latin is almoſt as univerſally ſpoken as the Sclavonian, there being a ſchool in every village for the teaching it; and the girls learn it in the nunneries. Their terms of art are chiefly German, and indeed there are whole towns and villages in Pruſſia which are of German extract, and ſtill ſpeak the German or High Dutch tongue. The Armenian, Perſian, and Tartarian languages are alſo ſpoken upon their frontiers; and the Jews have introduced the Hebrew in ſome places; but with all theſe languages, it is obſerved that their learning is but ſuperficial.

As to their divines, their learning, it is ſaid, conſiſts in adapting Ariſtotle's logic and metaphyſics to their ſchool divinity; and they value themſelves more on being verſed in the ſignification of logical terms, than in the nature of the things they reaſon about. They enquire but little into church-hiſtory, or the practice of primitive times, but ſeem to have an implicit faith, and to be entirely governed by the deciſions of the church of Rome: nor will they ſuffer any perſon to inquire into the reaſonableneſs of their tenets.

There are few native Poles that ſtudy phyſic. The phyſicians are generally Germans, French, or Italians. An illiterate quack of this kingdom, Doctor Connor mentions, however, who lived in a wood about ſix miles from Warſaw, undertook to cure the venereal diſeaſe in ſeven or eight days by bathing and ſweating. In the water the bath was made of, he boiled ſeveral plants, which the man made a ſecret of; but the doctor ſays, as well as he could diſcover, the chief of them were hellebore, aſter, and the capillus veneris, or maiden-hair. That he bathed his

his patients in a hot decoction of these herbs for four days together, and made them drink of it while they were in the bath frequently; that for four days afterward he laid them over the tub to receive the hot steams, covering them with blankets, and making them drink of the decoction as before. And thus by sweating, bathing, and drinking, he was assured he had done many wonderful cures in venereal cases; and for the whole cure demanded but two rix-dollars, which is less than ten shillings English. They seldom use salivation in this country, though venereal distempers are very common.

The disease peculiar to the Poles, is that called the Plica, in which the hair of the head is matted together, and grows so long, that it sometimes reaches down to the middle, covering their backs; but generally it hangs in twisted ropes: others have their hair only matted close to their heads, without growing to any length. If the hair be cut off it occasions a dimness in the sight, and sometimes a total blindness; it also occasions pain in the head and limbs, and pustules to come out all over the body. Foreigners that have been infected with this disease relate, that they have cut off their hair without any inconveniency attending it. The bishop of Posen acquainted doctor Connor that he was afflicted with this distemper in his youth, and that cutting off his hair, unknown to his friends, he felt a thousand racking pains, which left him as his hair grew again, but then the distemper returned. He observed also, that on the cutting off his hair he could sensibly perceive a volatile matter pass in great abundance through the tubes of his hair, which twisted and contracted the locks; that when he put a cap on his head, it occasioned an intolerable pain and heat, which he supposed proceeded from the pressure, by which the humours were repelled, and forced back upon the head. As to other diseases, it seems, the Poles are very little troubled with them. The scurvy, or malignant

lignant fevers, and pleurisies, are seldom of such ill consequence in Poland as in other countries.

By the laws of Poland, the estate of the father is equally divided among his children, except any of them go into a monastery, and then their parts are equally divided among the rest; and the young children here, as in other Popish countries, are encouraged by their parents to take the vow upon them, that their estates may be preserved entire to the eldest son, which would otherwise dwindle away to nothing, where there happens to be a numerous issue.

We are so apt to be biassed in our sentiments, by what happens in our own times, and as it were under our own eyes, that we can scarcely bring ourselves to think things ever were otherwise than as we now perceive them. But it is certain, that as restless and turbulent as the Poles now are, they were formerly of a different disposition, and very much attached to the persons and families of their princes. Thus for several ages they obeyed the family of Piastus, who was raised to the throne by his merit; and upon the death of Lewis, king of Poland and Hungary, the last male-heir of his family, they chose his daughter, and resolved to bestow their crown upon her husband, who was Jagello, duke of Lithuania. He took upon him the name of Uladislaus; and by his posterity they were governed till the death of Sigismund II. who was the last of that family, and died in 1574, when they chose Henry de Bourbon, afterward Henry III. of France, for their king; upon a promise that he would marry the princess Anne, sister to their late monarch. When he abdicated, they made choice of Stephen Batori, prince of Transylvania, who actually married the princess before mentioned, but had no issue by her. Upon his death in 1586, they made choice of Sigismund de Vasa, prince of Sweden, because he was the nephew of Sigismund II. and consequently by the mother's side of the race of their antient kings. The last of his race was Casimir,

 who

who abdicated the government and retired to France: and in 1670 they chose Michael Wielnowiſki, whoſe ſucceſſor was John Sobieſki; upon whoſe deceaſe in 1696, the Poles, contrary to their uſual cuſtom, rejected his family, and made choice of Auguſtus, elector of Saxony.

The preſent king of Poland, Staniſlaus Auguſtus, was choſen with unuſual unanimity, on September 7, 1764; he is a native of Poland, and before his acceſſion to the regal dignity, was count Poniatowſki, grand plancher of Lithuania, and was the only nobleman the Poles wiſhed to have for their king: his father was well known for his attachment to Charles XII. of Sweden, and for the ſignal ſervices he performed for him.

This monarch being himſelf a Pole, will conſtantly reſide in his kingdom; and having no foreign dominions, will of courſe enter into no foreign connections, but with a view to the intereſts of his people. His natural endowments and acquired advantages have united to form in him the compleat gentleman; and there is a paſſage of a letter ſaid to be wrote to him on his promotion, by the king of Pruſſia, which cannot be unwelcome to the reader in this place. It is as follows:——' Your majeſty muſt reflect, that as you enjoy a crown by election, and not by deſcent, the world will be more obſervant of your majeſty's actions, than of any other potentate in Europe; and it is but reaſonable. The latter being the mere effect of conſanguinity, no more is looked for, though much more is to be wiſhed, from him, than what men are endowed with in common. But from a man, exalted by the voice of his equals, from a ſubject to a king! from a man voluntarily elected to reign over thoſe by whom he was choſen! every thing is expected, that can poſſibly deſerve and adorn a crown. Gratitude to his people is the firſt great duty of ſuch a monarch; for to them alone, under providence, he is indebted for being one. A king, who is ſuch by birth,

birth, if he acts derogatory from his station, is a satire only on himself; but an elected one, who behaves inconsistent with his dignity, reflects dishonour on his subjects. Your majesty, I am sure, will pardon this warmth; it is the effusion of the sincerest regard: the amiable part of the picture, is not so properly a lesson of what you ought to be, as a prophecy of what your majesty will be.'——

Nothing shews more clearly the folly of that kind of modern policy, which consists in weakening and distressing our neighbours, than the present state of Poland. This country, as well by its situation, as from the natural genius and disposition of its inhabitants, is the proper bulwark of Christendom against the Turks; whom they have resisted with as much success, and over whom they have gained greater victories than almost any other nation. If we consider them in this light, it is very easy to see that it can never be the true and natural interest either of the house of Austria, or of the Russians, to promote troubles in this kingdom, because the more powerful and formidable the Poles were, the less able the Turks would be to alarm either of these potentates. The grand signior indeed has shewn a true spirit of policy, in never attempting to disturb this nation even in its lowest circumstances; but contented himself with the security that he reaps from their confusions: since, if he had ever attacked Poland, it would probably have put an end to them; and though at first he might have made great conquests, when the spirit of the nation was once roused, he would have been quickly driven out of them, as he knew, from the experience of former times.

If the Poles could once so settle their affairs, as to have time to consider the advantages that might result to their country by the extending their commerce, it is not at all impossible they should succeed therein, though they have neglected it so long. A project was formed by the late king Augustus, for opening a trade with Asia by the help of the Crim Tartars, and transporting the commodities that are brought from the Black Sea, by the Niester and the Bog. He had other great views with regard to Russia, and though at present they seem to have died with him, the time may come when they shall revive again, and be carried into execution by some other enterprising Polish monarch.

The country of Poland abounds with natural commodities, if the inhabitants knew how to make use of them; and with a numerous and laborious race of people, who would soon become rich if they were properly employed. We have reason to expect, therefore, that some time or other, awakened by their own necessities, or provoked by the example of their neighbours, they will think of improving their lands, working up their commodities, and vending them in different parts of Europe: which, whenever they do, will infallibly make them a rich and happy nation.

A SHORT ACCOUNT OF THE UKRAIN, And of its Inhabitants the COSSACKS,

Collected from the Writings of Mr. Beauplan, and others.

According to some authors, the word Cossack, in the Russian tongue, signifies free-booter or banditti; others derive it from Cosa, signifying a goat, because of their nimbleness. Some say that Cosa, in the Sclavonian language, signifies a scythe, their

their ordinary weapon. They are thought to have come first from the islands of the Boristhenes, near the mouth of that river, and were called Zaporowski, or Zaporienses, from the Porowis, or cataracts and rocks in the Nieper. The Turks usually call them Russians. They dwell in a part of Red Russia in Poland, and in Basserabia, betwixt the rivers Boristhenes and the Niester. They are terrible to the Turks, because of their invasions by the way of the Black Sea. In 1548, in the time of Sigismund I. king of Poland, these Cossacks were only volunteers of the frontiers of Russia, Volhinia, Podolia, and the other provinces of Poland, who assembled together, partly to defend themselves from the Tartars, by securing the passes of the Nieper, and attacking them as they returned with their prey; and partly to rob upon the Black Sea, where getting rich booty, they drew more into the association. Sometimes they made descents upon Natolia, and plundered the great towns, as Trebisond and Sinope; at other times they have advanced within two miles of Constantinople, and brought off booty and prisoners.

At first they were about six thousand, under Eustachicus Doscovitus their general; but their numbers were quickly increased by their neighbours, because of the gain they made by their piracies, part of which they laid up in their magazine, and the rest they brought home to their houses. About the end of the season, these adventurers separate, and agree upon the time and place of rendezvous next spring in the isles and rocks of the Nieper, whence they return to their piracy. Stephen Batori, king of Poland, who began his reign in 1576, considering the service that might be made of those thieves, for guarding the country and frontiers against the inroads of the Tartars, formed them into a regular body; and they served him as foot-soldiers; for the Polish army consists chiefly of horse. He gave them the town and territories of Tetchtimorow, about eighty miles in

 length,

length, in the palatinate of Kiow, upon the Boristhenes; which town they made their magazine, and the residence of their governor-general.

The Cossacks being thus brought into good discipline, did considerable service to the crown of Poland; but have since done the republic much mischief by their frequent rebellions: for the Cossacks knowing their own strength, and of what importance they were to the Poles, began to set up for themselves, and would not obey the orders of their superiors, and acknowlege the power of the Poles over them.

It was chiefly owing to them that the Muscovites got possession of the provinces of Smolensko and Siberia; and the greatest part of the palatinate of Kiovia, which were confirmed to them by the treaty of Olivia, in 1666. They have since those days suffered many changes of fortune, as well as diminution in numbers; but at this time however they are tolerably free, some under the protection of the Turks, others under the Poles; but the greatest part of them own themselves subjects to Russia. We will next consider the country in which they live, and which from the flatness of it, has been supposed, not without great probability, to have been left partly by the sea, and partly by the great rivers that run through it; in the same manner as the antients report of Lower Egypt; and as we know that track of country was certainly left, which is called Marshland, in the county of Norfolk.

The word Ukrain signifies a frontier country, and lies betwixt 48 and 52 degrees of north latitude; the Niester is their western, and the Nieper their eastern boundary. According to some authors, Kiow is the chief town, and belongs to the Muscovites; being taken from the Poles in 1633, by the confederate army of the Muscovites and Cossacks. This city gives name to the palatinate of Kiow, which had princes of its own till it was reduced to a province by by Casimir III. who began his reign in the year 1333. The ruins of the walls shew it to have been eight miles in compass: here are to be seen still the ruins of many arches, high walls, churches, and the sepulchres of many kings, with Greek inscriptions. The church of St. Sophia, whose walls are lined with mosaic work; and that of St. Michael, remarkable for its gilded roof, are still in a tolerable condition.

The Ukrain is a very fertile country, though the third part of it is scarcely cultivated; it produces such a vast quantity of grain of all sorts, that the inhabitants are at a loss how to consume it: they cannot export any of it, because their rivers are not navigable. They abound in honey, wax, wood, cattle, fowl, and fish. Hungary, Transylvania, Wallachia, and Moldavia, supply them with wine; they also make good beer, and aqua vitæ, out of their corn; they have much mead; the salt-pits near Cracow furnish them with salt; they have also some out of the country of Pokutia, on the borders of Moldavia and Transylvania, where there are salt-springs: their houses are of wood, and their fortifications of earth and wood, which they account better against cannon than brick walls; but they are soon set on fire.

The rivers of note here are the Boristhenes or Nieper; the Bog, Tyras or Neister, the common border betwixt them and Wallachia; the Dezna, the Ross, the Horin, the Souez, and the Ster; near which was fought the last battle between the Poles and Cossacks, in 1651; which obliged the Cossacks to seek protection among the Muscovites and Turks. The language of the Cossacks is a dialect of the Polish tongue, as the Polish is of the Sclavonian; but that of the Cossacks is much more smooth, and full of diminutives, which makes it very agreeable.

The common people are of the Greek church: their worship is the same with that of the Russians;

their metropolitan resides at Kiow, is consecrated by the patriarch of Constantinople, and subject to him. The whole almost of their religion consists in feasts and holy-days; but the greater part of the gentry are Papists, and a few Protestants. It is very common in this country for maids to woo the men: if a young woman be in love with a young man, she is not ashamed to go to his father's house, reveal her passion in the most tender expressions, and promise all obedience if he please to accept of her in marriage: if she be rejected by the young man, because he is too young, or not disposed to marry, or the like; she tells him that she is resolved never to go out of the house till he consent, and accordingly takes up her lodgings there. To force her out would be to provoke all her kindred: nor would the church suffer them to use any violence to her without inflicting heavy penance, and branding the house with infamy: so that after two or three weeks the parents, or the young man himself being moved with the constancy of the woman, accommodate matters as well as they can, and make up the match.

Their manners are like those of soldiers, they are not solicitous for what is to come, but spend freely what they have among their companions, and leave futurity to shift for itself: they are very inconstant, mutinous, and pursue their present advantage rather than their faith and promise. They are great drinkers; but by reason of their labour and hardships, they have so much health that physicians are of little use among them. They are of a good stature, strong, nimble, great lovers of liberty, uneasy under any yoke, and indefatigable: they are much given to fishing and hunting. None know better the way of preparing saltpetre, and making gunpowder; their country abounds with it, and several parts of Europe are furnished from thence. This territory was almost a desart, till improved by the industry of the Cossacks, and other colonies: the many rivers which run through it add much to its fruitfulness.

They

They have ſome animals peculiar to their country, ſuch as a beaſt called Bobac, not unlike a Guinea pig; it makes holes in the earth, which it enters in October, and never comes abroad till April; within theſe holes there are many little apartments for their proviſions, lodgings, and dead: eight or nine herds of thoſe beaſts live together in ſuch caves; they are eaſily tamed, and are very diverting. When they go out for proviſions they place a centinel, who, as ſoon as he ſpies any body, gives a ſignal, and they all run to their caves. The Jounaky is a kind of goat, remarkable for his beautiful furr, reſembling ſattin, and a white ſkin and ſmooth horns: he has no horn in his noſe, as ſome report, but as he feeds goes backward. They have many wild horſes, of no value but for their fleſh, which they ſell in their markets, and think it better than beef or veal: when thoſe horſes come to be old, their hoofs, never pared, ſo contract their feet that they cannot go. In ſummer they are mightily incommoded with flies and graſhoppers, in ſuch vaſt numbers, that they form a cloud of five or ſix leagues long, and three or four broad; darkening the air in the cleareſt day, and deſtroying all the corn they light on in leſs than two hours time.

When they rendezvous upon the iſlands of Scarbniza Waſkowa, the firſt thing that they do is to chuſe their general for that expedition; and to make their boats, which they call colna, of about ſixty feet long, twelve feet deep, and as many wide. They are built very light, one plank pinned on the edge of another, and widening upward. They have a ſtern at each end, and about twelve or fifteen oars at a ſide. They have no deck; but to prevent their ſinking, though full of water, they compaſs them round with a border of reeds, as big as a barrel, tied together, and faſtened to their boats with ropes: they have a ſorry maſt and ſail, but ſeldom uſe them, except in very fair weather. Their proviſion is a ton of biſket, which they take out of the bung as they uſe it;

a barrel

a barrel of boiled millet, and another of paſte, made with water, which they eat with their millet. Every boat carries about ſixty perſons; every man having two guns, and each boat five or ſix falconets or ſmall pieces of cannon. They ſet out about the beginning of June, and return about the 1ſt of Auguſt.

They wait for a dark night, that they may paſs undiſcovered by the Turkiſh galleys which lie at Oczakow to intercept them. With theſe boats they cruize over all the Black Sea. If they ſpy a galley, they keep at a diſtance till night, obſerve the courſe of the veſſel, and when it is dark come up and board it. They take out all the cannon, money, and merchandize, and then ſink the ſhip, becauſe they have neither ſkill nor opportunity to uſe it. No ſooner have the Turks intelligence that the Coſſacks are at ſea, but the alarm is taken immediately, which reaches quickly to Conſtantinople; from thence couriers are diſpatched to the coaſts of Natolia, Romelia, and Bulgaria, to bid them be upon their guard: but the Coſſacks are generally too nimble for them, and are forty hours on the coaſts before them. If a galley ſpy them in the day-time (which is very uncommon, for their veſſels are not above two feet and a half above water) they avoid fighting, by rowing away from her, or retiring to ſhallows among reeds where the gallies cannot follow them.

This was their way of living, till the grand ſignior obliged Sigiſmund, king of Poland, to prohibit thoſe piracies. It was bad policy in the Poles to let them chuſe their own general; for this general being abſolutely their own creature, is forced to comply with their methods. They handle their guns very dexterouſly, and have ſcythes ſet long-ways upon poles, with which they fight very fiercely, and at the ſame time ſkilfully; ſo that regular troops are often beat by them. They are very indifferent horſemen, but excellent ſoldiers on foot. They are inured to all manner of fatigues and hardſhips, obedient to their commanders,

commanders, active, and dexterous in intrenching themselves, not only in the ordinary way, but alſo by making a fence of their baggage waggons, which cover them as they march. Theſe moving intrenchments are abſolutely neceſſary for them, when they march without horſe in open plains in the deſarts of the Tartars, againſt whom they are forced to ſtand wherever they meet them. There have been ſeveral inſtances, that one thouſand Coſſack foot, marching between their chariots and waggons, have, in a plain, repulſed five or ſix thouſand Tartars on horſeback. Their horſes, though ſwift, are but weak, and ſtopped by the leaſt barricade. But however, this way of marching, in the midſt of their baggage and ammunition waggons, would ſcarcely be practicable in any other country but Poland and the deſarts of Tartary, which lie upon a level.

It is eaſy, from theſe accounts, to form a juſt notion of the original and ancient ſtate of the Coſſacks; but ſome farther explanations will be neceſſary, in order to have a juſt idea of the condition of this people at preſent. We will begin with what is requiſite to be ſaid of their country. In its utmoſt extent it may be conſidered as three hundred miles long, and in ſome places above a hundred broad; but then this comprehends the territory inhabited by all the Coſſacks; for they are, at preſent, diſtinguiſhed into various nations. When we reflect on the manners of the Muſcovites, Poles, Turks, and Tartars, and remember that their dominions border upon each other, we ſhall very eaſily conceive that the frontiers could not afford very ſafe or pleaſant habitations, and ſhall not be ſurprized to hear that they were deſart. Hence it was, that this otherwiſe large and conſiderable track of country came to be ſtiled the Ukrain, which, in our language, properly ſignifies the Marches. The people who firſt ſettled on the rocks in the Nieper were vagabonds from all countries, who built their huts in the moſt inacceſ-

ſible

ſible places, and were from thence called Coſſacks or goats, becauſe, like them, they dwelt out of reach.

But, by degrees, as theſe people became numerous, they began to plant and improve their country, which is one of the richeſt and fineſt in Europe: but from its very ſituation, it is ſo liable to be ranſacked and eaten up, whenever any wars break out among the neighbouring nations, which are none of them polite or well governed, that we cannot expect it ſhould ever be brought into any tolerable condition. Beſide, the Coſſacks, like the buccaneers in America, were planters only by accident; they looked upon living at home as a hardſhip, unleſs in the time they wanted winter-quarters; for their proper buſineſs was war, and they grew rich, not by induſtry, but plunder. They were from hence regarded as barbarians, and in that ſenſe very juſtly; becauſe, to live by ſpoiling others is the higheſt barbarity; inaſmuch as it is that ſort of life moſt repugnant to reaſon and the laws of humanity.

It has been before laid down that war was their buſineſs; and this was of two kinds, defenſive by land, and offenſive by ſea. In reſpect to the former, the country round about them was flat, and the enemies they had to deal with were Poles and Tartars, who brought great bodies of horſe into the field. To oppoſe theſe with inferior bodies of light-armed foot, the Coſſacks invented the Tabor, or waggon; in theſe they carried their baggage, ammunition, and proviſions upon a march; and when they encamped, they took care to have a river in front, and a moraſs in the rear; covering their flanks with an intrenchment of waggons. By the help of this diſcipline, they have defeated troops that would have appeared terrible, even to the moſt regular armies. Nay, to ſuch a degree they carried this art of fortifying with waggons, that field-marſhal Munich, who was an officer of great ſkill and experience, thought fit to adopt their method in his laſt war againſt the Turks;

and

and that with ſuch ſucceſs, as enabled him to come off with honour and victory, when attacked by the moſt numerous armies the Ottoman power could bring into the field.

In their offenſive wars, which, as we have ſhewn, the Coſſacks carry on by ſea, the invention of their boats is admirable; for, in the firſt place, they are very light, ſo that they may be tranſported from rock to rock with great eaſe; in the next place, they are capacious, ſo as to hold a great number of men, which gives them ſuch a power in boarding and attacking places on the ſea-coaſts, as it is hardly poſſible to reſiſt. Their method of building without keels, and ſheathing with reeds, defends them from ſinking, even if full of water. Beſide this, it makes their boats, when filled with men, lie ſo deep in the water, that they are not to be ſeen at any great diſtance, and yet they go at a prodigious rate, ſo as to be in no danger when purſued by any kind of ſhipping in uſe among the Turks.

If indeed we take theſe bark-boats out of the water, and conſider them independent of the Coſſacks who uſe them, they will appear very poor and deſpicable things, and the ſame may be ſaid of their waggons; but notwithſtanding this, when all circumſtances are duly weighed, when we remember that theſe people are poor, weak, and defenceleſs, in compariſon of their neighbours; have very few fortreſſes, and thoſe compoſed only of wood and earth; and that notwithſtanding theſe advantages, they have made a ſhift to cover their country ſo well, and defended themſelves ſo obſtinately, as to make the Poles and Tartars weary of their wars with them; we muſt allow them ſome merit with reſpect to military ſkill. On the other hand, when we call to mind, that they have no trade, no veſſels, no ports to receive them, if they had any; no yards, little timber, no docks, carpenters, or ſeamen; we cannot help owning that the naval exploits of ſuch people, are in a great meaſure aſtoniſhing.

Their

Their government is entirely military, insomuch that, in time of peace, they have hardly any magistrates or laws; but when the nation, by whom they are protected, (and at present some of them are under the Poles, some under the Turks, but the far greatest part of them under the Russians) propose they should rise and take the field; the first step is to give them leave to elect a general, who in their language is called Hetman, or Hatman. This some modern writers have mistaken for a proper name; whereas, in reality, it is the stile of office, and answers to that of Imperator amongst the ancient Romans: he has the absolute command so long as the war continues; neither is it easy to depose him afterward; for in this, as well as in all other countries, power has in it something so pleasing, that no small difficulty is found in reducing him who has been once a prince, to the rank of a private man.

In the histories of the wars in the north, from the beginning of the present century to the death of Peter the Great, emperor of Russia, the Hatman is often mentioned, and some of them made a great figure: but of late, and indeed in all times of peace, we hear of no such person. But it is right to enquire after, and have some tolerable knowlege, even of the most obscure nations, that when those accidents, which are always in the womb of time, bring them upon the stage; we may not be amazed at their names, or in doubt about their force.

It was the praise of Ulysses, the wisest man in his day in Greece, that he had seen and was acquainted with the laws and customs, the manners and modes, of different places and people. And this was a great commendation, worthy the pen and pains of the immortal Homer, who has justly celebrated the labours and travels of that excellent man: but it is the felicity of modern times, that every man may be an Ulysses in his closet; may sail over the ocean in his elbow-chair, and travel all the world over in his study.

Neither

Neither is this a flight of oratory, a lively or extravagant picture; but a plain, certain, and undeniable truth: books and maps will do the work effectually; a small degree of application, and that only for a few months, will enable us to acquire more real and useful knowlege than it was possible for any of the ancients to become master of in the course of his life. Therefore if we do not excel them, is not more their glory than our fault: 'he who has never travelled,' say the Turks; (he who has never read, may we say) 'thinks all the world like his father's house.'

We are now to look abroad into more civilized countries, where every thing has a softer air, and where the inhabitants are learned and polite. It is true, that the visiting such countries seems to be most expedient for modern travellers, who are sent abroad to acquire a genteel manner, and a correct taste: but for such as travel at home, the knowlege of the power, circumstances, and the rising and falling of nations in the balance of sound policy, seems to be the great, if not the only rational end of such inquiries.

A DESCRIPTION OF THE SEVEN UNITED PROVINCES OF THE LOW COUNTRIES,

From MISSON's Travels, &c.

IN order to render our account of the Low Countries more entertaining and descriptive than is to be found in any one writer, as these provinces furnish many articles for observation; to what Mr. Misson

ſon relates from his travels through them, we ſhall occaſionally add ſuch particulars from other travellers as may appear capable of illuſtrating the ſubject. A liberty, which, for the greater information and amuſement of our readers, we ſhall continue to take, wherever it may contribute to either of thoſe purpoſes. Mr. Miſſon appearing to give the beſt connected general obſervations on theſe provinces, we ſhall adhere principally to him, taking in what is ſaid by others collaterally. We ſhall, however, firſt premiſe, that what is comprehended under the general name of the Netherlands, extends along the German Ocean 400 miles from north to ſouth, and 500 miles from eaſt to weſt, lying between 50° and 54° north latitude, and between 2° and 7° eaſt longitude: they are divided into ſeventeen provinces, ſeven of which are united into one free republic, which we are now to travel through: the others are diſtinguiſhed into the Auſtrian and French Netherlands. The Seven United Provinces, as they are ſtiled by way of eminence, are, 1. Holland. 2. Zealand. 3. Frieſland. 4. Groningen. 5. Overyſſel. 6. Guelderland and Zutphen. 7. Utrecht. Of theſe, Holland is the moſt noted, the aſſembly of the ſtates meeting there.

Holland, ſays Mr. Miſſon, being a flat country, like a continued meadow; as we approached the ſhore, the pinnacles of the ſteeples and the trees appeared as riſing out of the water. The whole country is cut into canals and ditches, with incredible labour, without which the ground would be ſo ſoaked with water as would render it not habitable; whereas now, by the induſtry of its inhabitants, it is the richeſt and beſt peopled in the world, in proportion to its extent: ſome make their number amount to two millions five hundred thouſand ſouls, in the ſingle province of Holland.

The cities of Holland are generally very neat and beautiful, their inhabitants ſparing no pains or coſt for

for that purpose, as appears by their constantly washing them, and having the insides of their houses curiously painted, and their windows generally of glass, as clear as crystal: their cleanliness extends even to their shops and stables, which are kept neater here, than the best apartments are in some countries. Their streets are so clean, that you see the women walk almost constantly in slippers; and the canals being on both sides planted with trees, afford a most delightful shady passage through all the chief streets of the cities, and of some of the towns and villages also. They reckon in the United Provinces, one city, (Amsterdam) of the first rank, about twenty of the second, and upwards of thirty of the third, two hundred large towns, eight hundred villages. But to return to their canals.

These are very convenient for travelling, which is generally performed in large boats, covered against the injuries of the air, and drawn by horses, which go off and bring you to your journey's end exactly at certain hours; they serve for the transportation of commodities from one place to another: and some of these canals afford tolerable store of several kinds of fish.

Notwithstanding all these advantages, there are many things wanting in Holland; their supplies of wines, nay, even of corn, and most other things necessary for the sustenance of life, are derived from foreign countries: this occasions their having such a prodigious number of ships, that some have computed them equal to all the rest that Europe can produce. But as on one side they are chiefly obliged to the sea for their riches, so on the other hand it proves the occasion of almost irreparable desolations; for though they take all possible precautions to maintain their dams and mills for the emptying of the water, yet sometimes the impetuosity of this element breaks through all these fences, which has cost at several times the lives of some millions of people.

Thus, April 17, 1429, a hundred thousand people were drowned about Dort. In 1446, there were fifteen parishes overflowed in the village of Scheveling, 121 houses were carried away. and the church, now close by the sea-side, stood in the middle of the place. [In 1530, a great part of Zealand was overflowed. In the same century seventy two villages on the coasts of Holland and Friezland were swallowed up, and near twenty thousand people perished; and in 1665, an inundation broke down the dyke of Muydenburg, and laid the whole country round Naarden, and many places in the province of Utrecht, under water. The dyke between Amsterdam and Haerlem, and many others, were also broke: but the calamity was no sooner over, than the inhabitants, in a great measure, repaired the damage.]

Another inconveniency is, the sudden change of weather from heat to cold, a thing not agreeable to those who are not used to it. Their impositions are also very heavy, which consequently occasions a dearness of all sorts of victuals; but their plenty of trade seems to make them a sufficient amends for this and every other inconveniency.

We were not a little surprised with the first sight of Rotterdam; for its canals being, for the most part, so deep and broad, that they are capable of receiving vessels of a great bulk; this affords the most agreeable prospect of a mixture of trees, tops of lofty houses, and masts, which at a distance appear wonderfully beautiful.

The city of Rotterdam has not always been in the same flourishing condition, which makes it now challenge a place among the cities of the second rank; its port is both large and commodious, the city rich, populous, pleasant, and extremely flourishing; their store-houses for the navy, the town-house, and the bank, are beautiful structures; their glass house, (famous through all the seven provinces) manufactures abundance of little enamelled bowls, and such like

like baubles, curiouſly done, which are ſold for prodigious profit to the ſavages in the Indies.

There are two French churches here: the ſtatue of braſs of Eraſmus is fixed on a pedeſtal of marble in the place called the Great Bridge, ſurrounded with iron rails. Eraſmus is dreſſed in his doctor's robe, with a book in his hand; and near it you ſee the following diſtich, wrote over the door of a little houſe where he was born, October 27, 1467, but died at Baſil, June 12, 1536.

Ædibus hic ortus, mundum decoravit Eraſmus
Artibus ingenuis, religione, Fide.

There has been due care expreſſed in this reſpect, for the firſt ſtatue was erected 1540, of wood; after that another of ſtone, 1657; and this of braſs, 1662.

[Lady Wortley Montague gives the following entertaining character of Rotterdam and the Hague. On her arrival at the Briel, ſhe ſays, 'I was charmed with the neatneſs of that little town; but my arrival at Rotterdam, preſented me a new ſcene of pleaſure. All the ſtreets are paved with broad ſtones, and before the meaneſt artificers doors are placed ſeats of various coloured marbles, ſo neatly kept, that I aſſure you, I walked almoſt over the town yeſterday, incognito, in my ſlippers, without receiving one ſpot of dirt: and you may ſee the Dutch maids waſhing the pavement of the ſtreet, with more application than ours do our bed-chambers. The town ſeems ſo full of people, with ſuch buſy faces, all in motion, that I can hardly fancy it is not ſome celebrated fair; but I ſee it is every day the ſame. 'Tis certain no town can be more advantageouſly ſituated for commerce. Here are ſeven large canals, on which the merchants ſhips come up to the very doors of their houſes. The ſhops and warehouſes are of a ſurpriſing neatneſs and magnificence, filled with an incredible quantity of fine merchandize, and ſo much cheaper than what we see in England, that I have much ado to persuade myself I am still so near it. Here is neither dirt nor beggary to be seen. One is not shocked with those loathsome cripples, so common in London, nor teized with the importunity of idle fellows and wenches, that chuse to be nasty and lazy. The common servants and little shop women here, are more nicely clean, than most of our ladies, and the great variety of neat dresses (every woman dressing her head after her own fashion) is an additional pleasure of seeing the town.——

'Sure nothing can be more agreeable than travelling in Holland. The whole country appears a large garden; the roads are well paved, shaded on each side with rows of trees, and bordered with large canals, full of boats, passing and repassing. Every twenty paces gives you the prospect of some villa, and every four hours that of a large town, so surprizingly neat, I am sure you would be charmed with them. The place I am now at, (the Hague) is certainly one of the finest villages in the world. Here are several squares finely built, and, what I think a particular beauty, the whole set with thick large trees. The Voor-hout is, at the same time, the Hyde-park and Mall of the people of quality; for they take the air in it both on foot and in coaches. There are shops for wafers, cool liquors, &c. I have been to see several of the most celebrated gardens, but I will not teize you with their descriptions.']

We made a little journey from hence to a small village called Leckerkeck, about three leagues from the city, upon the river Leck, where the lord of the manor told us, that the salmon-fishing (the fifth part whereof belongs to him) used formerly to produce twenty thousand livres per annum for his share, but of late years, the salmon having left that river, the fishing (which they are forced to continue only to maintain their right) does not defray the charges.

The

The tower of the great church here is very remarkable. It leaned formerly on the nave of the building; that is, bent toward the north-east three feet and a half; but by opening the foundation, they have found means to set it up quite straight, as appears by a prose inscription in Dutch; which also acquaints us the ground was opened September the 25th, 1651, and was closed again April the 22d, 1655. The architect who performed this singular piece of work was one Nicholas Jeremy Persoons. Dion Cassius, under the reign of Tiberius, mentions something of the same sort done, and that the artist was but ill rewarded.

The ordinary passage-boat carried us in two hours to Delft, a city that holds the third rank in the assembly of the states of Holland. One of the chief curiosities they shew you in this city is the tomb of William prince of Orange, assassinated here by Balthasar Gerard, 1584. The arsenal, the town-house, the stadtholder's palace, the grand-place, and the great hospital, with its gardens, are well worth the sight of a traveller. The canal betwixt this city and the Hague is not above a league in length, in sight of Reswyck and Voyerburgh, two pleasant villages, and adorned on both sides with most delightful summer villas, fine walks, and noble gardens.

The Hague, being without gates or walls, is reckoned among the villages; notwithstanding which, as it enjoys the privilege of a city, so its grandeur and beauty seems to deserve that name; being beside this the residence of the princes of Orange when stadtholders, of all the foreign ministers, and the place of assembly of the States General: beside that, the great concourse of foreigners of all sorts, renders the people more obliging and sociable than in any other place of Holland. Add to this, that the air is very good, the wood near the town extremely delightful, and the walk from thence to the village of Scheveling, near the sea-side, very diverting. Here they shew a chariot furnished both with wheels and sails, which is carried along by the wind upon the sea-shore, very pleasant to walk on, it being both hard and level.

Its situation is certainly the most pleasant of any place in Holland, having the before-mentioned wood to the north, very fertile meadows to the south, good arable lands to the east, and the sea to the west.

The princes of Orange keep their residence in the palace of the antient earls of Holland; but that called the Old Court, where they formerly lodged, is by much the more regular structure; the houses of pleasure about the Hague are generally very beautiful.

We took, among other things, a view of the church of the village of Losdun, so famous for the two basons of brass preserved there, in memory of the three hundred sixty-five children of the countess of Henneberg, daughter to Florent IV. earl of Holland, that were baptized in them. The story goes, that the said countess having reproached a beggar-woman with having too many children, the poor wretch, by way of imprecation, wished her as many children as there were days in the year; which being fulfilled, they were all christened, (the boys by the name of John, the girls Elizabeth) and buried in the church of Losdun. The whole history is painted at large in the said church, on both ends of which picture the two basons are fixed. The truth of it is attested by Erasmus, Vives, Guicciardini, and others.

From the Hague we went forward to Leyden, a place not so much frequented by courtiers and officers, nor so much disturbed with business and traffic as the Hague and Rotterdam; but exceeding charming by its intrinsic beauty and quiet, so that you seem to enjoy the benefit of a country life in the midst of a great city: its chief trade consists in the woollen manufactory; which, together with the university, makes it one of the most considerable cities in Holland. There are commonly about 1500 students.

In the Anatomy-hall they shew you a great many skeletons

ſkelétons both of men and beaſts; abundance of plants, fruits, animals, arms, habits, pictures, mummies, urns, images, &c. and among the reſt, the picture of a Pruſſian peaſant, who having ſwallowed a large knife, the ſame (as they tell you) was cut out again of his ſtomach, and he lived eight years after.

In the gallery of the phyſic-garden, and the adjoining cabinet, called the Indian Cabinet, we ſaw divers natural curioſities; among the reſt a winged cat and ape; the hand of a mermaid; a vegetable Priapus, a moſt curious plant; a monſter produced from a hen's egg; a piece of money of paper, made during the ſiege of Leyden by the Spaniards in 1574, with this inſcription on one ſide, *Hæc libertatis ergo*; on the other, *Pugno pro Patria:* an Eaſt India ſerpent, on whoſe ſkin are to be ſeen, as ſome fancy, ſeveral natural figures reſembling Arabic characters; beſide a great number of animals, inſects, and other things, preſerved in vials filled with ſpirit of wine.

Before I take my leave of Leyden, I muſt not forget to give you an account of the Rhine, which is loſt near its mouth, where moſt other rivers are at the largeſt: for the Rhine dividing itſelf into two branches near Schenkerſchontz, one of them takes the name of Wakle, the other a little above Arnheim, that of Yſſel; and continuing its courſe about ſeven or eight leagues below that city, as far as Duarſtadt, is there again ſubdivided into two other ſmall channels, the chief whereof takes the name of the Leck. The other rivulet, which turns more to the right, retains the name of the Rhine; till coming to Utrecht, it emits another branch, which taking its courſe to the north, is known by the name of the Vecht; and the other continuing its courſe, by the name of the Rhine, to Worden, it at laſt loſes itſelf by two or three canals at Leyden. The cauſe of this odd fate of the Rhine is attributed to an earthquake, which throwing part of the Downs into the mouth of this river, ſhut it ever ſince; the waters were driven back, and consequently enlarged and deepned the channel of the Leck as we see it now.

They shew you here the shopboard belonging to that noted taylor called John of Leyden, (where he was born) the chief of the Anabaptists. His true name was John Bucold.

From hence to Haerlem is five hours travelling by the passage boat, the canal being lined by a great number of country-seats and summer-houses.

Haerlem is a large and pleasant city, and, for its agreeable situation, may challenge the preference before Leyden, most of its canals being mixed with the little river Sparm. This city is chiefly famous for the linen manufactory, and that of tape, though of late years they have made also great quantities of silk stuffs. The great church (the largest in all the seven provinces) and the town-house, are stately structures; and the wood without the city is a great addition to its pleasant situation; for which it is deservedly admired.

Lawrence Coster, who challenges the first invention of printing, was a native of this city; though John Guttenbergh of Strasburgh, and Conrade and Arnold, two brothers of Mayence, challenge that honour before him. However, those of Haerlem, in respect to their townsman, keep in their town-house the first book that ever was printed, in a silver case wrapt in silk, the keeping whereof is committed to the care of several of the magistrates; and the statue of Lawrence Coster is to be viewed in the same place. This inscription is to be seen in golden letters over the door of the house where the said Lawrence Coster lived.

MEMORIÆ SACRUM,
Typographia ars artium omnium Conservatrix, hic primum inventa circa annum 1440.

Meyer assures us, that in 1403, a mermaid was cast ashore by a tempest near Haerlem, who was brought

brought to feed upon bread and milk, taught to ſpin, and lived for many years. John Gerard of Leyden adds, that ſhe would frequently pull off her cloaths, and run toward the water, and that her ſpeech was ſo confuſed a noiſe as not to be underſtood by any body: ſhe was buried in the church-yard, becauſe ſhe had learnt to make the ſign of the croſs. He ſpeaks this upon the credit of ſeveral perſons who had ſeen her.

As it would require a long continuance in the city of Amſterdam to learn every thing that belongs to it, and a large volume to deſcribe it all, I will content myſelf with giving rather a ſketch than a deſcription of a place, which is, beyond all diſpute, one of the moſt beautiful and conſiderable cities in the world: however, for its extent, it is in no wiſe to be compared to London, there being, according to a good calculation, in London about ſeven hundred thouſand ſouls, but in Amſterdam not above two hundred thouſand. But for riches and trade it may vie with any city in the world; witneſs their Eaſt India company, which was founded in 1594, and has waged wars againſt very potent princes, without any conſiderable interruption in their trade.

This city is built upon piles fixed in the marſhes on the ſouth-ſide of the river Ye or Tye, which is a branch of the Zuyder-Zee. Its fortifications are very conſiderable, conſiſting of many baſtions faced with brick, ſurrounded with a ditch eighty paces broad, filled with running water, which, together with the ſluices, whereby they can lay all the adjacent country under water, render it almoſt impregnable: beſide the ordinary garriſon, the militia or trained bands of the city conſiſt of ſixty companies of a hundred men each, commanded by citizens.

Mr. Hanway's account of this city is as follows. 'The wonderful city of Amſterdam, as well as many other towns of the Netherlands, is a work of art and labour, not inferior to the greateſt monuments of human

human induſtry in paſt ages. It is ſituated about two hundred and twenty Engliſh miles from London, and derives its name from the river Amſtel; it being formerly called Amſteldam, or the dam of the Amſtel, which is the name generally given to it in authentic records. Our author obſerves, that it was then reckoned about four hundred years from its firſt beginning, and two hundred and ſeventy from its being incloſed with walls. In 1570 the Dutch began to lay the foundation of their wealth and naval ſtrength About twenty years before that time, they embraced the doctrines of Calvin and being provoked by the oppreſſive meaſures of Romiſh bigotry, they ſhook off the Spaniſh yoke. The Spaniards exerted themſelves upon this occaſion, from religious as well as political motives; but they were unable to render that confederacy abortive, which at length united the Seven Provinces, and formed a powerful republic.

About the year 1600, the love of liberty and gain cauſed ſuch a conflux of people thither, that the walls were extended; and ſince that time they have been farther enlarged, ſo that they are now about three leagues in circumference. The city is generally eſteemed near one third as populous as London or Paris. Within the walls are reckoned 26,500 houſes, and about 240,000 inhabitants, beſide thoſe in the ſuburbs, which are ſmall. The greateſt ſtrength of the place is in the difficulty of acceſs both by ſea and land; but the numerous ſhoals that render the entrance of the Texel difficult, have not obſtructed the progreſs of commerce. One remarkable proof of œconomy is obvious in the fortifications of the city; for the baſtions, which are very numerous, have each a windmill.

Moſt of the ſtreets are extremely clean; but except thoſe that have canals, they are much too narrow. However, they are rendered leſs incommodious by the hired coaches being ſet on ſledges drawn by one horſe.

horſe. Merchandize is alſo drawn on ſledges, which are not only the moſt convenient vehicles for the inhabitants and their trade, but are calculated to preſerve the houſes, which being built on piles, might in time be damaged in their foundations, by having a great number of wheel-carriages. Gentlemen's coaches are however, for the moſt part ſet on wheels, but for this liberty they pay a conſiderable tax. The principal ſtreets, or rather quays of the canals, are agreeably planted on each ſide with trees; but the canals ſometimes ſmell very offenſively. The houſes are rather neat than elegant or commodious: the nature of the climate renders it neceſſary to waſh them often; but the greateſt part of the people carry this kind of cleanlineſs ſo far as hardly to afford themſelves time for the neceſſary care of their perſons. The entrance of the houſes is generally by ſteps, which riſe four or five feet from the ground, and the paſſage into the rooms, which runs very deep, is floored and pannelled with marble, which has an air of grandeur in miniature. They have much neat, and ſome rich furniture, which ſeems rather occaſioned by an antient cuſtom of neatneſs and elegance, than the effect of a luxurious and expenſive taſte.

Of all the buildings in Amſterdam, the town-houſe is the moſt diſtinguiſhed. It is two hundred and eighty-two feet in front, two hundred and thirty-two deep, an hundred and ſixteen high, excluſive of the cupola. It coſt three millions of guilders, or three hundred thouſand pounds ſterling, when money was more valuable than it is now; which will be leſs ſurpriſing, if we conſider that it is founded upon thirteen thouſand large piles. This is a very grand and uſeful building, and yet is neither elegant nor agreeable. It contains the offices and tribunals for the execution of the laws, in the ſeveral branches of the military, as well as civil government. It is very obſervable that the entrance of this building is very mean; but had the doors been proportioned to the edifice,

edifice, they would have been more ſubject to be forced upon occaſion of thoſe tumultuous aſſemblies of the people, that are not unfrequent in this country. The ſtadthouſe is guarded in the night by a body of the burghers, who are thus charged with the care of the great reſervoir of the wealth of the United Provinces. In the lower apartments is the bank, in which is ſaid to be depoſited immenſe ſums.']

[Dr. Brown tells us, that 'their Raſp-huys, or houſe of correction is alſo worth obſervation; having at its entrance two lions bridled, with this inſcription:

Virtutis eſt domare quæ cuncti pavent.

'A proper emblem for the purpoſe it was intended, viz. to bridle the inſolencies of ſuch as are riotous in the ſtreets, or commit diſorders; and the extravagancies of the ſons of citizens, who are paſt the government of their maſters and parents. They are employed in gaining their bread by raſping Braſil-wood; and if they refuſe to perform their taſk, and become incorrigible by blows, they (as we were told) put them in a large ciſtern, with a pump by them, and ſo letting in the water upon them, force them to work for their life.

'Their Spin-huys is intended for the correction of young women, ſuch as live looſely, or are taken in the ſtreets, and other ſuſpicious places: ſometimes the citizens ſend their daughters hither for chaſtiſement, and theſe have chambers allotted them; I ſaw above an hundred women in one large room, ſome of which were very well dreſſed. In the hoſpital for children are ſix hundred orphans, well educated and looked after. The Dol-huys is like our Bedlam, intended for delirious perſons; the Gaſt-huys, an hoſpital for the ſick; as the Mannen-houſe is an hoſpital for old men. They have beſide this, a laudable cuſtom throughout all Holland; which is, that upon the appointment of any meeting at a tavern, or any other

other occasion, certain forfeitures are put into a box, kept in all public houses, for the use of the poor; which is the reason that scarce ever any beggars are seen in the streets.']

The Roman Catholics enjoy liberty of conscience, as in other parts of the Seven Provinces, though their number is not so considerable as some have endeavoured to persuade us; for I have been informed by persons of knowlege and credit, that the Roman Catholics, and all other sectaries together, do not make a fourth part of the inhabitants of Amsterdam.

In this city remains still a convent of certain nuns called Beguines, an order erected A. D. 1207, composed of maidens and widows, who have no children, and who need no other qualifications to be admitted into this society, than a testimonial of their good behaviour, and competency to live upon, either by themselves, or in conjunction with one or more of the sisters, as they find it most suitable to their purpose. Their convent (which contains about a hundred and thirty sisters) is built like a little city, with a wall and ditch about it, within which stands a church, where they are obliged to perform their devotions at certain hours. They wear an odd looking black habit, receive and pay visits, and quit the convent when they please.

The music-houses of Amsterdam, so much talked of, are public-houses or taverns, where young fellows come under pretence of dancing, but in effect to pick up lewd women, who resort thither in great numbers, and carry them to other convenient lodgings; these being intended only for their meeting-places. They are generally visited by strangers, out of curiosity; and you must either drink what they offer, or pay as if you did.

The exchange of Amsterdam is two hundred feet long, and a hundred and twenty broad: the galleries above are supported by forty-six pillars, but are not

not ſo ſpacious; nor are the ſhops ſo many as thoſe over the London Exchange.

The academy, ſtiled the Illuſtrious School, is alſo an elegant ſtructure, divided into ſeveral ſchools for divinity, philoſophy, hiſtory, law, and phyſic.

There are five high towers in this city, which have each a great clock, and are placed at ſuch a convenient diſtance, as that the hours of the day are ſhown all over the town.

[The eſtabliſhed religion (ſays Mr. Hanway) is that of Calviniſm, for which there are eleven churches for the Dutch, one for the Engliſh, two for the Germans, and two for the French; but the Roman Catholics are ſaid to have near thirty places of worſhip. Beſide theſe there are Lutherans and Baptiſts: the Jews are alſo numerous, and have their ſynagogues as in London; but none of theſe religions, except the Calviniſts, are allowed the uſe of bells: and the ſtates invalidate all marriages not performed according to the rites of the eſtabliſhed church, unleſs the parties firſt engage themſelves in form before the civil magiſtrate: and then they may perform the ceremony according to their reſpective religions.]

We paſſed ſeven hours upon the canal betwixt Amſterdam and Utrecht very pleaſantly; leaving on the right-hand the old caſtle of Abeow, and the village of the ſame name, the boundary of the province of Holland on that ſide, about three leagues from Amſterdam. We no ſooner came to Utrecht, but we found it to fall much ſhort of that extreme neatneſs we obſerved in the province of Holland. This city is famous for its antiquity, its univerſity, and the union made here in 1579, which was the foundation of the whole Dutch republic. The ſteeple of the cathedral is very high, and the church contains many relics highly valued by the Roman Catholics.

The Mall and the walks about it, without the gates of the city, are infinitely pleaſant, being upon that

ſcore

ſcore ſpared by the French king's expreſs command, when his troops ravaged all the country round about. A certain gentleman of Utrecht told me, that there were no leſs than forty-eight towns within the reach of a day's journey from this city, and among them thirty-three to which you may go and come back the ſame day. The country about Utrecht has a far different face from what you ſee in Holland, their fields being, for the moſt part, ploughed lands incloſed with ſtrong hedges.

Two hours from Utrecht we paſſed in ſight of Zeiſt, and of the caſtle on the right-hand: it is a very handſome ſtructure, incloſed with a ditch full of running water, adorned with labyrinths, gardens, ſtatues, fountains, and other ornaments, being built not many years ago, by one of the richeſt lords of this country. The fields betwixt Rhenen and Arnheim are for the moſt part planted with tobacco, propped by ſtakes; and at Reincom, a village three hours on this ſide of Rhenen, you ſee a ſtone, which is the boundary betwixt the lordſhip of Utrecht and the province of Guelders.

Arnheim has nothing remarkable but its fortifications. Two hours and a half beyond it we paſſed the Yſſel, divided into three branches near each other; and afterward continuing our journey through Doeſburgh, (a little city on that river, in the province of Zutphen) we dined in a poor village, if milk with biſcuit may be called a dinner: but the worſt is, that our fare was no better at night, when we lodged at Yſſelburgh, a ſmall diſmantled town upon the borders of Cleves.——

[To theſe particulars concerning the country, our readers will not be diſpleaſed to ſee ſome remarks relating to the inhabitants, from our ingenious countryman Mr. Ray; which are contained in the enſuing extract: with ſome additional obſervations which himſelf introduces.

'As to what relates to the common people of Holland, it muſt be confeſſed they are ſurly and ill-bred, which is the reaſon that no ſtrangers that know the country will deal with inn-keepers, waggoners, boatmen, porters, and ſuch-like, without bargaining beforehand. The men are generally very large boned and bulky, and theſe, as well as the women, are conſtantly eating as they travel. At their common entertainments, a ſallad leads the van, a kind of ſtewed meat is the main part of the dinner, and it concludes with ſome boiled and buttered herbs. The chief food of the ordinary people is cod-fiſh and pickled herring, which they cure better than the Engliſh. In the public houſes you commonly meet with ſmoaked beef, but in thin ſlices, good bread and butter, and four or five ſorts of cheeſe. Their ſtrong drink (they call it Dick-beer, and very properly, for it is ſeldom clear) is ſold for three-pence a quart; the dearneſs of which ariſes partly from the heavy exciſe laid upon this, as well as all other proviſions: partly from the plenty of money in thoſe provinces, which makes land ſold here at between thirty and forty years purchaſe. Moſt of their beds are made cloſe like cabins, narrow and ſhort, and yet you pay an exceſſive rate for them in the inns. Their houſes are kept exceeding neat, even to the outſide of pots and pot-hooks; nay, the very tiles of the pent-houſes: yet has it been obſervable, that in dreſſing their meats, they are not ſo clean and curious as the Engliſh. They uſe organs in moſt of their churches, collect money for the poor in ſermon time, with a purſe faſtened to a ſtick, and a bell hanging to it. The pſalms to be ſung are ſet down upon ſlates, hung upon the walls of the church for that purpoſe. They ſeldom travel on horſeback, but generally in waggons, ſome covered, others not, but moſtly by water; and this on Sundays as well as other days. Beggars are ſeldom ſeen in Holland, notwithſtanding the vaſt multitude of people; this province containing no leſs than

than twenty-four walled towns and cities, ſix of which (beſide Amſterdam) are bigger than any in England, except London. And upon this occaſion, ſome obſervations made by Francis Barnham, eſq; who was in Holland with my lord ambaſſador Hollis, have been eſteemed ſenſible and curious.

"There is, ſays he, a continual watch kept on the ſteeples in all the cities of the United Provinces: the differences ariſing among boatſmen and waggoners, who ſhall go firſt, are decided by caſting a die. They gather the rain-water by pipes from the houſes, and preſerve it in ciſterns, as they do in Venice. The Dutch ſtand much in awe of their ſuperiors, becauſe juſtice is done there without delay. They are ſtrangely addicted to novelties, and mightily taken with any thing that is gay. They are extremely greedy of profit, yet very juſt in their bargains. The knowlege how to get money is what they eſteem above all other things, and ſcarce ever apply themſelves to any thing beſide that and politics, in which they are generally well verſed; the meaneſt of them being qualified by his birth-right to become a burgomaſter. They fight bravely at ſea, though naturally they are of a phlegmatic temper, and conſequently not fit for brave exploits by land. They allow of liberty in religion, but keep a watchful eye over it to ſecure the public peace; which is the reaſon that it is more difficult to hatch a plot here than in any other parts: though at the ſame time the people ſay and print almoſt what they pleaſe, the ſame being included within the general notion of liberty. Moſt of them have little ſenſe of honour or generoſity, being guided merely by the proſpect of advantage or intereſt. They don't proſecute murder with ſo much violence as theft. The Dutch are always careful to ſolemnize any great action done by them, with all the public marks of honour and rejoicings, to imprint into the common people an idea of the ability and wiſdom of their go-

 vernors;

vernors; which is the reason they frequently erect monuments to those who have deserved well of the commonwealth. The ordinary sort of women (if not all) seem to be more pleased with obscene discourse than the English or French; they have also the reputation of making not so severe an account of chastity before marriage, but of being very faithful to their husbands. Even the better sort of women are not backward of admitting men, though of very little acquaintance, to a salute; and kissing passes current here, not only at parting and returns, but also in frolics and familiar conversation. Most women are let into all the actions of their husbands, who seldom undertake any thing without their knowlege and approbation. They have abundance of chiming in their cities; and vast multitudes of storks build their nests upon the tops of the chimnies."] These remarks have the repute of being very just, though wrote some years since: corresponding greatly with the reports of all who have been in the Low Countries. And though some allowances must be made for those alterations in customs, which all nations, and especially commercial ones, are subject to; yet some national characteristics still distinguish the inhabitants of the same places at all periods of time: and if the manners of the Dutch have undergone any alterations, it is chiefly in departing from their antient frugality, and adopting some of the luxuries of their neighbours.

TRAVELS

THROUGH

GERMANY, HUNGARY, BOHEMIA, SWITZERLAND, ITALY, and LORRAIN.

By JOHN GEORGE KEYSLER, F. R. S.

MR. Keyſler was born at Thurnau, a town belonging to the count of Geich, in the year 1689. His father, who was one of the count's council, performed the part of a conſcientious parent in the care of his education; and the ſincere piety he imbibed from his mother, during his childhood, was deeply implanted in his mind during the whole courſe of his life. He was ſo well grounded in the principles of the Proteſtant religion, that he was never carried away with the torrent of corruption, nor tainted by the prevalence of cuſtom in a degenerate age. His inclination for learning being very early conſpicuous, was cheriſhed and increaſed by the careful inſtructions of the moſt able maſters. He ſtudied at the univerſity at Hall, a place famous from its firſt foundation for perſons of the greateſt eminence in literature: and he had ſcarcely left the univerſity before he was appointed ſub-preceptor to Charles Maximilian and Chriſtian Charles, counts of Giech-Buchau; with whom, in the year 1713, he returned to Hall; and afterward attended them in their travels. The firſt place they viſited was Utrecht, where he became acquainted with the learned Hadrian Reland, who, perceiving in him an uncommon capacity, contracted with him an intimate friendſhip. And to the perſuaſions of this great man it was owing, that Mr. Keyſler resolved to execute what he had before some thoughts of, namely, to write a history of the antiquities of his native country.

Mr. Keysler's sense of his duty to the two young counts, carried him from the delightful city of Utrecht sooner than he otherwise could have wished. In company with them he visited the principal cities of Germany, France, and the Netherlands: never failing, in every place, to increase his literary acquisitions. Mr. Keysler returned safe from his first travels with his pupils, and acquired such an uncommon reputation, that his abilities for such a charge were mentioned in the highest terms to baron Bernstorf, first minister of state to his Britannic majesty, as elector of Brunswick-Lunenburgh. This great man was at that time desirous of finding a proper person to whom he might entrust the education of his grandson, a youth of the greatest hopes. Keysler was pitched upon, and the happy consequences have demonstrated, that the baron could not have selected a more proper person. In the autumn of the year 1716 he came to Hanover, where his indefatigable application to his charge exceeded the most sanguine wishes of his Mecænas.

In the year 1718, Mr. Keysler obtained leave to make a voyage to England, to which, whatever commissions he might have to execute, he knew how to give the appearance of a philosophical journey: and the same free access to learned societies, before so advantageous in France and the Low Countries, rendered London and Oxford very agreeable to him. Here he obtained a very signal proof of the high esteem he had acquired in England, by being unanimously elected a fellow of the Royal Society; the only title which he ever enjoyed.

The two young barons Bernstorf, after being upward of ten years under the direction of Mr. Keysler, were, by his judicious instructions in all the useful branches of science, fitted for visiting foreign coun-

tries

tries with advantage: and it is to the tour he took with these pupils that we owe the following work.

Mr. Keysler, on several occasions, during his travels, gave such happy proofs of his singular learning, and remarkable sagacity, that he had very considerable offers of public employments made him by several courts to settle among them: but the extraordinary patronage of the two barons Bernstorf, together with the ease and tranquillity he enjoyed under their protection; by which he was enabled to devote great part of his time to the placid muses; appeared to him more eligible than external magnificence, so apt to affect short-sighted mortals. The younger baron being nominated envoy to the imperial dyet, by the king of Denmark, as duke of Holstein-Gluckstadt, Mr. Keysler attended him to the Danish court at Copenhagen, and afterward to Ratisbon. When the dyet was over, he returned and spent the remainder of his days with his elder pupil, whose generosity placed him beyond the frowns of fortune: and both the brothers settled a very handsome pension on him for life. He died in the 54th year of his age, on the 21st of June, 1743, of an asthma, at Stintenburg, an estate belonging to baron Bernstorf, in Saxelauenburg: and his body was interred with great magnificence (contrary indeed to his desire) in the church of Cassahn, in the territory of Bernstorf. The exact order in which he left his manuscripts, is a convincing proof that he quitted this mortal stage in a well prepared disposition.

Having given this brief account of Mr. Keysler, we shall present to our readers the most curious parts of his travels; occasionally enriching his descriptions with those which we may meet with in other approved travellers to the same parts.

—The first place I arrived at, says Mr. Keysler, was the city of Schaffhausen, (capital of the canton of the same name in Switzerland) which is very handsome, the streets broad, the houses magnificent, and pleasantly situated in a plain. The canton of Zurich, which commences at the other ſide of a ſtately bridge, is ſeparated from it by the Rhine, which waſhes the ſouthern parts of Schaffhauſen, and is of very great advantage to its commerce. I muſt not, by any means, at my firſt entrance into Switzerland, omit an obſervation, the truth of which I was ſufficiently convinced of by a former tour through theſe countries, namely, that great numbers of people have formed very falſe ideas of the inhabitants of this country and their trade. They imagine Switzerland to be hardly any thing better than a confuſed chaos of barren rocks, craggy mountains, eternal ſnows, and gloomy vallies; hardly ſupplying its wretched inhabitants with the means of ſupporting a laborious and miſerable life. But this is very different from the truth; the country produces all the neceſſaries of life, in ſuch abundance, as to enable the inhabitants to export large quantities. Their flax and linen are of the greateſt advantage, particularly to the inhabitants of Berne and St. Gall. Crapes, coarſe linen cloth, drugs, Geneva, and other ſpirituous liquors, are exported in large quantities to Germany and Holland. The cheeſe of Switzerland is famous in every part of Europe; and orders are conſtantly tranſmitted from all parts for their butter. There is found near Bex, in the diſtrict of Aigle depending on the Pais de Vaud, Sulphur Virgineum, which greatly excels that brought, as a great curioſity, from America. It is eſteemed good in diſorders of the breaſt and nerves.

The Switzers kill ſo large a number of cattle annually, that the hides, beſide what they uſe themſelves, make a very conſiderable article in their commerce. They alſo ſend prodigious droves of ſheep and oxen to diſtant parts; and as the cattle of Jutland and Holſtein are greatly valued; ſo in Bavaria, Auſtria, and even Hungary, perſons of ample fortune procure the Swiſs cattle at any price, notwithſtanding they degenerate

ſo

ſo ſoon as to render a conſtant ſupply neceſſary. Switzerland ſupplies Lombardy with the greateſt part of its coach-horſes, and Savoy with horſes both for the army and artillery; and the French have hitherto purchaſed the greateſt part of their horſes for military ſervice, of the Swiſs, ſometimes ten thouſand in a year; but at preſent they are very attentive to improve their own. The inhabitants of Switzerland reap a very conſiderable advantage from a war between France and Germany; for as the paſſes are guarded, and horſes prohibited from being ſent from Germany into France, the greateſt part of this lucrative branch of trade, amounting ſometimes to ten thouſand pounds yearly, is carried on through Switzerland. As the inhabitants are under no neceſſity of importing any kinds of goods, ſalt alone excepted, (their ſalt ſprings not being ſufficient wholly to ſupply them) from the adjacent countries, as Tyrol, Bavaria, and Franche Comte; they can never want either a briſk trade, or a large balance in their favour. But trade is not confined to neceſſaries alone; that luxury, pomp, and infatuation for foreign productions, which has infected moſt parts of Europe, has extended its contagious influence to Switzerland; and ſeveral wiſe regulations have been made, to ſtop this pernicious and extenſive uſe of foreign commodities. But theſe wholeſome laws have the ſame fate in Switzerland as in ſeveral other parts of Europe; the ſpirit is explained away by ſubterfuges and arbitrary interpretations, and, conſequently, they loſe their intended effect.

The ladies in ſome parts of Switzerland, are reſtrained in their dreſs by ſumptuary laws; but the conſequence is, that they impatiently wait the return of ſummer, in order to their viſiting the German Spaws, where they may indulge their gay inclinations, free from the reſtraints of the laws of their country: and ſo fond are they of theſe annual journies, that they are often made one of their marriage articles.

It having therefore been found impossible to restrain all abuses, especially in a sex so impatient of authority, by human laws; manufactures have been erected in several parts, in order to prevent, in a more effectual manner, the sending money out of the country for foreign commodities. This scheme laboured at first under very great difficulties, but time has removed most of them, especially in the Protestant cantons, which, in this respect, greatly excel those of the Romish religion: nor is there any probability that the latter will ever carry commerce to any great height. Excellent cloth is made at Zurich, and the silks manufactured in the Pais de Vaud, are of great advantage. The kind reception which the French refugees have met with at Geneva, have largely contributed to increase the number of ingenious artists in that city; and it would have been of the greatest advantage, if this humane example had prevailed in its full extent throughout Switzerland. Zurich, Basil, Geneva, and Schaffhausen are the four staple towns of the commodities of Switzerland; but Zurich vastly excels the others. Their foreign trade is greatly facilitated by means of the Rhone and the Rhine: they send their goods to France and the Mediterranean by the former, and to Germany, the Netherlands, and the North Sea, by the latter. The trade of Schaffhausen has however been declining for some time, so that at present few of the merchants carry on trade on their own account, the generality dealing by commission.

The number of burghers in Schaffhausen is said to amount to two thousand; and though the arsenal cannot be called large, it is sufficient for the purpose intended, that of supplying the inhabitants, in case of necessity, with arms. But it must be remembered, that the sword is here considered as a mark of their freedom, as well as an ornament, on which account every citizen, and even the peasants, appear at church in their swords; nor does any one dare to appear before

fore the magiſtracy without a cloak and a ſword. The inhabitants of that part of the diſtrict of mount Jura, dependent on the canton of Berne, attend divine worſhip not only in their ſwords, but alſo carry with them their bayonets and firelocks, which they either hang up in a particular corner of the church, or place by them. Perhaps this cuſtom owes its origin to the frequent diſturbances of former ages, and their almoſt continual wars with the inhabitants of Burgundy, againſt whom it was neceſſary to be always prepared. It muſt however be acknowleged, that the practice of wearing ſwords at church has been prohibited in a ſolemn manner.

Between Schaffhauſen and Baſil, the navigation of the Rhine is twice interrupted by violent cataracts or falls of the river; the conſequence of which is, that the veſſels are under a neceſſity of being unloaded, at theſe falls, and the goods put on board others. Near the village of Neuhauſen, on the Schaffhauſen ſide of the river, is an iron manufacture, which produces a very conſiderable revenue. Petrified muſcles and cockles are often found in the iron ore, with which the country abounds.

The famous caſtle of Hohentwiel, called in Latin Duellium, belonging to the duke of Wirtemberg-Stuttgard, is ſituated four leagues north-eaſt of Schaffhauſen. It is entirely encloſed by the territories of Nullenburg, not having an inch of ground belonging to it, and therefore of more honour than advantage. Indeed its being ſituated at ſuch a diſtance from any enemy that might invade the country, and conſequently being in no danger of an attack for ſome time, renders it very convenient, on any dangerous conjuncture, for depoſiting records, papers, jewels, and other valuable effects: but the inhabitants of Swabia would reap more advantage from it, if it ſtood in a more convenient place, as no hoſtilities from the neighbourhood of the Switzers can be apprehended.

The

The ſituation of Hohentwiel is on a lofty mountain in the midſt of a charming and fruitful country, ſurrounded with pleaſant villages and ruinous caſtles on the ſummits of lofty mountains; which together with the lake Boden, lying at about two miles diſtant, afford a moſt beautiful proſpect. The lower caſtle ſtands at a great height, notwithſtanding which, a good ſort of wine is produced from vines which grow on the ſides of the mountain to the very walls. The neighbouring country, when covered with fogs, appears to a ſpectator at Hohentwiel like a ſea, and as the miſt diſſipates, the mountains and caſtles gradually appear like iſlands in the ocean.

A cuſtom prevails here, that when any prince, or other perſon of diſtinction viſits this fortreſs, he is obliged to carry from the lower to the upper caſtle, a ſtone of ten pounds weight, a conſiderable number of which are now to be ſeen there, ſome of them having the initial letters of the names of thoſe who have taken the trouble of carrying them up.

Duke Ulrich being in exile in the year 1520, purchaſed of a widow belonging to the houſe of Klingenberg this caſtle, and it has belonged ever ſince to the dukes of Wirtemberg.

I made an incurſion from hence into the adjacent parts of Swabia, famous for the ſource of that noble river the Danube, and flatter myſelf that my journey has not been uſeleſs. The Danube, in a courſe of four hundred German miles, waſhes fifty populous cities, and receives the waters of twelve large rivers, and more than eighty rivulets: ſo that few rivers, not even the Nile itſelf, can be compared with it. The Turks, indeed, are for giving the preference to the Nile, for a very ſingular reaſon, namely, becauſe it has not been ſo often ſtained with human blood as the Danube. The ſource of this famous river is near Don Eſchingen, in the territories of Furſtemberg, and ſoon becomes a conſiderable ſtream by the conflux of ſeveral rivulets.

Near

Near Burlatingen, a hunting ſeat belonging to the prince of Hohenzallern, is a chapel, built by Mr. Conier, a captain of horſe in the emperor's ſervice; the ſituation of which is ſo remarkable that it muſt not be omitted. It is built on an eminence, and in ſuch a manner, that the rain, which drops from one ſide of it, is, by means of the Lauchart, conveyed into the Danube, and that falling from the other, into the Rhine, through the Starzel and Nectar.

The territories of the circle of Swabia are very different with regard to fertility; and hence complaints from ſuch diſtricts as imagine their aſſeſſments of the public contributions to be unjuſt, are continually preferred to the aſſemblies of the circles; and ſome attempts have been made to remove their cauſe, and proportion the aſſeſſments in a more equitable manner. But it is a natural conſequence of thoſe aſſemblies, that a vaſt deal of buſineſs muſt remain undetermined; nor is it reaſonable to think that every proceeding would have been approved by the Areopagus. For not to mention the princes, biſhops, counts, abbots, and the principal cities; ſeveral places, and the imperial towns in particular, are reduced to ſuch a low condition, that it cannot be expected their repreſentatives can all be properly qualified for the truſt committed to them; which muſt conſequently be the ſource of many abuſes.

A great variety of droll adventures are related, though very unjuſtly, of the Swabians; but their own good ſenſe have inſtructed them to be themſelves the firſt relaters of them; and I muſt ſay, that in general, as much good ſenſe, and, perhaps, a larger proportion of the frankneſs and honeſty of the old Germans is to be found in Swabia, than in many other parts.

I continued my journey from Schaffhauſen through Zingen to Rotolfszell, or, as it is for ſhortneſs called, Zell, where both we and our carriage embarked for Conſtance, paying ſeven Rhine guilders for our paſſage. The diſtance is computed at four leagues, but may be performed, with a fair wind, in two hours. In five hours after our departure from Constance, we reached Lindau, though the distance is about six German miles; but all are not favoured with so quick a passage, some having been eight days in performing it. The whole length of the lake of Boden, which reaches to Bregentz, is about eighteen leagues, and twenty-two from Schaffhausen to Bregentz.

Beside the fish usual in these parts, there is found near Lindau and Bregentz, a kind of salmon-trouts called Gangfischie, which, when full grown, are pickled, and exported as a great rarity. When arrived at their full growth they are called Rheinlanken, Innlanken, or Rheinlacher, that is, Rhine salmon; they are near two ells in length, and weigh from thirty to forty pounds. As it is not always possible to find a good market for fish of so large a size, the fishermen fasten a small piece of wood to the end of a line, which they pass through the gills of the fish, fastening the other end of it to a stake on the shore near their huts; by which means the fish has the liberty of swimming thirty or forty paces, and the fishermen in no danger of losing it. In this manner it is kept till an opportunity offers of selling it to advantage.

I have seen, between Constance and Lindau, an incredible number of chafers, some single, others in large heaps, consisting of many thousands, floating dead on the lake; but whether they were driven thither, or had attempted to fly over it, is uncertain; but, be that as it will, there they expired.

The passage from Zell to the island of Reichneau, situated in the middle of the lower lake, is generally performed in half an hour. This island is not improperly called Reiche Au, or Augia Dives, the rich island, from its fertility, and the richness of the abbey built there. The island is about a league and a half long, and a league broad; and must not be confounded with Augia Minor, for that is not the island Meinau, in the lake of Boden, as some have pretended,

tended, but the cloyster and abbey of Weissenau, near Ratisbon.

The abbey of Reichenau is a noble structure; but what has rendered it particularly remarkable is a large emerald, presented by Charles the Fat. It is not easy now to procure a sight of this famous gem, an attempt having been made about four years ago, to rob the abbey; since which the prior, for the greater security of this valuable stone, conceals it even from the greatest part of the brethren themselves. We waited a considerable time before this gem was brought into the prior's chamber, where we saw it; and the prior assured us, that it would not be removed till night, and then by himself only; adding that, in order to prevent a surprize, it was not always kept in the same place. It is contained in a red wooden frame, something larger than a folio book, and weighs twenty-eight pounds and three quarters. They have been offered six thousand five hundred and fifty pounds sterling per pound for it, by several jewellers; it is two inches thick, three spans and a half long, and a span and a half broad. On its surface are scratched the initial letters of several names; but nothing of that kind is now permitted to be done.

In this church is interred the body of the above liberal emperor Charles the Fat, once so great and powerful, but afterward abandoned by all; so that he lived in the greatest indigence, and died, or, according to some, was murdered by his servants in the year 888, at Neidingen, on the Danube.

The monks of this abbey pretended to shew one of the water-pots used at the marriage of Cana of Galilee: in the cathedral of Bamberg are two of the same kind, and another at Hildersham; others are shewn at St. Denis, Angers, Quedlinburg, and above twenty other different places. Six or eight of them, all of a different size, colour, and shape, I have myself seen. It is abundantly evident that the small ones, with a narrow neck, could never have been used by the Jews in their purifications, which was done by plunging the arms up to the elbow in the water; but in these pots, this is impossible.

Constance, called by the inhabitants of the adjacent country, Coschstantz, is a pretty large city, and toward Lindau, makes an elegant appearance. The burghers of Constance are supposed not to exceed five hundred and fifty, whereas those of Lindau amount at least to between six and seven hundred. The pulpit in the cathedral is supported by a statue of John Hus, who was here condemned to be burnt. The placing his statue in this manner was intended as a mark of infamy, but it seems more naturally to imply an honourable distinction. This is in some degree similar to a piece of superstition current among the vulgar, namely, that the very place where John Hus was burnt, still bears the evident marks of divine displeasure, as no grass will grow upon it. Our guide, who was a substantial citizen, but a professor of the Romish religion, was so fully convinced of the truth of this legendary tale, that he even asserted it at the very time we were walking on the place; notwithstanding its beautiful verdure, at this season, has procured it the pleasing name of paradise; so that ocular demonstration was not wanting, had we thought proper to have opposed him. It is not indeed impossible but he might have refused a decision of the senses, as those of his profession have rejected their testimony with regard to an article of much greater importance, in their disputes with protestants.

Constance was formerly a free imperial city, but the tumults on account of religion, and the iterim in the year 1551, obliged it to submit to the house of Austria; so that the bishop's residence is at Merspurg, on the other side of the lake, his power here being very inconsiderable.

A passage-boat, which they call Ledi, goes from Constance to Lindau every Tuesday, but I did not chuse to wait for it. Lindau, and its adjacent territories,

ries, merit the elegant map made thereof by John Andrew Rauken. The town itself is situated in the lake of Boden, and thence termed the Venice of Swabia. It is joined to the continent by a bridge of two hundred and ninety paces in length. The Heidenmaure, or pagan wall, is said to be a work of the Romans, and on that account, but no other, merits observation.

An odd custom prevails in the villages of the forest of Bregentz, which is situated in the neighbourhood of Lindau, that the unmarried sons or servants of the peasants are permitted to have carnal knowlege of a girl; but, if she proves with child, they are obliged, under the most severe penalties, to marry her. They call this species of gallantry fuegen, consider it as very innocent, and are so bigoted to it, that an open insurrection was like to have been the consequence of an attempt made, a few years ago, by the government to put a stop to such a scandalous practice; nor is the dispute yet determined. An old grey-headed peasant, at a meeting on this important occasion, rose up, and seconded the prosecution of this affair, in the following remarkable speech: "My grandfather "fueged, my father fueged, I fueged, and therefore "my son, and all his successors, shall do the same."

The country in general between Lindau and Tirol, is but indifferent; great part of it is mountainous, and covered with woods, and the roads, especially between Kempten and Kemptenwald, remarkably bad: this is in a great measure owing to the perverse humour of some travellers, who will make use of their own carriages; whence the ruts become too narrow, and consequently very inconvenient and troublesome to others.

The Tirolese chain of mountains begins about a quarter of a league beyond Fussen. The passports with which all travellers are obliged to be provided, are signed at the Kniepass, and as soon as they arrive at Reuten, a small town in the valley, these passes

must

muſt be delivered to the commanding officer, who in return ſigns a certificate; none being permitted to paſs through the Ehrenburgherclauſe, without ſuch certificate. The ſame precaution is obſerved at the other paſſes into this country, by which means the governor of Inſpruck is informed of every perſon who viſits his province in twenty-four hours after their arrival. This country is entirely ſurrounded with a continued chain of mountains, and the paſſes are ſo far from being eaſy, that you are often at a loſs to diſtinguiſh them; and when, after many turnings and windings, you have diſcovered a paſſage, you will find it well defended by forts. Mr. Forſtener the privy councellor, in the year 1712, was aſſured by Charles Philip, elector palatine, at that time governor of this country, that ſeven thouſand men were ſufficient to defend the whole province againſt any number of enemies. It is one of the moſt profitable countries to the emperor of all his dominions, ſo that Maximilian I. did not without reaſon compare it to a peaſant's frock, which was at the ſame time very coarſe and very warm.

The ſilver, and other mines in Tirol, are now almoſt exhauſted; but in its mountains are found many kind of precious ſtones. The country abounds in ſalt, but no vines are found in the central parts. A traveller at his entering this province from Germany is amazed when he obſerves the lofty mountains, which from Ulminſter, are, even in the month of July, covered with ſnow. It is not at all uncommon, eſpecially before noon, to ſee the middle of the mountain involved in heavy clouds, while the parts above it are entirely clear almoſt to the ſummit, which is alſo involved in clouds. The ſummits of theſe mountains, are in general no more than rocky precipices; nor are there any trees of conſequence on the lower parts, a few dwarf pines and ſhrubs being the chief production.

Tirol,

Tirol, as well as Saltzburg, produce the Chamoiſe goat. Theſe creatures during the ſummer are not moleſted, their fleſh not then being in ſeaſon. The huntſmen, in order to follow this ſwift creature among the rocks and precipices, have a kind of ſmall iron hooks faſtened to their ſhoes, and ſometimes to their hands. There is often a kind of ſtone found in the ſtomach of theſe animals, reſembling the bezoar, and which, in this country, are ſold from three to ten guilders.

The Tirol peaſants, eſpecially the meaner ſort, make almoſt as deſpicable an appearance, as thoſe people we call gypſies; both ſexes wear hats of all colours. But notwithſtanding theſe marks of poverty, they are very zealous with regard to religion, and preſerve the warmeſt affection for their ſovereign, of which they gave convincing proofs at the beginning of the preſent century againſt the duke of Bavaria. Their houſes, barns, and ſtables, when compared with thoſe of other countries, are very mean, the covering being only boards placed horizontally, with no other faſtening than heavy ſtones laid upon them.

There are ſix ſtages between Fuſſen and Inſpruck; but which may be performed in one day. The roads are very good, and in ſeveral parts a commodious paſſage is cut, at a prodigious expence, through the rocks. The road runs along the ſide of the mountain, and nearly at an equal diſtance from the top and bottom of it. The paſſage is however very ſafe, being incloſed with wooden rails, ſupported at proper diſtances with ſtone poſts; and in ſome places, that carriages may not miſs the road, nor horſes ſtart at the ſight of the precipice, a wall of an adequate height, is erected along the ſide of the road. This way reaches to the old caſtle of Wernſtein, whoſe ſituation is extremely romantic. On the right ſide of the way, near a cuſtom-houſe belonging to this

 caſtle,

castle, is a natural cascade, beautiful but small, the water of which is conveyed through a wooden pipe into a statue of our blessed Saviour, and issues out again with great impetuosity and noise through an aperture in his side.

During the last stage you pass through the small town of Zurl, situated a long league from Inspruck, and immediately after you come to the rock, separated only by the road from the river Inn, on which Maximilian I. climbed to such a height in his eager pursuit of a chamoise, that nothing less was requisite to deliver him from his imminent danger, than the presence of an angel. And there is still preserved in the castle of Ambras, the Ostensorium, in which, if we will believe tradition, a consecrated host appeared to him at a distance, to his inexpressible joy, as an earnest of the assistance of heaven. A wooden cross forty feet high, and near it two statues, as big as life, of St. John and the holy Virgin, are placed on the very spot where the emperor is said to have stood, which is a niche in the mountain of Zurl, called also from its almost perpendicular steepness, St. Martin's wall; at such a height that the cross appears to a spectator, at the foot of the mountain, not to exceed two feet. The ascent is however, since the erection of this monument, rendered something easier, and though little less than two hundred feet from the plain below, the country boys very readily climb along the sides of the rocks into this cavity. Pfinzing's account of this miraculous affair is no more than this, that the emperor in hunting a chamoise near Inspruck, was in very great danger; for having climbed the rock to a vast height, the shank, together with all the nails, except one of his foot-irons, used in hunting these creatures, had given way; but the one that remained, though much bent, still held, by which means he was preserved. Heinsius adds, that he was saved by the peasants, who let him down by ropes.

Inspruck

Inſpruck is an elegant city; the ſtreets are well paved, and the palaces, after the Italian manner, grand and flat-roofed. The Jeſuits college, and the Franciſcan monaſteries form ſeveral ſtreets. The governor's palace, and the town-hall, are elegant buildings. The labours of Hercules are finely painted in freſco, in the hall of the palace; in the garden are grand ſalloons for aſſemblies, and an equeſtrian ſtatue of duke Ferdinand, which, notwithſtanding it is wholly braſs, and conſequently of a prodigious weight, reſts entirely on the hind feet of the horſe. Over the balcony in the chancery, is the famous golden roof; it conſiſts of copper-plates, overlaid with gold, and is ſaid to have coſt near two hundred thouſand dollars. The country people are perſuaded that the copper is now, by its long coheſion with the gold, abſolutely tranſmuted into that metal.

My curioſity was gratified in viewing the caſtle of Ambras, ſituated half a league from hence. In this ſeat belonging to the archduke, are to be ſeen great numbers of curioſities, collected at a prodigious expence, by the former proprietors of this country, particularly by the archduke Ferdinand. There is to be ſeen a large quantity of armour for tournaments, part for mere parade, part for uſe and ſervice; ſome for diſmounting an antagoniſt from his ſaddle, and others for actual execution and real combat; to each armour is annexed the effigy of the perſonage who wore it, together with his name, titles, and other additions.

Several of the ſuits of armour which belonged to the archduke of Auſtria have a kind of iron ſhoes or caſes, ſet with very long ſpikes or points. It is probable that the champion drove theſe points into his antagoniſt's horſe, and immediately afterwards drew back his foot: but it is evident, from a variety of inſtances in the hiſtory of the middle ages, that ſhoes furniſhed with long prongs were commonly worn, and for that reaſon called "*calcei lunati, cor-*

"*muti, rostrati,*" &c. Some of these spikes were an ell long; so that they were obliged to restrain this enormous luxury by particular laws. The like fashion I have observed not only in some antique German statues, but likewise in various pieces of tapestry in the palace at Brussels, made in the time of Philip duke of Burgundy, surnamed the Good. In some places this foolish ostentation was carried to a still greater height, by fastening little bells to these spikes. This practice will, however, appear the less absurd and ridiculous, when it is remembered, that the illustrious persons of that age used to wear such bells about their clothes, in order to give notice of their approach. Of this the stone statues of several dukes and duchesses of Brunswick, which are to be seen in the Autorshofe at Brunswick, together with the pictures of those princes that are in the town-house of Lunenburg, are sufficient proofs.

Against the wall stands a wooden statue of one Aymon, a volunteer in the guards of the archduke Ferdinand, who was eleven feet high, but died at about forty years of age. The famous imperial minister baron Bentenrieder, who likewise did not attain to a great age, was eight feet and eight inches high. As he was travelling this way some years ago, he measured himself with this wooden colossus, whereby it appeared, that he hardly reached to Aymon's armpits. At his side stands the wooden statue of a dwarf, who lived at the same time in the archduke's court, and was only three spans high. As the diminutive figure of the dwarf was often the subject of Aymon's laughter, the former privately requested the duke to drop his glove at table, and order Aymon to take it up: in the mean time the dwarf placed himself under the archduke's chair, and as Aymon stooped to take up the glove, he gave him a blow on the face, to the great diversion of the whole court. Here also is to be seen a stuffed horse, which, in the time of archduke Sigismund, from a sudden fright,

fright, leaped ſixteen paces, at a place near the village of Ambras; in memory of which two ſtones are erected: the action however proved fatal to both the horſe and his rider. In a box here is kept a piece of the halter with which Judas hanged himſelf; and near it is a certificate in the hand-writing of one Schertch, importing, that at the ſacking of Rome under Charles duke of Bourbon, this was obtained, and that the remaining part he made a preſent of to his own family at Mauren in the dutchy of Wirtemberg. I had here an opportunity of making particular obſervations on the behaviour of ſome Roman catholics, with regard to relics: the keeper of the palace, entruſted with the care of all the curioſities, on perceiving that catholics of the mean ſort are mixed with the company, in order to ſee every thing remarkable, only ſays at opening the box, that here is preſerved a rope which had been uſed at Chriſt's ſufferings; which words are no ſooner uttered, than the zealous catholics immediately kiſs the rope with the higheſt reverence and devotion; but this is ſcarce over, when the keeper purſues his narrative, and explains by whom, and for what purpoſe this rope was uſed; upon which the whole affair ends, with the company's laughing at thoſe zealots, who had ſo readily employed their devotion on a miſtaken object.

The cloſets of the upper gallery contain the moſt valuable curioſities, among which they ſhew the horſetail of the grand vizier, who in 1683 commanded at the ſiege of Vienna; and ſome conſecrated caps and daggers which were uſually ſent by the pope to ſovereign princes or celebrated commanders. Beſide which, there are ſeveral cloſets enriched with antiquities, paintings, medals, relics, and variety of natural and artificial curioſities.

Young gentlemen who have acquired a ſufficient ſtock of ſcience for travelling, cannot fail of reaping great advantage from the ſurvey of fine muſæums or well regulated cabinets of rarities: whence a great deal of light is thrown upon the knowlege of medals, natural and political history, mechanics, mathematics and antiquities; and it were to be wished that persons properly qualified could always be found for superintendants of such valuable curiosities, for not only a great deal of patience is requisite, but likewise the necessary knowlege of the things committed to their charge, for the better information of others.

The distance of Ambras from Inspruck is indeed some inconvenience to the gratifying the curiosity of travellers. Ambras was formerly the proper residence of the officers of the palace, it being a delightful place, and enjoying the most beautiful prospect in all Tirol, extended from Inspruck as far as Hall in the lower Inthal, both which fine countries want no decorations except that of vines. But for some time past the air about Ambras has been very unhealthful, especially during the night, whence various feverish disorders and fluxes are produced. The reason assigned for it is this: the imperial exchequer had formerly a large lake, lying between Ambras and Inspruck, appropriated for the breeding of fish, but by an ill-timed parsimony, the lake is choaked up with mud, and is at present no better than a morass, the noxious exhalations of which extend over the neighbouring parts. Upon a representation of this, the present keeper of the palace is permitted to reside with his family at Inspruck. A regulation has also lately been made with regard to the fees for viewing the curiosities; to the keeper two ducats at least, to the under-servants, who open the door and closets, two guilders, and one to the two soldiers who attend the company through every apartment.

Hall, a pleasant town of Inthall, is situated at about three quarters of a mile from Inspruck, and is remarkable for its mint, where an hundred and fifty dollars are stamped in a minute; the engine, which consists of two steel cylinders, or rollers, being turned by water. One of those cylinders are covered

with

with the dies for one ſide of a dollar, and the other with an equal number of the dies for the other ſide of the coin. The gold and ſilver plates, after being prepared of a proper thickneſs, are applied to theſe cylinders, and driven through betwixt them by their motion. The violent preſſure of theſe cylinders not only ſtrikes a clear impreſſion on both ſides of the piece, but alſo cuts them intirely from the plate, ſo that they fall of themſelves as they come out from between the cylinders. This machine requires only one man to attend it.

About a large league diſtant from this town are very lofty mountains, in which are ſalt mines, that have been worked for above an hundred years. The ſalt is dug out of capacious ſubterranean pits, in large maſſes, reſembling alum, but of ſeveral colours: it is mixed with dirt, and other heterogeneous ſubſtances, which renders its taſte leſs pungent than that of pure ſalt. It is carried from the mines to pits, filled with freſh water, where it is diſſolved, and the brine conveyed, by wooden pipes, to Hall, at which place it is boiled in iron pans, into white ſalt. The neat annual produce of the ſalt to the imperial chamber is nearly two hundred thouſand rix-dollars, notwithſtanding the mines and boiling employ near a thouſand hands.

The imperial mine at Schwatz is ſituated about a quarter of a league beyond Hall. There are nine hundred labourers in the mine, and the whole number of perſons, great and ſmall, belonging to it, is little ſhort of two thouſand. The ore, however, is far from being equal in readineſs to what it was formerly. In proportion as the mine was extended, the earth over it was ſupported by wooden props; but as theſe are very ſubject to decay, they now erect ſtone pillars in their ſtead, which is certainly an excellent method. Thoſe who viſit the parts of this mine that lie very deep, are conveniently carried along the level paſſages in ſmall carriages. It is computed, that forty pounds of copper are produced to every mark of silver. Few naturalists visit this mine without carrying away with them some of the flowers of iron and copper; the latter are remarkably beautiful, resembling large flakes of snow on an emerald ground.

There is, at some miles distant from Schawtz, in a mountainous part of the country, where ice continues all the year, a copper mine belonging to the lords of Sternbach. The metal produced by this mine is naturally so soft and malleable as to be used in the lace manufacture at Lyons; but may be hardened at pleasure.

The poorer sort of inhabitants of Tirol find very little employment at home, except in the mines and salt works; and being, like the inhabitants of other mountainous places, very prolific, are obliged to seek for bread in other countries; on which account it is a common practice among those who send their children abroad young, to prick some image on their arm with a needle, or the point of a knife; which punctures being rubbed over with a particular kind of black ink, the image never wears out, but many years after proves the means of discovering their family.

The persecuted Waldenses found a secure retreat in the desarts of the Tyrolese mountains toward Trent, and those of Saltzburg. In these desolate valleys the unhappy Waldenses pitched their habitations, and propagated a system of religion, which, in many points, agrees with that of the protestants. But one of these vallies lying in the diocese of the bishop of Brixen, his fiery zeal obliged those indigent people, whose religion had hitherto remained a secret, to abandon their habitations in the year 1681, and disperse themselves among the protestant states of Germany. And in 1688 the inhabitants of the valley of Tefferecker underwent the same fate.

The Bavarian salt-works are at Reichenhall, between Uncken and Saltsburg; and the salt-spring is so very considerable, that notwithstanding the great

quantity

quantity of ſalt-water uſed here, beſide that conveyed over the mountains to Traunſtein, a great deal is ſuffered to run to waſte. A ſtream of freſh water iſſues from the rock near the ſalt-ſpring; this current of freſh water is of great uſe, as it turns the wheels of their water-engines; but as both thoſe ſprings are ſurrounded by mountains, the place was often in danger of being overflowed by the conflux of theſe waters; to prevent which, an aqueduct was, about three hundred years ago, conſtructed at a prodigious expence. It is indeed a ſurpriſing work, the waters being conveyed in a channel half a league in length, under the town of Reichenhall, and under ſeveral fields and gardens, twelve fathoms below the ſurface of the ground. At the end of this channel the waters break out with great impetuoſity, into open day. Boats paſs through this canal in about a quarter of an hour; but there is a neceſſity for lighted candles, the motion being ſo rapid, that a great deal of care is requiſite in guiding the boat. The general depth of the water is between four and five feet, but it is often ſo much augmented by rains, that there is ſcarce room for the paſſengers to ſit upright in the boat. This canal is five feet in breadth, and the bottom of it is, every eight or ten years, cleared from ſtones, which either the floods have carried thither, or have been thrown down through the openings, or apertures built in the form of towers, and through which you may, from the walls of the city, ſpeak to thoſe who are paſſing in a boat through the aqueduct. The roof or arch which covers the aqueduct, is built of freeſtone, and coated over with a very hard ſpecies of roſin, ſo that it appears like one intire ſolid piece, and ſeems to promiſe to continue till the end of time. You deſcend to this ſubterraneous canal by a flight of ſtairs near the ſalt ſpring, the ſuperfluous water of which runs near fifty paces before it joins the ſtream of freſh water. The whole aquatic tribe avoid the ſalt ſtream before it mixes with the freſh; but after the two ſtreams are united, and the water, by that means, only brackiſh, it abounds with very fine trout, and ſeveral other ſorts of fiſh.

The ſalt of Reichenhall and Traunſtein in Bavaria, though not ſo pure and white as that of Hall in Swabia or of Saltſburg, is much cheaper and very ſtrong. The inhabitants of Saltſburg have anciently entered into ſeveral contracts with the Bavarians, by virtue of which they are to furniſh each other at a ſettled price; the former with ſalt, and the latter with corn: otherwiſe Saltſburg would often be in want of a market for its ſalt; as Auſtria on the one ſide, and Bavaria on the other, might prohibit the exportation of it. Notwithſtanding this, the elector of Bavaria has a very good price for the Saltſburg ſalt; the annual revenue of which amounts to ſome tons of gold. This ſalt is not conſumed wholly by his own ſubjects, large quantities are ſent abroad into France, Swabia, Bohemia, Switzerland up the Rhine, and Italy. Ratiſbon may be conſidered as a magazine for ſalt, from whence this neceſſary commodity is forwarded, by means of a little river, to Amberg and the upper Palatinate, and by the Danube to the countries adjacent.

Saltſburg is a very fine city, the houſes in general being five ſtories high; but the ſtreets are narrow, paved after the old faſhion. One part of the city is ſituated on a ſteep rock, whence the ſmall houſes on the bank of the river Saltz appear to be faſtened to thoſe on the rock, in the form of martins neſts.

In the area of the palace, oppoſite the new apartments, is a fountain, eſteemed the largeſt and grandeſt in all Germany. All the ſtatues are of white marble, but in the groteſque taſte. The circumference of the reſervoir, excluſive of the ſteps, is one hundred and ſeven feet. The water ſpouts from the mouths and noſtrils of four large horſes, but not in ſuch large quantities as from the ſtatues placed above them. The whole is above ſixty feet high, and from the top a column of water, ſeveral inches in diameter, is projected to the heighth of eighteen feet.

The palace is magnificent, containing a great variety of elegant pictures, tables of inlaid marble, grand ſtoves of all colours, and adorned with ſtatues. The tapeſtries, though nothing extraordinary, age having deprived them of their beauty, are valuable on account of the gold and ſilver. Near the palace, on a high mountain, ſtands the citadel.

The ſtables form three very long and lofty diviſions, arched; the mangers, out of which the horſes, being one hundred and fifty, eat, are of white marble. A ſtream of water is twice a week turned through the ſtalls on both ſides, by which means all the filth is carried away. Before theſe ſtables is a pond for watering the horſes, ninety-three feet long, in the center of which ſtands a large marble ſtatue of a horſe, the water flowing from his mouth.

A covered bridge leads you from the lower part of the city to the archbiſhop's palace of Mirabella, the middle part of whoſe capital-ſide is formed by an elegant chapel. Fronting it is mount Parnaſſus, having at the top a Pegaſus of braſs; but the water falls from this mount in caſcades, as in a wilderneſs. The grand ſtair-caſe of the palace is of white marble, and finely painted. The great hall is adorned with exquiſite landſcapes, elegant fiſh-pieces, and other paintings. The floors are inlaid with red and white marble, like thoſe in the city palace. The tapeſtry and other furniture are, in general, red, embroidered with gold and ſilver. The garden is very beautiful, being laid out within the fortification, in an elegant manner.

The city of Saltſburg is fortified with eleven baſtions. The troops of the archbiſhop amount to about a thouſand men, whoſe common uniform is white, faced with red; but ſometimes plain brown only. The life-guard and other officers are dreſſed in black, with red facings, and laced with gold.

Kleſheim

Klesheim is another palace belonging to the archbishop, and is situated three quarters of a league from the city: and about a quarter of a league from Saltsburg is another seat belonging to the archbishop, called Helburn. The edifice itself has nothing remarkable; but here are a great number of springs in this garden, and over one of them the statue of a monster, having a cock's comb, and eagle's feet, but in every other particular resembles a savage, or wild man. Under this statue is the following inscription:

"The original of this monstrous figure called a "forest-devil, was caught by the hunters near Havensburg, when Matthew Lang was cardinal and "archbishop; the skin of this monster was yellowish, "had all the marks of a savage disposition, but never "looked on any one, endeavouring to conceal himself in corners; his face resembled that of a man, "with a beard; his feet those of an eagle, with "lion's claws; he had a tail like a dog, and on his "head grew a large comb like that of a cock: he "would never, either by gentle or violent methods, "be prevailed upon either to eat or drink, so that "he soon died with hunger."

There are, in the menagery, some cranes, and a pelican, which is in reality only a species of bittern, having at his throat a large bag, in which he can deposit a large quantity of provisions. Beside these there are rock-eagles, lynxes, and two beavers, which have a young one; they live in the water, and are fed with the barks of trees, and small fish.

I was so fortunate as to arrive at Munich soon enough to be a spectator at the celebration of Corpus Christi festival. The procession consisted of many thousand persons, and continued a full hour and a half before the last passed by. Deputies from all the handicraft trades attended, having rich flags carried before them. The same thing was also done by the religious fraternities, not a member being absent at the solemnity. Children richly dressed exhibited the most remarkable religious hiſtories, in a great number of triumphal chariots. St. George and St. Maurice in Roman habits rode before their reſpective fraternities, among whom were many of the principal courtiers. A young lady dreſſed in a Roman habit repreſented St. Margaret, behind her a large dragon, in which two men were incloſed to give the figure its neceſſary motions. The four mendicant orders preceded the ſacred hoſt, which was carried under a rich canopy; and immediately after followed the elector, with his conſort on his left hand, both carrying in their hands a lighted taper. Next to the electreſs came her maſter of the houſhold, who was followed by ſome court ladies, and after theſe the whole court. The proceſſion was incloſed by the ſoldiers, burghers, and peaſants; and during the time the proceſſion ſtopped for the clergy to give their benediction to the people, which was done at four different places, eight pieces of cannon were fired from the fortifications.

The ſtreets through which the proceſſion paſſed were boarded, and in many places ſtrewed with herbs and flowers; but as it was continued along the Fauſſe-braye and round the city on the inſide of the walls, the exceſſive heat of the ſun muſt have made it very uneaſy to the prince and his conſort, as well as to the quality in general. The ladies of the court were dreſſed in the Spaniſh manner; but their complexions are greatly impaired from conſtantly attending the electors proceſſions, parties of pleaſure and hunting-matches, in exceſſive heat and cold, in rain, wind and ſunſhine. The electreſs is remarkably fond of her huſband, and generally in his company. She eats and plays with him, accompanies him to the ſtables, ſhoots excellently either at a mark or the game, and it is not uncommon for her in hunting to be up to the knees in a moraſs. If her coachman can by any means bring her in at the death of a ſtag, he is ſure of receiving a piece of gold to the value of ſeven guilders and a half. But endeavouring to do this a

few

few weeks ago he overturned her twice in one morning; but her electoral highneſs not only gave him the cuſtomary gratuity, but likewiſe procured his pardon from the elector, which he the leſs deſerved, as the electoreſs was then well known to be pretty far advanced in her pregnancy. In hunting ſhe wears a green coat and a little white wig, the dreſs in which ſhe made her firſt appearance in this country, and in which her picture is drawn at Kleſheim. She is exceſſively fond of dogs, as may be more eſpecially obſerved from the ſcarlet damaſk tapeſtry and the beds at Nymphenburg. The ſmall Engliſh greyhounds are her greateſt favourites at preſent; of which great numbers ſtand round her table, and one on each ſide of her highneſs ſnatching at every thing within their reach. The elector has alſo a vaſt many hounds, which was ſo much his father's taſte, that even when affairs obliged him to retire into France, he kept the fineſt pack of hounds in that kingdom. Louis the XIVth, obſerving a favourite bitch belonging to the elector, ſaid jeſtingly to baron Freyburg, the elector's great huntſman, "I have been told, "that your bitch often loſes ſcent of the game." To which the baron, with ſome warmth, replied, "How! She's as ſure as the goſpel."

At preſent the elector has only a few regular troops; but can in a ſmall time bring into the field a powerful army raiſed in his own dominions.

The trade in corn, beech maſt, white beer and ſalt, produce conſiderable ſums. At Munich from ſpring till the beginning of June they brew a ſort of white beer, called Ambock, which is very ſtrong, and in taſte reſembles the fine Engliſh ale, but will not keep ſo well. The monopoly of this liquor produces above a million of guilders yearly.

The electoral palace at Munich conſiſts of four courts: that called the prince's, which is adorned with great numbers of braſs ſtatues, and another termed the emperor's, are the moſt beautiful: the

conſtruction

construction of the latter is adapted to exhibit the combats of wild beasts. But the largest is that called the kitchen-court; in which a very splendid tournament was held at the elector's marriage. The old square is reckoned the meanest of the four, though far from being inelegant.

By permission from his serene electoral highness, his first gentleman of the bedchamber, Mr. du Lac, shews the musæum, which was indeed before the last unhappy commotions and disturbances in Bavaria, much richer than at present, though few in Europe can even now be said to equal it.

On the left hand, near the door of the old part of the palace, lies a large black stone, and some German verses on the wall near it, importing, that in 1409, duke Christopher of Bavaria took up this large stone weighing three hundred and forty pounds, and threw it to some distance. About a year ago a Bavarian country girl raised this stone about a hand's height from the ground. Near the same door are also three iron nails driven into the wall with German lines denoting that the first of these nails, which is twelve feet from the ground, shows the leap of duke Christopher; the second, which is ten feet and a half, was reached by Zundritt; the third, which is nine feet and a half, indicates Philip Springer's activity.

King Gustavus Adolphus was so charmed with the beauty of the city of Munich, that he said he wanted only rollers to remove it to some other place, well knowing it would be impossible to keep possession of this country. But had it been the fortune of this prince to have seen the city in its present condition; its straight broad streets adorned with many stately structures, both churches and palaces equalled by few cities in Europe, must have rendered this capital still more charming, in his opinion.

With regard to the ecclesiastical buildings, the churches of St. Anne and the Theatine are worth

seeing,

ſeeing, on account of their ſtucco-work. In the laſt on the left hand ſtands a holy ſepulchre; and on the right a ſcala ſancta, conſiſting of twenty-eight ſteps, the ſame as at Rome. No perſon is permitted to touch them with his feet, thoſe who aſcend them muſt do it on their knees, ſaying on each a certain number of Pater Noſters and Ave Marias. This muſt be extremely painful to thoſe whom I obſerved aſcending with extended arms and the moſt intenſe devotion, as they cannot perform it in leſs than half an hour. Before I ſaw this religious exerciſe, I was at a loſs to underſtand what the beggar boys meant, by promiſing, that for a few pfennings or farthings, they would ſay the Pater Noſter for the welfare of their benefactors with their arms fully extended.

The church of our Lady is decorated with two large towers, and in it is the magnificent monument of the emperor Lewis of Bavaria, conſiſting of black marble, adorned with ſix large, beſide ſeveral ſmall ſtatues of braſs. At a little diſtance from one of the doors is a ſtone with a mark upon it, from whence a ſpectator cannot, by reaſon of the great number of pillars, ſee a ſingle window in the church. But it muſt be owned, that this ſtructure cannot boaſt of being the moſt illuminated in Europe; and it is ſurely of greater advantage to a church that a great number of windows may be ſeen, than for every one of them to be concealed.

The roof of the jeſuits church is remarkably lofty, and about thirty-three common paces in breadth. It is generally conſidered as a raſh undertaking, but much leſs ſo than the new bridge which Sauli has undertaken to build at Genoa. This college is large, and the library well furniſhed with ancient books, but very few modern. A gallery between ſeven and eight feet in height runs quite round it, and renders the books eaſy to be conſulted. In the college they ſhew one joint of St. Chriſtopher's backbone; but ſhould the creature to whoſe body this piece actually be-

longed

longed appear, instead of a benevolent saint, I am persuaded we should see some frightful elephant or whale.

In a house situated near the Augsburg gate, is painted the story of a wheelwright, who about twenty years ago laid a wager, that he made a wheel at Augsburgh in the morning and drove it to Munich before sun-set, though these two places are nine miles asunder, and actually performed it.

The great resort of people to celebrate the feast of Corpus Christi, furnished me with an opportunity of seeing the various dresses worn by the peasants of Bavaria; among others the women inhabiting the wilds or forests about eight leagues from Munich, engaged my attention; they wore broad felt hats or bonnets, on which was a small knob or prominence behind near the neck, no bigger than a walnut. On holydays the servant maids of the large inns at Munich, wear round their necks a silver chain, consisting of three rows; and their breasts are likewise laced with two other chains of the same metal.

I observed that it was a general custom here to place before every house containing the corps of an unmarried person, a large green garland on a bundle of straw. The same custom prevails also in some places of Brabant, bordering upon Holland; and in Overyssel they hang a large lanthorn without a candle at the door of a house in which there is a dead body.

The number of inhabitants at Munich is said to be forty thousand.

The distance between Munich and Sleisheim is about three leagues, but you are seldom more than an hour and a half in performing the journey: the elector is but half that time. For several miles round Munich, the road is level, but the soil gravelly.

The palace of Sleisheim has a very good entrance; both the pavement and rows of pillars are of red and grey marble. The red marble is produced in Bavaria, but the green, several columns of which beautify the

 stairs,

ſtairs, is brought from Brixen. In the firſt hall are two large paintings, one repreſenting the raiſing the ſiege of Vienna, and the other the battle of Hagaz. Contiguous to it, in the victory hall, are paintings of the battles of Belgrade, Peſt, and other places, where the late elector gained ſo much honour, done by Bruch, who is ſtill living. The freſco paintings were performed by Amadoni. The furniture of the bed-chamber of the electreſs is yellow damaſk embroidered with ſilver; and at a ſmall diſtance from the bed of her highneſs is a little tent and cuſhion of the ſame for a favourite dog. On one ſide is a half length Jeſus, crowned with thorns, made in Latour's loom, but as natural and elegant as if it had been painted. In another chamber is alſo a picture of Penelope, with her women, attentive at their work, performed in 1503 by Abraham de Lele. In an apartment over it, is a cabinet of ſtucco-work, ſo highly finiſhed, as to appear equal to the fineſt marble. On the other ſide toward Munich is a grand gallery of pictures, the largeſt of which are hunting pieces by Rubens.

But the greateſt collection is in a particular apartment, the walls of which are covered with ſmall pictures; though only the nobleſt productions of that find a place in this repoſitory. The late elector, who made this collection, poſſeſſed a great variety of excellent pieces, having at one time purchaſed in the Netherlands a quantity of pictures, to the value of two millions of guilders.

The lower ſtory is hung with elegant tapeſtry of ſilk, from Flanders and other places. There is alſo here a table of caſt ſilver, and a muſical clock which imitates an organ; a ball within ſide moves in very different directions as in a labyrinth, till it ſeems to loſe itſelf; but immediately, like the power of a perpetual motion, aſcends to repeat its former courſe.

The bed-chamber of the elector is directly under that of the electreſs, and has a communication with it by a flight of ſtairs. A ſort of kennel for a dog is placed

placed near the elector's bed, and in a fine closet adjoining, are the like for twelve others.

Behind the palace of Sleisheim is an elegant garden. The middle walk has on each side a canal, in which are several small fountains. The garden at Sleisheim is entirely surrounded with moats and rows of trees.

The hunting-matches, held by the present elector's grandfather, have afforded subjects for several capital pieces preserved at Lustheim; the persons represented in these pieces were all drawn from the life.

About a league from Munich, on the other side, is situated the palace of Nymphenburg; which, though inferior to Sleisheim in grandeur, greatly excels it as a summer's retreat, by its elegant gardens and waterworks.

The mall and bowling-green are on the side of this building farthest from the palace, and contiguous to the former is the Pagodenburg, whither the elector, after violent exercises at these games, retires to change his linen and apparel. In this little structure are several small cabinets, resembling those of China, with many other pieces adapted equally to ornament and use.

Between Pagodenburg and the palace, is a small hermitage, so naturally resembling a building in ruins, that it cannot fail of attracting the admiration of the spectator. It appears in some places as if it had been repaired with lime and stones; the cracked walls and bricks hardly hanging together in another part, seem to threaten every moment to bury you under their ruins. In short, art has here so well imitated the ravages of time, that one of our company, who had never before visited this place, asked our guide seriously, and by way of contempt, who was the architect of so inelegant a work? To this place the late elector had some thoughts of retiring, in order to employ his whole time in religious contemplations, with no other attendants than his father confessor and a valet de chambre; but death prevented him from putting this design in execution. There is in this structure, which is situated in a kind of desart, a large grotto, containing a consecrated altar, on which are placed two candlesticks and a crucifix, all three made out of the horn of an unicorn. The other apartments are destitute of any ornament, except a small collection of religious books bound in the French manner. The utensils of both the kitchen and cellar, are only a neat sort of earthen ware. The archbishop of Cologne consecrated the altar about a year ago, at which ceremony the company made themselves so merry that they broke a quantity of glasses to the value of two hundred dollars.

Starenberg, another electoral palace, is situated three leagues from Munich. The court often retires hither to enjoy a particular diversion called water-hunting, which is performed in this manner: a stag is forced into a large lake in the neighbourhood, and pursued by the dogs, the huntsmen following him in boats, and their highnesses in a splendid barge, mounting twenty-four brass guns. There is a large piece of painting at Nymphenburg representing this kind of hunting.

Here also the court is amused with hunting the heron; and a custom has long prevailed at the conclusion of it every year, to set at liberty a heron which has been fortunate enough to be taken alive; putting on its leg a silver ring, on which is engraved the name of the reigning elector. Last spring they took one of these birds a second time, there being found on it a ring bearing the name of Ferdinand, grandfather to the present elector; and, consequently, this bird must have survived its former adventure sixty years at least. After putting on it another ring, containing the name of the present elector, they again set it at liberty. An eagle, after being confined one hundred and four years, died at Vienna in the year 1719; and it seems natural to think that birds of this

kind

kind which enjoy their freedom, live a much greater number of years.

The Wallersee, which lies not far from Benedict-Bavaria, is another natural curiosity of this country. It lies on an eminence, and both its banks and adjacent ground are so porous, that the water finds a passage through to another lake beneath it, called the Knochelsee. Mass is said every day in the place called the grotto of Munich, to implore the assistance of heaven in preventing any breach in the banks of the Wallersee, as the country adjacent would be in danger of an inundation from such an accident.

The protestants and papists are easily distinguished from each other by their manner of salutation. In the year 1587, Sixtus V. in order to introduce the salutation, 'Praised be Jesus Christ,' and the answer, 'For ever, Amen,' granted an indulgence of an hundred days to the use of it: but notwithstanding this indulgence, it was either never made use of, or entirely forgot till the year 1728, when the grant was renewed by Benedict XIII. The Italians however have neglected to adopt this form of salutation, but in the German catholic provinces, stiled by the Italians, *Terra Obedientiæ*, the land of obedience, it entirely prevails, except among the courtiers: the commonalty, nobility, and even the ladies very punctually observe it. That this custom tends much more to the abuse of the name of Christ, than to the honour of it, will sufficiently appear to any one passing by the public houses in the evening, where I have frequently heard fellows who were so drunk as to be scarcely able to stand, stuttering at leaving their companions, 'Praised be Jesus Christ,' and the company within answering, almost inarticulately, 'For ever, Amen.' But a late action of count N——, is still more extraordinary. He sent for a prostitute to his lodgings, and the lady on entering his chamber, said, 'Praised be Jesus Christ,' to which he answered, 'For ever, Amen; down with your breast-lace.'

It is impracticable to leave Munich with post-horses, without obtaining from the marshal of the court, or his deputy, a written order, which will cost twelve kreitzers (near six-pence sterling.) This is not, however, the only place where this imposition is practised, it being done in several others, particularly at Cassel and Paris.

From Saltsburg to Augsburg there are large tracks of level land; and I particularly observed a large extent of arable land, interspersed with woods, without a single mountain; yet I had not the pleasure of seeing a single vineyard.

Augsburg is a fine city*, but, like Munich, not equal to what it was formerly. Its trade was once the most considerable in all Germany, but it has suffered extreamly from the declension of that of Venice. In this city are reckoned to be six thousand burghers. The council consists of an equal number of Lutherans and Roman catholics: the latter daily increase in this city; and it must be owned, to their praise, that they live with more œconomy. The dress of the professors of both religions is different, whence they are easily distinguished.

The council house is esteemed the finest in all Germany; and the main-guard of the city, with six field pieces, mount here. The walls are decorated with brass bustos of the first twelve Roman emperors.

In the center of an adjacent square, or near the Perlach tower, is an elegant fountain, adorned with four statues of brass representing the four seasons, and in the middle, another of the emperor Augustus, with proper inscriptions. In the wine market there is likewise a fountain, with a metallic statue of Hercules. The bishop's palace, otherwise but a mean building, contains the hall, in which the Augsburg confession was presented to the emperor Charles V. in 1550, [by Luther and Melancthon.] It can however beast

* Augsburg is the capital of Swabia.

of

of no other furniture at present, than a few old tables and benches.

On the brass door of the cathedral, among other scriptural histories, the Virgin Mary is represented as forming Eve out of Adam's rib. The revenue of this bishopric is so considerable, that the younger princes of the electoral houses of Bavaria and Palatine generally enjoy it.. A canonship is worth from a thousand to a thousand seven hundred guilders annually, according as corn is cheap or dear.

The monks belonging to St. Ulrick's convent, dispose of a kind of dust or powder, which they call St. Ulrick's earth, from that holy man, who, they tell you, commanded all the rats in the city and neighbourhood to retire into a hole, which to this day is shewn in the church of that saint. They dig this powder near the place where he was buried, and pretend that it owes its virtue to its having lain near his sacred bones.

But it should be remembered, that the earth of the church-yard of Herzenberg, three leagues from Tubingen, is used as an antidote against rats in the same manner as that of St. Ulrick. That the bones of dead bodies drive away some sorts of vermin from mankind, is beyond all dispute; and very probably the earth of other church-yards, where several corps have mouldered away, may prove an effectual preservative against rats. But be this as it will, experience tells me, that St. Ulrick's earth, however successful at Augsburg, cannot boast of its virtue when carried to other places.

In Mr. Cosmo Conrad Cuno's Musæum, I had the pleasure of seeing a great variety of curiosities; and among others, several pieces of wood, in the inside of which, a crucifix, the name Maria, with other words and figures were conspicuous. These figures did not however owe their origin to supernatural causes, but to deep incisions made in the bark while the tree was young. The circles annually formed by the accretion of the tree, extend themſelves under the bark, and receive that figure which was impreſſed on the part and contiguous wood; ſo that in proceſs of time, the external bark with the inciſion made therein, cloſe up. From the bare inſpection of the wood, it ſufficiently ſhews that this was the real cauſe. Mr. Cuno has in his poſſeſſion, a ſmall piece of the fuſtian manufactured by the Fuggers in 1461; but a larger piece is preſerved in the Weaver's-hall. He alſo has a collection of above ſeventy different kinds of birds neſts: I remember to have ſeen the ſame among the king of Poland's rarities at Dreſden. I likewiſe obſerved here ſuch minute chains, that ſome of them were not too heavy for a flea; alſo cups of ivory, having a ring round the middle, but ſo ſmall, that they cannot be ſeen without the aſſiſtance of a microſcope, and a hundred of them may be put into a peppercorn. There is, however, no art required in making theſe, they being formed at one ſingle impreſſion, and almoſt in an inſtant, with the proper tools. The artiſts of Augſburg, as well as thoſe of Nuremberg, have always been very famous; nor are they at preſent wanting here.

Among the public ſtructures the Einlaſs, or entrance, as it is called, is very curious: it was invented by a Tiroleſe peaſant, and is managed by two men only. This contrivance has removed the trouble and danger they were formerly expoſed to, when they opened the city gates in the night for courtiers or travellers. A great many, either foot or horſe, may be admitted as well as a ſingle perſon. For this purpoſe a draw-bridge goes up and down; and as often as one gate ſhuts, another opens with a loud noiſe. In ſhort, both for convenience and ſecurity, the contrivance cannot be mended.

The road between Augſburg and Ulm is, in general, ſandy and the great number of ſloughs in the ſecond ſtage, render travelling ſo very tedious, that a journey

journey of nine ſhort German miles, requires a number of hours to perform it.

Ulm, when compared with the adjacent cities, may be ſaid to be well fortified. The Patricians have here an excluſive privilege of walking on the ramparts, nor will they ſuffer either the burghers or ſtrangers to appear there without paying a guilder. This practice proceeds more from avarice than from any apprehenſion of a clandeſtine correſpondence; for the hay and fruits growing on the ramparts belonging to the Patricians, they are very careful in guarding againſt every thing that has a tendency to diminiſh their profit.

The proſpect from the cathedral ſteeple, which is four hundred and one ſteps high, is remarkably beautiful, the whole country round lying on a level. It appears from an inſcription on the wall, that Maximilian I. in the year 1492, climbed up to one of the upper galleries; ſome add, that ſtanding on one foot, on the edge of the wall, he made a croſs in the air with the other. Sixty-three large copper kettles filled with water are hung up in ſeveral parts of the tower, and along the roof of the church, that in caſe any accident ſhould happen from fire or lightning, they may always have water ready at hand. There is alſo a machine, by the help of which the watchmen on the tower draw up their proviſions and other neceſſaries.

The city of Ulm muſt not, however, be ſuppoſed to be equal to what it formerly was; though this declenſion is not peculiar to Ulm, but common to many other imperial free towns. I am ſatisfied from obſervations I made during a former excurſion through this country, that the ſmaller and poorer the imperial towns are, the more the inhabitants abandon themſelves to a voluptuous way of living, and a variety of expenſive diverſions; without once reflecting on the inevitable conſequences, or ſhewing the

leaſt

least regard for the public happiness. The neighbouring states of greater power, sometimes indeed, rouse them from their lethargy: but as the managers of the finances can depend on the favour of the judge, and the assistance of their fraternity, they soon relapse into their former state.

Excepting some few mountainous parts in the Schwartz or Black Forest, and those on the Alps, the Dutchy of Wirtemberg may be classed among the happiest countries in Germany; and with regard to the pleasant intermixture of hills and vallies, may very justly be compared with Transylvania. This dutchy is said to contain fourteen prelates and abbots, four of whom are jointly superintendants-general, and thirty-six particular superintendants, and about five hundred and seventy ministers of parishes; seventy-two small towns and districts, twelve hundred villages, and about four hundred and fifty thousand inhabitants.

The duke of Wirtemberg, immediately after the repeal of the edict of Nantz, might have drawn very considerable advantages from granting reception to the French refugees; not only as there were many rich people among them, but also as several profitable manufactures, which have enriched Brandenburgh and other places, might have been introduced into this country: but a blind zeal for religion, and the clamours of the clergy, who gave out that it was better to admit Mahometans than Calvinists, filled the assembly of the states with such fears and jealousies as utterly frustrated the good intentions of the court. A cool reflection afterward opened the eyes of the people; but it was now too late, and they had only the mortifying prospect of seeing what a valuable opportunity they had lost.

On the death of the last Duke of Mompelyard, this princely territory, together with the seignory of Etoban and Magni d'Anegon, as being German fiefs, reverted to the illustrious house of Wirtemberg

Stutgard;

Stutgard; but the four lordships of Blamont, Clemont, Chatelot, and Hericourt, which produce an annual revenue of above four hundred thousand French livres, are still possessed by the French.

On my arrival at Stutgard, I had the honour of paying my respects to the duchess, and could not help admiring her singular goodness and resignation. The duke is of a majestic presence, and his noble qualities have gained him the love and esteem of his subjects, who incessantly offer up their prayers to heaven for an heir to their hereditary princes: well knowing that a catholic succession must be attended with very fatal consequences to that country.

The house of Wirtemberg, among other privileges, enjoys the court-judicature, a jewel of equal value with that of the court of appeal among the electors. The learned treatise written by Mr. Schoopf, relating to it, explains very minutely the manner of proceeding in this court, and sufficiently shews they might be advantageously introduced into higher courts of judicature. One advantage peculiar to this tribunal, is the speedy dispatch of justice; all pleadings here must be verbal; nor is sentence ever delayed till the succeeding day.

I never knew so many commissions for trivial matters issued in any country as in this; by which means many delays are occasioned in national affairs, the state and commission counsellors being mostly absent on such commissions, so that very often three or four only belonging to this court shall be at Ludwigsburg. Such tedious and expensive inquiries only tend to ruin the subject, and enrich the commissioners. Mr. Culpis used to call the territories of Wirtemberg, *Regnum Pharisæorum et Scribarum*, "A land of Scribes and Pharisees;" and probably this might be one, perhaps the principal, reason for such a sarcasm.

The duke's troops amount to four thousand men, including the contingent of the circle, which is eighteen hundred.

The

The order of hunting was founded at the beginning of the present century; and its statutes renewed and enlarged in 1719. The companions of this order enjoy the particular privilege of being preferred before any others to commanderies, each of which is worth about five hundred guilders per annum. The ensign of this order is a hunting horn, being the usual arms of the former counts of Urach, in which family the office of great huntsman of the Holy Roman empire was made hereditary; and whose lands, some hundred years ago, fell to the house of Wirtemberg. The knights of the order have a privilege of being present at all public solemnities, and particularly at the royal hunting matches, and also those of the master and companions of the order. Beside an arbitrary number of princes and persons of rank, this order consists of twelve antient counts of the empire, thirty knights, and a secretary. The emblem of the order is a cross of pure gold, resembling that of Malta, adorned with rubies, having at each corner an eagle of solid gold, and between the middle and lower point of each, a hunting horn; in the center is a circular shield of green enamel, on one side of which is a golden W, surmounted with a ducal coronet, the emblem of Wirtemberg, and on the other side the arms of that dutchy, being three gold hunting horns twisted together. This cross is commonly pendant to a very broad crimson ribbon watered, worn over the left shoulder, and hanging down to the right side. On the left breast of their coat they wear an embroidered silver star, in the center of which is the emblem of the order, and round it the motto, *Amicitiæ virtutisque fœdus*, "the bond of virtue and friendship," embroidered with gold on a green circle. The festival on which the general chapter is held, is that of St. Hubert's day; and wherever the sovereign of the order happens on that day to be, there is a grand hunting match. Those who cannot possibly appear at the chapter, must, if possible

possible, celebrate the day with a hunt, and other expressions of loyalty. If any knight be seen in public, without the cross, he forfeits to the informer a pair of elegant pistols, and also twenty rixdollars to the poor. But whoever neglects, during a year and a day, to wear the ensigns of the order, is degraded.

The duke is very fond of hunting, and from the nature of his country, has better opportunities of indulging that passion, than almost any prince of Germany. It is the customary method in London, Paris, and other large cities, to calculate the number of inhabitants from the bills of mortality; in the same manner a conjecture may be formed, of the prodigious quantity of deer in this country, from the number that perish in a severe winter: it is said, that during the winters of 1731 and 1733, above twenty thousand head of red deer and wild boars were destroyed.

The number of hunting seats belonging to the duke of Wirtemberg is considerable; and these he visits alternately, according to the seasons for hunting the deer or wild boar; by which means he visits his principal forests once in five years.

A very ancient custom prevails through the whole country of Wirtemberg, of decorating their apartments and galleries with large horns of deer; and it is natural to imagine that these decorations are not wanting at hunting seats. At Waldeburg, over the largest horns are written the names of those persons who shot the deer: and the dexterity of the reigning duke, has filled some rooms with them. At the hunting seat of Einsidel in Schonbuch, about half a mile distance from Tubingen, among others are to be seen two remarkable horns of deer, which in rutting time the creatures thrust into each others branches, in such a manner, that it was impossible to disengage them, so that both the creatures died on the spot. A curiosity of the same kind is deposited in the Royal Musæum at Copenhagen. At Einsidel is a large hawthorn, raised from a twig, brought by Everhar-

dus

dus Barbatus in his hat from the Holy Land, upward of two hundred years since, and set here with his own hands. In the time of Crusius, this thorn had spread to the circumference of fifty-two ells; its branches were supported by forty stone pillars, and its stock could not be grasped by any single person. Hence a superstitious notion has been propagated, that the house of Wirtemberg will decline in proportion as this thorn decays. It is however many years since this thorn has been damaged, both in its trunk and branches, and is at present but in a very indifferent condition.

All the princes of the house of Wirtemberg Stutgard seem born for heroic actions. Prince Maximilian, when scarcely fourteen years of age, accompanied Charles XII. of Sweden in all his campaigns; and even then attacked, sword in hand, at the surprize of the town of Pultausk, an old Saxon trooper, who turning on his heel with surprize, said, "Thou little son of a whore, art thou already for cracking the skull of an old experienced soldier?" and with that would have given the prince his quietus, had not Charles XII. rescued him. The prince himself, at the request of certain persons of distinction, related the whole affair, till he came to the trooper's speech, which he thought reflected on his honour, and therefore broke off the narrative, adding, "You cannot be ignorant of what the trooper said."

In the year 1703, during the darkness of the night, this prince riding full speed before the king, stopped short at a large pit: the king imagining he did this through fear of the enemy, called out, Forward, forward: accordingly, the prince immediately clapping spurs to his horse, leaped into the pit. The king was so close behind him, that he also shared the same fate, falling with his horse upon the prince, who was taken out almost dead. This action rendered him so dear to the king, that he sat up by him during the whole night. At the unfortunate battle of Pultowa,

where

where he commanded the Schonen regiment of dragoons, he had the misfortune of being taken prisoner. The czar offered him a commission, but he answered, "While I have a drop of blood in my veins, I will employ it in the service of my benefactor the king of Sweden." The czar was so charmed with this generous answer, he gave him his liberty; and also presented him with the sword he then wore. Whether, from an ill-timed gratitude to the Russians, he drank too liberally at parting, or whether the fatigues of the preceeding campaigns broke his constitution, is not certainly known: however the prince, on his return to Wirtemberg, was in the same year, namely 1709, seized with a violent fever, of which he died in the 21st year of his age, when youth was in its highest bloom, and his hopes well founded, that by his marriage with the princess Ulrica, he should one day fill the throne of Sweden.

The inhabitants of Wirtemberg carried on formerly, and even at the beginning of the present century, a considerable trade to Bavaria with their Necker wines. Both provinces found their account in this commerce; the Bavarians, instead of ready money, paying the value of the wine in salt. But when the imperialists became masters of Bavaria, affairs were conducted in a different manner, and this electorate furnished with wines from the neighbouring countries of Austria, Tirol and Franconia.

The importation of Franconian wines was greatly promoted by the imperial minister; count Lowenstein, as it was of the greatest advantage to his estates lying in that country: and this trade still continues, notwithstanding it is doubly detrimental to the Wirtembergers; for the wines will not keep any long time, and they are obliged to purchase salt with ready money.

This country, beside its arable lands and vineyards, has likewise excellent mineral springs, of which I shall only at present mention the baths and waters of Boller,

ler, Zaisenhauser, Wild, Teinacher, Liebenzeller, Rithenauer and Goppinger.

I must however add, with regard to the policy of this country, that in all the cities, towns, and large villages, they have a certain kind of officers, called private overseers, who inspect offences, clandestine meetings, and other enormities of their fellow burghers, making a report to the magistrates of the place, in order that a further inquiry may be made. These private censors or inquisitors are absolutely unknown to all but the magistrates, and are sworn to discharge their office faithfully. They have no salary, but are always preferred before any other persons, to some place or employment in the magistracy. As the accuser is constantly concealed, it may be productive of several abuses, should their bare reports ever be esteemed sufficient evidence, instead of information. This regulation has a near affinity with the denuncie secrete, or secret informations at Venice; and I much question whether any such thing is to be met with in all Germany beside.

Stutgard is situated in a pleasant country, interspersed with gardens and vineyards; so that, had the money expended at Ludwigsburg, been employed here in building a stately palace near Berge or Caustadt; it would have been equal to most in Europe, with regard to the beauty of its situation. Little notice is however taken of that truly noble palace at Stutgard; this is already particularly perceived in the banqueting-house, where the ridottos were formerly kept. This structure merits the observation of every traveller, on account of its hall, with which few in Europe are comparable: it is two hundred and twenty feet long, eighty in breadth, and ninety in height; without having a single pillar to support its arched roof, which is very ingeniously fastened together by means of wooden screws. The cieling is decorated with scripture histories; but the sides, with views of all the forests belonging to the dutchy of

Wirtemberg, and ſome merry adventures that happened at the hunting matches.

There is at preſent nothing remarkable in the ducal palace but the main ſtair-caſe, which aſcends ſo gradually without ſteps, that one may ride up or down it.

Ludwigſburg, which is two leagues diſtant from Stutgard, was formerly only a ſtall, or houſe for breeding of cattle; nor is there any probability that the duke at firſt intended to lay out ſuch quantities of money as he has done, ſince the counteſs of Gravenitz gained the aſcendant; and his highneſs began to conceive, by degrees, a greater diſlike to Stutgard, where his conſort the ducheſs reſided. It muſt be allowed that the palace is one of the fineſt buildings in Germany. And many are of opinion, that it is at preſent carried beyond perfection, as the prodigious height of the new buildings intercept the proſpect of the gardens, and by that means leſſen its former beauty. On account of the continual carriage of ſtone, timber, lime, &c. no pavement has yet been thought on, ſo that a perſon is greatly incommoded, either by the great quantity of duſt flying, or in rainy weather by the mud and clay; notwithſtanding which, moſt of the chambers have already been moved hither, to the great detriment of thoſe officers who have houſes of their own at Stutgard.

The palace is quite new furniſhed: and in particular the looking-glaſs and lackered cloſet, are worth ſeeing; as alſo the large ſtair-caſe for ambaſſadors, its beautiful cieling, and the gallery of paintings. Among theſe are ſome exquiſite night-pieces, and a great variety of fine pictures of dogs and horſes, eſpecially that of a black wolf, which had long been kept at court: he was called Melak, followed the duke every where, and ſlept near his bed. He was once with the duke in the army upon the Rhine, but the campaign continuing till the weather grew cold, Melak was tired of the field, and found very unexpectedly at Ludwigſburg, before the duke's chamber-door; no body knowing how he croſſed the Rhine. In the ſame manner he ſtole away from Frankfort, without taking his leave, probably not much liking the firing of ſo many guns at the emperor's coronation in 1711. Whatever his fidelity might be to the duke, he was ſly and miſchievous to others; and once bit a large piece out of colonel Forſtner's back, when no ſuch thing, was expected.

The chapel of the palace is very elegant, but ſomething too ſmall, and has this great inconvenience attending it, namely, that near the veſtry ſeveral common ſewers meet together. One would almoſt believe that this was done on purpoſe by the Popiſh architects, among whom Friſoni was the chief; it muſt however be owned, that theſe Italians are ſuch ingenious artiſts, that they commit very few miſtakes in ſuch ſtately ſtructures.

The duke expends a great deal of money in ſtuds of horſes, of which he is a great lover, and a good judge. At preſent he has three ſets of horſes, each conſiſting of eight, which the coachman, without the help of a poſtilion, can manage, though at the ſame time they perform all the curvets of the manege; and ſometimes the duke himſelf is ſeen on the coach-box. In honour of this prince it muſt be ſaid, that hard drinking is not ſo much in repute at his court as formerly it has been: however, any one who deſires to be honoured after the ancient cuſtom, will not be long here, before he finds perſons ready to gratify his inclinations.

The caſtle of Hohin-Tubingen is at preſent conſidered only as a hunting ſeat, whither the duke uſually retires with his court once in five years. The city of Tubingen, which is ſituated near the mountain, conſiſts of about five thouſand ſouls, and is celebrated for its univerſity. The vallies of Ammer, Stecker, and Luſtenauer, render the ſituation of this place as agreeable as moſt in Germany. In the caſtle are good

6 apart-

apartments; and formerly it muſt have been looked upon as a place of conſiderable ſtrength, being, beſide the declivity of the mountain, encompaſſed with a deep foſſe. It is vaulted underneath, and among other cellars, there is one which cannot be equalled; being dug in the rock, and lined with free-ſtone, three hundred feet in length, and upward of twenty in heighth. The thickneſs of the vault is two and twenty feet, and at one end of this ſtands an empty wine-caſk, which was made in the year 1548, four and twenty feet long and ſixteen high. This cellar communicates with another, where there is a large well of fine clear water, walled in, and three hundred fathoms in depth, ſo that there is no poſſibility of coming at the water. The reverberating ſound cauſed by throwing a ſtone into it, or firing a piſtol, has ſomething awfully aſtoniſhing.

On the Tubingen foundation, including thoſe who are in the country vicarages, there are conſtantly three hundred ſtudents of divinity, on whoſe application and good behaviour a ſtrict eye is kept. They meet twice a day in the greateſt order and decorum at their meals, at which times, one of them by turns preaches a ſermon.

According to the fundamental laws in the dutchy of Wirtemberg, all officers, civil and eccleſiaſtical, from the higheſt to the loweſt, muſt, at their admiſſion into employments, ſubſcribe the Formula Concordiæ; but, for ſome years paſt, this has not been ſtrictly inſiſted upon.

Among the curioſities of the univerſity library at Tubingen, upward of ſeven thouſand ſermons are ſhewn, which the celebrated Cruſius wrote in Greek, from the mouth of the miniſter, though they were delivered in German.

How far a rational principle, mutual affection, and compariſon of ideas may be aſcribed to animals, I will not at preſent determine; but aſſure you that the following adventure of a tame ſtork, ſome years ago in the univerſity of Tubingen, is literally true. This bird lived quietly in the court-yard, till count Victor Gravenitz, then a ſtudent there, ſhot with ball at a ſtork's neſt adjacent to the college, and probably wounded the ſtork then in it, as he was obſerved for ſome weeks not to ſtir out of the neſt. This happened in autumn, when foreign ſtorks begin their periodical emigrations. In the enſuing ſpring, a ſtork was obſerved on the roof of the college, and by its inceſſant chattering, gave the tame ſtork, walking below in the area, to underſtand that it would be glad of its company. But this was a thing impracticable, on account of its wings being clipt; which induced the ſtranger, with the utmoſt precaution, firſt to come down to the upper gallery, the next day ſomething lower, and at laſt, after a great deal of ceremony, quite into the court. The tame ſtork, which was conſcious of no harm, went to meet him with a ſoft chearful note, and a ſincere intention of giving him a friendly reception; when, to his great ſurpriſe, the other fell upon him with the utmoſt fury. The ſpectators preſent, indeed, for that time drove away the foreign ſtork; but this was ſo far from intimidating him, that he came again the next day to the charge, and during the whole ſummer, continual ſkirmiſhes were interchanged between them. Mr. G. R. v. F. had given orders that the tame ſtork ſhould not be aſſiſted, as having only a ſingle antagoniſt to encounter: and by being thus obliged to ſhift for himſelf, he came to ſtand better on his guard, and made ſuch a gallant defence, that at the end of the campaign, the ſtranger had no great advantage to boaſt of. But next ſpring, inſtead of a ſingle ſtork came four, which, without any of the foregoing ceremonies, alighted at once in the college area, and directly attacked the tame ſtork, who indeed, in the view of ſeveral ſpectators ſtanding in the galleries, performed feats even above human valour, if I may uſe that expreſſion; defending himſelf by the arms nature had given him, with the utmoſt bravery; till at length being overpowered by ſuperior numbers, his ſtrength and courage began to fail, when very unexpected auxiliaries came in to his aſſiſtance: all the turkies, ducks, geeſe, and the reſt of the fowls that were brought up in the court, to whom, undoubtedly, this gentle ſtork's mild and friendly behaviour had endeared him, without the leaſt dread of the danger, formed a kind of rampart round him, under the ſhelter of which he might make an honourable retreat from ſo unequal an encounter: and even a peacock, which before never could live in friendſhip with him, on this emergency, took the part of oppreſſed innocence, and was, if not a true bottomed friend, at leaſt a favourable judge on the ſtork's ſide. Upon this, a ſtricter watch was kept againſt ſuch traiterous incurſions of the enemy, and a ſtop put to more bloodſhed; till at laſt, about the beginning of the third ſpring, about twenty ſtorks ſuddenly alighted in the court with the greateſt fury; and before the poor ſtork's faithful life-guards could form themſelves, or any of the people come in to his aſſiſtance, they deprived him of life, though by exerting his uſual gallantry, they paid dear for the purchaſe. The malevolence of theſe ſtrangers againſt this innocent creature, could proceed from no other motive, than the ſhot fired by count Victor from the college, and which they doubtleſs ſuſpected, was done by the inſtigation of the tame ſtork.

For the conveniency of the duke's hunting-ſeats, and the horſes he keeps among the mountains, ſome good water-works have been conſtructed near Urach, where experiments may be made of the petrifying quality of theſe waters, by ſuſpending different bodies therein, which gradually become cruſted over with ſtone. Theſe water-works are about the middle from the mountain, near two contiguous ſprings, the one entirely clear, but the other gravelly; the latter of which works the engine. The whole mountain ſeems almoſt entirely to conſiſt of Stalactitæ, and in ſome of its caves the tops and ſides are adorned with very beautiful pieces, exactly reſembling ſugar-candy and white coral.

As I have mentioned Urach, I muſt not paſs over in ſilence a ſingular machine, kept up at a great expence, near the lower palace: it is called the Holzrutſche, or ſliding roller; and is compoſed of an iron canal or tube, above nine hundred feet in length, through which the wood felled on the hinder part of the Alb, or in the foreſt beyond Urach, where there is great plenty of beech and fire-wood, after being cut into pieces or logs, is carried down through this ſmooth, and entirely cloſe canal, from a ſteep eminence, with a violent force, and moſt hideous noiſe. By this contrivance, a tedious and troubleſome circuit is ſaved, and Stutgard furniſhed with fuel from the mountain. In ſpring and autumn, when the waters are high, the wood is floated from the foreſt down the Neckar, and landed at Berge near Stutgard. They have erected ſalt works at Suly; but have hitherto only been able to furniſh two or three neighbouring diſtricts with that commodity.

The firſt town I arrived at after my departure from Stutgard, was Durlach, a place which has experienced almoſt the ſame turns of good and bad fortune. Here the conſort of the reigning margrave, a ſiſter of the duke of Wirtemberg, keeps a ſolitary court, with the moſt placid reſignation under her troubles.

Karlſruh, to which the margrave has removed his reſidence, lies half a league farther toward the Rhine: it is a regularly built town, of above three hundred houſes, both which, and the palace, are built only of timber and brick. The houſes immediately round the palace are the largeſt, and provided with piazzas, where perſons may walk at all times.

Notwithſtanding the foundation ſtone of this palace was laid as early as the year 1715, half of the right wing is ſtill wanting, the work having been intermitted

termitted for ſome years. The main object attended to here, is the turret on the body of the building, from whence there is a proſpect, not only into all the principal ſtreets which are divided by three other croſs ſtreets, but alſo into twenty-five walks, ſome planted with trees, and others cut through the woods; in which reſpect, no other prince's ſeat can be compared with this; and beſide, the woods are planned out into a variety of other curious walks; ſome of which bear the names of thoſe miniſters who ſerved his highneſs at that time, as moſt of the ſtreets in the town are called after princes.

Raſtadt lies two ſtages and a quarter from Karlſruh; but no traveller will repent his turning a little on the left hand, toward the Favorita, built by the lady dowager of the late margrave of Baden-baden, of the moſt modern taſte. Here is a chamber of very fine porcelain, and a looking-glaſs cabinet containing numerous curioſities, both of nature and art: among others, are above forty good pictures of the ſaid lady, in the different maſquerade dreſſes ſhe wore on ſeveral occaſions in her youth. The ſame look is every where obſervable, amidſt the ſeveral alterations in the complexion and beauty, through ſuch a long ſeries of time. I do not know of any better ſet of portraits; and they alſo may be juſtly compared to Ruben's performances in the Luxemburg gallery, where queen Mary de Medicis is exhibited in a great variety of repreſentations and habits.

In the lower rooms, one ſees with great pleaſure the excellent order of the kitchen, larder, diſpenſary, waſh-houſe, &c. and accordingly the lady dowager takes a particular pleaſure in bringing her gueſts through theſe ſubterranean offices. At the end of the little orangery, to the left-hand, is a pheaſant garden, and to the right, a wild thicket leading to the hermitage. The houſe is ſituated in the middle of the wood; and the outſide walls of it are covered with pretty large pieces of bark. The door ſeems to rest on old stocks of trees; and within are only to be seen coarse statues of the Messiah, of Joseph and Mary, a mean bed without any curtains, an altar without ornaments; and at the corners of the narrow walks in the garden stand wooden statues of old hermits as big as life, and some of them in hairy habits: the niches for these, like the door, are supported by old and decayed trunks of trees. This hermitage is directly the reverse of that at Nymphenburg, which exhibits some grandeur under a concealed pomp: whereas, on the contrary, that of Baden derives its agreeableness from the exact imitation of natural simplicity, and unartificial disposition of a solitude, calculated for religious contemplation.

A league from the Favorita lies Rastadt: it is regularly built with streets and squares. The palace is a stately structure, and has from the center a view of three streets, the middlemost of which terminates in a long walk. The palace indeed is not yet finished; and the garden particularly will require a good deal of labour to render it equal to the building.

Few people are seen in the streets, and every thing wears the aspect of solitude.

The palace of Rastadt was built by the late margrave, of whose great skill in military affairs, even prince Eugene declared, "that had he himself the margrave of Baden's experience, or the margrave his good fortune, one of these two must be the best general in Europe."

Formerly many valuable paintings were deposited in the palace of Rastadt; but their number was very much diminished through the zeal of father Meyer, who at first had a great ascendancy over the marchioness dowager of Baden, till this influence sunk under the power of cardinal S****. The zeal of this ecclesiastic was such, that pictures above fifty thousand guilders value were burnt by his order, because they appeared to him too naked or immodest.

Every

Every traveller ſhould viſit the fine Scala Santa in the new chapel of the palace. The margrave's revenue, beſide what he has from his mother, is computed at four hundred thouſand guilders.

It is but one ſtage from Raſtadt to Stollhoſen; and the whole country through which you paſs is very fertile and delightful; turnips, in particular, abound here. Kehl is reckoned half a ſtage diſtant from Straſburg: and at a French toll-houſe upon the bridge, every box pays ſix creutzers.

Straſburg is a large and ancient city, but it has no fine buildings. It is an hour and three quarters walk round the ramparts; but remarkably pleaſant, a row of trees being planted all around; and in ſome places, two or three rows together. At preſent they are carrying on ſome new works on the ſide toward Kehl fort, in order to join more cloſely the city to the citadel; and for this purpoſe the burghers are obliged to give up the interjacent fields and meadows, for which indeed they are promiſed payment; but when they ſhall receive it, time alone muſt diſcover. After the taking of this city, which was in the year 1681, the inhabitants were obliged in the ſame manner to relinquiſh ſome part of their fruitful meadows for the new fortifications; but hitherto they have been ſo far from receiving the promiſed ſatisfaction, that thoſe who were fortunate enough to procure any thing, were forced to content themſelves with half the value. An engineer, after ſome years aſſiduity, has lately finiſhed a wooden model of the whole city, in which every particular houſe is ſo diſtinctly deſcribed, that ſcarce a window or chimney is omitted. This model was ſome time ſince depoſited in a large hall; but is now at Paris.

The new citadel toward the Rhine, as well as the town, ſtands on a plain; and the fortifications of both make no very ſtriking appearance.

Kehl may be cannonaded from the citadel, in which are laid up the old arms taken from the burghers in

1681. The neighbourhood of some marsh lands formed by the Rhine, renders the air of the citadel so unhealthful, that distempers rage among the inhabitants most part of the year. It is, however, at present, an academy for above an hundred cadets, or young gentlemen, who are instructed in mathematics and fortification. The innate ardour and fire of the nation, together with the volatility and usual wildness of youth, which does not subside in the French, till they are pretty far advanced in years, occasion continual broils among themselves, and still more with other people; for which reason they are locked up, as it were, in the citadel, and only a few permitted to go out at a time. They have here, however, the best opportunity for improvement, not only from the excellent masters that must of consequence be found among so great a number of engineers, but also from the advantage of viewing those excellent fortifications of Landau, Fort Lewis, Brisac, &c. in the neighbourhood of Strasburg; where the celebrated Vauban, Cohorn, and other great masters in this science, exhausted all their art.

The garrison of Strasburg commonly amounts to between eight and ten thousand men; and from the officers pay a monthly deduction is made for the support of the theatre; for which reason they always have a free admittance into the pit: and it is thought that such amusements are provided for them from prudential reasons, as they prevent many other disorders, and more pernicious meetings. Sometimes a company of officers agree to act some famous comedy or tragedy themselves; and in which they succeed much better than in the order of knighthood they lately instituted here. The members of this order call themselves Chevaliers de la Providence, "the Knights of Providence." The rules of their institution were, that every thing should be in common, and if any person of the society had two necessary things of the same kind, in his possession, he was to

bestow

beſtow one of them on an indigent brother; but every kind of ſuperfluity was to be burnt and deſtroyed. It may eaſily be imagined that few rich perſons entered into this ſociety, and conſequently this order, how commendable ſoever, could not long ſubſiſt.

The river Pruſche runs through the city, and the Ill waſhes its walls. The manners and cuſtoms of the inhabitants change with the times. The dreſs of the Straſburg young ladies, with their rich hats, broad over their foreheads, and terminating on each ſide in a peek of conſiderable length; together with the multiplicity of plaits in their gowns, are now out of faſhion, they all affecting to dreſs according to the French mode.

The cathedral is the principal ſtructure in Straſburg that merits obſervation. It was, after the ſurrender of the city, taken from the Lutherans and given to the Roman Catholics. The foundation of this church ſtands in water, and a ſort of clay. And not many years ſince, there was a paſſage round the lower vaults for a ſmall boat; but at preſent it is walled up. The whole ſtructure was finiſhed in the year 1449; ſo that the Proteſtants are not at all chargeable with the ſatiric pieces of ſculpture, which, a few years ago, were to be ſeen on the cornices of this church, and repreſented monkies, aſſes, hogs, &c. in monkiſh habits; and among others, a monk taking very indecent freedoms with a nun lying by him; but at preſent the greateſt part of theſe indecent images are defaced.

[Biſhop Burnet's account of the figures is as follows. ‘There is a proceſſion repreſented, in which a hog carrieth the pot with the holy water, and aſſes and hogs in prieſtly veſtments follow to make up the proceſſion. There is alſo an aſs ſtanding before an altar, as if he were going to conſecrate; and one carrieth a caſe with reliques, within which one ſeeth a fox;

a fox; and the trains of all that go in this proceſſion are ſupported by monkies. This ſeems to have been made in hatred of the monks, whom the ſecular clergy abhorred at that time, becauſe they had drawn the wealth and the following of the world after them; and they had expoſed the ſecular clergy ſo much for their ignorance, that it is probable, after ſome ages, the monks falling under the ſame contempt, the ſecular clergy took their turn in expoſing them in ſo laſting a repreſentation to the ſcorn of the world. There is alſo in the pulpit a nun, cut in wood, lying along, and a friar lying near her, with his breviary open before her, and his hand under the nun's habit; and the nun's feet are ſhod with iron ſhoes.']

The ornaments preſented to this cathedral by Lewis XIV. are very rich and ſplendid. It is ſaid that fifty perſons were employed about them eleven years, and that they coſt ſix hundred thouſand dollars. This preſent, beſide three ſets of prieſts veſtments and altar furniture, conſiſts of ſix large ſilver candleſticks, which require a ſtrong man to carry each of them, and a crucifix of double the weight. The whole ſeven pieces weigh ſixteen hundred marcs.

In this church is likewiſe a large clock, which exhibits the various motions of the planets: the common people are highly pleaſed with the images ſtepping forward, and a cock crowing, though very hoarſely. I rank this among the ingenious pieces of antiquity, rather than a clock I formerly ſaw in the chamber of Lewis XIV. at Verſailles; over one ſide of which a ſilver eagle trembles and ſhakes at the hourly crowing of a cock oppoſite to it. Whether ſuch a petty and pompous triumph over an enemy is conſiſtent with true greatneſs of mind, I leave others to determine. The invention of introducing a cock crowing in clock-works, was doubtleſs borrowed from the incident recorded in the hiſtory of our Saviour's paſſion: but to repreſent the king of birds as trembling at the crowing of a cock, is abſolutely repugnant

nant both to the principles of natural philoſophy, and ſymbolical repreſentation. Nor can ſuch inventions be pleaſing to any, but thoſe whoſe minds are poſſeſſed with the ſame weakneſs as Lewis XIV. who was ſo infatuated with flattery, that in operas, and prologues of plays, he uſed to join in ſinging the moſt extravagant airs in praiſe of himſelf: and who, even after the hard conditions of peace, to which queen Anne forced him to ſubmit, in the year 1713, ordered, or at leaſt permitted a marble ſtatue of himſelf to be erected; and which is ſtill ſtanding in the orangery at Verſailles, with the following arrogant inſcription:

Pace beat totum qui bello ſerruit orbem.

Peace he vouchſafed who ſhook the globe with war.

The ſteeple, or tower of the cathedral, is juſtly reckoned one of the higheſt in Europe, there being about ſix hundred and fifty-four ſteps from the pavement to the top: its geometrical height, ſome compute at five hundred and ſeventy-four feet; but others only at five hundred. After aſcending three hundred and twenty-five ſteps, you arrive at a ſpacious area, where water is continually kept, to be ready in caſe a fire ſhould happen in the tower. The earthquake of the 3d of Auguſt, 1728, which was felt here, and through all Swabia, raiſed this water between three and four feet high, and threw it about ſixteen or eighteen feet from the ſide; in commemoration of which, a particular monument is to be erected on the laſt ſtep. In the gallery round the church is alſo ſhewn a kind of crooked braſs horn, which is ſounded twice every night, for perpetuating the infamy of the Jews, who, in the year 1349, intended to betray the city, and had made this horn on purpoſe, to give the enemy notice when to begin the attack. The great bell in the ſteeple weighs above ten tons; and another called the Silver Bell, as being moſtly made

made of that metal, forty-six centenars, or two tons six quintals. The latter, except on particular occasions of rejoicing, is only rung twice a year, namely on St John's day, and fourteen days after Christmas.

The city hospital, which some years ago was burnt down, is now rebuilt in a very magnificent manner. On the left-hand of the entrance into the old part of the building, is placed in the wall a figure in relievo, having on its belly a prominence, resembling in some measure a middling cannon-ball, but with several ramifications of veins on its surface. Some think this statue represents a patient with a large plague sore, formerly belonging to this hospital; others imagine it to be a spider which was found in the wine-cellar. But both opinions are equally incredible.

In the cellar they have wines of the growth of 1472, 1519, and 1525: the second of these wines, for historical commemoration, is distinguished by the name of the Wirtemberg-war; and the last, by that of the Peasants-war. It is said, that no addition can be made to any of these wines, a thick crust or pellicle being grown over the surface of the liquor, so that infusion is rendered impossible: beside, upon mixing a few drops of any other wine with this, it immediately becomes black. The taste is not much better than that of sour lees; and a drop of it rubbed on the hand, leaves a smell which continues several hours, notwithstanding the spot be often washed with water. It is however sold very dear, a few drops only can be obtained for a guilder: and as each vessel is supposed still to contain eight awmes, the three must be considered as a very considerable fund to the steward of the cellars.

The royal hospital for invalids, and the Jesuits college, must be classed among the principal buildings of this city. The latter has a fine library, with a good collection of antiquities. The academy is also well

well provided with books, which are lent on giving an obligation for the return of them.

The anatomical theatre or hall is worth ſeeing: and the phyſic-garden, next to thoſe of Leyden and Paris, is looked upon as the beſt in Europe.

In the Pfennigthurme are kept the public records of the city; and among others, a parchment diploma of the emperor Charles IV. to which is appended a ſeal reſembling that of the Golden Bull at Franckfort, only that this of Straſburg is not of gold. Here alſo is kept the large ſtandard, about which ſuch frequent mention is made, in the diſputes for the office of ſtandard-bearer of the empire. It is eight ells and a half in height, ſeventeen and a half in breadth, and adorned with gold to the value of eighty ducats. In all probability, this is only ſome particular ſtandard belonging to the city of Straſburg, and never was the chief banner of the whole German army.

In St. Michael's chapel at Straſburg, was formerly a ſtatue of caſt braſs, between two and three ells in height, called Krutzmanna: it reſembled very nearly the figure of Hercules. A wooden cut of it by M. Daniel Specklin the architect, may be ſeen in the M. Hoſea Schadæus's particular deſcription of Straſburg cathedral, printed in 1617; but by taking off the cut, the ſtatue is reverſed, and the club appears in the left-hand, and the ſhield in the right. In the year 1525, this, with other ſtatues, was removed; but to what place, is not at preſent known.

The diſtance between Straſburg and Baſil is about twenty five ſhort leagues. The country near Biſenheim, between Old and New Briyſack, is very pleaſant, being entirely level. The proſpect toward France is terminated by the mountains of Burgundy; but on the other ſide, by the Black Foreſt, beyond the Rhine. The roads of Alſace are likewiſe very good, being generally cauſeways, having a deep ditch or channel on each ſide, to carry off the water.

A part

A part of Old Briyſack lies on an eminence, from which is a fine proſpect over the adjacent country. The bridge of boats, formerly at this place over the Rhine, has been demoliſhed ſome years, and its place is now ſupplied by a ferry.

On the ſide toward the Black Foreſt are vaſt numbers of wild boars, eſpecially in the marſhy parts of it, bordering on the Rhine; nor was it an eaſy matter to unharbour them, till, ſome years ago, a happy diſcovery was made, of burning brimſtone on the tops of ten or twelve long ſtakes, planted at ſome diſtance from one another, and on that ſide whence the wind blew; the hunters being poſted, with the proper weapons, on the oppoſite ſide. The wild boars, it ſeems, cannot endure the ſmell of burning brimſtone, but immediately fly from it; by this means they were driven to the other ſide of the moraſs, and within reach of their enemy's fire. The author of this contrivance ſeems to be no ſtranger to hog-ſtealing, a ſpecies of theft often practiſed here: theſe fellows, by holding ſome lighted ſulphur under the noſe of the animal, he immediately dies without the leaſt ſqueak. The peaſants of this country have alſo another method of taking wild boars. They know that theſe creatures frequently croſs the Rhine in the night; they therefore watch in their boats, and as a boar ſwims near them, they lay hold of his hinder-legs, and raiſe them ſome diſtance above the ſurface of the water: by this means his head is plunged under it, and he is ſoon ſuffocated; after which they pull him into the boat.

New Briyſack, built by Lewis XIV. lies over againſt the old town, and ſo near, that their forts are within cannon-ſhot of each other. The former ſtands wholly in the plain; all the works are new; and the ſtreets built in ſuch a manner, that from the great market-place the four gates of the town may be ſeen.

The road from hence to Baſil is extremely delightful, on account of the extenſive proſpect on the left-

hand

hand beyond the Rhine, into the margraviate of Baden. This little ſpot is indeed only four leagues in length, and the ſame in breadth; but very pleaſant and fruitful, eſpecially in wine, which they export into the neighbouring countries. It belongs to the houſe of Baden-Durlach, and is properly the old frontier province of Germany, toward Arelat; for which reaſon the family of Baden bears the title of margrave; their other territories having never anciently been the boundary of that country.

The new fortreſs of Hunningen, built by the French in the preceding century, lies within cannon-ſhot of Baſil; as the French, after finiſhing this place, once made an experiment, the ball lodging in the gate of Baſil. The city returned the compliment with another, which beat down a ſmall tower in Hunningen; upon which the French thought proper to make an excuſe for their firing firſt; alleging, that it was not done with any intention of damaging the town: and the garriſon of Baſil admitted the pretence. Hitherto indeed Hunningen has not offered ſince to moleſt the town of Baſil; which depends more on its union with the other Swiſs cantons, than on the ſtrength of its fortifications.

Baſil is ſmaller than Straſburg, but larger than Franckfort, and the largeſt of all the towns in Switzerland; having two hundred and twenty ſtreets, ſix market-places, and twenty-nine wells. Its ſituation is uneven, moſt of the ſtreets crooked, and the pavements rugged; being compoſed of ſharp ſtones, in order to prevent the horſes, which carry heavy loads up hill, from ſlipping. The clocks in this place go an hour faſter than any where elſe: this odd phænomenon ſome aſcribe to the diſcovery of a plot, the meaſures of which were diſconcerted by the alteration of the clock: others ſay, it had its origin during the time of the council; which after ſitting here ſeventeen years, ended in 1448, and was contrived to make the holy fathers either get up an hour ſooner in the morning, or ſit an hour leſs at dinner; their time of meeting in council being two o'clock.

Trade ſtill flouriſhes here, particularly that of ſilk ribbands, ſeven or eight houſes of merchants ſending each annually to the fairs at Franckfort, to the value of thirty or forty thouſand guilders of that commodity. The police of this place is under excellent regulations: moſt of the offices are beſtowed by lot, among well qualified perſons, none elſe being admitted as candidates for them; and even the very lucrative poſts are ſo often changed, that one perſon rarely continues in them above three years. No perſon without the city is to wear lace of gold or ſilver on his cloaths, under the penalty of three guilders for each offence. All young women, unmarried, are prohibited from wearing ſilks: the neareſt relations only, are invited to marriage-feaſts; nor does their number ever exceed fifteen or twenty: whereas, in former times, and even a few years ago, the number of gueſts at a marriage-feaſt, often amounted to upward of two hundred: by this means young people were led into unneceſſary expences, and contracted a very extenſive acquaintance. The burgomaſters and principal members of the council, contributed greatly to this regulation; for being always invited as gueſts, to every great wedding, and not being able to come off under a Louis d'or, the old cuſtom ſubjected them to an annual tax of at leaſt fifty ſuch pieces, which they ſave by this new law.

The bridge over the Rhine is two hundred and fifty common paces long; and makes a good appearance. On the tower, ſtanding on the ſide toward Switzerland, is a crowned Moor's head, which every minute thruſts out, and draws in again, its long red tongue. This figure, however ridiculous it appears, is more tolerable than a filthy repreſentation in a little houſe, ſtanding about the middle of the bridge, before which the common proſtitutes baniſhed the town, are brought and treated in a very indecent manner. That part of the city lying beyond the Rhine, on the ſide of Germany, called the Little Town, has its own particular juriſdiction, but in ſubordination to the city. The privileges of Baſil were formerly greater than at preſent, many of them having been abridged, on account of its declaring once for the houſe of Auſtria. This little town has no fortifications, and thoſe of the greater are of little ſignification. St. Peter's ſquare, which is decorated with rows of lime-trees, is the beſt walk in the great town. The cathedral is an old ſtructure, with two ſimilar towers. The empreſs Anne, conſort to Rudolph of Hupſburg, his ſons Charles and Eraſmus, were buried here; and in honour of the latter, there is a prolix, but inelegant inſcription, on a red and white marble tablet.

Over againſt the French church, on a long covered wall, is painted the dance of Death; where the king of terrors is repreſented as mixing with all ranks and ages of both ſexes; and complimenting them in German verſes on their arrival at the grave. The figures are all as big as life, and the author of it ſaid to be the celebrated Holbein, a native of this place, who painted another piece of the ſame kind; and alſo copied this on another houſe, but which the deſtructive hand of time has now entirely obliterated. But there are good reaſons for ſuſpecting that the dance of Death, near the French church, was done by one Bock, and not by Holbein. However, nothing of the original beauty of this piece, except the attitude of the figures, remains, the colours being ſo faded, that they were obliged to be retouched a few years ago; ſo that it is in vain now to look for the fine ſtrokes and touches of the old painting. The ſame misfortune has alſo attended the picture repreſenting the laſt judgment, on the ſtair-caſe of the council-houſe. In this piece, though done before the reformation, namely in 1510, yet even popes, cardinals, monks, and prieſts, are repreſented in the torments of hell. There is alſo in the council-houſe an exquiſite piece of the ſufferings of Chriſt, in eight departments, on two window-ſhutters, done by Holbein. Not only the beauty of the colours is very well preſerved, but likewiſe every motion and paſſion expreſſed with the utmoſt energy and propriety. Maximilian, elector of Bavaria, is ſaid to have offered the town thirty thouſand guilders for it. Connoiſſeurs particularly extol that department which repreſents the ſeizing of Chriſt in the garden: and both the colouring and artful conduct of the Claro-Oſcuro are ſo exquiſitely performed, that they would do honour to any of Raphael's ſcholars. In the court of the council-houſe ſtands a ſtatue of Munatius Plancus, a Roman general; who, about fifty years before the birth of Chriſt, built the antient city of Auguſta Rauracorum, near Baſil. This ſtatue was erected in the year 1526, by Beatus Rhenanus.

There is nothing remarkable in the phyſic-garden at Baſil, excepting a cherry-tree, which produces the ſame ſort of fruit thrice a year.

In the arſenal is ſhewn the armour in which Charles the Bold loſt his life; as alſo his kettle-drums and trumpets, together with the furniture of his horſe. The muſeums of Eraſmus and Amerbach belong to the univerſity, that ſeat of learning having, for nine thouſand dollars, purchaſed them from the heirs of the latter.

The diſtance from Baſil to Solothurn is commonly reckoned eighteen leagues, and to Bern twenty. Three leagues from Baſil lies the little town of Liechſtall, encompaſſed with a wall, and having a good road to it, through a delightful valley planted with vineyards and orchards. Five leagues from Baſil, beyond Holſtein, begins the craggy mountain, called Hauenſtein, which continues for ſome leagues, and is extremely troubleſome to travellers. On both ſides of the road are ſtill higher mountains: thoſe on the right extend to a great diſtance; but thoſe on the left-hand terminate in a large plain. On the mountain of Grindelwald is the celebrated Gletſcher, or ice mountain. It is ſaid that the ice on this mountain never melts; but, on the contrary, augments every year both in height and circumference. From this uncommon height of the country proceed the purity and subtility of the air in Switzerland: so that the Switzers, when in foreign countries, find, at times, a kind of heavy disquietude, and uneasy longing to breathe the fresh air of their native country, without being able themselves to give any particular reason for this restless anxiety. M. Scheuchzer at least makes use of this to excuse his countrymen's Nostalgia, Pathopatridalgia, or home-sickness, which particularly affects those of Bern. We have abundant instances, that upon the recruits from Switzerland having begun to play or sing the Kuhreiae, or cowbrawl, a tune usual among the Alpine boors when tending their cattle, the old Swiss soldiers have been so struck with the remembrance and passionate desire of returning to their native country, that they have fallen into lassitudes, anxieties, watchings, nauseas, and slow hectic fevers: for which reason their officers have been obliged strictly to prohibit the singing or playing this tune for the future. And those Switzers who are in the Piedmontese service, are condemned to run the gantlope for acting contrary to this order.

Upon entering into the territories of Bern, about a quarter of a league from Fravenbrunn, on an eminence, where a sentinel is always posted, I met with a stone pillar, on one side of which was a German inscription, in verse; importing that, on St. John's day, in the year 1375, the English captain here, called Gugler, or Juggler, was repulsed, with the loss of above eight hundred men on the spot.

On the other side are Latin verses, signifying that Cusin, an English nobleman, after having transported hither a considerable body of forces to demand his wife's portion from the archduke of Austria, her brother; and, committing many ravages; was here defeated with great slaughter by the inhabitants of Bern.

In this plain, all along the road, and likewise as far as Geneva, and even into Savoy, are planted vast numbers of walnut-trees, from the fruit of which an oil, used in physic, painting, and for burning in lamps, is prepared as follows: the shelled nuts are placed at a small distance from one another, in order to dry them thoroughly: then the kernels are taken out, pounded, and boiled in a kettle, and without any other preparation, put into a thick hair-cloth, placed under the press, and the oil expressed from them. Fresh nuts produce considerably less oil than those which have been gathered some time; but then it is of a much finer taste, and, at the same time, so strong as to intoxicate. It is entertaining to see what vast numbers of country-people, on Sundays and holidays, in autumn, meet together under the walnut-trees, and regale themselves with the fruit.

The wealthiest peasants in Switzerland are those of the territories of Bern; it being difficult to find a village without one, at least, who is worth between twenty and thirty thousand guilders, and sometimes even sixty thousand. The bailiff, or chief magistrate of Hutwil, is reckoned worth four hundred thousand. He has three sons, who are also farmers, and one daughter, whom her father has married to a peasant, notwithstanding she was courted by several gentlemen of Bern.

The common people of both sexes wear straw-hats; and the women's petticoats are tied up so near their arm-pits, that hardly a hand's-breadth is left for their shape. The inns throughout Switzerland are very good, and abound with trouts, carp, beef, veal, fowl, pigeons, butter, cheese, apples, peaches, turneps, sugar-bisket, &c. with good wine very plenty, and at a very reasonable rate, when compared with the bills of fare in Swabia, Tirol, and Bavaria.

There are Switzers in the service of most of the princes in Europe; but that of France seems the most profitable: for a captain, who has a whole company, generally

generally makes ten thouſand livres a year of it; but moſt of them have only half a company. At preſent the Swiſs, in French pay, amount only to fourteen thouſand men.

Before you come to Bern, it is neceſſary to deſcend a mountain, near the foot of which, but on the aſcent of another, the city is ſituated. The entrance is at firſt very narrow, but widens as you aſcend; and at the top, where it is almoſt level, opens into fine large ſtreets. The houſes are moſtly built of white free-ſtone, and in ſuch a manner, that the foot-paths in the principal ſtreets are under piazzas, or arches, one ſide of which is taken up with the ſhops and houſes of tradeſmen. Theſe piazzas, at the ſame time that they ſecure you from the weather, and render the walking very commodious on the free-ſtone pavement, deprive the houſes of the ornament of a portal; and the pillars raiſed from the ſtreet to the firſt ſtory, for its firmer ſupport, make an inelegant appearance.

The ſtory of the bear, taken on the day the foundation of the city was laid, and thence gave occaſion to its name, is well known. This creature is not only borne in the coat of arms, but they likewiſe ſtill keep in the upper part of the city ſome live bears, in two incloſures, where are high trees for them to climb up for their diverſion.

The burgherſhip is divided into two parts; thoſe qualified for the government and magiſtracy of the city, and the perpetual inhabitants. The latter, who obtained their freedom ſince the year 1635, are incapable of being admitted into the council, or holding any public employment, but enjoy all other privileges; the former hold all civil offices, as the deſcendants of ſuch as were made burghers before that year. The city was indeed built in the year 1191, in order to check the nobility in their violent career. But this precaution was not ſufficient to hinder ſix very old and noble families from getting them-

 ſelves

ſelves ranked in the number of the qualified burghers, who are reſpected more than any of the others; and when any one of this claſs is elected into the ſenate, or little council, he has the honour of taking place of every other counſellor, though his ſenior in office, and likewiſe of walking next the tribunes of the people, of which there are four.

Great ſtruggles were formerly made for obtaining the governments of the cantons in the country, on account of the conſiderable profits ariſing from theſe poſts; but to terminate all cabals and intrigues, a law was paſſed in the year 1711, whereby theſe, and other lucrative places, are to be determined by lot. A ſingle man is incapable of obtaining a country government, or of holding any other lucrative employment.

In the middle of the city is erected a large ſeat of juſtice, encompaſſed with iron rails, upon which the acting prætor ſits, with two members of the council, when ſentence of death is to be paſſed on any criminal.

The manners of this country, within theſe fifty years, have, in many reſpects, been greatly changed; inſtead of the plainneſs and honeſt ſimplicity of their anceſtors, the love of ſuperfluous expence and high living very greatly prevails: many vices are not, however, ſo common as in other large places, where they are only laughed at: and the clergy, from the pulpit, have ſtrenuouſly, and with becoming ſpirit, inveighed againſt theſe crying enormities; nor did they even ſpare a certain privy-counſellor, who, labouring under a venereal complaint, ſent for the celebrated Nauman from Paris to cure him.

The canton of Bern [which biſhop Burnet ſays comprehends above a third part of Switzerland] draws conſiderable advantage from the public granaries, which are erected both in town and country, for the uſe of the ſubjects. The great quantity of corn continually depoſited in them, not only ſerves the preſ-

ſing

ſing exigencies of a time of war, but whenever any bad harveſt happens, the rich are prevented from oppreſſing the poor, by raiſing the price of grain. The elegant building erected for this purpoſe in the city of Bern, near the Dominican church, is of free-ſtone, ſupported on lofty pillars; the piazza under which might ſerve for a commodious exchange. They have alſo great revenues ariſing from their ſalt-works at Bevieur, Roche, and Paner, in the Pais de Vaud.

In Bern, French is the general language; but here, as at Baſil, their pronunciation is very guttural, which renders their ſpeech diſagreeable.

The large church is a beautiful ſtructure. On the ſides of the great door are ſtone ſtatues of the five wiſe and five fooliſh Virgins, as large as life, with the paſſions of joy and deſpair, finely expreſſed. Over the door is the laſt judgment, together with ſeveral ornaments of foliages, fruits, and feſtoons, all in ſtone. The ſculptor has here, like the painter of the famous picture in the council-houſe at Baſil, repreſented the pope in hell.

After aſcending two hundred and twenty-three ſteps up the tower, you arrive at a gallery, from whence there is a charming proſpect over the city towards the Aar. The church ſtanding high, and the part of the city contiguous to it toward that river lying very low, they have found it neceſſary to ſupport the foundations of the tower and church, for between fifty and eighty paces on three ſides, with a wall, ſtrengthened with ſeveral pillars and arches. This work is ſome hundred feet in height, and the area being filled with earth, levelled, and planted with limes, is a moſt beautiful walk; from whence there is an enchanting proſpect over the artificial caſcade of water, made at a very great expence, for driving the city-mills. Some pretend that this terrace is equally elegant with that built by Solomon, near the Temple in Jeruſalem. In 1654, one Theobald Weinzapflein, a ſtudent in divinity, being intoxicated

toxicated with liquor, fell, together with his horſe, from this terrace: his horſe was killed on the ſpot, but the rider had only his leg broke; lived thirty years after the fall, part of which time he was a miniſter in the country. The memory of this eſcape is preſerved by a German inſcription placed in this walk.

In the Dominican church is always ſhewn to ſtrangers, a hole in the wall, through which there was a communication between a cell of one of the monks in the adjoining monaſtery, and an image of the Virgin in the church; by which means the ſcandalous impoſition of making the image appear to ſpeak, was carried on. The author of this fraud was condemned and burnt at Bern, in the year 1504, (a full account of which may be ſeen in Burnet's Travels, p. 53.) and the convent turned into a houſe of correction. In the city library are preſerved the tent and ſome beautiful tapeſtry belonging to Charles the Bold, which the Swiſs took in 1476, at the battle near Morat, together with a great number of other curioſities and antiquities.

None are permitted to ſee the arſenal without a licence from a particular counſellor, who rarely grants the favour. There are, it is ſaid, arms in it ſufficient for a hundred thouſand men; this may be true, provided each be contented with a ſingle weapon of any kind; but were they to be compleatly armed, I imagine, that thirty thouſand would nearly exhauſt it. Near the entrance ſtands a painted wooden image of a bear rampant, dreſſed in a cuiraſs, with a ſword by his ſide, and by treading on a piece of wood near it, he moves his head. In the firſt long hall are depoſited fifty-ſix pieces of cannon, ſeveral ſtandards, and two large horns of buffaloes, uſed in war by the canton of Uri, inſtead of trumpets, and were taken from the Roman Catholics in the year 1712. Hard by alſo hang the groteſque dreſſes of thoſe who blew them. The inhabitants of Uri, who boaſt their deſcent from the

the old Taurifci, bear a buffalo's head in their coat of arms: and the perfon who blows the great horn in time of war is called the Bull of Uri. At the end of this hall are two large pieces of cannon, which belonged to Charles the Bold, together with a great number of halters and gibbets carried by that prince to the battle of Morat, in order to hang up the Switzers, after defeating them.

In the upper hall are the ftatue and arms of Berchtold von Zahringen, the founder of the city, together with tents for forty thoufand men, and mufkets for forty-fix thoufand. Here are alfo three fwords, with which the fame number of executioners have procured their difcharge; in order to which it is requifite to have beheaded a hundred and one perfons with the fame fword; or three perfons of the fame family in a quarter of a year. Our guide affured us, in a very grave manner, that executioners of this kind were doctors; but at prefent they keep the fword themfelves, paying the republic fifty ducats as an acknowlegement for this favour.

A wooden ftatue of the famous William Tell is placed at the end of this hall. He is reprefented as taking aim at an apple placed upon the head of his little fon, who ftands oppofite to him. The hands and eyes of this wooden ftatue are finely expreffed. If we may judge from this piece, he was a man of an open, honeft countenance, very tall, and large boned, but thin. According to the fafhion of the times, one half of his coat is red, the other yellow and black, in long alternate ftripes. His breeches and ftockings are of one piece; and an arrow is fticking in his doublet behind his head; the boy is reprefented fmiling, as if he had nothing to apprehend on this occafion. A great number of ancient arms, fome curioufly mounted with ivory, and belonging to the life-guards of Charles the Bold, are depofited here; together with a mufket of a new invention, having fix fcrew-barrels.

But

But these are not the only stores; the castles where the country-governors reside are not only furnished with cannon and muskets, but every subject has his necessary arms. No young man is allowed to be married before he is master of a sword and musket, of which he must bring a proper testimonial to the clergyman who performs the ceremony. In every district or government, a corporal and six men continually watch on the highest mountain, near two large piles, one consisting of dry wood, and the other of straw; upon the least alarm of the appearance of an enemy, they set fire to one of these piles, according as the invasion happens, either in the day or night; if in the former, the straw, but in the latter the wood. By this means, in an hour or two, the whole country is in arms, the signals being continued from one mountain to another, and every one knows the place of rendezvous. Experienced officers and soldiers are never wanting; the foreign service, from which many are constantly returning into their own country, affording a continual supply. The people of the country are daily exercised: and the canton of Bern alone has at present forty thousand regular troops. But, as I have already observed, with respect to the trade and revenue of this country, so in military affairs the protestant cantons are greatly superior to the catholics.

At the distance of a league from Freyburg, in a wilderness of woods and rocks, is a remarkable hermitage, consisting of a church, an oratory, a steeple, a hall, a dining-room, a kitchen, chambers, stairs, a cellar, a well, and other conveniencies, all hewn out of a rock, even the chimney and steeple, notwithstanding the latter is fifty-four feet high. A work like this cannot fail of filling the mind of every spectator with astonishment: but when it is known that this work was wholly performed by only one man and a boy, the astonishment will be greatly increased. Nature indeed had provided a crystal spring, but the artist, by means of several channels, conveyed the

water

water from the rock into ſmall reſervoirs; and he alſo fetched from diſtant parts of the mountain, earth ſufficient to make a ſmall kitchen garden. Every one muſt be pleaſed at the ſight of this ſurprizing curioſity; nor is it hardly poſſible to ſuppreſs a ſigh for the fate of its unhappy, ingenious and induſtrious architect; who, in the year 1708, in conveying back ſome young people, who had attended the conſecration of his little church, was unhappily drowned in the river Sane, which runs near this hermitage, and on which, by the help of a ſmall boat, he uſed every week to fetch proviſions, and other neceſſaries, from the city.

A ſtructure in ſome meaſure ſimilar to this, we meet with in the biſhoprick of Heidelſheim, called Lippels-Hole, from its firſt poſſeſſor. It has a well, a ſtable, a low and long entrance leading to a large room, all hewn out of a rock, in a cavern of the mountain. The intention of the latter was, however, quite different from that of the former; Lippel uſing his as a place of retreat after committing murders and robberies; but it could not protect him from falling at laſt into the hands of public juſtice.

The chapel called La Salutation, at Freyburg, merits the obſervation of travellers, and the Jeſus College is looked upon as the fineſt in all Switzerland. At the diſtance of ſix leagues from Bern, by the neareſt road, which leaves Freyburg on the left hand, is Murten, which may be termed Little Bern, from the ſimilarity of the houſes and piazzas. A quarter of a league farther, on the right hand of the road, is a chapel, whoſe windows are ſecured with iron bars, but without any glaſs. In this ſmall ſtructure are depoſited the bones of the Burgundians, ſlain in the year 1476, and which formerly filled it to the very roof, but are now ſunk to half that height. This decreaſe is not owing entirely to the mouldering of the bones; the Burgundians, who travel this road, take away many, either out of devotion, or to keep as relics: and, what is more ſtrange, ſome of the country people, out of mere ſimplicity, uſe theſe bones medicinally.

In ſeveral parts of this country, as far as Lauſanne, you frequently meet with public gibbets, with vanes, on which are the arms of the canton, in whoſe juriſdiction the place is ſituated.

Lauſanne is ſituated in a valley, but the roads ſo rocky and uneven, that the wheels of carriages, though ſhod with iron, are ſoon demoliſhed. Contiguous to the eaſt ſide of the town is a very pleaſant walk, with a charming proſpect of the city and lake of Geneva, which indeed appears to be in the neighbourhood, but is at leaſt half a league off.

[We are farther informed by Mr. Addiſon, that Lauſanne was once a republic, but is now under the canton of Bern, and like the reſt of the dominions of that canton, is governed by a bailiff ſent them by the ſenate of Bern every three years. It is remarkable that there is one ſtreet in this town, in which the people have the privilege of acquitting or condemning any one of their own body in affairs of life and death, and as every inhabitant of this ſtreet has his vote, houſes ſell better here than in any other part of the town. They relate that not many years before a cobler had the caſting vote for the life of a criminal, which he graciouſly gave on the merciful ſide.]

In the wall of the principal church is a fiſſure, which was formerly large enough for a man to creep through, occaſioned by an earthquake in 1634. The celebrated old profeſſor Picket uſed to ſay, that he had often laid his cloak in it, when a boy, and at play in the church-yard with his companions. But about thirty years ſince it was almoſt cloſed again, by another earthquake, and the ſmall crack, which remained, being hardly an inch in breadth, filled up with mortar. The tower is an elegant piece of architecture; but by being unfortunately twice ſet on fire, the half of it only is now ſtanding. A ſmaller tower of the church was alſo ſet on fire, near its top, by lightning, upon which the inhabitants very wiſely determined

termined to beat it down with a chain-ſhot, in order to ſave the body of the church; ſince which a new ſpire has been raiſed upon it. In the church is a marble monument, erected to the memory of a knight of the houſe of Granſon; and another to that of Charles duke of Schomberg, who, in the year 1693, was killed in Piedmont. This church is on one ſide ſurrounded with a walled terrace or walk, like that at Bern; the latter has indeed a much higher wall, but the former greatly excels it in its inchanting proſpect of the lake, and level country about Geneva. Indeed this whole country is ſo ſituated, as at once to charm the eye with its pleaſing proſpects, and the mind, by the liberty enjoyed by the inhabitants. In ſhort, the charming contraſt of hills and vallies, corn-fields, meadows, vineyards, and woods; together with the vicinity of the lake, and its mild government, draws perſons of all ranks and countries to the Pais de Vaud; ſome indeed ſpend only the ſummer and autumn there; but others purchaſe eſtates, and become conſtant inhabitants of this delightful country.

Hither perſons of diſtinction from Geneva, and the canton of Bern, men of ſenſe and knowlege in every branch of ſcience, gentlemen who have travelled, experienced merchants, and other perſons of various conditions, reſort, as a kind of aſylum, or refuge from the perſecution of eccleſiaſtical and civil tyranny; and affording the beſt opportunities for improvement, and ſpending the time in the moſt agreeable company. Even ſtateſmen of the greateſt talents, who have conducted the affairs of their country in the moſt eminent courts of Europe, with applauſe, have choſen this country for the place of their retreat: and by converſing with perſons of literary merit, find that ſatiſfaction and real pleaſure which they formerly ſought in vain, amidſt the tumults of a court, and the embarraſſments of a conſpicuous ſtation.

The diſtance between Lauſanne and Rolle, by the road of Morge, is reckoned five leagues, or five hours journey, but it may be very well performed in four.

Aubonne, situated on the right, is at present a territory belonging to the canton of Bern, but was formerly a seigniory appertaining to the marquis Du Quesne, which he bought of Joh. Tavernier, the so much celebrated traveller, and afterward sold it to Bern. Tavernier, on being raised to the honour of nobility by the king of France, purchased this seigniority with a view of spending here the remainder of his life: but sending a relation of his to the East Indies, with a rich cargo, which cost him two hundred and twenty thousand French livres, and which must infallibly have produced him a million in return, had the voyage been prosperous, and his relation honest; but this not being the case, his relation embezzled the cargo, which so greatly involved him in debt, that he was obliged to sell his whole estate, and end his days in poverty and want. The marquis du Quesne was the eldest son to the famous admiral Abraham du Quesne, the only person then in France capable of opposing Ruyter, the Dutch admiral. It is commonly reported, that these maritime heroes had so high an esteem for each other, and under such apprehensions of losing the honour they had gained before, that they continually endeavoured to avoid each other, and even sent private intelligence what course each of them intended to steer: till at last du Quesne being prevented, by contrary winds, from continuing the course he had signified to Ruyter, it happened that, contrary to both their inclinations, they fell in with each other, near Messina, and were under a necessity of engaging. It is added that, from a false motion made by the Dutch admiral's ship, du Quesne concluded that Ruyter commanded no longer; and immediately encouraged his men, assuring them Ruyter was dead. In this he was, however, mistaken, for Ruyter lived several days after receiving the wound.

Du Quesne never abandoned the protestant religion. And, in his advanced age, when Lewis XIV. endeavoured to prevail upon him, to embrace the

Roman

Roman catholic religion, he frankly anſwered, *Sire, j'ai rendu aſsés long temps à Cæſar, ce que eſt dû à Cæſar; il eſt temps que je rende auſſi à Dieu ce qui lui eſt dû.* "I have, Sire, for a conſiderable time, "rendered to Cæſar, the things that are Cæſar's; "and it is now high time for me to render to God, "the things that are his." This reply, the king ſo little underſtood, that, turning to thoſe about him, he ſaid, *Eſt ce que la tête tourne à cette homme? veut il ſervir l'empereur?* "Is the man deprived of "his ſenſes? does he intend to ſerve the emperor?" When the edict of Nantz was repealed, he was the only perſon ſuffered to enjoy his religion, without quitting his country; the crown of France perceiving that his preſence was abſolutely neceſſary at that time. The heart of this celebrated admiral lies interred in the church of Aubonne, with a pompous marble monument, erected to his memory by his ſon. The ſpirit of perſecution would not admit that the whole remains of this great man ſhould be carried out of France.

Whenever a foreigner intends to ſtay any time in the towns belonging to theſe diſtricts, an officer of the place immediately waits on him, in the name of the governor, with a preſent of wine, for which the bearer of the meſſage is generally diſmiſſed with a piece of money.

From the ſea, the Pais de Vaud appears like a pleaſant amphitheatre, where the eminences riſe gradually to the eye. By land the road from Lauſanne to Genoa, is a pleaſant day's journey; and the territory of Savoy directly facing it, is not without its beauties.

The river Rhone diſembogues itſelf near Villeneuve into the Leman, or Geneva lake. This lake is eight German miles in length, but, if meaſured along its winding banks, it is near ten. The ſhorteſt ſide is that toward Savoy, which, with its meanders included, is not above ſeven ſuch miles. Its greateſt breadth is near Rolle, where it is about five leagues.

It is as rarely frozen as the Bodensee: there was however an instance of it in the year 1572. The abundance of fish formerly in this lake, has suffered some diminution; especially within these forty or fifty years past, by a species of ravenous fish, unknown here before that time. The natives call them moutela; but whether they came into this lake from those of Neufchatel or Yverdun (which last, by means of a canal, and the little river La Venoge, has a communication with the lake of Geneva) or from a large pond in the neighbourhood of La Venoge, through a subterraneous passage, or from some inundation, is uncertain. Trouts were formerly taken in this lake, weighing between fifty and sixty pounds; but at present, the largest do not exceed twenty or thirty. I have often wondered that there are here no gondolas or pleasure-boats, for taking the air on the water; but this, in all probability, proceeds from the well regulated police, and the strict precaution they take to cut off all incentives to unnecessary and exorbitant expences. In the lake, not far from Geneva, is a large stone, near the basis of which is a capacious cavity. They call it la Pierre de Neiton, Neiton's stone; a name given to the Neptune of the antient Celtæ and Gauls. That it was used as an altar for sacrifices, is apparent from several utensils for such purposes being found in its cavity about fifty years ago.

The Rhone, near its mouth, forms an island, upon which, and the banks on both sides, the city of Geneva is situated in latitude 46° 12′ north. That part of the city on the right hand, called St. Gervais, from a church of that name, is far inferior both with regard to extent, and the beauty of the structures, to that on the rising ground to the left hand of the river. In general, however, great improvements have been made in the city, and every day, during these twenty years past, has increased its lustre. The new and extensive fortifications, now erecting, have drawn hither great numbers of masons and other artificers; but

but as various methods have been difcovered of procuring excellent materials for building at a very cheap rate, the conftant works carrying on, inftead of increafing, had reduced the private buildings.

[Our countryman Mr. Addifon gives a defcription of the fituation of Geneva and its lake, to the following effect.

The greateft part of the city of Geneva is fituated on a hill, and has its view bounded on all fides by feveral ranges of mountains; but thefe are at fo great a diftance, that they leave open a furprizing variety of beautiful profpects; and from their fituation cover the country they inclofe from all winds, except the fouth and north; and to the laft of thefe winds the inhabitants of this city afcribe the healthfulnefs of the air. For as the Alps furround the city on all fides, forming a vaft bafon, within which is a well watered country, there would here be a conftant ftagnation of vapours, did not the north winds put them in motion, and fcatter them from time to time. From this fituation the fun rifes later at Geneva, and fets fooner, than in other places of the fame latitude; and the tops of the neighbouring mountains are covered with light, above half an hour after the fun is down at Geneva. Thefe mountains alfo much increafe the heats of fummer, and form an horizon that has fomething in it very fingular and agreeable. On the one hand, a long range of hills diftinguifhed by the name of mount Jura, is covered with pafture and vineyards; and on the other, huge precipices formed of naked rocks rife in a thoufand odd figures, and being cleft in fome places, difcover high mountains of fnow, at the diftance of feveral leagues behind them. To the fouthward the hills rifing more infenfibly, leave the eye a vaft uninterrupted profpect; but the moft beautiful view is that of the lake, and its borders, that lie north of the town.

This lake refembles the fea, both in the colour of its waters, in the ftorms that are raifed on it, and in the ravages it makes on the banks. It alfo receives

 different

different names from the coasts it washes, and has in summer something like the ebbing and flowing of the tide, occasioned by the melting of the snows, that fall more copiously into it at noon, than at other times of the day. It has five different states bordering on it France, the dutchy of Savoy, the canton of Bern, the bishoprick of Sion, and the republic of Geneva.

I made a little voyage, says Mr. Addison, round the lake, and touched at the several towns on its coasts, which, though the wind was all the way pretty fair, took up near five days. The right side of the lake from Geneva belongs to the dutchy of Savoy, and is extremely well cultivated. The greatest entertainment in coasting it, was from the several prospects of woods, meadows, vineyards and corn fields, which lie on its borders, and run up all the sides of the Alps; where the barrenness of the rocks, or the steepness of the ascent will permit. The wine on this side of the lake is, however, much inferior to that on the other, on account of the vineyards being less exposed to the sun.

The lake on its approaching Geneva gradually decreases in breadth, till at last it changes its name into that of the Rhone, which turns all the mills in the town; and notwithstanding its being very deep, is extremely rapid. It rises in the very midst of the Alps, and has a long valley that appears as if hewn out on purpose to give a passage to its waters, from its numerous rocks and mountains that are on all sides. This brings it almost on a direct line to Geneva, where it would overflow all the country, were there not one particular clift that divides a vast circuit of mountains, and conveys it to Lyons. From Lyons there is another great rent, which runs across the whole country, in almost another straight line; and notwithstanding the vast height of the mountains that rise about it, gives it the shortest course it could take, to fall into the sea.]

In the lower part of the town are several streets, having a kind of arched walks or piazzas, where a

 person

person may be sheltered from rain; but they are higher, and project farther than those at Bern. Such conveniencies are very necessary in a city like this, where no coaches can be procured.

The church of St. Peter, is the principal structure, dedicated to religion, in the whole city. It has a monument erected to the memory of Henry duke of Rohan. In this, and most other churches here, Calvinists, or reformed ministers, perform the sacred offices in French. The families which formerly fled hither from Italy, maintain an Italian church for themselves, and for such as may still be obliged to quit that country on account of religion. The German Calvinists have also their own reformed minister. Lutherans have for these twenty or thirty years past, been permitted to keep a pastor of their own; but at present their congregation is but small; the minister's wife is the only woman they have among them. The members of this society are protected by the duke of Saxe-Gotha, who nominates their preacher. Near the entrance into the council-house, are some inscriptions relative to the reformation of this church, in the year 1535; some in commemoration of the alliance entered into between the cantons of Bern and Zurich in 1184; and others relating to the attempt of the Savoyards to surprize the city, which proved abortive. The stairs, or ascent to the council-house, is without any steps, being only a pavement composed of small pebbles, as the most commodious for persons either to ascend or descend.

In the armoury are shewn the ladders, a loaded petard, and other implements, provided by the Savoyards for the famous escalade of the city, which was intended to have been executed by night, in the year 1602.

The city has but a small extent of territory belonging to it; so that the quantity of grain produced is far from being sufficient for the consumption of the inhabitants. The republic thereby well knowing, that the importation of it from the neighbouring countries, might be prevented either by a bad harveſt, infectious diſtempers, or war; they wiſely erected, as a ſecurity againſt a famine or ſcarcity, large granaries at the public expence: in theſe are continually hoarded up about ninety thouſand centers or quintals of grain; a quantity reckoned ſufficient to ſupply the inhabitants two years. But no perſon is under any neceſſity of purchaſing corn from theſe magazines, as is cuſtomary at Rome, where every one muſt buy it from the pope's ſtore-houſes, at an exorbitant price; while, at the ſame time, thoſe who ſell corn, are obliged to deliver it at a very low rate. The bakers, inn-keepers, garriſon and artificers, employed by the city, are indeed obliged to buy corn from the magazines belonging to the republic. The annual conſumption amounts to about ſixteen thouſand quintals, and is productive of two advantages; a ſmall profit ariſing from the inconſiderable advance of the price; and a circulation of the corn every ſix years, ſo that a freſh ſtock is brought into the granaries.

The juriſdiction was from time immemorial lodged in the people, conſiſting of about 1500 burghers; the chiefs of which form the four ſyndics, who, with twenty-one counſellors, compoſe the ſupreme judicature of twenty-five; in which two perſons of the ſame family can never ſit at the ſame time as members. Next to this is the ſeverer council of ſixty, and after them the grand council of two hundred.

The republic, for the maintenance of credit, has enacted a particular law, by which a ſon who refuſes to pay his father's debts, is rendered incapable of any office in the ſtate. With regard to matrimonial contracts, there are alſo ſome ſingular regulations in Geneva. No marriages are permitted where either party profeſſes any other than the proteſtant religion. All previous promiſes, obligations, and contracts, between a Calviniſt and a Roman catholic, are not only declared null and void, but alſo the promoters, and the conſenting parties are liable to be puniſhed according to the nature and circumſtances of the offence.

offence. A woman of forty years of age must not marry a man less than thirty; if she exceed forty, her husband must at least be thirty-five. Nor must a man above sixty, marry a woman who is not at least thirty. A widow must not alter her condition in less than six months after her husband's decease. The man is under no particular limitation with regard to time, but enjoined by the laws not to connect a new engagement too soon, with this remarkable addition, not to be met with in any former laws; *tant pour obvier au scandale, que pour montrer, qu'il a senti la main Dieu.* "Not only to prevent scandal, "but to shew that he hath felt the hand of the "Almighty."

A particular chamber is appointed for the suppression of luxury, and the maintenance of a well regulated police. And I cannot help remarking, that they have here discovered an uncommon revenue, arising to the city from the dirt gathered in the streets: whereas, in other places, they are paid for carrying it away. One person has the sole right of removing this soil, which proves excellent manure for the adjacent lands, and pays annually to the city for this privilege, eight hundred Geneva livres.

The French protestants, who were obliged to quit their country, on account of their religion, have supplied Geneva with excellent workmen and artificers, in almost every branch of trade: so that, at present, here are reckoned upward of three hundred, employed in the watch-trade, and its several branches. Nor are the watches made here, inferior in beauty to those of England. The silver watches sell here for thirty Rhenish guilders, and those of gold, and chased, for fifty rix-dollars.

The library belonging to the city is well furnished with excellent books, and has a curious collection of medals and petrifactions. The principal manuscripts are, an old copy of Terence, the four gospels, written in the ninth century, and an entire Latin bible, in a large folio. This manuscript has that passage in

St. John's epiſtle about the three who bear record in heaven, only the verſes are tranſpoſed; and the title of the epiſtle runs *ad Spartos*, of which ſome make *ad Sparſos*, or *diſperſos Fideles*, agreeing with the uſual title of catholic; but others read *ad Parthos*, becauſe St. Auguſtine, under this name, quotes ſome places of St. John's firſt epiſtle.

In the muſeum, are many other pieces of antiquity, ſome large Roman amphoræ, or pitchers, with narrow necks; the image of an antient Gauliſh prieſt, in bronze, with a cann in his right-hand; a large table, having in the center of it a piece of Florentine marble, two feet in length, and one in breadth, repreſenting in the moſt beautiful manner, a perſpective view of the country, with the demoliſhed fortifications of a city, and an old caſtle ſtanding on an eminence. Every perſon is allowed free acceſs to this library, ſome hours in a week; nor do they refuſe to lend the books on certain conditions.

I was favoured at the houſe of Mr. Lullin, the miniſter, with a ſight of St. Jerom's ſermons, wrote in Latin, on the Egyptian papyrus, or a kind of paper made from the bark of trees; and Montfaucon, by a writing under his own hand, prefixed to the manuſcript, declares it to have been written in the ſixth or ſeventh century.

The kings of France and England are conſtantly mentioned in their public prayers. The clergy of Geneva, whether we conſider their chriſtian deportment, or pacific temper, may be a pattern to many others of the ſame communion, who differ from them in points of doctrine. Both the clergy and laity are unwilling to enter into any diſcourſe about the proceedings againſt Servetus, and earneſtly deſire, that the whole tranſaction may be buried in eternal oblivion. It muſt indeed be acknowleged, that the manner of proceeding againſt Servetus, however perverſe and pertinacious his ſpirit might have been, cannot be juſtified on the genuine principles of the proteſtant religion. The place where Servetus was burnt, is a

ſhort

ſhort half league from the city, over delightful meadows, and the walk to it is called Plainpalais; where, on a ſmall eminence, was formerly a ſtone monument, with an inſcription; but ſome years ſince ſecretly taken away.

It would be an injuſtice to the republic not to obſerve that the ſcandalous and abſurd proceſſes with regard to indictments and ſentences againſt witches and ſorcerers, one of the relics of popery, were much ſooner exploded here, than in ſeveral other countries, where the proteſtant religion is profeſſed; none having ſuffered ſince the year 1605. Nor are thoſe ridiculous ſtories, ſo common in other countries, believed or even related here.

On the Plainpalais, near the gate where the Savoyards attempted to ſurprize the city, in the year 1602, is the common burying-ground for the uſe of the city; ſome few families are indeed interred in the church of St. Gervais, ſituated in the ſuburbs, and among the reſt, the remains of Beza. All allow that Calvin is buried in the church-yard on the Plainpalais; but the Geneveſe, to ſhew their deteſtation of ſectariſm, will neither mention him, nor give any information concerning the place where his remains are depoſited. The celebrated preacher, M. Galliton, informed me, that once a Scots preſbyterian came to him, and earneſtly deſired to ſee Calvin's grave. But he aſſured him he did not know himſelf where it was. This reply ſurpriſing the Scotchman, Galliton added, that it had been long ſince forgot; though they always expected, that a ſuperſtitious preſbyterian would one day make more inquiry about it than the thing deſerved. The Lutheran miniſter, however, ſhewed me, on the right hand, as one enters the church-yard, a mark in the wall of the peſt-houſe, which ſtands in the middle; and oppoſite to this, at the diſtance of ſome few paces, the body of Calvin is interred. He added, that ſome time after, one Reuber, a Lutheran clergyman, was alſo buried there, contiguous to Calvin.

About ſeven long leagues from Geneva, between Fort Ecluſe and Mount Credo, the Rhone totally loſes itſelf under ground. The road thither is troubleſome; but leſs ſo to thoſe who travel on horſeback, than to thoſe who perform it in any other manner. Fort Ecluſe is ſituated on a rock, at the foot of which the river directs its courſe: and as this is the only road to Lyons, travellers are ſtrictly examined at this place. After ſome gentle falls, the river diſappears at once, directing its courſe under ground, ſo that one may ford it over. When the water is low, the opening in the earth is viſible, but intirely covered when the floods are out. Betwixt eighty and a hundred paces from this place, are ſeveral ſprings and whirl-pools, and ſoon after this, almoſt half the river appears, but the other half ſtill flows in its ſubterranean channel.

All young perſons ſhould viſit Geneva before France, as they cannot fail of reaping conſiderable advantage from the converſation of ſo many perſons of diſtinguiſhed abilities both among the clergy and laity; many of whom hold aſſemblies ſeveral times in a week, where the diſcourſe turns on the ſciences; nor is it any difficulty for ſtrangers to procure admittance. All opportunities and incentives to a licentious way of life are reſtrained, and as much as poſſible, ſuppreſſed by their police; not a theatre is permitted among them. Several languages are ſpoke here, particularly the French; and thoſe who are deſirous of arriving at perfection in the academical exerciſes, will here find opportunities ſufficient for that purpoſe. The ſcholars ride four or five times a week, at the riding ſchool; and the firſt month's expences are five piſtoles, but the ſucceeding, together with gratuities, amount to only four. Thoſe who teach the languages, and other branches of literature, charge a piſtole a month, or for ſixteen leſſons: and at ſome profeſſors houſes you have an opportunity of boarding, for which, with lodging, fire and candle included, you pay about forty Rheniſh

guilders

guilders a month. Greater improvement may be reaped at Geneva, from the conversation of the ladies, than in any other place. Their manners are free and open like the French; but being strengthened by a virtuous education, the exhortations of their clergy, the salutary laws of their police, and at the same time not exposed to examples of immorality and licentiousness; they habitually contract an irreproachable virtue: so that should any one, from the freedom of their behaviour, conclude that little trouble would be sufficient to contract an immodest familiarity, he would find himself wretchedly mistaken; whereas the French ladies, especially the Parisians, are very free, and at the same time possessed but of little virtue.

Almost the only method of travelling from Geneva to Italy, is in a kind of sedan, or post-chaise, half covered at top, large enough to hold two persons, and room behind for two trunks. It has only two wheels, is drawn by two horses, one of which goes between the shafts, and bears the greatest part of the burden. It is commonly said, that in order to have a good chaise, the shafts should be made at Venice, the wheels at Geneva, and the iron-work at Milan. You cannot travel in four-wheeled carriages through Savoy, without a great deal of trouble, on account of the rocks, and the narrow and short turnings often met with in the mountains. As there are frequent opportunities at Geneva of return chaises for Turin, the whole expence for the carriage, living on the road, the charges of a mule and servant to attend it over mount Senis, will not amount to more than eight or nine pistoles: but it will be necessary to agree for eating and lodging together, as the inn-keepers are very apt to impose upon strangers; postboys know both the price of wines and provisions; and the landlords are willing to oblige them on account of their constant custom. This caution is unnecessary in other parts of Italy; it being sufficient to tell your host, that you will eat *al pasta*, or at the ordinary, which costs each

each person thirty Piedmontese sols, or three paoli, and at supper for bed and chamber forty sols, or four paoli; and for a servant half that sum. If a man would live *al conto*, or bespeak any thing for himself, he seldom fares better, notwithstanding the innkeeper charges what he pleases. The usual entertainment in Savoy is the same as in Italy, and commonly consists of a soup, boiled or roasted pullets, pigeons, chesnuts, butter, cheese, and some fruit. On fast-days the ordinary is very indifferent, old salt-fish being one of the principal dishes. The Savoyard wine is of a dark red colour, and has some roughness on the palate. There is, indeed, a sweet wine, called *vini amabili*; but less wholsome than the *vino brusco*.

You cannot well travel from Geneva to Turin in less than six or seven days. The river Arve runs at about the distance of a quarter of a league from the former, and is on that side the boundaries between the republic of Genoa, and the dutchy of Savoy. After passing this river, every thing which a traveller is desirous of not having frequently searched, is sealed at a Savoy custom-house, and a certificate given, that they have examined it at Novalese.

The prodigious mountains called *Montagnes maudites*, " the cursed or infamous mountains," and nearer Anecy, the *Glacieres*, " or ice houses," you leave on your left hand. They are situated at about three days journey from Geneva, and being perpetually covered with snow and ice, the searching for rock crystal in their clefts, is always dangerous and often fatal.

In these mountains, particularly those of Faucigny, are the sources of the river Arve, which, at about a musket-shot from the city of Geneva, falls into the Rhone; and, according to the diversity of seasons, either swells or sinks very suddenly. Some particles of gold are found in the sand; but not in quantities sufficient to compensate the tedious task of collecting it; no person being able to earn above a quarter of a dollar a dollar in a day. In the adjacent villages it is rare to meet with any, except women, throughout the year. The men, especially those that are young, being scarcely two months of the year at home, the poverty of their native country obliging them to seek their bread in foreign countries, by sweeping chimnies, carrying about marmottes, and the like: but they never fail to bring home part of the little they procure, to maintain their families. And as the men both set out and return at one particular season; the women commonly lie-in about the same time. At Marlie, a quarter of a league from Geneva, I observed the first paper windows so common in Italy, and even sometimes in the palaces of the great; but cannot recommend them as ornamental. The paper is soaked in oil, in order to render it more transparent, and, at the same time, to keep out the external air, which, in several places, especially in the night-time, is very unwholesome. The dearness of glass may be one reason why paper windows are so common in Italy; to which must be added the above-mentioned property of keeping out the external air, and its not refracting the sun-beams; for in a hot summer the refraction of the sun beams through glass, would render the rooms insupportably hot.

Rumelie is situated a quarter of a league from Marlie; about half way, on the left hand, are high mountains, covered with snow, and at a small distance Anecy, an episcopal see, situated on a beautiful lake. This place affords a most delightful residence; both on account of the many elegant prospects that surround it, and the good company to be met with in it. French is universally spoken in Savoy; and from that language they have taken most part of the names of towns and villages; but the disposition and temper of the nation, are more of a German turn, distinguishing themselves from their neighbours, who inhabit the southern and western districts, by what they call the old German honesty. This, in all probability, is greatly promoted by the poverty of the

mountainous

mountainous part of the country, where a peaſant poſſeſſed of a pair of oxen, two horſes, four cows, a few goats and ſheep, with a ſmall ſpot of cultivated land, is eſteemed a man of ſubſtance. It therefore is no wonder, that they ſend their children abroad, in order to get their livelihood, by ſhewing marmottes, cleaning of ſhoes, ſweeping chimnies, or the like. They ſay, there are about eighteen thouſand Savoyards, young and old, at Paris. Among theſe, the boys clean ſhoes, and during winter, between forty and ſixty of them lodge together in one room; but in ſummer, the ſtones at the threſholds of houſes, ſerve them for pillows. They are, however, notwithſtanding their poverty, ſo honeſt, that you may truſt them to change gold. If they are even fortunate enough to procure a ſufficiency for opening a little ſhop, they are ſuch conſummate maſters of œconomy, that they ſcarce once fail of acquiring a conſiderable fortune. The rich banker and financier, Croizat, whoſe daughter married count d'Evereux of the houſe of Bouillon, was originally one of theſe Savoyard boys. The love of their native country is, however, often ſo prevalent, that when they have amaſſed ſome money, they return home. Once a year an old man goes through all the villages, and gathers all the lads together, ſo that in ſome reſpect, he may be compared to the rat-catcher of Hamel. Frequently the children committed to his care, are ſo little, that they are carried off in baſkets. This man alſo brings letters from the Savoyards at Paris, Lyons, and other places, to their parents, relations and friends; and ſometimes, likewiſe, a little money, needles, and the like trifling preſents; which encourages the old people at home to entruſt him with new colonies; and he himſelf reaps ſome profit from theſe emigratory travels, eſpecially while he continues in Savoy, where he has every thing provided for him, without any expence.

Three leagues from Rumeli ſtands the city of Aix, very famous for its hot baths, which are free to all, only

only paying the attendant or rubber a trifle of money, to which office a certain number of perſons are appointed. The loweſt bath has a ſulphureous ſmell, and iſſues from a very plentiful ſpring. The upper has no ſmell, and madame Royale ordered a large open bath to be built a little below it; but this is already diſuſed. No fiſh or other animal will live in theſe hot waters. But, when ſtrangers come to ſee this bath, it is cuſtomary for little dirty ſwarthy boys to ſwim about in it, and dive under the water like ſo many frogs, in hopes of acquiring a little money, as a reward for their dexterity.

Chamberry, the capital of Savoy, lies about two leagues, or two hours journey, on the other ſide of Aix, in a charming valley. It is pretty large, but affords little remarkable to gratify a traveller's curioſity, except the fountains in the market-place, where four dogs ſpout the water out of their mouths, may be called a curious piece. The chapel belonging to the palace, dedicated to St. Michael, has a beautiful front, enriched with elegant ſtatues and grand pillars.

Three leagues from Chamberry lies mount Melian, formerly ſo famous for its fortifications, but which are at preſent entirely demoliſhed; and three leagues farther is Aigues-belles, about half a league from which begins a narrow valley, extending to mount Senis. La Chambre is four miles further. A little before you reach St. Jean de Morcienne, two leagues diſtant from La Chambre, they have mended the rough and ſtony roads, and built a large, high, and paved ſtone bridge over a narrow valley; but amidſt theſe tremendous mountains reſembling thoſe of Tirol, both with regard to height, and their ſummits being immerſed in clouds, the roads are far worſe than thoſe of Tirol. We paſſed a river betwixt five and ſix times in one day, travelling ſometimes on this, and ſometimes on that ſide of the valley, over craggy rocks, which about a quarter of a league on this ſide of St. Michael, are remarkably ſteep and narrow. Theſe high rocks do not, like others, conſiſt of one hard

hard ſtone, but of ſeveral huge maſſes, not connected with one another, but heaped confuſedly together. So that, in rainy and ſtormy weather, they are eaſily ſeparated, and large maſſes often tumble into the road, ſome veſtiges of which I have ſeen; and once a whole waggon was cruſhed and buried under a diſruption of this kind. They incommode the way ſo, that one is obliged to travel on the other ſide. And the poſt-boy, who generally travels this road every week, aſſured us, that it was only a few weeks ſince that they were rolled away. As ſoon as the valley begins to augment in breadth, we meet with ſmall vineyards, ſupported with a dry ſtone wall, reſembling a breaſt-work.

Near St. Michael, on the right, are ſome mountains, which make a very beautiful appearance, being extremely lofty, and covered with paſtures and arable fields to the borders of the ſnow. But being inacceſſible to carriages, the manure is carried to them by women and aſſes. The wine produced on ſuch a barren and craggy ſoil, cannot be expected to be the moſt excellent in the world; but that of Mont Melian is eſteemed the beſt in the country.

There is very good accommodation in a ſpacious inn at St. Michael's, ſtanding by the road-ſide; it formerly belonged to a nobleman, but he was at laſt obliged to abandon it, on account of the great expence of procuring water. Over the doors of the chambers, are ſtill ſome excellent moral inſcriptions in Latin. And it would be no diſagreeable amuſement to travellers, if all inns were furniſhed with ſomething of the ſame kind, which could not fail of entertaining travellers very agreeably, when obliged to wait for their meals being got ready, or for the baiting of their horſes. But with regard to the ſallies of fancy, commonly wrought by young perſons upon window-panes, they are generally either trifling or vicious.

The continual cataracts or falls of water, and the rapidity of the Arc, are ſufficient demonſtrations, that the land is greatly elevated; but its acclivity ſtill continues

continues to the very foot of mount Senis. The white froth, and green tincture of the waters, form a very beautiful contrast; and the cascades which it forms over the huge rocks fallen down from both sides of the mountains, are often as elegant as those made by art: beside, the numerous springs and streams which tumble down the mountain, greatly increase, by their lustre and confused murmur, the pleasure of this romantic scene. But, on the other hand, the road is every where so narrow, and in some places so steep, that the most secure way is to alight, and walk on foot. A little on this side of St. Andre, the road passes over a rising ground, where, in some places, it is supported by a breastwork, and others by wooden rails, but not of strength sufficient for the purpose; so that this place nearly resembles the pass near Cismone, in the Lower Tirol. What increases the terrible aspect of the road is, the high impending rocks, from whence dissevered pieces threaten every moment to follow those fragments which have already rendered the road so difficult to travellers.

Modane, St. Andre, Termignon, and Lanebourg, are but mean places. At the last of these, measures are taken for crossing mount Senis: and as five hours are requisite to accomplish this journey, a traveller should be careful to set out early in the morning, or at least before noon; for the night will be very uncomfortable, if any accident should oblige him to put up on the mountain, at La Ramasse, or La Grande Croix. At Lanebourg, one takes a mule to La Grande Croix, where the baggage and chaises are taken to pieces, and carried over the mountains upon mules and asses. The vetturrini, or carriers, have chaises on each side of the mountains, so that they have no occasion of being at the expence, or trouble, of taking them to pieces. The horses which they take with them, by frequently going over this road, become as well acquainted with it as those belonging to the natives; so that between Lanebourg and Novalese, you may safely let them go as they

 please.

please. From La Grande Croix, to Novalese, travellers take the carriers they hired at Lanebourg. In travelling from Piedmont, the journey is performed on mules, from Novalese over the steep mountain, till one comes to La Grande Croix, and also over the plain to La Ramasse, where the Novalese carriers take up and forward the travellers to Lanebourg. In going down the mountain, mules are not so secure from slipping, nor does one sit so well upon them as in going up; for which reason, it is necessary to be carried by men. In the inn at Chamberry I met with a learned Franciscan, from Turin, who made it a point of conscience not to be carried by men, asserting, that in his opinion, it was a violation of that equality, nature had placed between all the human species, and which should, as far as possible, be maintained. Accordingly, he travelled from Ramasse to Lanebourg on foot; but assured me, that he would not for the future regard such scruples, as the prodigious steepness of the mountain often put him to the greatest difficulty of keeping himself from falling.

Lanebourg is situated in such a manner among the mountains, particularly mount Senis, which lies so near it on the east and south; that the inhabitants never see the sun from the end of November till the 17th of January: at which time he makes his first appearance over the summits of the mountains. On the left hand near Lanebourg, is Bonaise, a very high mountain, whose top is entirely covered with snow, and where they hunt the chamois, during the summer season. From Lanebourg to the top of mount Senis, is reckoned a league, but you cannot reach it in less than an hour. From thence it is two leagues, over a plain, to La Grande Croix, and requires upwards of an hour and a half. Then you have two leagues farther, on a declivity, one of which brings you to Fertiere, and the other to Novalese.

In winter, when the snow lies on the ground, the plain on the summit of mount Senis is passed in sledges drawn by a horſe and mule. The declivity from La Grande Croix to Novaleſe, you paſs in all ſeaſons in chairs; the huge ſtones, crooked ways full of pits, and dangerous precipices, not admitting ſledges. But you may paſs the deſcent from mount Senis to Lanebourg, during the winter, in another manner. At the beginning of the declivity, ſtands a houſe called La Ramaſſe, where, being placed in a ſledge, you deſcend to Lanebourg in ſeven or eight minutes; but with ſuch rapidity, that it is with difficulty you can keep your breath. Theſe ſledges contain only two perſons, the traveller and guide, who ſits forward, and ſteers with a ſtaff. On each ſide of him he has an iron chain, which he drops like an anchor, whenever he is deſirous either to moderate or ſtop the motion of the ſledge. This, as well as the carrying in chairs, they call *Ramaſſer les gens, aller à Ramaſſer.* Some travellers, eſpecially the Engliſh and Germans, are ſo pleaſed with this rapid deſcent, that they take mules from Lanebourg, and ride up again to La Ramaſſe, in order once more to enjoy the pleaſure of ſuch a quick deſcent. The horſe road from Lanebourg, up the mountain, is in a continual winding courſe; which the mules and aſſes are ſo far from miſſing, that they know how to pick out the beſt track, and avoid the ſtones; ſo that the rider may truſt himſelf to them without any danger.

From Lanebourg to Novaleſe are two roads, the old and the new. The latter is indeed the worſt, but at the ſame time the ſhorteſt, and therefore followed by thoſe who ride on mules, or are carried in chairs. One would be apt to think, that the men of Lanebourg and Novaleſe, on account of the heavy loads they almoſt daily carry, and their continual paſſing up theſe ſteep and lofty mountains, muſt ſoon become conſumptive. In Germany, what a noiſe and buſtle our chairmen make, if they are obliged to carry any bulky perſon a few hundred paces. But the Lanebourg carriers climb up, like cats, a ſteep mountain, for the ſpace of an hour, without the leaſt difficulty of breathing, or reſting themſelves; and on the plain at top, get the ſtart of us again; and as ſoon as they have put their chaiſes in order, which they do in a few minutes, they carry the company over the worſt part of the road for two hours, without reſting more than a few minutes at four different times. But ſuch is the effect of habit, and ſimple diet, and to the ſame cauſes may be attributed their longevity, many of them arriving at a hundred years of age. Their common drink is milk, and they ſeldom taſte any wine. To render them leſs liable to ſlip, they have no heels on their ſhoes, and their ſoles are rubbed with a compoſition of roſin and wax. The machine in which travellers are carried down hill, is a kind of ſtraw chair, with a low back, two ſupports for the arms, but no feet; inſtead of which a board is faſtened before with a cord for the traveller to reſt his feet upon. The ſeat, which conſiſts of bark, and pieces of ropes twiſted together, is faſtened to two poles, and carried like a chair or ſedan, by means of broad leather ſtraps.

La Grande Croix lies on the ſide next to Piedmont, where the high plain of mount Senis terminates, and the deſcent of the mountain begins. The only buildings here are an inn and a chapel; in the latter, thoſe who periſh by cold or ſnow on theſe mountains are buried, provided a roſary, or any other token of their being catholics, is found about them. The wooden croſs erected near the houſe, ſeparates Piedmont and Savoy from each other; ſo that the inn belongs to both countries. After we had taken chairs at this place, and were carried over ſome very dangerous places, we arrived at a ſmall plain ſurrounded with lofty rocks, and called La Plaine de St. Nicholas, where are alſo ſome breaſt-works, compoſed of looſe ſtone, which in the laſt war ſerved the troops of both ſides as a kind of defence. The French wanted to penetrate farther on the ſide toward Lanebourg, and the

the Germans kept their post on that toward Novalese. In this plain we walked above a hundred paces on foot, till we came to the large cascade of the river Semar; the bottom of which is so deep, and the rapidity and force of the water so great, that nothing which falls into it ever appears again, as happened last winter to a loaded mule.

Fertiere lies half way between La Grande Croix and Novalese, and, in my opinion, is nearly on the same horizontal level with Lanebourg. From this it may be concluded, how much lower Piedmont lies than the other parts of Savoy, contiguous to mount Senis. From Chamberry you begin again to ascend, and it is sufficiently evident from the rapid course and frequent cascades in the river Arc.

On the left hand between Fertiere and Novalese is mount Rochemelon, supposed the highest of all the Italian Alps. From this place indeed it seems to unite with the adjoining chain of mountains, but they are separated by a valley, and it is a whole day's journey to gain its top. I at first could clearly see its summit, but in less than a quarter of an hour it was shrouded in a cloud. Such changes occur very frequently, and it often happens, that after the toil of climbing this prodigious acclivity, you are obliged to wait for fair weather, before you can come down again. But when the sky is clear and serene, the labour is very well compensated, by a most astonishing prospect of the territories of Milan, Trevignan, Venice, and other states. Whence some have imagined, that this was the mountain from whence Hannibal shewed his army the glories of Italy, to animate them to pursue their march. Upon firing a musket on the top of this mountain, the report is not louder than that of breaking a piece of wood. Formerly a statue of Jupiter was placed on the top of Rochemelon, but at present there is one of the Virgin Mary, and every year, on the 5th of August, mass is said here, at which many thousands of people aſſiſt, from all their neighbouring parts; notwithſtanding they are obliged, even at that ſeaſon of the year, to clamber over ſnow and ice, and paſs at leaſt one night on the mountain, where they lie on the bare ground or naked rocks. They therefore have need of mantles, and other good covering, to protect them from the ſeverity of the weather.

Between Fertiere and Novaleſe, you are ſometimes obliged to alight from theſe ſtraw chairs, and walk about forty or fifty paces on foot; not from the dangerouſneſs of the road, but the narrow paſſes between the ſteep rocks, which will not permit the chairmen to carry their chairs on their long poles; but bear them either on their arms, or aloft in the air, for they are very light. One of theſe defiles is called *le Pas de Diable*, that is, "the devil's ſtep." The path is often ſcarcely a foot broad, having on each ſide very ſteep precipices. Sometimes indeed it happens that theſe chairmen ſtumble and fall down, but ſeldom or never, in places where there is any danger. Whenever an accident of this kind happens, it is moſt adviſeable to throw themſelves on the ground. They go a very eaſy pace; and as the weather was fair and ſerene, I was very well pleaſed with my day's journey.

Suſa lies a full league beyond Novaleſe, and on this ſide of it ſtands fort Brunette, erected fifteen years ago, and cannot perhaps be paralleled in the whole world. It conſiſts of eight baſtions; and was, together with all its outworks, hewn out of the rock. All communication between the baſtions and the other works is by ſubterranean paſſages, cut through pure rock; theſe paſſages are of ſuch a breadth, that large waggons and heavy cannon, drawn by ſeveral horſes, may commodiouſly and ſafely go from one place to another. No houſes are to be ſeen in the whole fortreſs, and but a few centinels belonging to the garriſon. Cannon and mines would be of no conſequence to this ſtrong place, as being compoſed of one entire rock;

rock; and two thousand men, well supplied with provisions and ammunition, might defend it against a powerful army.

When you are past Susa, the road is good, the valley opens, and discovers a beautiful prospect of arable lands, decorated with rows of walnut-trees, excellent meadows, and extensive vineyards. Four leagues and a half beyond Novalese, lies Bossulens, a mean place, but, like many others, of no consideration. Veillane lies four leagues from Bossulens, and from it there is a fine prospect terminated by Superga, a new church built on a high mountain, a league and a half beyond Turin. About a league from Veillane stands the royal palace of Rivoli, about three short leagues from Turin. It is impossible for imagination itself to form a pleasanter road than this last, it being a straight avenue, and sufficiently capacious for six carriages to go a-breast. The trees on both sides are indeed but young; the French, during the last siege of Turin, having destroyed every tree in the whole country. The palace of Rivoli is situated on an eminence, at the beginning of the avenue, near Susa, and at the other end the prospect is terminated by the city of Turin, over one part of which Superga appears. The avenue leading from Mechlin to Louvain has, it must be owned, its beauties, and is extended three leagues in length; but the ground is more uneven and hilly than this of Turin.

It would perhaps be difficult to find a place where arbitrary power is carried to greater height than at Turin; where the personal qualities of his majesty impart a greater authority to his commands, than an army of regular troops could do in another country. His dominions being situated between two powerful neighbours, the house of Savoy has thence politically augmented both its dignity and power. Some indeed pretend, that such a conduct would not appear in the most favourable light, if strictly examined by the unerring rules of justice and morality; but others are of opinion, that when the exigencies and urgent neceſſities, under which the court of Savoy has often laboured, are conſidered, theſe difficulties which may give umbrage to a tender conſcience, will totally vaniſh.

It muſt, however, be acknowleged, that the greateſt œconomy is obſerved in all the expences of the court. In Turin no marſhal's table is kept; and even at la Veniere it is ſerved with diſhes from the king's table. The king dines only with the prince of Piedmont and his conſort; expenſive diverſions are ſeldom known, and the account of all diſburſements ſo clearly ſtated, that the king, at one view, may ſee the whole amount of his annual expences. Upon any alteration, or extraordinary diſburſements, the cauſe of the difference muſt be fairly entered in a particular book; and this is obſerved in ſuch ſmall articles, as wood and candles, &c. The king is ſo intimately acquainted with the price of every commodity, that formerly he uſed to bargain with his tradeſmen, and would even point out thoſe articles wherein they impoſed upon him; as alſo the profits ariſing from each commodity. It is known, that he has himſelf bargained for hats, ſtockings, &c. both for himſelf and family, with the dealers in thoſe commodities, whom he cauſed to wait perſonally on him. He once commanded all the millers in his dominions to aſſemble and repair to him; reaſoned with them himſelf, and raiſed the rent of their mills in one forenoon, three hundred thouſand livres. While the chapel Royal, called the Holy Sudary, was repairing, his majeſty uſed to repair conſtantly every morning early to La Conſola, to hear maſs; and took the opportunity of viſiting the markets, and inquiring ſtrictly of the country people the prices of their partridges and hares, whereby he acquired a very particular knowlege in the value of theſe commodities, and never failed to give his caterers the neceſſary cautions. Perhaps the difficulties under which he laboured, might greatly

contribute

contribute to render him ſo conſummate an œconomiſt. In the mean time, it muſt be acknowleged, that inſtances of his liberality are not wanting. Some years ago, the opera at Turin being directed and ſupported by a ſubſcription of merchants, the king only required a ſmall box for himſelf, and even came but very ſeldom to the opera. However, at the end of the carnival, he preſented the company with thirty thouſand Piedmonteſe livres.

It is owing to his majeſty's great wiſdom and penetration, that the whole country has not been over-run with ſuperſtitious notions of ſorcery, and perſons pretending to be poſſeſſed by evil ſpirits. A young girl in Turin being troubled with hyſteric fits, which threw her body into ſuch poſtures and agitations, that ſeemed ſupernatural, the jeſuits, who are always attentive to every thing that has a tendency to promote themſelves, or turn to their advantage, ſoon flocked about her, attended by phyſicians in their intereſt, who alledged, that ſhe was actually poſſeſſed, and conſequently, not to be cured by medicine. Accordingly, the exorciſts were aſſembled, and the girl previouſly inſtructed for the better carrying on the impoſture. The affair made a great noiſe, people came from all parts, and the old tales of witchcraft and ſorceries were revived; and others produced, who were alſo poſſeſſed. Dr. R. nobly oppoſed theſe proceedings, and declared the girl's cauſe was entirely owing to natural cauſes, ſupporting his opinion by reaſons and inſtances, which he had heard of in Holland and England, where he had reſided many years. The jeſuits furiouſly attacked him as an infidel, whom they would infallibly confute from the teſtimony of his own ſenſes. The doctor conſented to attend them, and while they were performing their prayers and exorciſms, appeared very devout. When they had finiſhed, he deſired the two eccleſiaſtics, who were entruſted with the management of the affair, that they would order their patient to anſwer him a few

few queſtions, which they granted, on condition he aſked nothing unlawful, and commanded the devil to anſwer. Accordingly, the doctor ſaid to her in Engliſh, What is my name? This being a language, to which both the girl and the jeſuits were ſtrangers; ſhe anſwered in plain Piedmonteſe, that ſhe did not underſtand the queſtion propoſed. But according to the received opinion, as well as the ritual; the knowlege of all languages, the ſupernatural ſtrength of body, and foretelling things to come, are the proper criteria of a real ſatanical poſſeſſion: the devil therefore ought to underſtand all languages; and it is eaſily conjectured, that this ignorance did not a little mortify the jeſuits. They, however, did all in their power to elude the conſequence, by pretending that the doctor had put an unlawful queſtion to the evil ſpirit, and they had forbid him to anſwer any of that kind. But the phyſician ſoon confuted their allegations, by explaining the queſtion he had aſked; and immediately repeating the queſtion in Piedmonteſe. But the poſſeſſed, to whom he was unknown, could ſay as little to this as before, when the ſame queſtion was propoſed in Engliſh. The doctor, highly pleaſed at this ſucceſs, ran to court in triumph, where he ridiculed the ignorance of their devil; the king and prince of Piedmont joined in the laugh: and the latter, for the more effectually ſilencing this jeſuitical devil, fetched a Chineſe pſalter from his cloſet, ſent him by the cardinal Tournon, as a curioſity. This pſalter has indeed a Latin tranſlation, but the Chineſe leaves could be taken out ſeparately from thoſe containing the tranſlation. With one of theſe leaves Dr. R. was again diſpatched, to aſk the devil the contents of it, and in what language it was written. The fathers, who did not deſire any more of Dr. R.'s viſits, were for keeping out of his way; and the devil threatened, if he came again, to expoſe the minuteſt tranſactions of the doctor's life. A Theatine, who was an accomplice of the jeſuits, acquainted the doctor's tor's ſiſter with this circumſtance; and ſhe, from an implicit veneration for the clergy, was very urgent with her brother, not to have any further concern with this devil; but to no purpoſe. I am indeed apt to think, that could the devil have expoſed all the particulars of Dr. R.'s life, one would have been diverted with many ludicrous ſcenes. The doctor, however, had no great opinion of the devil's omniſcience, and told the king, that if the devil knew all things preſent or abſent, there would be no neceſſity for princes to be at ſuch immenſe expences in envoys, agents and ſpies; they need only maintain a poſſeſſed perſon or two, from whom they might conſtantly have immediate intelligence of every tranſaction. After this remark, the doctor haſtened to the houſe of the poſſeſſed, where he found the jeſuits with the girl. On entering the room, after the uſual compliments, he acquainted them that having been informed, that a detail was to be given of every tranſaction of his life, he was deſirous of hearing it himſelf, and began to defy and challenge the devil to begin his ſtory; adding, that if he did not, he would brand him, and all who favoured this pretended poſſeſſion, for knaves or fools. This reſolute ſpeech, thunder-ſtruck both the patient and the jeſuits; but the latter pretending to ſhew the doctor the neareſt way out of the houſe, he ſoon ſilenced them, by producing the commiſſion, and inſiſted, in the name of the prince, that the poſſeſſed ſhould declare what was written on the leaf he exhibited, and what language it was written in. The two jeſuits, who were, doubtleſs, not the moſt artful of their order, pretended that the characters might be diabolical, and therefore refuſed to anſwer the queſtions. Dr. R. anſwered, that it did not become them to violate the reſpect due to their prince, by ſuch a ſcandalous ſuſpicion; and inſiſted, in the name of the king and prince, that they ſhould no longer amuſe him

him with ſuch weak ſubterfuges. The two jeſuits, after whiſpering to themſelves, anſwered, that an affair of this kind muſt be introduced by prayer, and a long ſeries of devotion; wherefore it was neceſſary to defer it to a more convenient opportunity. Dr. R. replied, there was now time ſufficient for the purpoſe, and that he would pray with them; ſo that they were at laſt, notwithſtanding their evaſions, obliged to begin their ceremonies. During the exorciſm, the girl threw her body into ſtrange contorſions, and hideous looks, which the jeſuits inſiſted upon were ſupernatural; but Dr. R. promiſing to mimic her actions in a manner ſtill more horrible, orders were given to the poſſeſſed, to anſwer truly to all interrogatories. Accordingly, the leaf was laid before her, with the above-mentioned queſtions. Upon this ſhe ſcreemed in a terrible manner, deſiring it might be taken away, for ſhe could not bear it. At laſt, after the moſt preſſing arguments, ſhe ſaid it was Hebrew; and that it was a blaſphemous writing againſt the holy Trinity. This was ſufficient for the doctor, who, after ſhewing them plainly how ignorant their devil was, he returned to court to give an account of his proceedings. The two jeſuits were baniſhed, the two phyſicians recanted in public, and the parents and relations injoined, on pain of being ſent to the gallies, never to mention this affair as a diabolical poſſeſſion. With regard to the girl, ſhe was ſoon cured by the uſe of proper medicines, and is at preſent in good health, and chearful. Thus ended this impoſture, and with it all notions of ſorceries, witchcraft, and fantaſtical poſſeſſions, with which the minds of the people were infected. The jeſuits, indeed, threatened to write againſt Dr. R. but he gave them to underſtand, that in leſs than twenty-four hours they ſhould receive ſuch an anſwer as would prove their eternal diſgrace. At preſent they treat him in the moſt polite manner, but

he

he is wiſe enough not to place any great confidence in their profeſſions of eſteem, and is even ſuſpicious of their feigned civilities.

We may be convinced of the little faith his majeſty places in ſtories of ſorcery and witchcraft, from an inſtance which happened about nineteen years ago. A certain perſon having made a taliſman to repreſent the king, endeavoured, by certain ſuperſtitious ceremonies and incantations, to deſtroy his majeſty by means of that image; but the deceived magician was ſoon apprehended, and convicted for his diabolical intention. The king turned the manner of perpetrating his death into a jeſt, ſaying, he did not remember he had ever enjoyed a better ſtate of health, during his whole life, than during the time the magician was uſing all the means in his power to deſtroy him: and that, if there was in reality any ſuch thing as witchcraft, he was perſuaded that the Almighty would never give ſuch vile perſons a power over the lives and deaths of princes. As the king perſiſted in ſuch ſentiments, the council was obliged to repreſent ſeveral times to his majeſty, that though the power of the villain ſhould be denied, yet, as his intentions were actually criminal, he ought to be puniſhed as an example, to deter others from ſuch proceedings, which muſt be conſidered as ſcandalous to ſociety; eſpecially, as he had often, in his magical incitations, profaned the Euchariſt, a crime which even his majeſty himſelf could not pardon. The king, at laſt, yielded to theſe reaſons, and ſentenced the villain to be ſtrangled, and afterward ſuſpended by one of his legs before the gate of the priſon. It is, however, very probable, that the ſentence would not have been ſoon put in execution, had not the court of Rome, by taking cognizance of the affair, put at once a final period to the tranſaction, and life of the criminal.

They are more ſtrict at Turin, with regard to prohibited books, than in any other part of Italy; thoſe which

which contain opinions differing, though ever ſo minutely, from the tenets of the Romiſh church, and which are publicly ſold at Rome and Naples, no prudent Roman catholic would chooſe to aſk for at Turin.

They have at the court of Turin a particular privilege, called *la grande entrée*, or admittance to the prince. But this privilege is limited to the knights of the ſeveral orders, the archbiſhops and biſhops, the maſter of the ordnance, the generaliſſimo of horſe and foot, and the ambaſſadors and envoys from foreign princes and ſtates. This privilege conſiſts in the above perſons, and all others who have an honourable employment at court, together with the officers upon guard, who are admitted every morning after ten, when the king is at Turin, and propoſes to aſſiſt at maſs; of having admittance into his majeſty's chamber, and of walking out before him, whilſt all others wait in the anti-chamber, and only ſtand on both ſides, whilſt he paſſes. His majeſty is daily to be ſeen both here and at maſs, but he rarely ſpeaks to any one, unleſs a private audience be deſired, a favour ſeldom aſked for by travellers.

The Italian language is rarely ſpoken here, thoſe of France and Piedmont being generally uſed both at court and in the country; but ſome ladies underſtand only the latter, which often renders it difficult for a ſtranger to converſe with them. None are admitted to the court of Turin in bags or ſhort wigs, nor without a long cravat. The only winter amuſement, at court, is the opera. but this is only continued during the carnival. The king's theatre is, indeed, the place of performance, but a private ſociety defrays the expence, which this year amounts to ſeventy-five thouſand livres. The expence of a ſeat in the pit, is three Piedmonteſe livres, and a box for the whole time of the carnival, in the Rang de la Courone, which is the ſecond row upwards, ten Louis d'ors. The theatre is a very grand ſtructure, having five

five galleries, one above another, beautifully ornamented with gilding and ſculpture. When any of the royal family are preſent, no clapping, hiſſing, or noiſy indications of applauſe or diſlike are permitted; a decorum which cannot fail of being approved of by every curious ſpectator. With regard to the Italian muſic, I ſhall ſuſpend my obſervations on it, till I have heard the maſters in other parts of Italy.

The only aſſembly, at court, is the circle abovementioned, but they are frequent in town, particularly at the palaces of the princeſs de Francheville, and madame de Cavaillair. A ſtranger finds no difficulty of gaining admittance to theſe aſſemblies, provided he is willing to play; but he ought to be very careful if he does venture; for though he has nothing to apprehend from any foul play, they being perſons of the ſtricteſt honour, yet unleſs he is a very expert gameſter, he will certainly loſe his money: for the Piedmonteſe are initiated into this art in their infancy, and by a conſtant practice of it, acquire ſuch a degree of perfection, that few are able to play with them. Here was formerly a very celebrated coffee-houſe for gaming, called l'Academie de Pompejo, where Mr. Law, the famous projector, met with the accident to which you are no ſtranger; but that famous gaming-houſe is now in no manner of requeſt; Boiri's coffee-houſe in the Rüe Neuve, being the only place where baſſet is played. According to the manner in which that game is played at Turin, the bank has always forty per cent. advantage over the Pointeurs, as Law has ſufficiently demonſtrated. You will, therefore, not be ſurprized, that fifty Louis d'ors were this year paid to the managers of the opera, for the liberty of ſetting up a bank there during the carnival.

I ſhall now proceed to give a deſcription of the royal palaces, both in and near the city of Turin. With regard to the former, it conſiſts of two principal wings, having a communication with each other by by means of a gallery. The first stands in the square called Place du Chateau, and was the residence of Madame Royale till her death; but is at present, not only uninhabited, but unfurnished. The front, which is very magnificent, was built after a design of Don Philip Juvare, architect to his majesty; but the other side shews, by its large round towers, that it is no modern performance. From the spacious and beautiful Place du Chateau, one passes through a gate, into what is properly the court of the palace, and out of which is a passage through the Corps de Logis, or main body of the palace, into the back court, contiguous to the garden. On the left hand is the main stair-case, on which is a brass statue of duke Victor Amadæus, mounted on a white horse, very curiously formed out of a single block of marble.

The halls before the king's apartment, and the other chambers, are hung with large tapestry, on which are represented the principal actions of Cyrus. They were made by Jacob van Zeunen, a native of the Low Countries, and presented by the emperor Charles V. to the house of Savoy: they are esteemed invaluable on account of their beauty, antiquity, and the number of pieces. The king's apartments are elegantly furnished, and in his bed-chamber is a curious piece of tapestry, representing the battle *ad Brancum deletis Lotharingicis*, &c. as the inscription expresses it. In the gallery is a beautiful marble busto of cardinal Morigi, who was descended from the house of Savoy, and a wooden model of the Charteruse, situated three Piedmontese lines from Turin: but the chief curiosity, are the marble statues, of which there are upward of three hundred, and chiefly antique, covering both sides of the gallery. The king also resides in this story, but opposite to the court. The chamber where he confers with his ministers, is contiguous to the chamber of audience. A passage from his apartments leads to a beautiful gallery of paintings, the largest and best of

6 which

which were done by Paul Veronefe. The frefco work on the wall, and particularly that on the cieling, is exquifitely beautiful, and was performed by the chevalier Daniel, a German, who died in this monarch's fervice.

A flight of ftairs leads from his majefty's and the prince's apartments to the library and repofitory of the archives. The number of books, in the former, is not now remarkable, feven thoufand volumes, together with the manufcripts having lately been given, as a prefent to the univerfity library; but it has ftill a confiderable number, particularly a collection of the choiceft pieces both in hiftory, and the conftitutional laws of Germany.

The royal archives are kept in very good order, in oaken repofitories, carefully locked; and upon fome of thefe are printed titles; for inftance, *Lettres de Milan, de Rome*, &c. *Ceremoniel et Prerogatives de la Maifon de Savoye*; *Negociations à la Cour de Rome*; *avec la France, l'Empire*, &c. *Vicariat du St. Empire en Italie*; *Juftifications des Reliques*, &c. "Letters from "Milan, Rome, &c. the Ceremonial and Preroga- "tives of the Houfe of Savoy; Negotiations at the "Court of Rome; alfo thofe with France, the Em- "pire, &c. the Vicarfhip of the Holy Roman Em- "pire in Italy; the Vouchers of Relics, &c." The inftruments relative to domeftic affairs are feparated according to the refpective diftricts and towns. In every repofitory is a particular lift of all the pieces it contains, and confequently the keeper of the archives, may, in an inftant, find whatever he wants. At the end of the year the minifters of ftate are obliged to fend in to the chamber of archives, all written inftruments they have no farther occafion for.

His majefty had formerly a valuable collection of medals, but they were by degrees all given away to the countefs de Verüe, who carried them with her into France, and afterward difpofed of them to the regent at a very confiderable price.

St. Suaire's chapel, situated on the left hand of the wing of the palace near the garden, is built of a blackish grey marble, that it might in some measure be adapted to the melancholy relic deposited in it. The plan was drawn by P. Guarini; and is said to have cost four millions and a half of Piedmont livres. The linen-cloth, in which Christ (as the clergy here pretend) was wrapped after his crucifixion, and which has the bloody figure of a man imprinted on each side of it, is preserved in the middle of the chapel, in a tabernacle secured by iron-rails; and is exposed to public view only on high solemnities; as the marriage of the hereditary prince, and the like.

The pretended sudary of Christ is likewise shewn at Mentz, Lisbon, and in upward of twelve other Roman catholic places. To this objection, they commonly answer, that from the account of Lazarus's resurrection, it is plain, that a great many linen-clothes were made use of in wrapping the body of the deceased. But this subterfuge, though it might be admitted, if the small bandages used for the arms, feet, or head, are included, can by no means solve the difficulty with regard to the large pieces of linen, on which the intire figure of the person is represented. All they can allege, therefore, is, in truth, no more than this, that large pieces of linen were used without the least necessity, much smaller being equally adapted to answer the same intention; and that our Saviour, after his resurrection, had thought proper to imprint, in a miraculous manner, his intire figure upon every such piece. The clergy of Besançon must necessarily maintain this position, for they boast of being possessed of a sudary which was only wrapped about our Saviour's head; though it exhibits his intire image; and is six geometrical feet, wanting three inches in length. It should, however, be remembered, that all the other holy sudaries produce the very same authorities; and in support of that kept at Cadorn in Perigord, they produce fourteen papal testimonials

timonials and bulls; whereas the ſudary of Turin claims only four. But notwithſtanding this, the veneration paid to it at preſent is ſo great, that Philip of Spain, at the time of his marriage with the princeſs of Savoy, could not obtain the liberty of taking a copy of it, till after repeated ſolicitations, and even then with the greateſt difficulty. Nor was it thought proper to take a copy, without performing, at the ſame time, ſeveral religious ceremonies. The painter performed his work on his knees, and eight biſhops continually read maſs, at eight different altars. Father Valfré was honoured with extraordinary reſpect, ſome threads of this Turin ſudary being given him as a preſent, which he very religiouſly kept continually in his breviary.

Rivoli is a royal palace, ſituated three leagues from Turin toward Suſa. The road is extended all the way in a direct line through fields, meadows, and vineyards, and has not perhaps its equal in the world. It was laid out in the year 1712, after the ſiege of Turin; the French, during their hoſtile incurſions, having rooted up every tree in the whole country. Nothing can ſurpaſs the proſpect of this walk. At one end of it, on a riſing ground, is the palace of Rivoli; at the other, the city of Turin, and two leagues beyond it, in a direct line, the magnificent church of Superga. The palace of Rivoli has the beſt apartments and paintings; and the royal family are lodged more commodiouſly than at La Venerie, or Turin. The air is always ſerene and healthful, creating a good appetite; but, on account of its ſharpneſs, not ſo agreeable to ſleep in. This palace is ſo far from being compleat, that upward of five millions of Piedmont livres are yet wanting to finiſh it.

Formerly, the palace of Valentin, only half a quarter of a league from the city on this ſide Porte Neuve, was the place where moſt of the diverſions of the court were performed. It has the name of Valentin from these obsequious gentlemen, who, as count de Grammont informs us, were pitched upon to attend each lady. Both names derive their original from St. Valentine's day, which happens in the month of February; when it is customary, in most parts of Italy, for those ladies who are single, to chuse a guardian or gallant, by way of amusement, from among her friends or acquaintance; who, in return, presents her with nosegays and other trifles, and is obliged to attend her both in company, and when she walks abroad. This ceremonious attendance continues only a year, is not liable to any exception, and often terminates in a real marriage. The parents, in the mean time, have a watchful eye over the conduct of their daughters; and every thing is performed with so much honour and decency, that even the monks themselves make no difficulty of taking upon them the office of a Valentine. Perhaps they are particularly interested in recommending such pleasing intercourse between both sexes.

The king's territories on the continent contain sixteen bishoprics; among which are the archbishoprics of Turin and Tarantaise. Three hundred and forty towns and villages, beside the city of Turin, are subject to the former; and as every Roman Catholic is obliged, not only to receive the sacrament at Easter, but also to deliver to the priest an exact account of his children and family, it is not difficult to make a pretty exact calculation of the number of inhabitants in such countries. And on this principle the number of the king's subjects in Piedmont, Savoy, and his other dominions on the continent, have been computed at above two millions. Savoy, Piedmont, and the conquered places on the continent are said to contain above two hundred towns.

The king's power, in civil affairs, is greater and more unlimited than that of any monarch in Europe; and few potentates, of the Roman Catholic persuasion, have exercised so great an authority in ecclesiastical matters.

matters. The pope, indeed, has always been treated with the greatest complaisance; and even the legend or bull of Gregory VII. in which he has arrogated to himself the power of dethroning princes, is at present highly extolled as truly heroic; and, though the French vigorously opposed it, the Piedmontese have declared it orthodox: but it must be remembered, that, upon a change of interest, it can as readily be abrogated. The king, in the mean time, has obtained every thing he desired from the pope; and not only nominates to most of the ecclesiastical benefices, in Savoy and Piedmont, but also to those in the bishopric of Alessandria: he has likewise the power of a nomination to a cardinal's hat, of which we have an instance in cardinal Ferreri. The pope had indeed, in this, an opportunity of actually gratifying his personal friendship for Ferreri and was thence the more readily induced to bestow upon the house of Savoy so important a privilege, which, in the church of Rome, is equally attended with profit and honour.

The Piedmontese have, from the transactions of the last forty years, contracted a martial spirit; and, during the late war, such noble exploits were performed by their troops, as would have reflected honour, even on the old Romans themselves. Near the close of the preceding century, marshal Catinat having made an irruption into the Piedmontese territories, it was of the last importance to the king, then only duke of Savoy, to march to Turin before the marshal, in order to put that city in a proper state of defence. Accordingly, he sent major de Santena, since a general, with a body of some hundred men, to the old castle of Avigliano, three German miles from Turin, that commands the valley and road from Susa. Santena, at the approach of the French army, consisting of thirty thousand men, disputed the passage, though he had only a few pieces of cannon in the castle. Catinat, equally surprised and provoked at at ſuch a daring attempt, ſent a trumpet to the caſtle, threatening to hang up the commanding officer, if he did not immediately ſurrender up the place. Santena anſwered, that the commanding officer would never be in his power alive; and that it would be in vain to expect the ſurrender of the caſtle before their cannon arrived. Catinat, ſtill more enraged, cauſed a battery to be raiſed, and a ſecond time ſummoned the caſtle to ſurrender. Santena anſwered, that a breach muſt firſt be made. Accordingly the artillery began to play upon the caſtle, and a breach being made in the walls, Santena deſired to capitulate. Catinat ſent a lieutenant into the caſtle to ſettle the capitulation; but inſiſted that the ſoldiers ſhould be made priſoners of war, and the officers hanged up immediately. Santena, on receiving this meſſage, conducted the lieutenant to his room, ſhut the door, and taking him by the hand, led him between two barrels of gun-powder, near which two lighted matches were laid. Santena took one of the matches in his hand, and ſtepped upon one of the barrels, deſiring the lieutenant to do the ſame; adding, that if he muſt periſh, many of the French ſhould, with him, viſit the aerial regions, before all the Piedmonteſe officers in the caſtle loſt their lives. This compliment not being at all agreeable to the lieutenant, he begged Santena to abandon ſo deſperate a reſolution; promiſing, at the ſame time, that he would do all in his power to obtain an honourable capitulation for the garriſon. On this aſſurance, Santena ſuffered the lieutenant to return; and Catinat, on hearing this reſolute anſwer, ſaid, "I muſt ſee ſo extraordinary a man," and allowed the commander and his men to have the honour of marching out with their ſwords. As Santena paſſed by, the marſhal told him, that in juſtice he deſerved to be hanged: but, being willing to demonſtrate that he was a friend to courage, even in an enemy, he ſhould come that day and dine with him. At table, ſome French officers,

among

among other things, rallied Santena, on the duke's having entered into a league with heretics againſt the moſt Chriſtian king. Santena continued ſilent for ſome time, but at length aſked the marſhal, whether he would give him leave to anſwer? And Catinat permitting him, he replied: "It is true, my maſter has, for his own defence, taken up arms againſt the king of France; and made an alliance with heretics, namely, England and Holland; and, what is ſtill more, ſent an ambaſſador to Conſtantinople to negotiate a treaty with the Turks; but was unfortunately diſappointed, his moſt Chriſtian majeſty having previouſly concluded an alliance with the infidels." Catinat was highly pleaſed with Santena's anſwer, laughed at the officers, and told them, he hoped they would have more wiſdom and generoſity for the future, than to inſult brave men under misfortunes. In the mean time Santena, by his prudent management and behaviour, obtained for his maſter a ſuſpenſion of arms for ſome days.

The long and brave defence of the marquis d'Enteyve, at Verua, againſt the French in the laſt war, is well known. The camp of the allies was near the place, on the banks of the Po, from whence the preſent king of Sardinia often threw bombs, filled with Louis d'ors, into the place, to encourage the garriſon to make a vigorous defence; but, being deſtitute of proviſions, they were obliged at laſt to ſurrender. At their marching out, d'Enteyve cauſed an ammunition loaf to be carried on a pike before him, and as he paſſed by the French general, ſaid to him, "This piece of bread was the only proviſions left in the place; had there been ſufficient for ſubſiſting the garriſon two days longer, you ſhould have bought the place at a much dearer rate."

Nor have the Piedmonteſe failed to diſtinguiſh themſelves by their gallant behaviour in foreign ſervice; of which we had a noble inſtance in the imperial general, St. Amour, who was the ſon of a poor peaſant. Upon his obtaining a regiment, the officers who valued themſelves upon their birth, ſo highly reſented it, that four of his captains ſucceſſively challenged him, all of whom he killed on the ſpot. Upon his diſpatching the laſt of the four, he ſaid, "There are now only eight left." But theſe, it ſeems, thought it more adviſeable to conceal their reſentment. This gentleman deſerves the higheſt regard, both on account of his courage, and his generous diſpoſition; for he never forgets the meanneſs of his extraction. Having, while the army was in Piedmont, invited the chief officers to an entertainment; his father happened to arrive juſt as they were ſitting down to table. Notice of his father's coming being ſent up to the general, he immediately aroſe, informed his gueſts of his arrival, adding, that he knew the regard he owed them; but at the ſame time begged leave to withdraw, and dine with his father in another room: which he accordingly did, notwithſtanding the importunity of his gueſts, who were very deſirous of having his father ſit at their table. Thus he diſcharged the duty he owed his father, and, at the ſame time acted politely toward ſtrangers of diſtinction.

General Roſſallerie ſtill preſerves his great reputation, and has, on ſeveral occaſions, given ſignal proofs of his valour; particularly at the ſieges of Verua and Turin. An accident that happened to him, while he continued in the emperor's ſervice, gave him no great opinion of the Germans One of his horſes dying in the ſtable, he ordered his ſervant to drag out the carcaſe: but the ſervant being unable to perform it, he took hold of the rope himſelf, and aſſiſted him. This action, which, either in Italy or England, would not have been in the leaſt regarded, his ſubalterns conſidered as ſo derogatory to his rank, that they refuſed to ſerve under him. The duke of Lorrain, then generaliſſimo, hearing of the affair, iſſued orders that no perſon ſhould dare to inſult him on this account, and at the ſame time invited him

him to dinner. This order, however, failed of its intended effect, and the general found himself obliged to quit the imperial service.

One action more, performed by a Piedmontese, must not be omitted, and cannot fail of appearing very extraordinary to the world, and intitle its author to the greater applause; as his birth was mean and obscure, and himself deprived of the advantage of a liberal education, the sources from whence most of those actions we stile grand and heroic derive their origin. At the siege of Turin, in the year 1706, the French had forced a passage into one of the largest subterraneous galleries of the citadel; and the engineer, for the great importance of the action, was rewarded with two hundred Louis d'ors. The French now no longer doubted of their being able to penetrate, by means of this passage, into the very center of the citadel; and accordingly planted two hundred grenadiers at the entrance to secure the gallery. This being perceived by one Mica, a peasant of Piedmont, who at first, out of pure necessity, had served as a pioneer, but by his natural sagacity and long experience, was so well acquainted with the art, that he had been made a corporal of the miners, and was then at work in the very place, with about twenty men, in order to finish a mine. On hearing the French busy over his head, in securing the possession of the gallery, he was convinced that it would be of no manner of service to continue his work, the enemy being masters of a place which must inevitably prove the destruction of the besieged. He was also, at the same time, convinced that it would cost him his life to hinder it, his mine having no saucisson or train by which he might fire it with safety. As there was no time to deliberate, he immediately came to the following resolution: he commanded the pioneers who were at work with him, to withdraw immediately out of the mine, and as soon as they were in a place of safety, to fire a musquet as a signal; desiring firing that they would inform the king, that Mica implored of his majesty a maintenance for his wife and children. The signal was accordingly given, and Mica immediately set fire to the mine, by which means, the post occupied by the French, and their grenadiers, together with Mica, perished by the same blast. I shall leave this action, and only add, that the king has not only made a compleat provision for Mica's widow and children, but also settled an annual pension of six hundred livres for ever on his posterity.

Turin is not very large, but populous; and I was assured by one who had seen the account, delivered yearly to the king, by the marquis del Borgo, that, at the end of the year 1728, the number of inhabitants amounted to fifty-four thousand six hundred. The misfortune of one place often turns to the advantage of another; thus, the plague that raged at Marseilles, and the adjacent parts, proved of the greatest benefit to Turin, as several manufactures were introduced, some of which were entirely new to that city; and others, though already there, were but in a languishing condition. Within the city are forty-eight churches and convents, and seventeen in the neighbourhood. The titular patrons or saints of the city are, St. Francis de Sales, St. Francis de Paola, St. Philip Neri, St. Antony of Padua, St. Secundus, and St. Valerius; whose several festivals are celebrated with particular grandeur and devotion. If Turin continues to encrease in grandeur, as it has hitherto done, it will doubtless exceed any city in Europe. Even at present I know not any, either in Italy, France, England, Holland, or Germany, equal to it in that particular. But here I would be understood to mean the new city, containing the king's palace, the Rüe Neuve, and the Rüe de Po, both very grand and beautiful. From the palace gate you have a view of one thousand and seven hundred common paces in a direct line, over the area of the court, and the Place de St. Charles, through the Rüe Neuve to the port Neuve. Le Place de St. Charles is a fine ſquare, and the houſes have all piazzas, under which a perſon may walk without being incommoded in the heavieſt rain.

Proprietors have the liberty of finiſhing the inſide of their houſes as they pleaſe; but the outſide muſt be built according to a certain plan preſcribed them, that all the parts, expoſed to the public view, may be ſimilar and uniform. When the proprietors, either from inclination or inability, refuſe to build, an impartial eſtimate, both of the ground and houſe is made, and the lieutenant of the police purchaſes both, on account of the city: but, to hinder the charges from falling too heavy on the public, the king has taken care to ſettle every thing relating to the contract with the ſurveyors and directors.

The fineſt buildings in the city are the palaces of count Paeſane, count de Gouarene, and the Marquis de Granieri; the Jeſuits college, the hoſpital of St. John, and the palace of Carignan, built after a deſign of father Guarini. The palace of count Paeſane is ſaid to have coſt fifty thouſand Louis d'ors. Beſide theſe, there are many fine buildings lately erected near the Port de Suſa, and the parts adjacent to the Caroline-ſquare. Theſe expenſive decorations of the city are greatly facilitated, by an order, that every one who intends either to rebuild or enlarge his houſe, may oblige his next neighbour, provided his houſe be of leſs value than what he intends to erect, to diſpoſe of the whole, or a competent part of his ground to him, at a reaſonable price.

The cleanlineſs of the ſtreets is remarkable, and owing to the following contrivance: a canal is cut from the river Doria to the covert way, between the citadel and Porte de Suſa; and from thence the water is conveyed, by means of an aqueduct, over the town-foſſe into the city, and afterward diſtributed at pleaſure through every part of the ſtreets, and cleanſes them from all filth and ſoil. They can alſo, by this means,

means, clear the ſtreets from any ſnow that may happen to fall during the winter; but ſometimes they are not permitted to do this, becauſe the hereditary prince often diverts himſelf in riding on it in a ſledge.

The eccleſiaſtical buildings in this city are very ancient, and not to be compared with thoſe already deſcribed, which were all erected during the two laſt reigns.

The chapel of Corpus Chriſti, which ſtands in the herb-market, is much frequented on account of a miracle ſaid to have been performed there. In the year 1453, the Savoyards plundered Exiles; and, among other pillage, a conſecrated Hoſt was brought to Turin. The aſs, in whoſe loading it was, ſtopped at this place, kneeled down, and would not go any farther. In the mean time the box with which the aſs was loaded opened of itſelf, and the conſecrated wafer flew up into the air, where it continued hovering in the ſight of numberleſs ſpectators, till the biſhop, who was ſoon informed of the miracle, arrived: immediately the ſacred wafer deſcended into his holy hand, and was by him placed in this church. In the year 1598, the adjacent country being viſited with a terrible plague, the inſide of this church was finely decorated with beautiful marble pillars and ſtatues; an elegant front was alſo added, at the charge of the city, as a votive offering for having eſcaped the contagious diſtemper.

On the other ſide of the bridge, over the Po, about half a league from the city, is the chapel of Notre Dame de Pilone, full of mean paintings and ſmall ſilver images, depoſited there as votive offerings. Among the laſt, is one repreſenting the bleſſed Virgin, who, according to the inſcription, appeared to a young girl of eleven years of age who had fallen into the Po, and though immerſed under the water, near the wheels and eddies of a mill, eſcaped without receiving the leaſt hurt; and this chapel was erected by the piety of the faithful, as a grateful monument of ſo happy a deliverance.

About three years ago, a child at Ulm fell into the Danube, and, after having been toſſed by the wheels of a mill, and carried a pretty way down the river, by the rapidity of the ſtream, was taken up without receiving the leaſt hurt. And an inſcription is engraved on a copper-plate, to perpetuate ſo remarkable an event.

The hoſpital for lunaticks merits the attention of all ſtrangers, on account of its excellent regulations. Here I ſaw the relation of a certain great general and ambaſſador, whoſe imagination is ſtrongly poſſeſſed with the notion of his being the legitimate ſon of Lewis the XIVth, his mother, (as he imagines) not having been the miſtreſs, but the wife of that prince. Accordingly, he inſiſted upon having a ſplendid court, and all the enſigns of royalty. But this being refuſed him, he became ſo furious, that they found themſelves under a neceſſity of ſending him to this hoſpital, where he has a particular apartment to himſelf, with a little gallery for walking, his brother paying eight hundred Piedmonteſe livres for his annual maintenance.

The king is very careful of obtaining exact intelligence with regard to the manner of executing the laws of the police; he has formerly been even known to walk about the ſtreets of the city alone, muffled up in a cloak, that he might ſee himſelf how affairs were managed in the city. He once took from a baker a loaf, which ſeemed to be both bad bread and ſhort of weight, and carried it to the ſenate, in order to have it examined. The baker laid the blame on the heavy duty, which obliged them to uſe ſuch meal; and, as the complaint was not entirely deſtitute of foundation, his majeſty cauſed ſome alteration to be made in that reſpect, and the exciſe to be lowered in proportion.

Thus have I given an account of what pleaſed me moſt in Turin; you will permit me to mention what I moſt diſliked: and in the front of theſe I muſt place the frequent thick fogs in autumn and winter, ariſing from the Po and other waters, which render the air thick, damp, and conſequently unhealthful. Theſe exhalations chiefly affect the inhabitants of the city, which is often covered with noxious fogs, when Rivoli enjoys, at the ſame time, the moſt ſerene and delightful weather.

The foul and muddy water, in moſt of the wells and reſervoirs in this city, is an inconveniency almoſt as bad as the fogs; eſpecially when it is remembered that this continues all the year. The badneſs of the water, in a great meaſure, reſults from their neglect to keep the wells and reſervoirs clean; dead animals, and other filth, being frequently thrown into them. There is, indeed, before the Po-gate, near the capuchin monaſtery, a well of excellent water, which they take care to preſerve from filth, by locking it up.

Another inconvenience is the vile regulation of the inns with regard to ſtrangers; the uſage being very bad, and the impoſitions intolerable. In ſhort, the entertainment at Turin is worſe than in any other part of Italy. The country produces plenty of good wine; but, unleſs you pay an exorbitant price, what they ſell at the public inns is the moſt wretched ſtuff in the world. The catholics in particular, on faſt-days, are very badly off; for, notwithſtanding the Po abounds with a great variety of excellent fiſh, as pike, carp, perch, trout, and ſturgeon, weighing from eighty to a hundred pounds; the avaricious landlords will not be at the expence of purchaſing freſh fiſh, but their gueſts muſt be contented with miſerably bad ſalt fiſh, or an aumellete of ſtale eggs.

Their manner of burying the dead is very unnatural and offenſive. They carry the corpſe in proceſſion to the grave, into which they put it without any coffin. I need not mention how diſagreeable a ſpectacle

tacle this must be, when the person died of the measles, small-pox, or the like infectious distempers. But the disagreeableness of the spectacle is not the worst consequence that attends it; we know the effluvia are infectious, and consequently must greatly tend to spread the disease. The masked fraternities, who often attend funerals, and whose eyes only can be seen, make indeed a frightful, but at the same time, a very mean appearance. The churches are also, by their negligence, often rendered offensive; for it is not uncommon, even when any contagious distemper rages, to see three or four dead bodies lying in them uncovered a whole day. Persons of distinction have their peculiar family-vaults in the churches and chapels; but the poorer sort are thrust into a kind of hole under ground, in their parish-churches, from fifty to a hundred and fifty together, without any coffins. The passages indeed into these deep repositories are vaulted, and have several doors between them and the church; but all is not sufficient to prevent the noxious effluvia from diffusing itself over the whole church. I well know, that this inconveniency is not peculiar to the churches at Turin, but a nuisance common to most of the large cities, especially in Romish countries. But, as it is a practice repugnant to reason, it ought to be universally rejected.

The celebrated Dr. Philip Verheyen, professor of physic and anatomy at Louvain, who died in 1710, in his lifetime, caused an inscription to be placed on his own tomb, importing, " That he had ordered his mortal part to be deposited in the church-yard, that he might not defile the church, or infect it with noxious steams." A caution, that certainly merits the most serious attention.

Nor can I be reconciled to the unbounded liberty which mountebanks and empirical quacks have obtained in Turin, as well as in other parts of Italy, of cheating the people both of their money and their

health.

health. The ordinances of the Turin academy, indeed, prohibit, under pain of death, any person from selling medicines, without a permission from the first physician of the country; but this prohibition is of no consequence, every place swarming with ignorant itinerants; unless the physician can be suspected of granting his licences, without knowing either the person, or the nature of medicines he has the confidence of selling to the common people. There are always in the Place de Chateau, several stages erected for these empirics, where each endeavours to excel his rival in music, antic tricks, and other fooleries, in order to augment the number of his audience. And it is shocking to hear what asseverations these impious wretches make use of to recommend their noxious preparations. Some days since I heard one of them begin his harangue in the following solemn manner: "Praised be the Lord Jesus Christ, of whom I desire no more than that he will deal with me according to his righteousness in the last judgment, in the same manner as I shall with you this day. I squander away my substance from an affectionate regard for your health; but the devil, that enemy of all good works, has so blinded your eyes, that you look upon a few sols as equal to a hundred scudi, and by that means neglect your own health, and that of your nearest relations, which might be established for so insignificant a trifle: if I take a single doit from you contrary to the dictates of my conscience, I wish I may be condemned to swallow your melted money through all eternity in hell, &c."

This detested empiric's panacea consisted of two powders, with which he pretended to cure infallibly the apoplexy, epilepsy, or falling-sickness, cholic, head-ach, consumption, and dropsy; though at the same time the price of both was no more than a single parabojoles or nine pfennings; whence a judgment may be formed of the excellent ingredients of which these medicines were compounded. Modesty, however,

ever, does not ſeem to be entirely baniſhed from the tooth-drawers; for they commonly aſſure their patients, that they will happily take their teeth out *con adjuto di ſanta Apollonia*, "with the help of St. Apollonia," the titular ſaint and patroneſs of the teeth. And, whenever ſhe is named, both the doctor and audience never fail to pull off their hats in token of reverence.

[To what is related by Mr. Keyſler, we ſhall add ſome farther particulars of a later date, and of a more familiar nature, from the ingenious Mr. Sharpe; whoſe letters from Turin are dated in May 1766.

"There are two theatres at Turin; the one for the ſerious opera, almoſt as large and magnificent as that at Naples; the ſecond, a ſmaller, for the three other kinds of ſpectacles: namely, the Comedie Françoiſe, the Comedie Italienne, and the Opera Comique. Theſe four exhibitions ſucceed each other, in the four different ſeaſons of the year; but the king and family never frequent any but the grand opera. I do not learn that his majeſty lays himſelf under this reſtraint, from any religious exception to a play-houſe, but merely becauſe it is the etiquette of the court. Should the royal family break through this ridiculous form, it would certainly tend to improve their ſtage, and render the ſpectacles more brilliant; but they have a cuſtom here, which will always preſerve elegance and decorum in their operas. There is a ſociety of forty gentlemen, anſwerable for every expence whatſoever, viz. the ſalaries of the actors and the orcheſtra, the purchaſe of the ſcenery, the dreſſes, &c. &c. ſo that the performers are ſure of their pay, though the operas ſhould not ſucceed. It is not ſo with regard to the Italian and French comedians; thoſe two companies taking the chance of good and bad houſes.

Whilſt I am at Turin, I go every day to the king's anti-chamber, to ſee him and his court paſs to chapel, and as conſtantly wait on them through the whole service: if meerly attending on public worship be a work of merit, I may vaunt with the Pharisee in the Gospel, of my great desert. You will wonder to hear so much of my perseverance in the pursuit of these religious ceremonies; but, as the folly I am enquiring after is infinite, were I to live here for ever, the search would likewise be endless. The good old king, in his latter days, gives himself up entirely to devotion; the rest of the family too are exceedingly devout: the church, therefore, is triumphant at Turin, and the chief splendor of this city is to be found in the king's chapel. He has a choice orchestra, at the head of which are Pugnani, and the two Bisoucis. He seldom prays to God; but as Nebuchadnezzar prayed to his God, with the sound of the sackbut, the psalter, and all kinds of musical instruments. Certainly, if a gilded church be an honour to the Deity, he is much more honoured in Italy than in England, and the catholic religion, if I may use the expression, is much more flattering to him than our plain home spun form of prayer.

On Saturday last, the whole mass was performed in the pantomime manner, the priest not pronouncing one word aloud, but only accompanying the music through the whole office, with a thousand unintelligible, (at least to me) ridiculous gestures. The day following being Whitsunday, there was a high mass, which continued exactly fifty minutes, and was celebrated both by music and by chaunting. The tricks played by the priests, and their attendants, during the celebration, are so whimsical, that, were I capable of describing them, you would imagine I had sat down to invent raillery, sarcasm, and caricature. To give you some idea of one part: conceive to yourself, four young men in scarlet banyans, and white nightrails, walking half the time of the service before the altar; one moment bowing like the judges in Bays's dance, to the king, the next moment to the altar; and presently after, to the ground; thus ringing

ringing the changes for fifty minutes: then each of them has a large lighted taper, which, for a certain length of time, they carry horizontally, walking solemnly one after another, with the same care as you would step along a narrow deal board, without touching the cracks of the floor. After this procession they bend both knees toward the ground, but not so far as to touch the ground, just in the method you have seen dancers on the slack rope, but something more deliberately; after this, they raise themselves from that uneasy posture, to an erect situation; but with so circumspect and gradual a motion, that they tremble and totter, not without some risk of falling: when the genuflection and elevation are finished, or, rather, during the operation, the tapers are thrown into various positions, as a soldier would exercise with a pike or a musket. How the fertile and foolish brain of man could invent all this foppery and nonsense is wonderful; but it would, perhaps, be curious, could we come at the history of its origin, and on what pretence these several practices were introduced. I am afraid to go on with my description, because I feel myself unequal to the ridiculousness; and, indeed, lest I should forfeit the character of veracity, by telling truths so very like falsehoods: but must not omit to mention, that, at a certain moment, (I think the instant after the elevation of the host) the two priests who officiate at the altar, embrace and kiss other priests who sit on the bench near the altar, with a solemnity and grimace truly ludicrous. I confess it is seldom pardonable, to deride the ceremonies of any religion sincerely professed by its followers; but, when the ceremonies of a religion are farcical, and so palpably the instruments of oppression and tyranny, by which the common sense and civil rights of the world are enslaved to a proud priesthood; it were virtue to laugh till men grew ashamed of their folly.

There is at Turin a famous violin, called Pugnani, in the higheſt reputation for his proficiency on that inſtrument; and, in the opinion of the Italians, and even the Engliſh here, ſuperior to Giardini. It has been my good fortune to hear him to the greateſt advantage; but, if I may hazard my ſentiments on this delicate point, I muſt tell you, though I am ſingular in my judgment, I prefer Giardini, and eſteem him a much more agreeable performer than Pugnani. It is ſaid, Pugnani draws out a louder tone from the upper part of the fiddle than Giardini does, and this, it muſt be granted, is his fort; but, with ſubmiſſion to Italian ears, mine were a little ſhocked in ſeveral parts of his ſolo. I wiſhed he had been a little more ſweet, though he had been leſs forte; and, from this example of ſo excellent a performer, it may be ſuſpected that a ſtring, of a certain ſhortneſs, will not admit of ſweetneſs beyond ſuch a degree of loudneſs. His taſte and elegance I thought by no means comparable to Giardini's; but, perhaps, I may have been miſtaken in all my criticiſms; however, I am perſuaded, though my judgment may be falſe, that it does not ſpring from a want of feeling; for the Biſoucis, both of them, (the hautbois and the baſſoon) gave me the pleaſure I expected from their fame; who, though they are extremely old, have ſtill the ſame powers as formerly. Moſt probably Pugnani will find his way to England ſome time or another; but, at preſent, I am told the king will not ſuffer it; for, though his majeſty has no reliſh for muſic, he will have the beſt hands he can procure for divine ſervice. I ſuppoſe, were a plain Chriſtian to aſk, why all this noiſe and parade in divine worſhip? why all theſe drums, trumpets, and clangor? Are not a good life, a devout heart, and a ſober prayer, the moſt pleaſing offering that can be made to the Deity? The men with ſhaved heads, holy water, ſweet burning incenſe, tapers lighted at noon day, and a wafer god, would treat him as a fanatic, a here-a heretic, a blaſpemer: and, in my opinion, conſiſtent enough with the reſt of their conduct, who are ſo abſurd and cruel, as to mutilate young lads, in order to render their voices and praiſes more acceptable to an Almighty Being.

The environs of Turin are nearly as pleaſant as thoſe of Florence; and, if you conſider the beauty of the river, fully ſo: the city itſelf is, certainly, much more regular and handſome than any other in Italy, and would be a delightful abode, were a man well recommended and introduced into the beſt company; for our notions and characters of places often depend on the little accident of falling into agreeable or diſagreeable ſociety. The young Engliſhmen here complain of the dullneſs and melancholy of the court, which throws a gloom over the whole face of Turin; as there is neither an Engliſh or a French ambaſſador here, the common reſources of amuſement and politeneſs, in the principal courts of Europe. The king, as I have intimated, prays much; the duke of Savoy not a little: the ladies in waiting are ancient, the ſame that adorned the drawing-room ſome thirty or forty years ago: then the duke is the father of nine children, a circumſtance which naturally renders a man ſomewhat ſerious in every ſtation of life. All theſe things conſidered, you will imagine Turin is not ſo gay as it might have been under other circumſtances. The women, however, are extremely beautiful and fair in this country, though, indeed, the ladies of Milan and Venice almoſt vie with them in complexion and features. It is a matter of aſtoniſhment, to what a degree this fairneſs of ſkin prevails in the northern parts of Italy. I can hearken to a reaſoner, who informs me, that the frequent mixture of the Moors, and their intermarriages with the Spaniards, during the ſeveral centuries they occupied ſo large a portion of Spain, will account for the olive complexion of that nation; but we are ſtill at a loſs to comprehend why the French are a browner people than the inhabitants of Piedmont and Lombardy, who live in nearly the same latitude. The common people are more olive-coloured than the gentry here; but that, perhaps, is owing to the heat of the sun: so that, in fact, they are rather sun-burnt than of a natural olive-colour. The women here, are so much handsomer than those in Naples, that, on the first thought, one wonders that a Neapolitan, of a large fortune, does not, for the sake of a fair offspring, seek a wife in these parts; but, when it is considered how little the charms of beauty, affection, society, and constancy, are required in marriage here; the wonder ceases: family connections, fortune, and an eldest son, seem to be the only objects of matrimony.

I go every night to the comedy. The company of comedians are from Venice, and perhaps are the best company in Italy; but, the drama all over Italy is in a very low state, and how a reformation should be effected, I can hardly conceive. Their plays are generally dull, where they are not farcical; and where they are farcical, they descend to the ribaldry of our jack puddings at Bartholomew-Fair. How, therefore, should they ever have good actors, till their actors are furnished with better compositions, and better heard; and, what is also of equal consequence, better paid than at present? I must not, now I am upon the subject of plays, any longer forget to tell you, that at Florence, women, as with us, sit in the pit: a custom, I believe, peculiar to that city.

In the great guard room, adjoining to the king's apartments, I see the same cobwebs I left there last year, and, which possibly have subsisted ever since the beginning of this century. Strange, that, in so elegant a palace, there should be so glaring, so nasty a deformity; but it is in England only, where a uniformity of grandeur, and cleanliness, bespeaks the riches of the master! In Italy you see some palaces

with

with pictures and ſtatues, to the value of ten or twenty thouſand pounds, and a bricked floor, you would be aſhamed of, in your kitchen; then the hangings, chairs, and curtains, are ſuch, as an Engliſhman would bluſh to put into his garrets. Another inſtance, a ſtriking one indeed, of parſimony mixed with royalty, is, that at this moment, both in the gardens at Parma, and Turin, they are actually making hay in the ſmall plots, or partitions; and I ſhould ſuppoſe, the quantity is rather an object of ſhillings, than guineas; for the abundance of meadow-grounds all through Piedmont and Lombardy, is really ſurpriſing.

I take pleaſure in ſurveying the fortifications of Turin. I conſider this ſtate as our natural ally, an enemy to France, from its ſituation; and it gives me the utmoſt delight, to ſee the exact order in which they are kept: it appears to me, that if a brick decay, it is immediately ſupplied with a new one. The repairs of ſo many fortified towns, in ſo ſmall a principality, muſt fall heavy on the king's revenue; but there is an œconomy here practiſed in government, an Engliſhman has no idea of: I have it from the beſt authority, that the appointments of the ſecretary of ſtate, are about four hundred pounds a year ſterling.

I think I have mentioned, how frequently I have bluſhed in England at the brutal cuſtom, which prevails amongſt the common people there, of boxing upon every little quarrel; and how often I have ſince bluſhed in Italy, that I ſhould have been aſhamed of my country, for a practice, which I now eſteem laudable, taking mankind ſuch as they are. I find, by experience here, that the ſudden indignation and tranſports of a choleric man, muſt be immediately gratified, and when a bloody noſe given on the ſpot, or the gentle and cooler method of challenging the offender to ſtrip, does not ſatisfy, aſſaſſination will take place, and ſtabbing will be the ſubſtitute of boxing. I am led into the repetition of this remark, by a ſtory, I picked up the other day, in this city, which pleaſes me extremely, as it characterizes ſo ſtrongly, the different geniuſes of the Italian, and the Engliſh common people. It ſeems, that a few weeks ſince, ſome Engliſh ſailors in the port of Nice, had got drunk at a public houſe, grew noiſy and quarrelſome, ſtript into buff, and fought it out; but the poor landlady, who expected nothing leſs, from the outſet of the fray, than blood and murder, had, in the very beginning of it, run for the guard of the town, to take them into cuſtody: the guard accordingly came; but, before this period, the ſailors had finiſhed their battle, and had ſet down to drink again, the beſt friends in the world; which they explained to the ſoldiers: but the ſoldiers, not having the leaſt comprehenſion of ſuch ſudden forgiveneſs and friendſhip, inſiſted they ſhould all go to the guard-houſe: this obſtinacy affronted our tars, who fell violently upon them, and, I think, broke two or three of their muſkets; but in the end they were overpowered, and one of them taken priſoner, the reſt eſcaping to their ſhip. The ſequel of the ſtory is, that the commandant put the priſoner into the ſtocks all night, which is an infamous kind of puniſhment here; for they do not ſit, but lie, (perhaps in the mud) on their backs. Now, the priſoner happening to be the boatſwain of the ſhip, he thought his dignity affronted, and lodged a complaint againſt the commandant, with the Engliſh *chargé d'affaires*, who reported it to the king. His majeſty was very gracious, condemned the precipitancy of the commandant, who, he ſaid, ſhould have ſent to court for his inſtructions, laughed at the ridiculouſneſs of the event, but told the *chargé d'affaires*, that no reparation could be made, in any kingdom of the world, to a man who had oppoſed the officers of juſtice, in the regular execution of their duty.

The frequency of ſtabbing in theſe countries, is not, however, meerly owing to the ungovernableneſs of the paſſions; for, were men under more reſtraint,

the

the crime, I am perſuaded, would be leſs common; but, here, beſide the ſanctuary which delinquents find in churches and holy places, there is another ſtill more open ſanctuary, I mean, the remiſſneſs both of law and proſecution. Mr. Murray, our late reſident at Venice, upon his firſt arrival there, loudly proclaimed, that ſhould any Engliſhmen be aſſaſſinated during his reſidentſhip, no expence, no interpoſition, ſhould prevent his bringing the criminal to condign puniſhment: the Venetian common people are all appriſed of his reſolution, and, that no Engliſhman has been murdered, he aſcribes to this meaſure. Sir James Gray, our late envoy at Naples, I am told, was once extremely active in bringing a criminal to the gallows, who had aſſaſſinated one of our countrymen. The example, perhaps, had a good effect on their behaviour, as there has been no ſuch other inſtance ſince that time; but it had little influence on their morals; for the day happening to be black and ſtormy, the common people believed that heaven was offended at the execution of a catholic for the death of a heretic; ſo far were they from imagining it was a proper juſtice, and a ſacrifice pleaſing to God. Could the church be prevailed on to recede from the right of ſheltering murderers, it would be a great ſtride toward a reformation of this enormous evil. At Florence, where Sir Horatio Man informed me, fewer capital crimes are committed than in any other city of Italy, my eyes were tired with the view of an aſſaſſin and another delinquent, who had taken refuge on the ſteps before a church contiguous to lord ———'s houſe. One could not look out of window, but theſe fellows preſented themſelves to your ſight; they ſauntered upon the ſteps all day, and retired into the church during the night. His lordſhip told me, they had led this life many months, and ſo badly do good people often judge of real charity, that it was eſteemed a matter of religion in the neighbourhood to ſupply theſe wretches every day with a ſufficiency of provision. I must not omit, however, to mention, that government, upon very extraordinary occasions, will sometimes encroach a little upon the privileges of the church. Not long ago, there was a murder, of a very atrocious nature, committed in that city, and the perpetrator, as usual, flew to a church for his asylum; upon which, the magistracy caused it to be surrounded night and day, with a guard sufficient to prevent any one from going to mass there, and, consequently, from carrying him any sustenance. In a few days, the criminal, from a certainty of present death, by starving, threw himself in the hands of justice, to take his trial, when he met with his deserts." We now return to Mr. Keysler.]

The genius, temper, and method of living among the Savoyards, having been already considered, it remains, that I now give you some account of the Piedmontese. A native of this country some time since drew up a comparison between them, but I am far from pretending to justify it. He pretended, that, among ten Piedmontese, one honest man might probably be found, but not one dishonest person among ten Savoyards. But whether this assertion be true or false, this is certain, that the Piedmontese are extremely artful, and it would greatly tend to promote their reputation, if they never employed their talents in an improper manner. They are, however, very careful to conceal the abuse they make of them under such plausible circumstances and artful appearances, that it is impossible not to admire their dexterity.

In 1695, a Piedmontese, under the borrowed name of count Caraffa, came to Vienna, and immediately waited on the imperial minister, pretending that the duke of Savoy had sent him to negotiate some weighty affair between themselves, without the knowlege of the French ambassador. He produced, at the same time, his credentials, in which both the hand-writing and seal of the duke were imitated to the greatest perfection.

tion. Accordingly, he was very favourably received; and ſoon after publicly declared himſelf envoy extraordinary from the court of Savoy. He was honoured with frequent conferences by the emperor's council; and was ſo well received in the genteeleſt aſſemblies, that on the captain of the guards refuſing him admittance to a private concert in the palace, he demanded ſatisfaction in his maſter's name, and the captain was commanded to aſk his pardon. To obtain the protection and friendſhip of the jeſuits, whoſe power, at court, he was no ſtranger to, was his firſt care. Accordingly, he viſited their church, and, obſerving that it was not finiſhed, owing, as they alleged, to the utter inability of the ſociety to proceed in the work, he aſked them what ſum of money it would require? The fathers, in anſwer to his queſtion, laid before him an eſtimate, amounting to two thouſand Louis d'Ors. Upon which the pretended Caraffa declared his particular attachment to their order, adding, that he thought himſelf extremely happy in meeting with the leaſt opportunity of ſhewing it publicly; that they might continue the building of their church, toward which, he that very day ſent them the two thouſand Louis d'ors. He was, however, ſenſible, that he could not long act his part without being diſcovered; and, not being willing to bear the whole expence of ſuch a piece of generoſity, he invited ſeveral of the firſt ladies of the court to ſupper and a ball. Every one promiſed him their company: but he pretended to complain that they had ſeveral times before diſappointed him, and, in a jocoſe manner, deſired a pledge from each lady, as a ſecurity for her fulfilling her promiſe, by honouring him with her preſence. Accordingly, one gave him a ring, another a pearl necklace, a third rich ear-rings, and a fourth a gold watch, with ſeveral things of value, ſo that the pledges amounted to near twelve thouſand dollars. All the gueſts appeared at the place and time appointed; but the diſappointment and chagrine of the

whole

whole company are much easier imagined than described, when they were convinced that their gay friend was no other than a sharper, and was retired from Vienna. The jesuits had likewise but little reason to boast of their good fortune: for, a few days before his departure, putting on an air of a deep concern, he threw himself in the way of the emperor's confessor, who, observing him to be remarkably melancholy, asked him the reason. The count answered, that he would venture to entrust him with the secret, which was, that he wanted money at the very time his master's affairs required a sum of eight thousand Louis d'ors, to render his negociation at the imperial court successful. The jesuits, who had so lately known an instance of his liberal disposition, made no scruple of furnishing him with the eight thousand Louis d'Ors; and, with this acquisition, together with the pledges of the ladies, he thought proper to withdraw. Some years after he was apprehended on a very different occasion, in the duke's territories, and that prince ordered him to be beheaded in prison. But I have been assured at Turin, that his sentence was changed into an imprisonment for life, the duke's council having pleaded very pathetically on the following maxim in the law, *quod excellens in arte non debeat mori*, "Whoever has uncommon skill in any art should not be put to death."

The late father Sacchieri, of Turin, was a remarkable instance of the strength of human understanding, particularly that faculty of the soul we term memory. He was very well versed in the higher geometry, especially in Leibnitz's Analysis Infinitorum; and, after reading over with attention a leaf in any printed book, he could, with the greatest ease, repeat it with fluency, both forward and backward. Upon hearing a sermon, provided the preacher did not exceed above an hour in delivering it, he could readily repeat it in the same order; though the Italian sermons seem to be less connected than any others, on account

account of the maxims and moral ſentences with which they abound. He could play at cheſs with three different perſons at the ſame time, even without ſeeing any one of the cheſs-boards. He required no more than that his ſubſtitute ſhould tell him what piece his antagoniſt had moved, and Sacchieri could direct what ſtep was to be taken on his ſide, holding at the ſame time converſation with the company preſent. If any diſpute aroſe about the place where any piece ſhould be, he could tell every move that had been made, not only by himſelf but by his antagoniſt, from the beginning of the game; and in this manner unconteſtably decide the proper place of the piece. This uncommon dexterity at the game of cheſs appears to me almoſt the greateſt inſtance that can be produced of a ſurpriſing memory. And, for the truth of the fact, I can appeal to witneſſes, whoſe veracity, as well as high rank, will not admit of the leaſt doubt.

But a quickneſs of parts is not only obſervable among perſons of faſhion and learning, but likewiſe among the common people in Piedmont, who are remarkable for their penetration: for which they are very probably indebted, both to the warm climate of Italy, and their proximity and intercourſe with the French nation, with whom they are ſometimes at peace, but more frequently at war. We muſt, however, except, out of the number of the king's ſagacious ſubjects, the inhabitants of the mountains of Aoſta, who ſeldom or never leave their vallies, and hardly believe that any part of the world is inhabited beſide the ſpot where they dwell. The greateſt part of them have wens or ſtrumous ſwellings on their throats, and the ſame diſtemper is alſo obſervable among their horſes, dogs, &c. Such excreſcences are therefore, in all probability, owing to the water they drink. The natives are ſo accuſtomed to them, that they are not conſidered as deformities. And it is ſaid, that a ſtrange lady, who had not a wen, coming

ing into a church in this valley, during the ſermon: ſo uncommon a ſight diſturbed the devotion of the congregation, and produced a general laugh. Even the preacher, after looking about ſome time for the cauſe of this uproar, could not contain his riſible paſſion; but, ſoon recovering his clerical gravity, he repreſented to his audience, that, indeed, in what they had done, they were not altogether culpable, though the natural imperfections of our neighbours were not proper objects of mirth and ridicule; that a Chriſtian, upon any ſuch occaſion, ſhould rather be thankful to providence for the gifts beſtowed on him, than inſult his neighbour for being deſtitute of them.

With regard to the manner of living among the ladies in Turin, it is extremely free; they continually talk to the men, and laugh ſo exceſſively, as would be liable to cenſure in other places. Each has her gallant and confident for carrying on intrigues; and with theſe they converſe at aſſemblies. But foreigners, who do not approve of living gaily, muſt not expect to have their company greatly coveted. Vanity and a love of praiſe make them extremely polite to ſtrangers, and, upon their coming into an aſſembly, they riſe, and talk with them about the weather, the opera, and the like; but never proceed any farther. The ſame behaviour ſhewn to ſtrangers, during the firſt week, continues the ſame for near a quarter of a year; but their complaiſance abates much ſooner, if they imagine their ſtay at court, or in the city, ſhould be longer. They ſpeak but little French, generally their own Piedmonteſe language, which is a medley of French and Italian: many words are intirely French, but ſpoken as they are written; for inſtance, *lait* (milk) is pronounced *laït*, and it is the ſame with *fait*, and other words.

Piedmont carries on a conſiderable trade in ſilk, which, for fineneſs and ſtrength, are reckoned the beſt in Italy. All the ſilk manufactures in Turin are as good as in any place, except the glazed ſilks, or brocades, and the gold and ſilver tiſſues, which fall far ſhort of thoſe of France. Many peaſants in Piedmont ſell, ever year, between four and five rubbs (each rubb weighing twenty-five pounds) of ſilk, which has not yet been wound from the balls; and each pound of theſe rubbs is worth betwixt twenty and twenty-five ſols. Theſe balls being thrown into warm water, the threads are readily looſened, and wound off without the leaſt difficulty, and without any waſte. Between three and four ſuch threads are wound off together, and theſe conſtitute the firſt fine threads. A pound of this fine ſilk is worth about a Louis d'or. After boiling the threads, they change from a yellow colour to a white. Some of the balls can never be rendered uſeful; this happens when the worm dies there, and the putrefaction of the inſect deſtroys the texture of the ſilk. Theſe are all put into a wooden veſſel, and trodden out with the feet; but, as this ſort of ſilk cannot be ſpun fine, it is only uſed for linings. It is not allowed to keep any ſilk-worms, at leaſt, in any conſiderable numbers, at Turin, they being looked upon as detrimental to health, the people imagining, that, from their ſeveral tranſformations, fermentations, and ſome degree of putrefaction, the air may be impregnated with pernicious particles, which are not ſo eaſily diſſipated in the city as in the country. Ever ſince the dreadful contagious fevers, which, during the year 1709, raged with ſuch violence at Peſaro, and which, according to the opinion of Joh. Maria Lanciſi, the pope's phyſician, proceeded from the putrid effluvia ariſing from water where the worms had been trodden out, it was ordered, " That ſilk-worms, in their balls, ſhould be dried in ovens, where bread was afterward to be baked; that they ſhould not be boiled in kettles, unleſs convenient pits or ditches were at hand to convey the infectious water from the city; that the dead worms ſhould be taken out of the cods of ſilk before they are boiled, and both the dead worms and the erucas ſhould not be thrown into the city-ditch, as it is without water, but carried to the Pharos, and thrown into the sea." It is not difficult to compute the number of silk-worms possible to be kept from the number of white mulberry-trees. The worms produced from an ounce of eggs eat between eighty and a hundred and forty rubbs of mulberry-leaves, according as the season has been more or less warm; for they eat less in cold than in warm weather. Mulberry-leaves sell from ten to twenty-five sols a rubb, or twenty-five pounds.

The papilioes, immediately after their leaving the pod, copulate, and, after eight or ten days, deposit their eggs, and die. The eggs are, during the winter, preserved with the greatest care; and as soon as the buds appear on the mulberry-trees, they are placed between two matrasses, and in forty days, by a gentle warmth are hatched. Some women greatly hasten the production of the worms, by carrying the eggs in paper bags in their bosoms.

The nobility of Piedmont have large quantities of silk-worms on their estates in the country, which, under certain restrictions, they commit to the care of their tenants. This task requires great attention, on account of the fresh air that must continually be let into the large rooms where they are kept, and the careful feeding of them at proper seasons. The nobleman provides the silk-worms eggs, which, in Piedmont, are generally worth between three livres and a half and five livres per ounce, together with the requisite quantity of mulberry-leaves; for which he has half the produce of the silk in return. The general produce of silk, from an ounce of eggs, if the worms work well, is about four rubbs of balls of unwound silk.

No good reason can be given why the production of silk is so greatly neglected in Germany, as it would save the country prodigious sums of money annually. France has, in this particular, shewn a good example to her neighbours, as the breeding of silk-worms and establishing of silk manufactures, dur-

ing

ing the reign of Henry IV. have proved inexhaustible sources of riches to that kingdom. The English, who import great part of their silk from Persia, and mix it up with that of Italy, are very sensible what advantages would result to the nation, could they propagate the silk-worm in their country, as, by the addition of Persian silk, which is preferable to all others, they would be able to carry the silk manufactures to as great perfection as they have done those of cloth, by mixing a small quantity of Spanish wool with that of their own production. Even in Italy the silks of English fabric are better esteemed, and sold at a higher price than the Italian: and it is very common for the Neopolitan tradesmen, in order, more particularly, to recommend their silk stockings, and other such goods, to declare they are of English manufacture. The ancient Romans, during a long series of years, never flattered themselves that the silk-worm could be propagated in their country. And the ancient Greeks never saw any silk till after Alexander the Great's conquest of Persia. From Greece this commodity was brought to Rome, but sold so extravagantly dear, as to be of equal value with gold itself. The Persians, being the only people acquainted with the secret of making silk, would not suffer a single egg or worm to be carried out of the country. And this was also the reason that the ancient Greeks and Romans were so little acquainted with the origin of silk, that they imagined it grew spontaneously on trees. The holosericum, or pure silk, was worn by the ladies only: men of quality and rank were contented with what they called subsericum, a stuff made of equal quantities of silk and flax; Heliogabalus being the first who made use of the former.

In Italy, the mulberry-trees produce leaves very early, so that the first brood of worms is over before the strong heats of the summer commence; but in Germany the worms are frequently hatched, before any mulberry-leaves appear; the consequence of which is, that the whole brood perishes. In order to prevent this misfortune, and retard the production of the worms, till nature has provided their proper food, the eggs should either be deposited in a chest wrapped up in white linen, or in a glass-vessel well stopped, and suspended over the water, in a well.

Where they have no mulberry-trees, they feed the silk-worms with lettuce; but great care is requisite not to give them above four or five of the tender leaves of the plant at a time, and that those leaves are thoroughly dry. That the climate even of the northern parts of Germany is adapted to the production of silk-worms, we have an ocular demonstration, from the practice at Berlin, where the white mulberry-trees have stood the sharpness of the severest winters, and the silk produced from them, by means of some particular methods of management, much preferable to that of many other countries, both with regard to strength and beauty.

Another article, of considerable profit to the peasants of Piedmont, is truffles, which are found in such plenty, that this country may be stiled their native soil. Several peasants are said to have earned between sixty and seventy dollars a year, purely by taking up this famous vegetable. Truffles are of three kinds, black, white, and streaked or marbled. When they are fine and large, they cost, here, from fifty sols to three livres a pound, the price increasing with their magnitude. At Casal, some time ago, a truffle, weighing twelve pounds, was sold for four Louis d'ors: and another of the size of a plate, quite sound, and weighing fourteen pounds, was presented to the princess of Piedmont.

Piedmont derives no small advantage from the great plenty of wine produced in most parts of the country. These wines, like all others in Italy, are very sweet while new, especially the white. But they have a kind of red wine, very different from the sweet, called vino brusco, esteemed proper to be

drank

drank by perſons of a corpulent habit; whereas the ſweet or vino Amabile is thought more proper for thoſe that are thin. At the inns the wine is exceſſively bad; but no judgment ſhould thence be formed of the wines produced here, which are very good, particularly in the neighbourhood of Aleſſandria. The fruitful mountains of Montferrat produce excellent wine, in large quantities.

Piedmont is a fertile country, abounding in every part with filberd, cheſnut, and mulberry-trees. The common people are great admirers of the large cheſnuts or marons, as they call them: theſe they put into an oven, and, when thoroughly hot, cool them in red wine; after which they are dried a ſecond time in the oven: when thus prepared, they are called biſcuits, and eaten cold. The fineſt country in the king's dominions is that lying between Turin and Coni, and which can, perhaps, no where elſe be equalled. About two leagues from Geneva is a wood of box, belonging to the marquis Coudray, covering two hundred acres of ground. The ſtocks of ſome of theſe trees are ſo large that few men can graſp them with their arms. Not many years ago part of this plantation was cut down, and the timber ſold for twenty-four thouſand dollars. Box is ſo plenty in Savoy that the beeſoms are made of it.

The breeding and fattening of cattle are articles of great value to the Piedmonteſe, the profits annually ariſing, being ſaid to amount to near three millions; beſide the great numbers of black cattle ſold yearly to the Milaneſe. Mules are bred in Savoy, though great numbers are brought annually from Naples, Sicily, and particularly from Auvergne, and ſold for between forty and fifty piſtoles a head.

With regard to the coin current in this country, the Louis d'or, or Spaniſh piſtole, paſſes for ſixteen livres and five ſols; but what they call the common piſtole is worth fifteen livres only.

A ducat is nine livres.

A zecchino, nine livres thirteen ſols and a half.

The ſilver French dollar, with three crowns, paſſes for five livres; and thoſe which have the ſmall armorial enſigns, for four.

The philippo of Milan is worth four livres thirteen ſols and one third; in Milaneſe money, it is equal to ſeven livres, the proportion betwixt the livre of Milan and that of Piedmont being as 3 to 2.

The livre is twenty ſols.

A douſon, thirteen ſols and a half.

A parabajola, two thirds of a ſol, ſo that three parabajoles make exactly two ſols.

Beſide theſe pieces, they have five-ſols pieces; and double deniers, ſix of which are equal in value to a ſol.

I cannot deſcribe the ſtate of the nobility of Piedmont, without the greateſt regret. The behaviour of the king of Sardinia toward the nobility, who are now deprived of their ancient privileges and dignity, has been the ſource of the misfortunes of a great many of them, and given great diſcontent to the reſt. Baron Forſtner ſhewing the duke of Savoy a map of the duchy of Wirtemberg, publiſhed by Meyern, in 1710, the duke was ſurpriſed to ſee the number of ſmall eſtates belonging to the imperial knights diſſeminated through all parts of the country; and aſked, "Why the houſe of Wirtemberg did not ſeize theſe "eſtates?" The baron anſwered, "That neither the "laws of the empire, nor the intereſt of his imperial "majeſty, would admit of it." But his highneſs replied, "That it was not impoſſible, without having "recourſe to compulſive methods, to obtain them, "as both he and his anceſtors had experienced by the "Piedmonteſe." The king has, indeed, in ſome of his late ordinances, dropped ſome tender expreſſions with regard to the welfare of his nobility, and enacted ſome laws for augmenting their number. The perpetual eſtabliſhment of the right of primogeniture, in all fiefs, is an inſtance of this; whereas in allodial eftates no nobleman can execute a *fidei commiffum*, or feofment in truft, farther than to the 4th degree of confanguinity. Burghers and plebeians are allowed to make very few feofments; and, though they may leave their whole eftate to one of their fons, yet that fon is not obliged to preferve and convey it intire and undivided to his children; an uneafy reflection to thofe who have the misfortune of feeing their fons infatuated with the gaieties of life, and defirous of having their eftates remain in their families. The daughters are allowed a competent portion, but excluded from fucceeding to a fief, till the male line is totally extinct; which greatly tends to fupport the grandeur of families. But notwithftanding all thefe regulations, the nobility of Savoy and Piedmont are [illegible] [illegible]effed than thofe of any other kingdom or ftate in Europe.

For the future all alienations of demefnes are prohibited, all efcheats or devolutions of fiefs annulled, and all expectancies or reverfions abrogated. The fovereign has indeed ftill the power of reftoring fiefs forfeited either by felony or treafon; and, in a cafe of neceffity, or as a reward for fome particular fervice, he may alienate or beftow a fief on any perfon; but the obligation ceafes at the death of the receiver.

The grandeur of the ancient nobility alfo gradually diminifhes, in proportion as their number is multiplied. Whoever buys an eftate to which the title of marquifate, barony, or the like, is annexed, is ennobled by the purchafe, and accordingly takes the title of marquis, baron, &c. Thefe honorary titles are eafily and cheaply obtained, fix or eight thoufand livres being fufficient to purchafe of his majefty a fief to which fuch titles are annexed.

As a conclufion, I fhall add the following remark with regard to the nobility of Piedmont and Savoy; namely, that, in common with the French and Englifh nations, thofe of the fame family affume, from their effects and fiefs, different titles; fo that often the hufband and wife have diftinct appellations. This custom renders it unnecessary, in a place where many of the family reside, to add the titles of their offices and other circumstances, by way of distinction. But, on the other hand, a foreigner finds it difficult to trace these intricacies of genealogy; and therefore should be very cautious of asking minute questions, or passing censures on any persons, as he may perhaps be a near relation to him with whom he is at that time conversing, notwithstanding they are known by very different names.

From the strong desire which I had for some time entertained of seeing the Borromean islands, situated in the Lago Maggiore, while the weather was favourable, I was induced, after my arrival at Turin, to make a short excursion into the Milanese, and found the best way of performing this journey was to take the post-horses.

Perhaps there is not a country in the world so well watered as the Milanese; and the corn fields and meadows, being every where separated by canals and ditches, are particularly adapted to the culture of rice. Immediately after the grain is sown, the ground is laid wholly under water, and continues so till the rice is ripe. But the noxious effects, produced by the effluvia of these marshy grounds, are sufficiently evident from the head-achs, vertigos and fluxes, which seize those persons who only travel, during the hot weather, the roads near these rice plantations. The soil in most parts of the duchy of Milan is so remarkably fertile, that it produces two crops annually. The wheat sown in the autumn of the preceding year is ripe in June; and, as soon as it is carried off the fields, they sow the ground a second time with barley, Turky wheat, rice, &c. and the crop of it is reaped in the month of October.

Novara, the first city on this side of the duchy of Milan, is regularly built, and has some good fortifications. The cathedral merits observation, both on account of its marble pillars, statues, and great va-

riety

riety of curious bronzes, and the silver chapel, as they call it. The tract of land between the city of Novara and the Lago Maggiore is under the jurisdiction of the bishop, for which reason he appears on horseback, with a sword. The country, as far as Sesti, is remarkably pleasant, both sides of the way being planted with rows of chesnut-trees. But the roads, which in other respects cannot be complained of, are lower than the adjacent fields, and therefore in rainy weather always full of water.

The carriages used by the peasants in carrying their goods from one village to another are called Berceaux, or cradles, being covered with the branches of vines.

The heavy rains that fell about this time deprived me of a great deal of pleasure I should otherwise have enjoyed in viewing so fine a country; but this was in some measure compensated by affording me an opportunity of observing the particular dresses used by the inhabitants, when they travel in the rain. Some who travel on horseback wore a kind of oil-skin petticoat tied about their waist, and a short mantle of the same stuff, which covered the upper part of their bodies. The foot passengers of the meaner sort wore a long cloak of straw, or small rushes, reaching to the calves of their legs, and fastened round their necks; their dress in some particulars resembling that worn by some of the savages of America. Many of the peasants, who wear this straw cloak, travel barefooted. A foreigner, at first sight of such uncommon dresses, will find it difficult to suppress his risibility.

Before you arrive at Sesti, you cross the Ticino in a ferry-boat. The distance, in a straight line, from Sesti to the Borromean Islands, is fifteen Italian miles.

Il Lago Maggiore, or, as it is otherwise called, Il Lago Locarno, is fifty-six Italian miles in length, about six in breadth, and the water in the middle of the lake is reckoned about eighty Bracci, or fathoms deep. Towards Switzerland it terminates in a canal, which is of the greatest advantage to trade. It takes up four days to perform the journey through Sion to Geneva, the roads being extremely bad.

The Lago Maggiore is intirely ſurrounded with hills, adorned with vineyards, and a great number of pleaſure-houſes. Above the vineyards are planted groves of cheſnut-trees, great quantities of their fruit being conſumed in the northern parts of Italy, eſpecially in the republic of Genoa, where the price of corn falls conſiderably, when there are plenty of cheſnuts. They keep in perfection till Chriſtmas, but the common people eat them till Eaſter, eſpecially when roaſted and ſteeped in red wine. The banks of the lake are adorned with fine rows of trees, and walks arched over with vine-branches. But theſe natural decorations are more particularly beautiful on the left ſide of the lake, near Leſco and Belgirada, where the vines, by the gentle declivity of the ground, and their full expoſure to the ſouth, produce an excellent wine, much admired at Milan. The inchanting proſpect, from a boat ſailing on the lake, is heightened by grand natural caſcades, which in ſeveral parts fall headlong from the rocky precipices of the mountains.

The lake begins to widen at the diſtance of two leagues from Seſti, and continues to increaſe in breadth to the entrance of the bay where the two famous iſlands Iſola Madre and Iſola Bella are ſituated. On the right hand are Intra and Palanza; the former belongs to count Borromeo, the latter to the emperor. Iſola Madre ſhould be viewed firſt, the mind generally making a falſe eſtimate of the value of one object, when filled with the idea of a more excellent one of the ſame kind. But, the wind not being favourable, we were obliged to land firſt on Iſola Bella. Some idea of theſe charming iſlands may be formed by comparing them with pyramids of ſweetmeats, adorned with foliages and flowers. The garden of Iſola Bella is decorated with ten parterres; the perpendicular height of which above the ſurface of the water

is

is ſixty ells, or one hundred and eighty ſpans. Each parterre decreaſes proportionally in circumference, as its ſituation is nearer the ſummit of the hill, reſembling ten parallelograms of unequal ſize, placed upon one another, and ſucceſſively diminiſhing from the baſis to the ſummit. From the upper parallelogram, or ſummit of the garden, is a delightful proſpect. It is paved with free-ſtone, ſurrounded with a baluſtrade, and every ſide is adorned with ſtone ſtatues of a gigantic ſize. The rain water falling on this area is conveyed to ciſterns underneath. There are alſo machines for raiſing water into them from the lake, for ſupplying the water works. Round each of the parterres is a delightful walk, and at the four angles are placed alternately pyramids and gigantic ſtatues. All the walls are covered intirely with hedges of laurel, eſpaliers of orange, citron, peach-trees, and the like. The laurel-trees continue all the winter in the open air; but the eſpaliers of citrons and oranges are covered with boards, when the cold is intenſe, and cheriſhed with an artificial heat by fires made in ſtoves of free-ſtone erected for this purpoſe; and are between five and ſeven paces aſunder. Both the covering and the partition, which is there continued from one poſt to another, conſiſt of boards a foot and a half in breadth, and ſeven feet in length. The gardener told us, that upward of two hundred thouſand pieces of wood were uſed for this purpoſe. The yearly expences attending this Borromean villa amounts to forty thouſand Piedmonteſe livres. But to make ſo delightful a place on theſe iſlands ſeems to ſurpaſs even the revenues of a prince; for it muſt be remembered, that this Iſola Bella was, about the middle of the preceding century, only a barren rock, and conſequently every baſket of earth, and whatever elſe is ſeen upon it, muſt have been brought by water at a prodigious expence. The garden has a ſouth expoſure, and each angle of its front decorated with a lofty and circular ſummer-houſe, the rooms of which are grand,

grand, and richly adorned with red and black marble. To the left of the garden, coming from Sesti, is a covered gallery on stone pillars, and shaded with lemon-trees. On the other side, toward the east, is a most beautiful walk of large orange-trees, in four or five rows; and near it two Latin inscriptions on marble, in commemoration of Vitaliano count Borromeo, who made all these improvements in 1671.

Not far from these inscriptions is a small, but delightful laurel grove, consisting of narrow walks, and a cascade falling down above twenty steps. Near it is a beautiful plantation of large pomegranate-trees. The lake washes the walls both of the gardens and the palace; so that you can only land on a small spot before the north front of the palace, which commands a delightful prospect toward Isella. On the east and west sides are very large arcades, which support the earth of the parterres already mentioned; whence this work may very well be compared with the pensile gardens of antiquity. These arcades serve at once to support the soil, and adorn the garden, each being formed into an elegant grotto. Near the palace in a boat-house are kept three fine gondolas, for the pleasure of sailing on the lake.

The palace is not yet finished, but already contains a great variety of pictures, vases, bustos, and other curiosities. Among the former are several, especially flower-pieces, some of which are painted on marble tablets, that are really admirable. In several rooms are portraits of cardinals descended from the Borromean family. The vaults which support the palace are formed into grottoes, and decorated with shells, marbles, &c. The floor consists of small stones, artfully placed in such positions, as to represent all manner of figures, like the mosaic pavements of the ancients. The continual undulating motion of the waters of the lake increases the pleasure every spectator must feel from this assemblage of the beauties of art and nature; so that imagination itself can hardly form a more

more charming ſummer retreat. Cloſe to the ſouthern front of the palace are five cypreſs-trees of uncommon bigneſs, and equal to the place in height; their trunks are covered down to the very ground with the thick foliage of ſcarlet oaks. On entering the garden, the ſmell is regaled with the blended odours of fruits and flowers. After aſcending a few ſteps, you arrive at an eſpalier of bergamot citron-trees, next to a very lofty range of orange-trees; advancing ſtill, you come to a lofty grotto, decorated both with water works and ſtatues. On the top of it is a very large unicorn, in a leaping poſture, and, on his back, a Cupid. On both ſides is an aſcent by ſteps to the upper area, which terminates the ten parterres already deſcribed.

The paſſage between Iſola Bella and Iſola Madre is generally performed in half an hour. Their great height, doubtleſs, makes the diſtance appear much leſs than it really is. Iſola Madre has ſeven parterres, which indeed are of an equal height with thoſe of Iſola Bella, but, lying ſloping, and at a conſiderable diſtance behind each other, they appear lower than thoſe of the other. The external foundation of Iſola Madre is for the moſt part compoſed of ſteep perpendicular rocks projecting conſiderably over the water; conſequently the maſon work was leſs here than at Iſola Bella. The houſe is nothing remarkable, that ſide of it only which looks toward Seſti and Iſola Bella being finiſhed; it is not, however, deſtitute of elegant paintings of flowers, portraits, and landſcapes, particularly a repreſentation of Vercelli, before it was demoliſhed. Nor is the garden without its beauties; among which is a fine eſpalier of citron-trees, a low contre-eſpalier of orange-trees, a cloſe walk of cedars, a ſmall eſpalier of jeſſamine, an eſpalier of the acacia, and another of roſemary, about eight or nine feet high, with ſtems equal in thickneſs to a man's arm. Beſide theſe, here are laurel-groves with walks cut through them; ſome of theſe trees are ſurpriſingly

 large.

large. A few years ſince, a laurel-eſpalier was planted here, and is now upward of eighteen feet high; the laurel hedges have attained the ſame height. Theſe, by the cloſeneſs of the leaves, make a beautiful appearance. Theſe trees, by the mildneſs of the climate, and their being defended from the cutting winds of the north by the neighbouring mountains, grow ſurpriſingly; ſix or ſeven years being ſufficient for theſe hedges to attain the height abovementioned. Great numbers of pheaſants are kept upon Iſola Madre, the great breadth of the lake rendering their eſcape impoſſible. They ſometimes, indeed, attempt to fly over it, but ſoon flag, and, falling into the water, are taken up by a boat, and carried back again to the iſland; but this is very rare: for the iſland being conſiderably larger than Iſola Bella, and provided with abundance of colliflowers and other garden productions, as alſo with fruit, underwoods, and convenient places for ſhade and ſhelter, they are too happily ſituated to deſire a change of habitation. There is a particular houſe erected for the young pheaſants, near which is a beautiful walk of very lofty cypreſs-trees, conſiſting of thirty-five in each row; their ſtems at the lower part are nearly of the thickneſs of a man's body. This is, in my opinion, the moſt beautiful part of the iſland; its gloomy and romantic ſcenes cannot fail of reviving in the memory the fabulous deſcriptions of enchanted iſlands and caſtles. One end of this walk terminates at a ſummer-houſe contiguous to the lake, where the late empreſs, who ſtayed ſome days here, landed. Her conſort, the emperor Charles VI. alſo ſpent a few days on Iſola Bella, but not at the ſame time when the empreſs was on this iſland.

Iſola Madre, among other natural curioſities, has a large ebony-tree; it reſembles the pine, but produces large red berries.

Painted flower-pots are placed all round the banks of both iſlands: and, when a foreign prince viſits theſe Borromean paradiſes, in the night, or ſtays there

any

any time, both iſlands are illuminated with lights of a variety of colours; a ſight which muſt be equally grand and delightful.

It may not be improper to remark, that thoſe who intend to viſit theſe iſlands, muſt be careful to take the neceſſary proviſions and wine with them from Seſti, as nothing can be purchaſed here.

The firſt part of the road between Seſti and Milan is very bad, the country being over-run with heath and buſhes. But this diſagreeable proſpect is ſoon changed into one of a very different kind: the country is level, and adorned with the fineſt meadows, gardens, cornfields, vineyards, and orchards. The main road is ſmooth, broad, and planted on each ſide with rows of trees; but, lying four or five feet lower than the contiguous fields, the beauty of the proſpect is greatly impaired; and, after any heavy rain, it is, for a conſiderable time, notwithſtanding the ditches on each ſide, filled with water.

[According to biſhop Burnet the city of Milan is one of the nobleſt in the world for an inland town, that hath no court, no commerce either by ſea, or any navigable river, and that is now the metropolis of a very ſmall country: for that, which is not mountainous in this ſtate, is not above ſixty miles ſquare, and yet it produces a wealth that is ſurprizing. It pays for an eſtabliſhment of ſeven and forty thouſand men, and yet there are not ſixteen thouſand ſoldiers effectively in it; ſo many are eat up by thoſe in whoſe hands the government is lodged. But the extent of the town, the nobleneſs of the buildings, and above all, the ſurprizing riches of the churches and convents, are ſigns of great wealth.]

Milan falls infinitely ſhort of Turin, both in beauty and conveniency, few of the ſtreets being uniform, and many of them are both crooked and narrow. The paper windows are more frequent than at Turin or Florence, and do not tend to augment its beauty. It is not uncommon to ſee the windows of grand palaces composed promiscuously of glass and paper, the latter being added to supply the vacancy of a broken pane. All the houses of the city are covered with wooden shingles. Statues, some of marble, but the greatest number of brass, are erected in different parts of the city, where the public processions stop; the number of these statues amounts to sixty. But, if Milan falls short of Turin in beauty, it excels it in largeness, its circuit round the walls being ten Italian miles; but it should be remembered that a great number of gardens, lying between the ramparts and the houses of the city, are included in this extent. The inhabitants are generally reckoned at three hundred thousand. It has twelve gates, six of which are large, and the other six small. The former terminates an equal number of broad streets, called il Curso, which are the grandest in all the city, but they are very remote from its center, and even from one another. Near the six large gates is a market every day. In Milan are a hundred and ten convents, a hundred oratories, for religious fraternities, a hundred and seventy schools, and two hundred and fifty churches, about a hundred of which are parochial. This city, though not situated upon any navigable river, nor commodiously in other respects for trade, still supports its grandeur; notwithstanding the vast number of misfortunes it has met with from the calamities of war and pestilence: for it was besieged more than forty times, taken above twenty, and almost utterly destroyed four different times. A like calamity it suffered in 1162, under the emperor Frederick Barbarossa, through the fault and insolent behaviour of its citizens; when the city, as far as the churches of St. Mary, St. Ambrose, and St. Maurice, was intirely demolished, and the ground plowed up and sown with salt.

In the Curso, before the east gate, on a pillar, stands a lion fronting it, as a memorial how far the Venetians once penetrated into this city.

Milan,

Milan, like all very large cities, is not capable of making any great reſiſtance, being encompaſſed only with a ſingle wall. The citadel, though at ſome diſtance from the city, encompaſſes a good part of it, being built in form of a creſcent. It has ſix baſtions, and the moraſſes toward the country ſecure it on that ſide from being approached either by trenches or mines. But it has few outworks, and thoſe prevented from exerting their whole force by the great number of contiguous buildings, eſpecially on the city ſide. Governor Colmenero pulled down a whole ſtreet, to remove, in ſome meaſure, this diſadvantage; and in the area two monuments, with long inſcriptions, are erected to his memory; but the buildings are ſtill too near in ſome parts. On the ſide next the city are two ſtrong towers, whoſe walls are twelve ells in thickneſs, and faced with large pieces of marble, cut angularly, like a diamond, which at once increaſes their ſtrength and beauty; with regard to the former they are cannon-proof. In the citadel is a foundery for cannon, and an arſenal furniſhed with arms for twelve thouſand men. There is an inſcription over the gate of the citadel, to the honour of Philip II. king of Spain, in which he is ſtiled defender of the faith. Before the governor's houſe is a ſtatue of white marble of St. Nepomuco, erected this preſent year.

The governor of the citadel may eaſily obtain a conſiderable revenue, ſome ſay, forty thouſand Piedmonteſe livres a year, by admitting contraband goods to be carried through the gate leading into the city, and of which he has the abſolute command. He is alſo quite independent of the governor-general of the Milaneſe. I was aſſured by M. de Corbeau, a Savoyard lieutenant-colonel, that —— N—— could not, during four generations, reckon a married perſon among his anceſtors, notwithſtanding his grandmother was a nun. It is not much regarded in Spain, whether a child is legitimate or not; and a ſingle man, who has the choice of two ſiſters, one of which is is lawfully begotten and the other not, will often chuse the latter, especially if nature has given her the least advantage in point of beauty.

We are also told, that the grand master of Malta always thinks it sufficient, with regard to the birth of a young nobleman of Spain, if he produces a certificate from his father, in the following terms, *Questo —— è il mio figlio.* "The bearer —— is my son." The old prince of Vaudemont, Charles Henry, who, at the close of the preceding century, was governor of Milan, and died in France in 1723, was a natural son of Charles III. duke of Lorrain, but never, during his being governor, endeavoured to conceal this blemish in his extraction. An Italian gentleman, dining with his highness, entertained the company with observations on the laws scrupulously observed in Germany, with regard to the admittance of noblemen's sons into canonries, and the difficulties frequently attending the requisite proof of their pedigree on such occasions. A gentleman who sat next the Italian, fearing he might, through inadvertency, say something that might give the prince offence, said to him in a whisper, *Prenez garde, à cause du prince du Vaudemont.* "Be careful what you say, consider the "prince of Vaudemont." The Italian very gravely answered, "Very well, very well;" but pursued the thread of his discourse; and, thinking to give the greater force to his harangue, he added, *Par exemple, on n'admettroit point un garçon comme cela.* "For example, even such a gentleman as that would not be "admitted," pointing at the same-time to the prince. This, however, so little offended his highness, that he was the first who laughed at the expression; and afterward used often to rally the Italian on his compliment. Indeed, the generosity and affability of this prince were equally remarkable, and endeared him to all ranks of people. Nor had he imbibed the least tincture of pride. Among many other instances, the following serves to shew how free he was from being the leaſt affected with that vice. Once, as he was ſigning a patent for a nobility, the privilege of which had been granted him with the ſovereignty of Commercy, he ſaid, *Ma foy, cette patente eſt plus grande qu'a ma ſouveraineté.* "Upon my honour, this patent "is larger than my whole ſovereignty."

The governor-general of the duchy of Milan always reſides in that city. The palace is indeed large, but old, and badly contrived. The theatre for operas and plays is in this place, a band of muſic being maintained by the governor, in conformity to the cuſtom of the dukes of Milan.

The yearly revenue of the government of Milan is two hundred thouſand guilders; and a new governor is generally ſent every three years.

The number of regular troops now lying in all this country is about eighteen thouſand men, the greateſt part of whoſe cloathing, arms, and other neceſſaries are of German or Auſtrian manufacture; at which the Milaneſe are not a little diſcontented, thinking it but right that the money which they themſelves furniſh for the maintainance of theſe ſoldiers, ſhould be again expended among them.

The council belonging to the city is compoſed of a preſident and ſixty doctors of law, who are all nobles, and not at all dependent on the governor-general. They are all dreſſed in the Spaniſh manner.

It is ſaid that the Spaniards have, in peaceable times, raiſed annually two millions of dollars from the dutchy of Milan; but all ſuch computations are ſubject to very great uncertainty, few having an opportunity of attaining an adequate knowlege of the neceſſary particulars.

Milan has often experienced the viciſſitudes of fortune; being ſometimes ſubject to the French, ſometimes to the Spaniards, and at other times to the Germans. Theſe changes have occaſioned troops to be ſent hither from all theſe different nations, whence a much freer way of living has been introduced in Milan,

 than

than in the ſouthern parts of Italy, and to this the fertility of the country and opulence of the nobility have greatly contributed. The following inſtance will ſhew, in ſome meaſure, the freedom and expenſive liberality of the Milaneſe ladies: a few days ſince a company of them, attended by five or ſix gentlemen, but not their huſbands, went on a party of pleaſure to Aleſſandria, having previouſly ſent thither their plate, rich wines, and all other neceſſaries for a gay and elegant repaſt: the ladies defrayed the whole expence, not only of the entertainment and diverſions, but alſo of the gentlemen, their ſervants and horſes.

Thoſe of the lower claſs among the fair ſex, whom fortune has denied the means of equalling the ladies in extravagance, imitate them as far as poſſible, and indulge themſelves in many freedoms denied in other parts of Italy. The ſhops here, like thoſe at Paris, are generally attended by women, who amuſe themſelves with embroidery and other needle-work; and, though theſe ſhops are, during the ſummer, intirely open, they are the rendezvous of the gay part of the gentlemen. Even the auſterities of the monaſtic life are as far mitigated as poſſible; ſo that gentlemen have not only the liberty of talking, rallying, and laughing with the nuns at the grate; but alſo of joining with them in concerts of muſic, and of ſpending a whole afternoon in their company. You will not therefore be ſurpriſed at the attempt of Mr. Preval, an Engliſh gentleman, who about two years ſince carried off the counteſs de Pietra from a Benedictine monaſtery, and conveyed her to Geneva.

The area before the cathedral was formerly the uſual place for walking in an evening; but for ſome years common people only have frequented it, the rich and gay viſiting the rampart betwixt Porta Orientale and the Porta Toſa, ſome in their coaches, and others on foot. This place was ſome years ago planted on both ſides with white mulberry trees, which become the city's property after the planter's death.

The

The walks are laid out in a ſtraight line, and their breadth ſufficient for three or four carriages to go a-breaſt. On one ſide is a delightful proſpect of the open country; and on the other, of the other gardens and vineyards between the ramparts and the houſes in the city. But the moſt charming part of theſe ramparts is behind the church of St. Maria della Paſſione.

The trade and manufactures of the city conſiſt principally in ſilk, hard-ware, and rock cryſtal; the laſt is often found in the neighbouring Alps, and wrought into lamps, tobacco-boxes, looking-glaſſes, and other toys at Milan. A looking-glaſs was ſome years ago made here out of a ſingle piece of cryſtal, which was a foot in breadth, and a foot and a half in length. A great variety of artificial flowers, compoſed of wax, paper, iſing-glaſs, feathers, and cotton, are made at Milan, particularly by the nuns, who excel in this imitative art. Gentlemen never wear theſe for ornaments, except at maſquerades, and during the carnival; nor are they much uſed by the ladies. But the altars in the churches, and the grand apartments in palaces and genteel houſes, are finely decorated with them; and great quantities exported. I muſt not forget to remark, that, in ſo large a city as Milan, gunpowder is ſold only in one place, and by one perſon.

The cuſtoms and duties at Milan are under very bad regulations. Goods of any kind may be diſpoſed of without any enquiry or ſearch, provided you give the officer a ſmall gratuity, which is always demanded in an open manner; whereas in Piedmont they are too ſevere, and give ſtrangers a great deal of unneceſſary trouble.

The cathedral of Milan, dedicated to the Virgin Mary and St. Thecla, is juſtly reckoned the principal religious ſtructure in the city. It is four hundred and eighty feet in length; its roof is ſupported by a great number of marble pillars, many of which can hardly be fathomed by three men, and is divided ino three ayles. The history of St. Charles Borromeo is represented in large paintings between the pillars, particularly that transaction of his selling the principality of Deria, and distributing in one day eighty thousand dollars among the poor. Near these are placed vast numbers of votive pieces in silver, weighing some thousand ounces, and representing heads, hearts, feet, hands, ears, and other parts of the human body, which, having been hurt or diseased, were restored to their original strength and soundness by St. Borromeo's intercession. Every goldsmith's shop abounds with votive pieces of various sizes; so that the person recovered may immediately pay his vow; perhaps delay might cool his zeal, and bury his gratitude in oblivion.

[Mr. Addison gives the following summary account of this structure. I could not stay long in Milan, without visiting the great church, of which I had heard the highest commendations; but was much deceived in my expectations at my first entering it, for I then saw only the front which was not half finished, and the inside was so smutted with dust and the smoke of lamps, that neither the silver, the brass work, nor the marble, appeared to advantage. This vast Gothic structure is all of marble, except the roof, which would have been built of the same substance with the rest, had not its weight rendered it improper for that part of the building. The outside of the church appears much whiter and fresher than the inside, from its being often washed with rain; this renders the marble more beautiful and unsullied, than in those parts that are not at all exposed to the weather. It is generally said that there are 11,000 statues about the church; but they reckon into the account every particular figure in the history pieces, and the small images that make up the equipage of those that are larger. There are indeed a prodigious multitude of such as are bigger than the life; I reckoned above 250 on the outside of the church, though I only told three ſides of it, and theſe were not half ſo thick ſet as was then intended. The ſtatues are all of marble, and generally well cut; but the moſt valuable is a ſaint Bartholomew new flead, with his ſkin hanging over his ſhoulders. This is eſteemed worth its weight in gold.]

At the entrance of this and all other churches in Milan, a great number of old women ſpinning, or buſy about ſome ſuch female work, place themſelves. They never beg, and therefore poſſibly they may imagine it to be a work of merit to ſpend their whole time, as it were, at the houſe of God. Women in black veils are often ſeen aſking alms; probably they are perſons who, on account of their rank or other circumſtances, are deſirous of concealing their poverty. The ſame diſguiſe was alſo formerly uſed by men; but, ſuch maſks having given riſe to ſeveral abuſes, the uſe of them to that ſex was prohibited by the archbiſhop.

The treaſury cannot be ſeen under four or five Piedmonteſe livres: it is extravagantly rich, both with regard to its gold and ſilver veſſels, and alſo in buſts, ſtatues, rings, chalices, crucifixes, and other curioſities of the ſame kind, where theſe metals are the leaſt valuable part. Brevity obliges me to omit a great variety of valuable pieces; but I cannot help mentioning a deſign of Raphael Urbino, repreſenting the adoration of the wiſemen. This cartoon is kept in a cloſet with the greateſt care. An altar-cloth of ſilk, embroidered by a young lady, called Lidovina Peregrina, about a hundred and fifty years ſince, merits the attention of every traveller; the embroidery is ſo finely executed, that it is difficult to diſtinguiſh it by the naked eye from an elegant piece of painting.

It is not judged proper to leave the treaſury without a watch during the night; and accordingly four young eccleſiaſtics, attended by ſome large maſtiffs, ſit up every night in the cathedral. In the roof of the choir is preserved, as they pretend, one of the nails by which Christ was fastened to the cross. It is set in rock crystal, and near it a particular machine, by which six persons may be drawn up to it at once. On the third of May, observed in commemoration of finding the cross, this relique is carried in a grand procession, at which ceremony all the clergy, the governor general, and the principal persons of the city assist. When the country labours under any extraordinary visitation, as a long continued drought, the plague, or other public calamity, the like procession is made, the archbishop carrying the holy nail under a very rich canopy. Some say that the emperor Theodosius made a present of this nail to St. Ambrose, in order to perpetuate his memory in the Milanese: but others entertain a very different opinion.

Among the other reliques in this cathedral, is a piece of Aaron's rod, notwithstanding the ecclesiastics belonging to St. John de Lateran, pretend that it is deposited intire in their church. Some pieces of this rod are likewise shown in the palace-church at Hanover, among the reliques which Henry, sirnamed the Lion, brought from the Holy Land: nor must it be forgotten, that a piece of Moses's rod is also there deposited.

The archiepiscopal palace, a grand and spacious building, is situated opposite to the cathedral. It consists of two courts, in one of which are the statues of St. Charles Borromeo and St. Ambrose; the latter has an iron rod in his hand, as a symbol of the noble opposition he made against the emperor Theodosius in Milan; perhaps the present clergy would equal St. Ambrose himself in this respect, were their power equal to their inclination. There is a subterranean passage from the archbishop's palace into the cathedral. The church of St. Alexander is, except the cathedral, the finest in the whole city, both with respect to sculpture, painting, gilding, and stucco-work; and St. Magdalen's chapel in it should be visited fited by every traveller. The church of St. Ambrose, situated near the Porta di Vercelli, belongs both to canons regulars and the Bernardines, called Cistercians, who follow the rules of St. Augustine. Both orders use the choir, which, when finished according to the specimen under the dome, will be elegantly adorned with Mosaic work. Four elegant pillars of porphyry support the tabernacle for the host, near which is a statue of brass; and on a marble pillar near the chancel is a serpent of the same metal. The vulgar are persuaded, that this is the serpent made by Moses in the wilderness; others maintain that this is not the original serpent of Moses, but formed out of the fragments of it; while others insist that it is only an hieroglyphical representation of Æsculapius. But, be its origin what it will, numbers of children in a languishing condition are placed before this image on Easter Tuesday, from a superstitious notion that their health will be miraculously restored.

Near the high altar, the body of St. Ambrose is deposited. For it should be remembered that this is the most ancient church in the duchy of Milan. The popes have always refused to let any buildings be erected near this church, from a persuasion, that in the adjacent ground great numbers of primitive saints have been buried, whose remains they will not suffer to be disturbed; and perhaps the bad condition of the pavement is owing to the same reason. If tradition may be credited, the gates of the grand entrance are identically the same which St. Ambrose shut against the emperor Theodosius, and would not suffer him to enter the church, till he had performed the penance enjoined him, for his cruel massacre of the Thessalonians, who had been guilty of seditious practices. These gates are held in high veneration, and few pilgrims visit the church without picking off some of the splinters, which they constantly carry about them; but I must confess myself a stranger to the virtue of these wooden reliques. Sixty or seventy monks continually reside in the Cistercian monastery, contiguous to the church of St. Ambrose. This monastery, together with its spacious gardens, occupy a very considerable area The library is large, and well furnished with books, and the large hall adjoining is finely adorned with statues. It is constantly open two hours in the morning, namely, from ten to twelve, and two hours in the afternoon, except the times of vacation. The number of printed volumes amount to forty-five thousand, but the manuscripts, which are said to amount to fifteen thousand, are its greatest treasure. I am, indeed, tempted to believe that the number of manuscripts is magnified beyond the truth; but, be this as it will, there are many valuable pieces among them.

There is also, in the Ambrosian college, a school for painting, where the students draw and form models after nature, during the summer.

The contiguous apartments are appointed for a musæum, where, among other curiosities, is the skeleton of a very beautiful woman, who desired her bones might be exposed to public view in Milan, for the good of others. Under the skeleton, is the following inscription:

Ut ægrotantium saluti mortuorum inspectione, viventes prospicere possint hunc σκελετὸν.

"That the living, by consulting the dead, may be enabled to recover the sick, this skeleton is here placed."

Several curious pieces of penmanship are shewn here, particularly a representation of the Lord's supper delineated on a large octavo leaf, and on the faces and among the hair of the persons sitting at table, and on the table-cloth, are written, in the most delicate manner, St. John's account of our Saviour's passion, the Lord's prayer, the creed, *confiteor*, *beatus vir*, *laudate pueri*, *magnificate*, the fifteen gradual, seven penetential, and many other psalms.

But

But the moſt excellent *depoſitum* in the whole collection, are the manuſcripts of Leonardo da Vinci, bound in twelve large volumes of mathematical and other drawings; which ſufficiently demonſtrate that, in the theory of anatomy, optics, geometry, architecture, and mechanics, very few, then, excelled that great maſter. Nor are his mechanical drawings delineated on three hundred and ninety-nine leaves, and containing ſeventeen hundred and fifty original deſigns, leſs curious than the former. The notes at the foot of the page are in a very ſmall hand, and wrote from the right to the left, ſo that few are able to read them without the aſſiſtance of a magnifying mirrour; and, accordingly, one is always placed near thoſe manuſcripts. King James I. of England ordered the earl Arundel to offer Galeazzo Arconati, who had then one of theſe volumes in his poſſeſſion, three thouſand piſtoles for it; but he refuſed the money, chuſing to preſent it to the Ambroſian college, where the reſt of that celebrated maſter's works were before depoſited. And the *conſervatores* of the college have perpetuated the remembrance of this magnificent gift by an inſcription on the wall.

Fronting the grand entrance of the church of St. Celſo, are two gigantic ſtatues of Adam and Eve, in white marble; they are both elegant pieces, eſpecially the latter, which is reckoned equal to any thing of the kind. Four beautiful ſtatues of the evangeliſts alſo of white marble, together with a great number of others, having their ornaments and pedeſtals of braſs, adorn the front; which was deſigned by Bramantes Lazari. On the top of this grand front are ſeveral pyramids, one of which is bent in a ſurpriſing manner, thought to have been gradually effected by ſtormy weather. The inſide of the church is adorned with ſeveral beautiful pieces of painting, and alſo with the tomb of Annibal Fontana, the celebrated ſtatuary, erected by the architects of this church in 1637.

They

They ſhew, in the ſacriſtry of St. Euſtorius, a gold medal, pretended to have been preſented by the Eaſtern wiſemen to our Saviour. As the monks previouſly inſiſt upon a promiſe of devoutly kiſſing it from all to whom they ſhew it, I did not ſatisfy my curioſity in this particular; but others, who have enjoyed that favour, aſſured me, that it has ſcarcely the traces of any impreſſion remaining on it.

The chapel of St. Giovanni de Caſarotti is ſmall, but elegant, and has ſeveral decorations in marble. On the left-hand is a paſſage and vault, where criminals. who periſh by the hand of juſtice, are buried. This beautiful chapel belongs to a devout fraternity, called de Cavaleri. They are deſcended from the beſt families in Milan, and enter into this order to demonſtrate their humility and devotion. They are diſtinguiſhed by a ſmall croſs which they wear on one ſhoulder of their upper garment. The only ſon of count Ferdinand Daun, governor-general, and a gentleman of the bed-chamber to the emperor, is a member of this fraternity. When any malefactor is to be executed, this order is under an indiſpenſable obligation of ſending ſome of its members to viſit him the night before, in order to prepare him for his awful paſſage into eternity.

When the criminal aſcends the ladder, one of the moſt eminent among them follow him, holding a crucifix before his eyes, and, at parting, pronounces the benediction; the Capuchins, who uſually attend criminals in their laſt moments, remain below. Two ladders are placed againſt the gallows on this occaſion, one for the criminal and executioner, and the other for the Cavaliere, who attends maſked, and cuts the criminal down, as ſoon as dead. Others of the ſociety aſſiſt in carrying the corpſe to the chapel, where it is interred. Whatever the fraternity make uſe of on this occaſion, as gloves, the cord, &c. are thrown into the grave with the malefactor. Nor is this humble office conſidered as the leaſt degradation to their

rank;

rank; but opportunities of performing these humble offices are not frequent at Milan; for the soldiers are not subject to the civil power, and even the poor are under no temptation to pursue dangerous courses, as they may easily acquire a comfortable subsistence by begging in the streets. Add to this the asylum granted to churches and monasteries, whereby many criminals are sheltered from the hands of justice, and it will be no wonder that executions are not frequent here.

Not far from the Porta Orientale, the commodious lazaretto, belonging to the great hospital, is situated. It is a spacious stone-building, of a quadrangular form, but greatly out of repair. There are three hundred and sixty chambers round the quadrangle, but all of them without inhabitants. Each has a window toward the country, and another toward the gardens, in the area of the lazaretto; and, also, a particular chimney and privy. The gardens in the area are let to poor persons, who maintain their families by cultivating gardens and vineyards. In times of pestilence, or any other contagious distemper, foreigners are obliged to depart the country, and the natives infected with the distemper brought to this lazaretto. On the outside of the several apartments or cells, is a piazza, supported on marble pillars, and inclosed with a palisado, to prevent the patients from going into the gardens. But, whenever the city is visited with such contagions, all the trees in the gardens are cut down, and an open octangular chapel erected in the center on pillars, and mass said in it every day, that the patients may, from their beds, have the opportunity of paying their adoration to the host. An idea may be formed of the area inclosed in the lazaretto by the length of one of its sides, which is six hundred paces. A swift stream of water runs under the whole quadrangle, and carries away all kinds of soil and filth; a conveniency of the last importance to buildings of this kind. In a marble pillar, facing the entrance, is a hole, a hole, representing a broken plague-sore in the flesh; the inside of it appears fresh and bloody, and the outside purulent and yellow. This phænomenon is said to owe its origin to a miracle of St. Charles Borromeo, who exorcised the plague from the people into this pillar. But those who have seen the pillars in the jesuits college at Genoa, well know that appearances of this kind may be easily given to a kind of Carrara marble.

It must be owned that the protestant countries cannot be compared to those where the Romish religion is professed, with regard to hospitals, lazarettos, and other charitable foundations. Perhaps, among other incitements to charities of this kind, the dread of purgatory is not the least; and it must be remembered, that the Romish clergy are very careful to inforce every motive that has a tendency to promote the great work of charity. At Leyden, however, there is still a lazaretto or pest-house kept up, in which are two hundred and fifty beds always in readiness, and, on occasion, nine hundred patients may be admitted; nor can the cleanliness and decency with which every thing is there conducted be any where exceeded: but it must be owned, that, as the patients have not each a separate room, but twenty, or more, lie in the same ward, very bad consequences may result from a contagious distemper.

The court of inquisition, established here, consists of an unlimited number of ecclesiastics, sixty noblemen, and a hundred and fifty wealthy merchants. Those unhappy persons who fall into the hands of the inquisition, never know their accusers, nor the reasons of their confinement. Nor can they ever flatter themselves with the hopes of being delivered from these nauseous dungeons, and other shocking hardships, but by voluntarily accusing themselves.

A priest, about three years since, severely felt the rigour of this court, for celebrating mass before his bull of ordination arrived. He pleaded, indeed, that

that the bull was ſigned at Rome, and actually on the road to Milan, before he preſumed to perform that office; but this plea was rejected, nor was the intereſt made by his relations of the leaſt effect. He was ſentenced to read maſs on a ſcaffold, erected before the church where the crime had been committed; but, as ſoon as he begun, the firſt leaf was torn out, his canonical robes ſtripped off, and his body delivered over to the ſecular power; by which he was condemned to be hanged; his thumbs, together with the fore and middle fingers of both his hands, between which he held the hoſt at the elevation, being firſt burnt to a coal. We ſhall not be at a loſs to account for this ſeverity, if we reflect on the dignity aſſumed by the prieſthood, and the diſadvantage that muſt accrue to the pope from perſons intruding themſelves into that office without a proper ordination. Hoſtienſis aſſerts that the ſacerdotal office is ſeven thouſand ſix hundred and forty-four times above the regal, that being the proportion between the magnitudes between the ſun and moon. According to the canon law, the prerogative of the mitre excells that of the crown, in the ſame proportion as gold does lead. But theſe proportions are far from ſatisfying Alanus de Rupe, a Dominican monk, who places the power of a prieſt above that of God himſelf; becauſe the latter ſpent ſix days creating the world, whereas the former, every time he celebrates maſs, by a few words, produces, not a creature only, but the Origin of all things, the ſupreme uncreated Being himſelf.

Lo Spedale Maggiore, or the great hoſpital, owes its foundation to Franciſco Sfortia, and is a grand and beautiful ſtructure.

Nineteen of the principal nobility inſpect this hoſpital; and one of the governors conſtantly attends every morning, and inquires into every tranſaction, viſits every ward, and aſks the patients, ſeparately, what treatment they have met with.

A fever

A ſewer or canal runs under every part of the hoſpital, to carry off all kinds of filth. And the baker, butcher, weaver, taylor, ſempſtreſs, and other neceſſary mechanics, have their ſhops within the walls of the hoſpital; which, in this particular, reſembles a city or ſmall republic, having very little connection with Milan. There are alſo paſtures belonging to it, in which oxen, ſheep, and other animals are fed for the ſlaughter: for it appears that near ſix hundred weight of butcher's meat is daily conſumed in this hoſpital, beſide other proviſions.

The method of receiving foundlings into this hoſpital is as follows: at the main entrance of the houſe is a kind of wicket, which two hours after ſun-ſet, is conſtantly opened; within this wicket is a copper machine, reſembling an oven, capable of containing a child of ſix or ſeven years of age. This machine turns on an axis; and every night, as ſoon as the wicket is opened, the aperture is turned toward the ſtreet. The perſon who brings the child places it in this machine, turns it round, knocks at the gate, and retires. The porter, who always watches in the room to which the aperture of the machine is turned, takes out the infant, and ſends it immediately to one of the nurſes. If the child has been baptized, a certificate is given in with it; but, if no certificate be ſent, that ceremony is immediately performed. Before this hoſpital was erected, the children were laid before the door leading to the ward appointed for the wounded; but this was a very inhuman practice, many of the children loſing their limbs, and ſome even their lives before they were diſcovered, and taken into the hoſpital. Seldom leſs than three children are brought every night to the hoſpital, but often four or five. The apartments, deſigned for the wet nurſes and other women, are ſeparated from all others; ſo that no men ever enter them, except in preſence of ſome officers, or thoſe appointed to attend ſtrangers: and in the walls of theſe apartments are apertures with turning boxes, like thoſe at the nunneries, by which they receive their proviſions and other neceſſaries. The boys are taught ſome handicraft trade, and the girls the neceſſary buſineſs of a family. Italy excels all the countries in the world, in the humanity and care with which the ſick and poor are attended. And if this hoſpital be deficient in any particular, it is, perhaps, in the abilities of its phyſicians and ſurgeons.

Formerly, the dead from the great hoſpital were buried without the city, in a particular church-yard; but their prodigious number infecting the air with a noxious and almoſt inſupportable ſmell, a grand building was, by the generous liberality of M. Annoi, a merchant of Milan, erected round the church, having a great number of vaults in the ſides for the uſe of this hoſpital. Fifty or ſixty bodies, covered with lime and other corroſives, are depoſited in each of theſe vaults; and, when full, the entrance is firmly cloſed up, ſo that the aſcent of any noxious effluvia is entirely prevented. Nor is there any danger that the place will ever be infected with the deleterious exhalations; for the number of vaults is ſo great, that the bodies buried in the firſt will be entirely conſumed long before the reſt are full.

The common method in other churches is to throw the corpſe into a common vault, to the amount of two or three hundred; which cannot fail of filling the air, in theſe edifices, with noxious effluvia. The Sextons, during the winter, empty theſe vaults, throwing the bodies, half-decayed, into large pits opened for that purpoſe behind the churches.

The church of St. Stephen, called alſo la Rota, is erected on the very ſpot where St. Ambroſe, then biſhop of Milan, is ſaid to have performed a very extraordinary miracle, after the firſt battle between the orthodox and Arians. The ſaint, it ſeems being at a loſs to diſtinguiſh the bodies of the true believers from thoſe of the heretics, commanded the latter to

turn

turn their faces to the ground, and the former, theirs toward heaven, which was accordingly done. They add, that the blood of the orthodox formed itſelf into a round maſs, reſembling a wheel, and was at laſt totally abſorbed by a ſtone, over which there is now a braſs plate, and contiguous to it a pillar, with an inſcription on it, to perpetuate the miracle.

Near this church is a chapel, called *Les Morts de S. Bernardino*, paved with the ſkulls and bones of thoſe ſlain in the above battle, reſembling, in ſome meaſure, the chapel of the eleven thouſand Virgins at Cologn. The ground-work is compoſed of bones, and the ſkulls form croſſes in it by way of decoration. A pyramid of bones, before which is an iron grate to prevent their falling, or being taken away, is erected on each ſide of the altar. A pair of colours, and a drum, reſembling thoſe uſed by the ancient Germans, hang up on the left-ſide of the entrance, and are ſaid to have been taken from the Arians in the ſame battle.

It is very common for young travellers, when they enter any of the taverns in Milan, to be aſked whether they chuſe a *Letto fornito*, or female bedfellow, who continues maſked till ſhe enters the bedchamber. The ſin is now, alas! little regarded; but ſurely they ſhould remember to what danger their health muſt be expoſed, when it depends on the ſcandalous choice of a mercenary landlord.

A ſtranger is ſurprized, in walking the ſtreets of Milan, to meet with ſuch numbers of deformed dwarfs, and people with wens of a prodigious ſize. I remember to have ſeen an old woman who had three wens, the leaſt larger than her head, which ſhe could not move at all. Some imagine that this deformity is owing to the ſnow-water from the mountains mixing with that of the ſprings and rivers; but it ſhould be remembered that the inhabitants of Switzerland uſe ſnow-water, both to prevent and cure theſe excreſcences. Others think that the ſtony particles with which

which the waters, in their deſcent from the mountains, are impregnated, cauſe theſe wens, by forming concretions in the minute veſſels of the neck; but it is well known that theſe deformities are hereditary, and affect infants before they have ever taſted any water.

The villa of the marquis de Creci, a few Italian miles from Milan, ſhould be viſited by all travellers who are pleaſed with beautiful ſtatues and paintings.

The marquis Simonetta's villa is remarkable for an extraordinary echo, produced by the ſound's being reflected between the parallel wings of the building, which are perpendicular to the front, and at the diſtance of fifty-eight common paces from each other, without either windows or doors for diſſipating the ſound. It is of the tautological kind, reflecting a man's voice above forty, and the report of a piſtol above ſixty times; but the repetitions ſucceed each other with ſuch rapidity, that it is difficult to count them, or even mark them down, unleſs the experiment be made early in the morning, or in the evening, when the air is remarkably calm and ſtill: but, when the air is either too dry, or too much loaded with vapours, the effect does not ſo well anſwer the expectation.

The ſmall town of Monza, ſituated a few leagues from Milan, is remarkable for the treaſure depoſited in the church of St. John the Baptiſt, founded by queen Theodolinda. Among other valuable curioſities is a cup of a conſiderable ſize, made out of a ſingle piece of ſapphire, and was the uſual drinking cup of that princeſs.

Here is alſo the iron crown, as it is generally called, with which the ancient kings of Italy, and afterwards the emperors of Germany, were crowned kings of Lombardy. The crown, however, is ſo far from being wholly of iron, that a ſmall fillet is the only part of it made with that metal, the reſt of it being gold, adorned with jewels; but it has neither

 ſpikes

ſpikes nor ornaments at the top, nor is it large enough to fit the head of any grown perſon. The fillet or iron ring, if the inhabitants of Monza are to be credited, was formed out of one of the nails which faſtened our Saviour to the croſs, which procured this crown ſo great veneration, that, in the year 1681, they erected a chapel for it in the church of St. John the Baptiſt, placed it upon the altar, and even carried it in proceſſion. The clergy of the cathedral at Milan were piqued at theſe proceedings, apprehending that the devotion paid to the nail kept in their church would be greatly leſſened, if a relique of the ſame kind ſhould be depoſited in the neighbourhood. The diſpute continued for ſome time, but was at laſt carried before the *Officium S. Congregationis Rituum*, at Rome, where in all appearance, it will always remain, without any definitive ſentence being ever pronounced; it being evidently the intereſt of that office to augment, rather than diminiſh the number of reliques.

That part of the country which lies between Milan and Pavia is extremely delightful; the fertile meadows, being interſected by canals, beautiful rows of trees, and luxuriant vineyards, feaſt the eye in the moſt elegant manner. The graſs, produced by theſe meadows, is ſo rich and ſucculent, that horſes fatten in a few weeks; but it renders the horned cattle ſo very weak, that they are not fit for labour: ſo that the inhabitants are obliged to have their beaſts of draught from Piedmont, where they are all entirely white, as on the contrary the hogs in the Milaneſe are wholly black.

Pavia is a ſpacious city, but old, and thinly inhabited. It is built on the river Teſſin, or Ticino, over which it has a ſtone bridge of ſix arches, and is three hundred common paces long; the road over it leads to Borgo. Its fortifications are very inſignificant, nor are there any veſtiges remaining of its having formerly been the capital of the powerful king-

kingdom of Lombardy. The cathedral is an old ſtructure, and built of brick, as are alſo moſt of the public buildings in this place.

A very ſingular method of aſking alms at the gates of Pavia muſt not be omitted. The beggar holds out a kind of diſh, in which is a human ſkull, the better to excite the charity of paſſengers.

The univerſity of Pavia was founded by Charlemagne, and repaired by Charles IV. Baldus, Jaſon, Andreas, Alciatus, and other celebrated civilians, formerly taught here with the greateſt reputation.

From Turin to Aleſſandria is eight ſtages, or thirty-five Italian miles; the diſtance between Aleſſandria and Genoa is near thirty Italian miles; which are accounted ſeven *poſte reale*, or double poſts, and are paid for accordingly.

You travel near Aleſſandria with as much expedition in the cambiatura, as by poſt in the territories of Venice, Piedmont, or Milan, and at half the expence.

The abbey of del Boſco is ſituated about midway between Aleſſandria and Novi. It is conſtantly inhabited by fifty or ſixty Dominican monks, who ſpend five hours and a half every day in performing the offices of the church, and only two in their ſchools. The building is, upon the whole, ſtately and convenient, but the library very indifferent. But what, in in their opinion, is the greateſt curioſity in the whole church, is a wooden crucifix, which, in the year 1647, turned itſelf to the right toward a chapel, wherein ſeveral reliques are depoſited, particularly a piece of our Saviour's croſs, and a thorn of his crown, at the very inſtant a thief had entered the chapel, in order to carry off the treaſure: but, being terrified by the noiſe made by the crucifix in turning itſelf about, he ran off without his booty. It remains to this day in the ſame poſition; but it ſeems to be no more than the natural conſequence reſulting from the warping of the wood, it being the bottom only, not the body of the croſs, which is turned about.

The country between Aleſſandria and Novi is entirely level; but from thence are ſeveral hills, which may be conſidered as a prelude to the adjacent Apennine mountains. The roads are, however, very good, and many of them paved. The Apennine mountains derive their name from Alpen, an old Gauliſh word, ſtill uſed in Germany, to ſignify a mountain in general.

Genoa is one of the moſt beautiful cities in Italy, but its ſituation the moſt inconvenient. It appears to the greateſt advantage to a ſpectator in a ſhip at about a quarter of a league diſtant from the city; for then all its ſtately buildings, which have procured it the name of Superba, form a grand amphitheatre, being ſituated on the gradual declivity of the hill. But this declivity, ſo advantageous to its proſpect from the ſea, together with the narrowneſs of the ſtreets, render the uſe of carriages very difficult; ſo that all the inhabitants, except the principal ladies of the city, who are carried in chairs, walk on foot. They ſay, that the narrowneſs of the ſtreets, and the loftineſs of the houſes, greatly tend to preſerve the health of the inhabitants, by intercepting the rays of the ſun, during the exceſſive heats of the ſummer. All the ſtreets in general are well paved, and ſome in particular with free-ſtone. The cleanlineſs of the ſtreets is partly owing to their being free from carriages, and partly to the ſterility of the neighbouring ſoil, which requiring large quantities of manure, they carefully gather up all the dung which the horſes, mules, and other animals leave there; ſo that the poor inhabitants of Genoa are as careful to pick up all the dung they meet with, as the Arabs are in preſerving that made by the camels returning from Mecca.

The roofs of the houſes in general are flat, and covered with lavagna, a ſpecies of ſtone reſembling ſlate. Thoſe areas are filled with orange-trees; and, from

from their ſloping ſituation, form a kind of penſile gardens, which add greatly to the fine appearance of the city.

The fortifications toward the ſea are remarkably ſtrong, being cut out of the rocks; in ſome places two or three baſtions of this kind are formed behind each other. The length of theſe fortifications, together with thoſe of the lower town, is near three Italian miles; and the number of ordnance mounted on all the works with which the city is defended, amounts to near five hundred. Toward the land the city of Genoa is encompaſſed with a double wall; that next the country, called the new wall, from its being erected long ſince the other, extends beyond the hill, beginning at the Final, and terminating at the river Biſagno. It is, in circumference, ten Italian miles; but ſuch is the ruggedneſs and inequality of the country, that you cannot ride round it in leſs than three hours. The great extent of this wall renders it of no great uſe, except as a defence againſt the attempts of banditti. All travellers, on their entering the city, are obliged to deliver up all their fire-arms, which, according to the laws of the city, ſhould not be re-delivered till their departure; but a piece of money prevails on the officers, who immediately deliver the arms to their owners. Nor is this remiſſneſs of the officers taken any notice of; and it muſt be acknowleged, that travellers are permitted greater liberty in obſerving every part of the city, than can reaſonably be expected in a republic, whoſe ſituation, with regard to the French and Piedmonteſe, muſt tend to render it jealous of ſtrangers. There is a fine ſtone-bridge over the Bonzevera, and another over the Biſagno; the former waſhes the weſt, and the latter the eaſt ſide of the city.

The harbour of Genoa, though large, is far from being ſafe; nor is it poſſible to defend it entirely againſt the ſouth-wind, without making the entrance ſo narrow, as to be very prejudicial to the commerce of the city. It muſt, however, be acknowleged, that neither care nor expence is wanting for rendering it as ſafe and commodious as poſſible; the mole, which is a kind of wall extended on the left-ſide a great diſtance into the ſea, has been lengthened this preſent year thirty-five paces; ſo that it is now ſeven hundred paces long, and is ſtill to be continued two hundred paces farther. There is alſo a mole on the right-hand near the Final, or light-houſe, extended ſeven hundred and ſeventy-four common paces into the ſea, and is defended from the fury of the waves by prodigious pieces of rocks. As the water is here ſo deep, that great part of the wall, near its foundation, muſt have been built by divers, aſſiſted by bells, and other inventions of that kind, the expence attending the work muſt have been immenſe. They alſo propoſe to extend this mole, in order to defend the ſhips in the harbour from the ſouth-weſt wind, which they call *Labeccio*, and is the moſt dangerous of any. In the middle of the harbour is a place called the Royal Bridge, to which water is conveyed by pipes from the mountains for the uſe of the ſhips. The dock for the republic's gallies, is within the harbour.

The naval power of Genoa, which formerly made ſo conſpicuous a figure, is now reduced to ſix gallies only, and even theſe employed chiefly in fetching corn from Naples and Sicily, and carrying out the ladies for the air. The largeſt gallies carry from ſixty to a hundred ſoldiers, beſide three hundred and twenty rowers, ſix on a bench, which alſo ſerves them for a bed. There are a great number of Turkiſh ſlaves in the Darſena; their aſpect is, in general, very moroſe, which the long whiſkers they wear, have not any tendency to leſſen. They wear a large coarſe cloak, having a hood to it like that of the Capuchins. They have their liberty in the Darſena, but not in the city, where they ſell cheeſe, cloth, and other things about the ſtreets chained together in couples. Their officers alſo permit them to keep public houſes and

ſmall

ſmall ſhops in the Darſena; and, when they go to Marſeilles, Corſica, and other places, advance them ſmall ſums of money for purchaſing different kinds of toys, which they ſell again at Genoa to very great advantage. The officers, however, take care to have themſelves part of the profits. Some of the ſlaves are alſo ſupplied with goods at the republic's ware-houſes, partly for ready money, and partly on credit. But none of them are ſuffered to be abſent at night from the Darſena, where they are then conſtantly muſtered and locked up. No perſon who takes any ſlaves from the Corſairs of Barbary, are hindered from keeping them; but this is rarely done, they being uſually ſold to the republic, which has the beſt opportunities both of employing and ſecuring them. They are chiefly employed in knitting ſtockings and caps, meeting with far more indulgence here, than thoſe unhappy Chriſtians, who have the misfortune of falling into the hands of the Corſairs of Barbary.

It is common to divide the rowers in the gallies into three claſſes: 1. Thoſe who, through poverty, ſell themſelves for a term of years, called by the French Bonavoglies: the Genoeſe give only ſixty or ſeventy of their livres to theſe poor people for two years ſervice. The criminals, who are ſentenced to the gallies for a longer or ſhorter term, according to the nature of their crimes. 3. The priſoners taken from the Turks or the piratical ſtates of Barbary. The latter, even if they embrace the Chriſtian religion, are not entitled to their liberty; though they often obtain it by means of their good behaviour, or, at leaſt, are ſettled in a way of getting a comfortable living. Whenever a galley engages an enemy, the Turkiſh ſlaves, and thoſe condemned for life, are placed in the middle of the bench.

The Fanal, or light-houſe, is a lofty tower aſcended by a hundred and ſixty-ſix ſteps, and built on a large fortified rock, on the weſt ſide of the harbour, near the ſuburbs of St. Peter d'Arena. Near the top of

 this

this light-house, and on the side next the sea, a lanthorn, containing thirty-six lamps, is suspended every night, except a few during the middle of the summer. When they expect a fleet of ships, they increase the number of lamps, which, at a distance, appear like a single star. When the watchman on the top of the light-house sees a ship at a distance, he hangs out a single bullet as a signal; when more ships than one appear, the number of bullets are increased, the number of bullets always equalling the number of ships, unless there are more than five, when he hangs out a bullet and a flag.

The badness of the harbour, and extravagant price of commodities greatly check the commerce of Genoa, which, doubtless, would otherwise be carried to a much greater height. The principal manufactures are velvets and damasks; but, beside these, they carry on a considerable trade in silks, brocades, lace, gloves, sweetmeats, fruits, oil, Parmesan cheese, anchovies, and medicinal drugs, from the Levant.

The English have a consul, but no merchants settled at Genoa, as they have at Leghorn. Great numbers of French Protestants have, however, made choice of Genoa for their asylum, where they are kindly received, notwithstanding their different tenets of religion; nor is any notice taken of the frequent visits paid them by the chaplain of the Protestant regiment generally quartered at Alessandria. They have, at Genoa, in common, with the other Italian states, a court of inquisition; but no very strict inquiries are made with regard to foreigners.

The inhabitants of this city, professing the Roman Catholic religion, are said to amount to a hundred and fifty thousand. Virgil, Silius Italicus, Ausonius, and other authors, are not very favourable in their accounts of the fidelity and honesty of the Genoese, formerly called Ligurians; and the following proverb is still applied to this country, and its inhabitants: *monte senza legno, mare senza pesce, gente senza fede, &* *donne*

donne ſenza vergogna, 'a mountain deſtitute of wood, 'a ſea deſtitute of fiſh, a nation deſtitute of honeſty, 'and women deſtitute of modeſty.'

It muſt, however, be allowed, that the policy of Genoa is much better executed than in many other ſtates of Italy. You may walk the ſtreets in the night with the greateſt ſafety, it being very difficult to find an inſtance of any perſon's being attacked by robbers or aſſaſſins. All ranks of people here are engaged in trade, ſuch aſcendancy has the deſire of riches over the mind of man. But exceſſive ſplendor and luxury are, in many reſpects, reſtrained by ſeveral ſalutary laws. No perſon, except foreigners and the eight counſellors of ſtate, is permitted to have more than one footman; ladies of conſiderable rank are indeed, beſide ſuch an attendant, allowed a page, but his age muſt not exceed fourteen years.

What ſeems not altogether conſiſtent with the regularity and diſcreet conduct of the female ſex, is, that the greateſt part of the married ladies of rank are conſtantly waited on by a gentleman, called Ciziſbeo, who walks before their chair in the ſtreets, holds the holy water to them at church, and performs all the little ceremonious offices uſual among lovers. Some ladies have ſeveral of theſe humble and obſequious attendants, among whom the little offices are divided; one attends her abroad, another provides for the table; a third directs the parties of pleaſure; a fourth the gaming-table, &c. And, in proportion to the number of theſe officious gentlemen, the lady is valued for beauty and wit. They all pretend to no more than Platonic love; and, indeed, one would almoſt be tempted to imagine, that the huſbands were really convinced that nothing was to be apprehended: for the Genoeſe, who are as jealous as any other Italians, muſt well know to what heights ſuch intimacies are often carried, as they themſelves perform the ſame offices to other married ladies.

dies. There is, however, no obligation for admitting this cuſtom; time and the general practice are all it has to plead.

The young ladies of Genoa are rarely ſeen, their youth being generally ſpent in the confines of a cloiſter. The married ladies generally wear black, either ſilk or velvet; for, after the firſt year of their marriage, they are rarely indulged in chuſing what colours they pleaſe.

There are two claſſes of nobility at Genoa, the old and the new. The families of Doria, Fieſchi, Spinola, Grimaldi, and Imperiali, are at the head of the former. Formerly, the Juſtiniani were of the ſame claſs, but they have lately abandoned it, and placed themſelves at the head of the new nobility, of which there are about five hundred families. Both claſſes are equally preferred to public employments; but the old, in other reſpects, look with contempt upon the new. All the families of both claſſes, thoſe of Doria and Spinola excepted, are engaged in trade, as merchants or bankers. But the moſt diſtinguiſhed for commerce, among the nobility are the Pallavicini. It muſt, however, be owned, that notwithſtanding the exorbitant wealth of many private perſons, the ſtate is far from rich. The new nobility have a particular walk on the left ſide of the exchange; and the old, on the right. The latter indeed, are not excluded from walking with the former, but neither they nor the citizens are permitted to mix with the latter.

The form of government at Genoa is ariſtocratical, and the nobles muſt be aſſembled before any affair of importance can be tranſacted. The doge has nothing more than a ſhadow of ſovereign power, and even that little expires, with his office, at the end of two years. When the diſputes in theſe biennial elections cannot be determined, they are often adjourned for eight days, during which interval, the oldeſt ſe-

nator

nator conducts the government. A person may be elected doge without being previously a senator; but no person can be a candidate for this supreme office of the republic, under fifty years of age. Frequently, the vote of a poor nobleman may be procured for fifty or sixty Louis d'ors: and it is reported at Genoa, that, some time since, a senator, in necessitous circumstances, being obliged to go a journey, asked a rich member, belonging to the same class, to lend him a cloak; but was refused. Soon after, the poor nobleman coming into the senate on the day of election, the wealthy senator, who wanted only one vote to be elected doge, applied to him, using all the soothing methods, attended with the greatest promises, to obtain his voice; but the poor senator declared, 'That, as his neighbour had lately suffered him to 'go a journey without a cloak, he intended, in return, to let him go home without a cap;' alluding to that worn by the doge.

The doge, with his family, resides in a palace belonging to the republic, having eight senators as a council to assist him in the government. His life-guard consists of two hundred Germans, at present commanded by baron Isengerde. Their uniform is red turned up with blue; but that of the Corsican corps, blue turned up with red. The bombardiers, who wear bayonets, have red coats and leather waistcoats; and the rest of the soldiers white coats faced with blue. The whole number of troops, maintained at present by the republic, amounts to five thousand; and these are continually in garrison at Savona, Sarzana, Novi, Gavi, Spezza, Ventimilia, and in the castles and fortified towns of the island of Corsica.

The doge, when he assists at processions, is dressed in a crimson velvet or silk, and the senators who follow him, in black.

During the doge's administration, he is stiled Serenita; but, after the expiration of his office, only Excellenza, a title common to all senators; and it is said,

ſaid, that the ſecretary of ſtate, when the doge's term of government is expired, makes him the following compliment: 'Your ſerenity having accompliſhed 'the term of your government, your excellency may 'now retire from the republic's palace to your own 'reſidence.' The nobles are ſtiled *illuſtriſſimi*; but, as they are never wanting in title, we commonly hear a perſon ſtiled *illuſtriſſimo & excellentiſſimo ſignore*, or, *illuſtriſſima excellenza*; the latter is given to all phyſicians, but is leſs honourable than *excellentiſſimo & illuſtriſſimo ſignore*, the latter including thoſe who are of noble extraction.

The palace appointed for the doge is both an ancient and elegant ſtructure, ſituated near the center of the city. The apartments on the left-hand are allotted to the doge, whoſe table, during the two years of his adminiſtration, is maintained at the public expence. In the court of the palace, on the left-hand of the large portal, is a white marble ſtatue of Andrew Doria, with an inſcription, in which that great man is ſtiled, the Reſtorer of the ancient liberty of the Republic.

The aſpect of this illuſtrious perſon has in it ſomething very martial, or rather fierce, which is increaſed by the enormous length of beard and whiſkers on the upper lip; ornaments long ſince diſuſed. Over againſt this ſtatue ſtands that of his kinſman and heir, John Andrea Doria, much in the ſame taſte, with an inſcription, calling him the Preſerver of his country's liberty.

The aſcent from the court to the great hall is by a flight of very low white marble ſteps: here the doge is elected, and public audience given to foreign miniſters. It is extremely beautiful, lofty, and well lighted. In this hall are ſix white marble ſtatues of perſons eminent for their liberality to the public.

In the ſummer council chamber, into which there is a paſſage from this hall, is an elegant piece, repreſenting the inhabitants of Genoa receiving the

aſhes

ashes of St. John the Baptist, painted by Solimene. Here is also a fine piece of the discovery of America, by Christopher Columbus, a native of Genoa. The expulsion of Justiniani from Scio, by Soliman, who inhumanly murdered all the children of that family, is finely painted on the middle of the cieling by Pordenone.

Over the entrance of the arsenal, to which there is a passage from the hall of audience, is a rostrum of a ship belonging to the ancient Romans. Its length is about three spans, and its greatest thickness two thirds of a foot. It was discovered in the year 1597, when the harbour was cleaned. Above twenty-five thousand muskets are deposited in the arsenal; and among other curiosities, a shield, in which are fixed a hundred and twenty pistol-barrels, forty of which may be fired at one time: and also the armour of several ladies of Genoa, who joined in a croisade to to the Holy Land, in the year 1301, under pope Boniface VIII.; and in the archives are deposited three letters of the prelate, concerning this expedition.

In the new square before the doge's palace, is a daily market, Sundays not excepted, for garden-stuff. And, what is very remarkable, green pease, artichokes, water-melons, together with hyacinths, and other flowers blown in perfection, are exposed to sale here in the middle of January.

The Strada Nuova is the finest street in the whole city; it was laid out, and the principal palaces in it built by Alexio Galeazzi, an architect of Perugia. Ten or twelve of these palaces are remarkable for beauty and magnificence, especially those of Doria, Pallavicini, Lercari, Carrega, &c. These palaces have elegant hanging gardens and orangeries, supported by stone pillars, equal in height to the first story, which opens into them. The following motto is placed over the entrance of the Doria palace: *Nulli certa domus*, 'We have here no settled habitation.'

Over the door of the doge's palace the ſame words are written, and ſeem very properly adapted to the ſhort continuance of that magiſtrate. The Pallavicini palace has this motto: *Sapientia ædificabitur domus*, 'A houſe ſhall be eſtabliſhed by wiſdom.' An elegant ſquare or market-place, where the Negroni have a beautiful palace, terminates the Strada Nuova.

The Strada Balbi is nearly equal to the Strada Nuova in beauty, and ſuperior in length and breadth. It is adorned with two palaces belonging to the Balbi family, the Jeſuits college, and the palace of Durazzo. The latter greatly excels every other private building in the whole city, and is an hundred and twenty common paces in front; nor is the furniture unequal to its magnificent appearance. Here are ſeveral capital paintings; and the third ſtory has round it an open gallery, from whence there is a beautiful proſpect of the harbour and the ſea, and leads to an elegant garden, decorated with fountains and groves of orange and citron-trees. A garden of the ſame kind may be ſeen at the palace of prince Doria, ſituated near the light-houſe: and behind the garden was formerly a ſtone wharf, from whence the family could ſtep into their barge. Charles V. lodged ſome time in this palace; and, during his ſtay, apartments were ſuddenly run up, at the end of which the emperor, to his aſtoniſhment, found a yacht ready to receive him, and a ſplendid entertainment prepared for his reception. All the gold and ſilver plate, when taken from the emperor's table, was, by prince Doria's orders, thrown into the ſea; but care had been previouſly taken to ſpread nets all round the veſſel. The Spaniſh noblemen in the emperor's retinue, ignorant of this contrivance, could not conceal their aſtoniſhment at ſuch extravagant actions; and, that they might not think any part of this prodigious quantity of plate borrowed, an inſcription, in Spaniſh, was placed on the front of the palace, oppo-

opposite to the Fanal, signifying, 'That nothing in 'that house was borrowed.'

In the middle of a fountain, on the right side of the walk between the palace and the garden, is the statue of a sea-monster, said to have been taken alive. Its forepart resembles a satyr, with two small horns; but behind, it has a double tail of a fish, placed in an erect position. Another fountain, much larger than the former, is decorated with several statues, particularly a gigantic one, of Andrew Doria, with the symbols of Neptune, in a triumphal car, drawn by three large horses. All the embellishments of this fountain, in the center of which the above group is placed, are cut out of one single block of marble.

Andrew Doria, after a life of ninety-three years, during which, he performed a series of the most honourable actions, died in the year 1560. And the senate, as a public testimony of their gratitude, for the many eminent services he performed for his country, sends annually, on the 15th of September, the captain of the palace, attended by two hundred soldiers, with the keys of the city, to the prince of Doria, who always entertains them in an elegant manner, and displays, on this occasion, his valuable collection of pictures, plate, tapestry, and other rich furniture of his palace. The princes of Doria enjoy another privilege, as a further mark of the republic's gratitude, being allowed to wear their swords in the city; a privilege denied to all except strangers, and the nobles when setting out on a journey.

The Doria family may boast of a succession of heroes, not easily paralleled in any other. The present prince is no stranger to naval affairs, and a few years since had a squadron of gallies; but, to avoid disputes with the republic, occasioned by his sometimes assisting the French, and at other times the Austrians, he sold his fleet. His annual revenue is said to amount to a hundred and fifty thousand philippi, each philippi being equal to four Piedmontese livres, fourteen sols and a half.

From the second story of the aforesaid palace is a passage, which goes over a little bridge into another garden, laid out in a beautiful variety of compartments along the side of the mountain. And, among other things, one sees, on its top, a gigantic statue of Jupiter, in stucco, with the left foot resting on a large dog, under which is an epitaph in Italian, importing, that his fidelity and good nature intitled him to that monument; and from the practice of both which good qualities while alive, it was thought but justice to deposit his remains near Jupiter, of whose royal protection he was truly worthy. He lived eleven years and ten months, and died September 7, at five in the evening, 1605.

Such as may be surprised, that a public monument should be erected to a dog, and even the hour of his death particularly mentioned, will doubtless think it more extravagant, that he had five hundred philippi a year settled on him for his maintenance. Spartian, in the 20th chapter of the life of Hadrian, relates, that this emperor was such a lover of horses and dogs, that he caused monuments to be erected to their memory. The heroic king of Sweden, Charles XII. was so fond of his dog Pompey, which always attended him, that, upon the creature's dying in Poland, he ordered his remains to be sent into Sweden, that he might have the honour of being interred in his native country. But those, who, from his care of his favourite dog, thought he could not fail of rewarding the services of his faithful subjects, were mistaken: for he never indicated the least emotion of pity for those who had sacrificed their lives for him at Stralsund, the island of Rugen, or other places. The lovers of well turned epitaphs on dogs will find sufficient matter of entertainment in Lipsius's Select Epistles, Golnitz's Itinerary, and Ferari's Works.

S. Pietro d'Arena, the ſuburbs on the Fanal or light-houſe ſide, is a moſt charming place, finely decorated with elegant gardens and ſummer-houſes: but the Villa Imperiale, where the preſent empreſs lodged twice, deſerves particular notice.

The celebrated muſæum of Micconi is ſtill at Genoa; but the owner being employed in moving his goods to another houſe, I could not have an opportunity of ſeeing it.

The buildings conſecrated to religion in this city are thirty-ſeven pariſh churches, of which twenty are collegiate, ſeventeen monaſteries, and two large hoſpitals.

In a chapel of the cathedral, which is dedicated to St. Laurence, are kept, with the greateſt veneration, the remains of St. John the Baptiſt. This chapel is on the left-hand of the entrance into the cathedral, and in it thirty ſilver lamps are kept continually burning. The altar is ſupported by five pillars of porphyry, and decorated with a painting by Vandyck.

In this church is a large emerald diſh, ſaid to be a preſent from the queen of Sheba to king Solomon, by whom it was afterwards uſed for the paſchal lamb; and by our Saviour at his laſt ſupper: and the republic of Genoa either received it as its ſhare of the plunder of the city of Cæſarea, in the year 1101, or is indebted for it to the generoſity of Baldwin, king of Jeruſalem. This valuable curioſity, which cannot be ſeen without permiſſion from the archbiſhop, is of a circular form, with a hexagonal rim. Its diameter is two common palms, and its circumference five palms wanting one inch. It is formed out of one ſingle emerald, and is entirely plain, without any carving or ſculpture. Perhaps the emerald I before mentioned, at the convent of Reichneau in Bodenſee, is the only one in Europe equal to this in dimenſions.

The church of St. Dominic is finely decorated with marble ſculpture; but it is more remarkable for a fine painting of Cæſar Procaccino, repreſenting the circumciſion of Chriſt. The tribunal of the inquiſition is held in the Dominican convent, to which this church belongs. The church of the ſame name, belonging to the Dominican nuns, near the church of St. Luke, ſhould alſo be viſited by travellers.

Between the Piazzo Sarſano and St. Mary's church is a broad ſtreet, belonging to the Sauli family; and at the end of this ſtreet is a ſtone bridge, connecting two eminences in the city, formerly ſeparated by a deep valley. It is impoſſible to view this bridge without aſtoniſhment, its height being near ninety feet; and conſiſts of one ſmall and three large arches; the latter are elevated ten or twelve feet above ſeveral houſes five or ſix ſtories high, being built croſs a large ſtreet. This extraordinary bridge is forty-five feet in breadth, and an hundred and ſeventy paces in length. The diameter of the middle arch, under which there are ſeveral houſes, is above thirty paces. One of the Sauli family, who is ſtill alive, but without any child, from a deſire of perpetuating his memory, finiſhed this work at a vaſt expence; and the republic, as a teſtimony of its gratitude, has erected, in the doge's palace, a ſtatue to his memory.

There are ſome fine Freſco paintings by Franciſchina de Bologna, beſide other pictures by Piola, in the church of St. Philippo Neri, belonging to the fathers of the oratory. In this church, every Sunday evening, during the winter ſeaſon, an oratorio, founded on ſome ſcripture hiſtory, is performed. This is ſucceeded by a ſermon of near half an hour; and the whole concludes with a grand piece of church muſic. There can be no great objection againſt a performance of this kind, as it is evidently calculated to prevent people from running into ill company, and, at the ſame time, to endeavour, by every method

thod of perſuaſion, to impreſs on their minds the duties of morality and religion; but the ſummer's diverſion by theſe fathers cannot claim an equal indulgence. They have, without St. Thomas's gate, near prince Doria's palace, a fine garden, in which is a beautiful ſtructure. Here ſeveral games, as draughts, cheſs, and billiards, are permitted every Sunday in the afternoon; they have indeed excepted cards and dice. It muſt however be owned, that they play only or *ave marias*, *pater-noſters*, *&c.* not for money; and, accordingly, when a ſet breaks up, the loſers repair to an image of the Virgin, and there, on their knees, diſcharge the debt. As ſoon as the evening approaches, all play ceaſes, and the fathers perform an oratorio; then one of them makes a ſpiritual exhortation, and the whole concludes with a ſolemn piece of church muſic. As the fathers endeavour, by theſe meetings, to prevent the commonalty from joining their riotous companions, and gratify their prepoſterous paſſion for gaming, without any prejudice to their families and fortune, the deſign itſelf cannot be condemned; but can the abuſe of the name of God in theſe laſt prayers, where the attention is not engaged, be juſtified? Surely they cannot be ſaid to be edifying, if indeed they are lawful.

When a ſingle perſon is buried, a kind of garland, formed of all ſorts of artificial flowers, is placed on the coffin. But, at the funerals of perſons of diſtinction, the religious fraternities walk in proceſſion, having white hoods drawn over their faces, and flambeaux in their hands, which they carry in an horizontal poſition, that poor children may earn a few ſols, by catching the wax which perpetually drops from them upon paper. The intention is doubtleſs commendable; but the ſolemnity is not greatly increaſed by the number of ragged boys every where mixed with the proceſſion.

Before I conclude it is necessary to observe, that though the entertainment at the inns of Genoa is so much preferable to that at Turin, yet a traveller will have no reason to boast; especially if he neglects to bargain for every thing before he receives it. Their wine is none of the best; but this is not to be attributed to the landlords; for they are obliged to fetch all their wine from the vaults of the republic, where it is delivered in sealed bottles. And as the innkeeper gains nothing more than the bottles in the sale of the wine, he always takes care to make himself amends in other articles.

The republic, beside this monopoly of wine, deals also in corn, none of that commodity being sold in the market, so that every baker is obliged to purchase it at the public granaries.

[Lady Wortley Montague gives several particulars and observations relating to Genoa, which will illustrate the foregoing account.

'Genoa is situated in a very fine bay, and being built on a rising hill intermixed with gardens, and beautified with the most excellent architecture, gives a very fine prospect off at sea; though it lost much of its beauty in my eyes, having been accustomed to that of Constantinople.——The Genoese were once masters of several islands in the Archipelago, and all that part of Constantinople which is now called Galata. Their betraying the Christian cause, by facilitating the taking of Constantinople by the Turk, deserved what has since happened to them, even the loss of all their conquests on that side to those infidels. They are at present far from rich, and are despised by the French, since their doge was forced by the late king to go in person to Paris, to ask pardon for such a trifle as the arms of France over the house of the envoy, being spattered with dung in the night. This, I suppose, was done by some of the Spanish faction, which still makes up the majority here, ſhere, though they dare not openly declare it. The ladies affect the French habit, and are more genteel than thoſe they imitate. I do not doubt but the cuſtom of Cicisbei's has very much improved their airs. I know not whether you ever heard of thoſe animals. Upon my word, nothing but my own eyes could have convinced me there were any ſuch upon earth. The faſhion begun here, and is now received all over Italy, where the huſbands are not ſuch terrible creatures as we repreſent them. There are none among them ſuch brutes, as to pretend to find fault with a cuſtom ſo well eſtabliſhed, and ſo politically founded, ſince I am aſſured that it was an expedient, firſt found out by the ſenate, to put an end to thoſe family hatreds, which tore their ſtate to pieces, and to find employment for thoſe young men, who were forced to cut one another's throats, *pour paſſer le temps*; and it has ſucceeded ſo well, that ſince the inſtitution of Cicisbey, there has been nothing but peace and good humour amongſt them. Theſe are gentlemen who devote themſelves to the ſervice of a particular lady, (I mean a married one, for the virgins are all inviſible, and confined to convents:) they are obliged to wait on her to all public places, ſuch as the plays, operas, and aſſemblies, (which are called here converſations) where they wait behind her chair, take care of her fan and gloves, if ſhe plays; have the privilege of whiſpers, &c.——When ſhe goes out, they ſerve her inſtead of lacquies, gravely trotting by her chair. 'Tis their buſineſs to prepare for her a preſent againſt any day of public appearance; in ſhort, they are to ſpend all their time and money in her ſervice, who rewards them accordingly (for opportunity they want none) but the huſband is not to have the impudence to ſuppoſe this any other than pure Platonic friendſhip. It is true, they endeavour to give her a Cicisbei of their own chuſing; but when the lady happens not to be of the ſame taſte, as that often happens, ſhe never fails to bring it about to

 have

have one of her own fancy. In former times, one beauty uſed to have eight or ten of theſe humble admirers; but thoſe days of plenty and humility are no more. Men grow more ſcarce and ſaucy, and every lady is forced to content herſelf with one at a time.

You may ſee in this place the glorious liberty of a republic, or, more properly, of an ariſtocracy, the common people being here as arrant ſlaves as the French; but the old nobles pay little reſpect to the doge, who is but two years in his office, and whoſe wife, at that very time, aſſumes no rank above another lady. It is true, the family of Andrea Doria (that great man who reſtored them that liberty they enjoy) have ſome particular privileges. When the ſenate found it neceſſary to put a ſtop to the luxury of dreſs, forbidding the wearing of jewels and brocades, they left them at liberty to make what expence they pleaſed.

I look with great pleaſure on the ſtatue of that hero, which is in the court belonging to the houſe of duke Doria. This puts me in mind of their palaces, which I can never deſcribe as I ought.—— Is it not enough that I ſay, they are moſt of them the deſign of Palladio? The ſtreet called Strada Nova, is perhaps the moſt beautiful line of building in the world. I muſt particularly mention the vaſt palaces of Durazzo, thoſe of the two Balbi, joined together by a magnificent colonade, that of the Imperiale, at this village of St. Pierre d'Arena, and another of the Doria. The perfection of architecture, and the utmoſt profuſion of rich furniture are to be ſeen here, diſpoſed with the moſt elegant taſte, and laviſh magnificence. But I am charmed with nothing ſo much as the collection of pictures by the pencils of Raphael, Paulo Veroneſe, Titian, Caracci, Michael Angelo, Guido and Correggio; which two I mention laſt as my particular favourites. I own, I can find no pleaſure in objects of horror; and, in my opinion, the more naturally a crucifix is repreſented, the more

diſagreeable

disagreeable it is. These my beloved painters shew nature, and shew it in the most charming light.'——

Dr. Smollet, who was at Genoa in 1765, furnishes us also with the following remarks.

'It is not without reason that Genoa is called *La Superba.*—The city is very stately, and the nobles are very proud. Some few of them may be proud of their wealth: but, in general, their fortunes are very small. Many Genoese noblemen are said to have fortunes of half a million of livres *per annum*: but the truth is, the whole revenue of the state does not exceed this sum; and the livre of Genoa is about nine pence sterling. There are about half a dozen of their nobles who have ten thousand a year: but the majority have not above a twentieth part of that sum. They live with great parsimony in their families; and wear nothing but black in public; so that their expences are but small. If a Genoese nobleman gives an entertainment once a quarter, he is said to live upon the fragments all the rest of the year. I was told that one of them lately treated his friends, and left the entertainment to the care of his son, who ordered a dish of fish that cost a zechine, which is equal to about ten shillings sterling. The old gentleman no sooner saw it appear on the table, than unable to suppress his concern, he burst into tears and exclaimed, *Ah Figliuolo indegno! Siamo in Rovina! Siamo in precipizio!*

I think the pride or ostentation of the Italians in general takes a more laudable turn than of other nations. A Frenchman lays out his whole revenue upon tawdry suits of cloaths, or in furnishing a magnificent *repas* of fifty or a hundred dishes, one half of which are not eatable, nor intended to be eaten. His wardrobe goes to the *fripier*; his dishes to the dogs, and after his decease no vestige of him remains. A Genoese, on the other hand, keeps himself and his family at short allowance, that he may save money to build palaces and churches, which remain to after-

 ages

ages ſo many monuments of his taſte, piety, and munificence; and, in the mean time, give employment and bread to the poor and induſtrious. There are ſome Genoeſe nobles who have each five or ſix elegant palaces magnificently furniſhed, either in the city, or in different parts of the Riveria. The two ſtreets called Strada Balbi and Strada Nuova are continued double ranges of palaces, adorned with gardens and fountains; but their being painted on the outſide, has, in my opinion, a poor effect.

The commerce of this city is, at preſent, not very conſiderable; yet it has the face of buſineſs. The ſtreets are crowded with people; the ſhops are well furniſhed; and the markets abound with all ſorts of excellent proviſion. The wine made in this neighbourhood is, however, very indifferent; and all that is conſumed muſt be bought at the public cantinre, where it is ſold for the benefit of the ſtate. Their bread is the whiteſt and the beſt I have taſted any where; and the beef, which they have from Piedmont, is juicy and delicious. The expence of eating in Italy is nearly the ſame as in France, about three ſhillings a head for every meal. The ſtate of Genoa is very poor, and their bank of St. George has received ſuch rude ſhocks, firſt from the revolt of the Corſicans, and afterward from the misfortunes of the city, when it was taken by the Auſtrians in the war of 1745, that it ſtill continues to languiſh, without any near proſpect of its credit being reſtored. Nothing ſhews the weakneſs of their ſtate more than their having recourſe to the aſſiſtance of France, to put a ſtop to the progreſs of Paoli in Corſica: for after all that has been ſaid of the gallantry and courage of Paoli and his iſlanders, I am very credibly informed that they might be very eaſily ſuppreſſed, if the Genoeſe had either vigour in the council, or reſolution in the field.

True it is, they made a noble effort in expelling the Auſtrians, who had taken poſſeſſion of their city; but

but this effort was the effect of oppression and despair; and if the insinuation of some politicians in this part of the world may be believed, the Genoese would not have succeeded in that attempt, if they had not previously purchased, with a large sum of money, the connivance of the only person who could defeat the enterprize. For my own part, I can scarce entertain thoughts so prejudicial to the character of human nature, as to suppose a man capable of sacrificing, to such a consideration, the duty he owed his prince, as well as all regard to the lives of his soldiers, even those who lay sick in hospitals, and who being dragged forth, were miserably butchered by the furious populace. There is one more presumption of his innocence, he still retains the favour of his sovereign, who could not well be supposed to share in the booty. *There are mysteries in politics which were never dreamed of in our philosophy, Horatio!* The possession of Genoa might have proved a troublesome bone of contention, which it might be convenient to lose by accident. Certain it is, when the Austrians returned after their expulsion, in order to retake the city, the engineer, being questioned by the general, declared he would take the place in fifteen days, on pain of losing his head; and in four days after this declaration the Austrians retired. This anecdote I learned from a worthy gentleman of this country, who had it from the engineer's own mouth. Perhaps it was the will of heaven. You see how favourably Providence has interposed in behalf of the reigning empress of Russia, first in removing her husband; secondly, in ordaining the assassination of prince Ivan, for which the perpetrators have been so liberally rewarded: it even seems determined to shorten the life of her own son, the only surviving rival from whom she had any thing to fear.

The Genoese have now thrown themselves into the arms of France for protection: I know not whether it would not have been a greater mark of sagacity to cultivate the friendship of England, with which the they carry on an advantageous commerce. While the English are masters of the Mediterranean, they will always have it in their power to do incredible damage all along the Riviera, to ruin the Genoese trade by sea, and even to annoy the capital; for, notwithstanding all the pains they have taken to fortify the mole and the city, I am greatly deceived if it is not still exposed to the danger, not only of a bombardment, but even of a cannonade. I am even sanguine enough to think, a resolute commander might, with a strong squadron, sail directly into the harbour, without sustaining much damage, notwithstanding all the cannon of the place, which are said to amount to near five hundred. I have seen a cannonade of above four hundred pieces of artillery, beside bombs and cohorns, maintained for many hours without doing much mischief.——

The few days we staid at Genoa were employed in visiting the most remarkable churches, and palaces.

In some of the churches, particularly that of the Annunciata, I found a profusion of ornaments, which had more magnificence than taste. There is a great number of pictures; but very few of them are capital pieces. I heard much of the Ponte Carignano, which did not at all answer my expectation. It is a bridge that unites two eminences which form the higher part of the city, and the houses in the bottom below do not rise so high as the springing of its arches. There is nothing at all curious in its construction, nor any way remarkable, except the height of the piers from which the arches are sprung. Hard by the bridge there is an elegant church, from the top of which you have a very rich and extensive prospect of the city, the sea, and the adjacent country, which looks like a continent of groves and villas. The only remarkable circumstance about the cathedral, which is gothic and gloomy, is the chapel where the pretended bones of John the Baptist are deposited, and in which thirty silver lamps are continually burning. I had a curiosity to see the palaces of Durazzo and

and Doria, but it required more trouble to procure admission than I was willing to give myself.——

Having here provided myself with letters of credit for Florence and Rome, I hired the same boat which had brought us hither, to carry us forward to Lerici, which is a small town about half way between Genoa and Leghorn, where travellers, who are tired of the sea, take post-chaises to continue their route by land to Pisa and Florence. I paid three Loui d'ors for this voyage of about fifty miles; though I might have had a felucca for less money. When you land on the wharf at Genoa, you are plied by the felucca men just as you are plied by the watermen at Hungerford-stairs in London. They are always ready to set off at a minute's warning for Lerici, Leghorn, Nice, Antibes, Marseilles, and every part of the Riviera.']

The roads between Genoa and Lucca are very bad, often infested with banditti; and the accommodation at the inns very indifferent, so that the journey is both troublesome and dangerous. Those therefore who have before seen Milan, will find it much more agreeable, especially during the autumn and winter seasons, to imbark in a felucca for Leghorn. The corsairs, during these months, rarely approach the shore, and, the wind being generally to the northward, the passage is performed in two days without the least difficulty. But you must not forget to take with you a certificate of health; and, with regard to the corsairs of Barbary, a pass from the consul of any nation at peace with these states may be of the greatest service.

The distance between Genoa and Leghorn is about an hundred and twenty Italian miles; and a private felucca may generally be hired for three or four pistoles, or about three pounds four shillings sterling. Feluccas are light open vessels, sufficient for ten or twelve persons, and make use both of sails and oars. They always keep near the shore, so that, in case of contrary winds, or the apprehension of meeting any corsair, they turn into some secure creek or harbour on the coast, where they continue during the night.

The

The diſtance between Genoa and Capo Fino, or Punto Fino, is fifteen Italian miles; and between them Nervi and Camogli are ſituated. Several houſes and villages, being erected along the coaſt, render it a very agreeable proſpect. Capo Fino is one of the head lands or promontories which form the bay of Rapallo: it is only a barren rock, extending a conſiderable diſtance into the ſea, and having on the eaſtern ſide of the ſummit a pretty ſtrong caſtle. Rapallo, being built in the form of an amphitheatre, affords a very agreeable proſpect. Glaveri, a large but irregular village, ſituated on the coaſt between Rapallo and Lavagna, is not mentioned in ſeveral maps. The coaſt between Lavagna and Porto de Venere, except thoſe ſmall towns mentioned above, is one continued barren rock, deſtitute of vines, graſs, and wood; nor have the inhabitants any other method of acquiring their ſubſiſtence than fiſhing.

The territories of Genoa are on one ſide terminated by the ſmall principality of Meſſa, the capital of which is Carrara, from whence the famous marble, dug from a quarry in the neighbourhood, derives its name. Near the river Magra are ſtill the ruins of the ancient Luna. Some imagine, that Gulfo di Spetia is the Portus Lunæ of the ancients.

Leghorn *, called by the ancients Liburnus Portus, was, a few ages ſince, but a mean and unhealthy place, and belonged to the republic of Genoa; who exchanged it for Sarzana, an epiſcopal city near Lerici, with Coſmo I. duke of Tuſcany. The former appeared, at that time, to have greatly the advantage; but the grand duke had before formed a ſcheme for rendering Leghorn a place of much greater conſequence than it had hitherto been. Nor was he deceived in his expectations; for, by cutting a great number of canals, and uſing other proper methods of cultivation, the ſoil is rendered fertile, and the

* The proper name of this place is *Liverno*: being called Leghorn by none but the Engliſh.

noxious

noxious exhalations almoſt totally deſtroyed; which, with the free trade it enjoys, have rendered it very populous. The city is, however, deſtitute of good water, which the inhabitants are obliged to fetch from Piſa.

[" Leghorn, ſays Mr. Miſſon, is about fourteen miles diſtant from Piſa, the country between them being very level, but woody, filled with oaks, cork-trees, and wild myrtles: they tell you, that theſe woods were formerly all covered by the ſea, which reached within three miles of Piſa, where you ſee a large church at the entrance of theſe woods, which, ſay they, was built in the ſame place where St. Peter was ſhipwrecked one day when he was fiſhing. Leghorn is a modern city, built on a level ground, and ſtrengthened with good fortifications faced with brick-work; its ſtreets are large, ſtreight, and uniform, the houſes generally of the ſame height, and painted on the outſide."]

Merchants of all denominations enjoy intire liberty of commerce, and the free exerciſe of their religion in private; but the only one permitted to be exerciſed publicly is that of Rome: though the Greeks, Jews, and Mahometans, have, in ſome meaſure, the ſame indulgence. The proteſtants have always opportunities of baptiſing their children, receiving the ſacrament, and performing the other duties of religion, either by means of the great number of Engliſh, Dutch, and Daniſh ſhips conſtantly in the harbour, or the chapel of the Engliſh factors erected here. Commerce is not obſtructed at Leghorn by high duties; every bale, how large ſoever, pays only two ſcudi, or piaſters, (about nine ſhillings ſterling) nor are the contents ever examined. The baggage of travellers is never ſearched; they are indeed obliged to deliver up their fire-arms, but theſe are reſtored, by procuring an order from the governor, which is not attended with any great difficulty. The Engliſh, of which there are thirty-ſix families, carry on the greateſt trade here of any foreign nation.

There

There are ſaid to be eighteen thouſand Jews in the city of Leghorn, which is termed their paradiſe; for they here enjoy the greateſt freedom, nor are they branded with any ignominious mark of diſtinction. The inquiſition is indeed eſtabliſhed at Leghorn, but its power is not extended to the Jews, but limited intirely to eccleſiaſtical affairs of its own communion.

The number of inhabitants in Leghorn, including the Jews, is ſaid to amount to forty thouſand; but, in my opinion, this eſtimate is too large. The ſtreets in general are ſtraight and broad; ſo that from the great ſquare, where the market is kept, there is a proſpect through the oppoſite gates of the city. The north part is called New Venice, from its cleanlineſs, the number of canals that interſect it, the elegance of the buildings; and its convenient ſituation for trade. The walks on the ramparts are very agreeable, there being on one ſide an extenſive proſpect of the ſea, and on the other of a country finely embelliſhed with gentlemen's ſeats. Beſide the citadel, there are two caſtles toward the ſea; ſo that the place is capable of making a good defence. There are at preſent about three hundred pieces of ordnance, the greateſt part of which are braſs, on the ſeveral fortifications; and the garriſon conſiſts of ſix hundred men.

At the mouth of the harbour, on the left hand, are two towers, ſaid to be the remains of a pier belonging to the republic of Piſa. Leghorn harbour is divided into two parts, called the outward and inward harbour. The latter, termed the Darſa, or Darſena, is appointed for the reception of the gallies belonging to the grand duke. Theſe are often ſent out on a cruiſe againſt the corſairs of Barbary; but it cannot be ſaid to compoſe a very formidable fleet, their whole number not exceeding five or ſix.

The former, or outward harbour, is defended from the violence of the waves by a pier-head of ſix hundred paces in length, compoſed of prodigious large ſtones; the top of it is paved, and on it the moſt

wealthy

wealthy citizens take the air in their coaches. The breadth of the harbour is near fifteen hundred paces; but the water, eſpecially in the middle, is not of a ſufficient depth; ſo that large ſhips are obliged, for the greater ſafety, to be faſtened to the ſide of the mole. There is good anchorage in the road at about one or two Italian miles diſtance from the mole; but the ſhips riding here are equally expoſed to the weather and the Barbary corſairs.

Civita Vecchia ſeems in ſeveral reſpects to be better ſituated for trade than Leghorn, and, ſhould the pope declare the former a free port, it muſt prove very diſadvantageous to the latter. Several popes have been convinced of the advantage that could not fail of reſulting from this ſcheme, but the intereſt of the Florentine cardinals, and large ſums of money properly diſtributed, have hitherto hindered its being carried into execution. The unhealthfulneſs of the air at Civita Vecchia is no objection at all; becauſe Leghorn itſelf is a ſufficient inſtance that it may be remedied; and the beſt of water may, by the help of pipes, be eaſily conveyed thither.

The Pharos, or light-houſe, where, during the night, above thirty lamps are conſtantly burning, is built upon a ſingle rock in the open ſea. Corſica, and even Sardinia, may be ſeen from this tower, in fine weather; the former is indeed viſible from the mole. The Lazaretto, where perſons and goods, coming from all places ſuſpected of contagious diſeaſes, perform quarantine, is ſituated near the light houſe, on the main land.

The Turkiſh ſlaves, and others condemned to the gallies, are every night ſecured in a kind of large priſon, called the Bagni, from a word uſed by the Turks for the place where they confine their Chriſtian captives. They are at liberty to quit the Bagni every day, and may follow any trade or buſineſs; but they muſt be ſure to return early in the evening. There are generally about two thouſand of theſe rowers, eight or nine hundred of which are Turks. There are also Turks in the city, which are no slaves, but are obliged to live in a particular quarter, near that appointed for the Jews. They have a great mosque in the Bagni, but it is generally shut up.

There is not a single church in Leghorn that merits the observation of a judicious traveller. The Greeks in this city are divided into two sects, and distinguished by the names of Latin Greeks and Eastern Greeks. The former acknowlege the pope's supremacy. The Armenians have also a church here; but the difference between their religion and that of the Roman catholics is very immaterial. The Jews and Turks are obliged to live in particular parts of the city; and the common prostitutes are forced to confine themselves to the district assigned them: nor are these unhappy wretches allowed to visit any other part of the city without leave from the commissary, which cannot be procured under a few sols.

But, notwithstanding all the advantages enjoyed by Leghorn, it is far from being a cheap place to reside at; for, beside the large duties on all provisions brought to it by land, the duke reserves to himself the monopoly of several commodities, especially brandy, tobacco, and salt: and so very strict are they with regard to the last article, great quantities of which are found on the sea-shore, that whoever has half an ounce of such salt in his custody, is sent to the gallies, without any regard to his rank or situation in life.

Barks go daily from Leghorn to Pisa, by means of a canal, except in winter, when it is sometimes frozen. This canal, which is sixteen Italian miles in length, is not only very advantageous to trade, but highly useful in draining the morasses, whereby the air is rendered more healthy than it otherwise would be.

Pisa was, some centuries ago, a famous republic, whose victorious fleet were a terror to the Saracens in the Holy Land, the coasts of Africa, the islands of Sicily and Majorca, and the republic of Genoa. But there

there is hardly the ſhadow of this mighty power now remaining; partly owing to their having fallen under the dominion of the Florentines, and partly to the opening of the neighbouring harbour at Leghorn. The city indeed is ſpacious, the ſtreets even, broad, and well-paved, and the houſes not badly built; but the life and ſpirit which ſhould actuate this well finiſhed body, namely, the number of inhabitants, are wanting to ſuch a degree, that the ſtreets are in many places full of graſs. The principal and richeſt families, ſince the republic loſt its liberty in the year 1406, have abandoned Piſa, and retired to different places, ſome even as far as Geneva; nor is there the leaſt appearance of this loſs ever being repaired. The air is however healthy, the water excellent, the adjacent country very fruitful, and the ſituation of the city pleaſant and commodious, on account of the river Arno, which waſhes its walls. The number of inhabitants in Piſa amounts at preſent to between ſixteen and ſeventeen thouſand; but was their number proportional to the largeneſs and other circumſtances of the place, it ſhould at leaſt amount to eighty thouſand.

The condition of the univerſity, founded here in 1339, is alſo but indifferent; though it is neither deſtitute of public endowments, colleges, or able profeſſors, who are nominated by the great duke. The exchange is a beautiful and ſtately ſtructure, built in 1605, but it is now frequented by a few merchants only. Shipwrights and other artificers however enjoy here one particular advantage, namely, the building of gallies, which the great duke has removed to Piſa, on account of the conveniency of the Arno; and the ſmall naval force of that prince is commonly ſtationed here.

Piſa has three bridges over the Arno, of which that in the middle is the moſt beautiful, and built of marble. The common people, who live oppoſite to the river, have annually a mock engagement on this bridge, like that on St. Barnabas's bridge at Venice, betwixt the Caſtellani and Nicoloti.

With regard to the botanic garden, I ſhall only mention, in general, that it lies near St. Steven's church, is very ſpacious, and, beſide a great number of plants, is decorated with ſeveral water-works. Near the entrance is the intire ſkeleton of a whale, and ſeveral parts of another. Over the door is this advice, often neceſſary in a garden, *Hic Argus eſto, non Briareus.* "Employ the eyes of Argus, but not the hands of Briareus."

In the repoſitory of natural curioſities, near the botanic garden, among other remarkable pieces, is a coral-ſprig growing on a human ſkull, and two pieces of cryſtal; in the center of one of which is a drop of water in continual motion, and in that of the other a fly. The ſight of theſe cryſtals brought to my remembrance a relique ſhewn by the Benedictines at Vendome, who pretend it is one of the tears which our Saviour ſhed at the grave of Lazarus; but, in fact, is no other than a mere curioſity of nature. I have elſewhere pointed out the miſtake of the ancients, in aſcribing the ſame original to cryſtal as to ice; and I believe I have alſo mentioned, that an amethyſt containing a drop of water may be ſeen in Sir Hans Sloane's muſæum at London.

Lucca is twelve Italian miles diſtant from Piſa; but the road is delightful, eſpecially in dry weather; when there is no neceſſity for travelling over the mountain of St. Julian, but keep entirely in the plain, which is divided into ſquare incloſures, and planted with beautiful rows of trees, round which the vines intwine their branches, and form, on the tops, luxuriant and beautiful cluſters and feſtoons. The beautiful appearance of this track of land cannot be exceeded either in ſummer or autumn; the mountain on the right being entirely covered with tall cypreſſes and olive-trees. The winters, in theſe parts, cannot be ſaid to be mild, for, at preſent, the froſt is often ſo

 intenſe

intense during the night, that the carriages make no impression on the ground, defended from the rays of the sun: but, notwithstanding the severity of cold, I observed, that several fields were sown with flax, which looked very green, and was upward of half an ell above the surface of the earth. It does not ripen till May; so that it must be extreamly hardy to bear so keen a frost. I also saw white cabbages and large turnips in other inclosures.

Notwithstanding the republic of Lucca is not above thirty Italian miles in circumference, yet the fertility of the soil and clemency of the government have proved such prevalent motives to settling here, that the inhabitants of the city, together with those of the hundred and fifty villages, of which the republic consists, are said to amount to one hundred and twenty thousand; thirty thousand of which are capable of bearing arms. The territories of the grand duke intirely encompass those of Lucca; so that a foreign force only can prevent this republic from falling under the yoke of the grand duke of Tuscany. Nor have those princes failed often to shew their desire of uniting this delightful spot with their other dominions, and of reducing Lucca to the same wretched circumstances with Florence, Sienna, and Pisa. It is no great difficulty to find plausible causes for a rupture between contiguous states; their respective boundaries, which can never be absolutely determined, will alone afford a perpetual source: but this is not the only one; the republic of Lucca have always refused to acknowlege the family of Medicis, grand dukes of Tuscany, the only title, they will allow those princes, being dukes in Tuscany. Such is the situation of Lucca, and, therefore, an universal harmony among the members of that republic is absolutely necessary, if they are desirous of transmitting to their posterity the blessings of liberty, their darling idol, with whose image they decorate their coins, their city-gates, and public buildings. The republic is governed by a council of ſtate, and a great council: the former is composed of the Gonfaleniere, or doge, and nine ſenators, who are all members of the latter, or great council. Theſe ſenators are termed Anziani or elders, have the title of *excellentiſſimi*; and, during their office, which continues only two months, have apartments in the palace of the republic, and are maintained at the public expence. And, whenever their own private affairs call them from the palace, they always go *incognito*, and in a cloſe ſedan, with the curtains drawn. A doge cannot be re-elected till ſeven years after the expiration of his office. The great council conſiſts of a hundred and thirty nobles and ten burghers, who enjoy their office two years. A corps of ſeventy-ſix Switzers form the doge's guard; the other forces belonging to the republic amount to about five hundred men; and its annual revenue to about four hundred thouſand ſcudi, or eighty thouſand pounds ſterling.

The city of Lucca is about three Italian miles in circumference, and is defended by eleven baſtions, on which two hundred and eighty pieces of cannon are mounted. Several rows of trees are planted round the walls, which render the walks on them very pleaſant. The city is ſituated in the middle of a delightful plain, which is every where terminated by a chain of mountains; and, from the diligence of its inhabitants in their ſilk and other manufactures, has acquired the honourable epithet of *induſtrioſa*, the induſtrious. They extract from a ſmall, but excellent ſort of olives, the fineſt oil of any in Italy; and from this commodity the republic derives conſiderable advantages. It would be unjuſt not to commend the inhabitants, of whom there are near four thouſand in the city, for their juſtice, candour, and polite behaviour.

The palace belonging to the republic is a large building, but contains nothing curious, except the arſenal, where arms ſufficient for twenty thouſand men are always ready for any emergency.

The

The bishop of Lucca is intitled to the pallium and cross, like archbishops, his see being under the immediate jurisdiction of the pope.

Over the grand portal of St. Pietro Maggiore's church is an inscription, signifying, that, in the year 1688, a gamester had his arm immediately broke, on having thrown dice at the image of the virgin. But this miracle must not be confounded with another commemorated by a monument in St. Augustine's church; whereby we are informed, that some years ago a statue of the Virgin, having her infant son in her arms, was placed in a niche of the wall on the outside of the church; and that a gamester, being unfortunate at play, threw a stone with such force at the image, that the infant would doubtless have been damaged, had not the virgin miraculously removed it from her right to her left arm, where it still continues: that, on the stone's striking the image, blood flowed from the wound, and the earth opened and swallowed up the criminal. The statue was soon after removed into the church, and the miracles commemorated by several inscriptions. They also shew the stone, and the opening in the earth, which, according to the vulgar, terminates in hell. This aperture has an iron cover, fastened with two iron bolts; but it is too small to admit of any, except a very small person.

Pistoja is situated twenty Italian miles from Lucca, and the road, during the first five, is through a most delightful plain; but the remainder, till within a few miles of Pistoja, is through a mountainous country: but the prospects are very agreeable, the mountains being cultivated to their summits, and adorned with parterres one above another. The parts of the road which lead over the mountains cannot be commended, but the other are good, and many of them paved. The plain country in the neighbourhood of Lucca cannot be exceeded; and even that of the Milanese is inferior to it.

Piſtoja was famous among the ancients for the defeat of Catiline; and, among the moderns, the factions of the Guelphs and Gibellines, rendered it remarkable: but it is now ſo greatly reduced, that the whole town, which is very ſpacious, does not contain above five thouſand inhabitants. The country is very fruitful, and proviſions remarkably cheap, which, in all probability, were the principal motives that induced near forty noble families to reſide in this city.

The fine new church of St. Proſpero was ſome years ſince preſented by cardinal Fabroni to the fathers of the oratory, together with a library, and other conſiderable benefactions. The library is open every day, and contains, excluſive of the manuſcripts, fourteen thouſand volumes. This donation was made in the year 1726; and the pope, in order to render it more extenſive, granted a permiſſion to the fathers of adding prohibited books, provided they ſecure them from being read by all, except ſuch as have obtained a licence from the ſee of Rome for that purpoſe.

The diſtance between Piſtoja and Florence is twenty-one Italian miles. Pope Leo X. of the houſe of Medicis, laid the foundation of a palace at Porggio a Cajano, ſeven miles and a half from Florence. The beautiful proſpect of the neighbouring mountains was the principal inducement for his making choice of this place; but he did not live to finiſh the building, that taſk being performed by Francis the grand duke.

In this country grow a kind of large reeds or canes, which they uſe inſtead of poles in the vineyards. The horned cattle are all totally white.

Between Piſtoja and Florence the road is very pleaſant, but, the country being deſtitute both of villas and plantations, which are chiefly in the neighbourhood of Florence, the proſpects are not ſo beautiful as in ſeveral other parts.

Florence, with regard to curioſities worthy the attention of a judicious traveller, exceeds every other city

city in Italy, Rome only excepted; ſo that Octavius Ferrarienſis has not improperly called it *Italiam, ipſius Italiæ*, "the Italy of Italy itſelf." But we ſhall not be ſurpriſed, that Florence contains ſuch an invaluable collection of the moſt beautiful pieces of every kind in the fine arts, if we conſider, that the family of Medicis have, for above two centuries, applied themſelves to the improvement of the ſciences and arts; in which they have expended incredible ſums. The literati, who too often imitate courtiers in flattery, blinded by their zeal for ſuch noble actions, ſeem to forget the enormous blemiſhes which diſgrace the actions of ſeveral princes of this illuſtrious family; or perhaps they are deſirous of hiding theſe defects beneath the veil of oblivion.

Foreign princes, who make the tour of Italy, find ſome difficulty in being admitted to the ducal family. A prince *incognito* is not denied a viſit; but the Italians are for ſtipulating what they ſtile a *mezzo-cere-moniale*, and are very artful in explaining every thing to their own advantage.

Il Palazzo Vecchio was formerly the palace in which the grand duke reſided. In this palace, which fronts a large ſquare, called la Piazza del Gran-Duca, is that curioſity termed the aerial tower. It projects out of the building, and the diameter of it is larger in one part than that of the baſe, but ſoon acquires a proper proportion. The top of it is ſupported with four pillars; but I could never obtain any certain information whether it owed its name to the firſt or ſecond of theſe circumſtances.

The duke's wardrobe is in the Palazzo Vecchio, together with the famous Florentine pandects, and the manuſcript goſpel of St. John; but you cannot procure admittance without a particular licence from the maſter of the wardrobe. In the ſame palace are alſo twelve large cloſets, containing a prodigious quantity of plate, great part of it finely chaſed; and, among the reſt, four bed-poſts of ſilver that belonged to the ſtate-bed of Coſmo III. Abundance alſo of Turkiſh arms and bridles, finely ornamented with jewels, are depoſited here, together with the crown with which pope Pius V. crowned the firſt great duke of Florence, Coſmo I. It is of gold, and richly adorned with jewels. But the moſt valuable piece in this wardrobe is a Palliotto, or altar-cloth, given, as we are informed by an inſcription over it, in letters formed with rubies, by Coſmo II. in conſequence of a vow. It is covered with pearls, rubies, and other precious ſtones; among which are two gems, called *aqua-marina*, of the ſize of a large walnut, ſaid to be of immenſe value. The arms of Auſtria and Florence are quartered on each ſide. Coſmo II. is repreſented in emboſſed work of gems and enamel, in the middle of the Palliotto, on his knees, before an altar or table, on which is a crown covered with diamonds; his robe is richly decorated with gems of the ſame kind.

The *Pandectæ Florentinæ* are contained in two folio volumes, bound in crimſon velvet; but now, eſpecially on the backs, greatly worn. Moſes, on the outſide of one of the volumes, with the two tables of the law in his hands, is painted in enamel; the writing on one of the tables is defaced, but that on the other, legible. On the other volume the arms of Florence, namely, a red croſs, is alſo painted in enamel; but now greatly injured. The word *libertas*, at preſent the motto of Lucca, is placed over the arms. The vellum on which theſe books are written, is almoſt as thin as ſilk paper; but, to preſerve the leaves from any injury, a piece of green taffety is placed between each.

Here are the original decrees of the council of Florence, held in 1439, and which were oppoſed to thoſe of the council of Baſil, by pope Eugene IV. They are written on a large ſkin of parchment, and ſigned by the biſhops and cardinals of the Latin church, and by the emperor and biſhops of the Greek church.

church. Beſide theſe, here are *Acta Concilii Florentini*, and two Greek manuſcripts of the goſpels; one of which, containing the four evangeliſts, is written on vellum, and bound in ſilver covers, adorned with pearls. The other contains only St. John's goſpel, and is ſaid to be an original performance of that evangeliſt himſelf; but what proof they have for this aſſertion I cannot ſay. It is in folio, written on vellum, in large and legible letters of gold, but full of abbreviations, and has two fine illuminations adapted to the hiſtory of the goſpel.

In the ſquare before the Palazzo Vecchio is a large and elegant fountain, erected by Coſmo I. after the deſign of Ammanati. It is decorated with Cupids, ſhells, cornucopias, and Tritons, and four other ſea divinities, in braſs, larger than life. In the center is a ſtatue of Neptune, ten ells high, in a ſhell reſembling a triumphal car, and drawn by four horſes, two of braſs, and two of white marble. In this ſquare is alſo the Fabrica degli Uffici, erected by Coſmo I. after a deſign of Giorgio Vaſari. The ground-floor of this ſtructure is appropriated to the city magiſtrates, who there live together, for the more ſpeedy diſpatch of buſineſs, and the better maintenance of the public tranquillity. Artiſts occupy the ſecond ſtory, and make here curious pieces for the duke's wardrobe and gallery. But among all the performances executed here, that ſtiled Florentine work is the moſt elegant; ſparks of precious ſtones and particles of elegant marble, are ſo diſpoſed as to repreſent the objects of nature in a very beautiful and ſurpriſing manner; but works of this kind require a prodigious time to compleat them. A flower piece, lately finiſhed, about a foot and a half in length, and half a foot in breadth, employed the artiſt above eighteen months. And a piece of emboſſed work, about the ſize of a common ſheet of paper, repreſenting the adoration of the Eaſtern magi, and a group of angels in the air, has already been forty years in hand,

and under the direction of several masters. They use only precious stones in these works, whereas they employ vitreous compositions in other kinds of mosaics, and even these are highly valued at Rome. They make also here those small ebony cases, which are set with precious stones, and represent birds, flowers, and the like, in basso-relievo. In these cases the great duke sends perfumes and essences, as presents to foreign princes.

The third or upper story of the Fabrica degli Uffici is divided into several museums, or apartments for curiosities. Here in particular is the duke's gallery, which would alone require a folio volume to describe it fully. The ceiling of the gallery is covered with paintings, representing the revival of the arts and sciences, with other historical pieces, in which are introduced the most eminent persons of Florence. The walls on each side are decorated with the portraits of the most illustrious members of the house of Medicis; and over these, on the entablature on one side, are small portraits of generals, ministers of state, and princes; and, opposite, the busts of persons celebrated for their learning. Groups of statues, busts, and figures, are placed on both sides of the middle part of the gallery, and cannot fail of highly pleasing the lovers of sculpture and antiquity, as all of them are originals. The passage from the gallery leads into several museums, filled with curiosities that merit attention. The first contains above a hundred and twenty portraits of the most famous painters, and chiefly executed by themselves. They are in gilt frames, and the names of each person over his respective picture.

In the next cabinet are deposited a great number of large and rich porcelain vases, and other pieces of that kind. There are also some vessels of a curious species of Egyptian clay, of a greenish colour, called Babbagauro, and two urns of Pucaro del Cile, a very clear sort of earth, brought from Mexico. They also

shew

ſhew here a large table, beautifully adorned with Florentine work, repreſenting birds, flowers, fruits, &c. This curious piece of work has employed 25 artiſts 14 years.

In a cabinet, on the other ſide of the gallery, is a very valuable pillar, formed out of a ſingle piece of oriental alabaſter, four ells in length, and almoſt tranſparent. Here is alſo a ſmall chimera in bronze; it is an antique, and reſembles the large one in the gallery, except that the tail is perfect in the latter, which is wanting in the former. Here are alſo great numbers of antique lamps, idols, a ſiſtrum, a tripod, a mural crown of braſs, portraits in needle-work, an image of Dante, the famous poet; a large painting on lapis lazuli, a buſt of cardinal Benbow, executed in moſaic; and alſo ſome inlaid works of precious ſtones, but vaſtly inferior to that now performed at Florence. In the middle of the chamber hangs a large branch, wholly compoſed of amber, and was preſented to the grand duke by one of the electors of Brandenburg; and has the heads of ſeveral princes and princeſſes of that auguſt houſe finely chaſed upon it.

In a contiguous apartment is a beautiful table, on which the harbour of Leghorn is finely repreſented in gems; the ground is lapis lazuli, which repreſents the ſea; and a border of agate is carried round the whole work, which is above a hundred years old, but charmingly executed. There are, beſide this table, ſeveral other antique performances, both in marble and precious ſtones; particularly a very capacious vaſe, formed out of one ſingle piece of oriental alabaſter; a large crucifix on a pedeſtal of *pietra paragonia*, or touch-ſtone. The croſs is of agate, and the image, excepting the arms, which are inſerted, formed out of a ſingle piece of ivory. A great number of pieces of turned ivory are depoſited in a particular cabinet; ſome of them valuable for the curiouſneſs of the workmanſhip, and others for being the performances of perſons of rank: among the latter are a round box,

turned

turned by the Czar Peter the Great; a pair of candlesticks, by prince Theodore of Bavaria: and, among the former, a large globe, with near a hundred others of small dimensions, turned within it; and a Curtius on horseback leaping into the gulph, in the Roman forum, which last is the finest piece in the whole collection.

They have also here a prodigious collection of pieces in amber, most of which have contracted, by time, a red colour; a circumstance common to all kinds of amber, especially when it has been steeped in rape or linseed oil. I will not pretend to say, that boiling of amber in the above oils will restore its colour; but I well know, that, if it be boiled in either of them for twenty-four hours, it will lose all its dulness, and appear as transparent as the clearest glass. I am indebted for this discovery to that ingenious optician Christian Portschinen, of Konigsberg, who makes amber spectacles. It should however be remembered, that this boiling greatly lessens its electrical virtue. In another cabinet is a great variety of curiosities in ebony, truly admirable for their workmanship, and the rather, as this species of wood is very difficult to carve in any curious manner in Europe.

Cujatamo Julio Zummo, an ecclesiastic of Sicily, has adorned the next chamber with the anatomy of a human head, and the gradual putrefaction of the body, in wax. On one side of these pieces sits Time with an old torn folio at his feet, and over them hangs the picture of the artist in miniature. The gradual putrefaction is shewn by several figures; the first is an inflated corpse, and contiguous to it another of a fallow hue; the third figure is that of a child, whose body, being disseminated with blue and yellow spots, indicates the near approach of corruption. Contiguous to this is a figure covered with suppurating ulcers, full of worms. The remaining figures exhibit an increasing series of ravages made by the worms, and the gradual progreſs of corruption, till at laſt the body is reduced to a bare ſkeleton. Notwithſtanding the ſhock which figures of this kind muſt give a perſon, who cannot think on his own diſſolution without horror; the various ſtages of putrefaction are ſo natural and delicately exhibited, that they cannot be viewed without pleaſure. The various ſtages and effects of the plague are exhibited in the ſame manner by this curious artiſt.

In an adjacent chamber you ſee a large collection of mathematical inſtruments, burning mirrours, and various machines for explaining the celeſtial phænomena, according to the ſyſtems of Ptolemy, Copernicus, and Tycho Brahe; together with a pair of globes above eight feet in diameter, a magnet of a foot long, near three inches thick, and ſix broad, and ſaid to lift forty pounds. Among other optical curioſities, are ſeveral heads, trophies of ſtandards, colours, ſpears, &c. painted on a table, but, being viewed through a glaſs tube, exhibit the picture of the preſent duke's grandfather. On the wall are all the territories belonging to the great duke.

I ſhall not dwell any longer on the pictures, deſigns, pieces of ſculpture, &c. which are not always in the order here deſcribed, being often transferred from one cabinet to another; but to proceed to that celebrated chamber, called la Tribuna, or l'Octogone, from its octangular figure. The diameter of this room is twenty feet, and has a cupola incruſtated with a ſpecies of mother-of-pearl; on the ſuperficies of which is delineated a kind of compaſs, on which the direction of the wind is ſhewn by an index. In the center of this chamber are ſix marble ſtatues, and, among the reſt, that famous one called the Venus de Medicis. All judges of ſculpture have conſtantly agreed that this ſtatue is the moſt beautiful piece of ſculpture in the world. It was formerly placed in the palace of Medicis, on mount Pincio, at Rome; but, by order of Coſmo III. removed to Florence. Thoſe

who

who were intrusted with the care of packing these statues, were so negligent in their duty, that the thighs, legs, and arms of the Venus de Medicis were broken off by the way; but they have been again replaced, and joined with so much art, that a very critical inspection is requisite to discover the least traces of that misfortune. An inscription on the pedestal informs us, that Cleomenes, an Athenian, son of Apollodorus, was the author of this celebrated piece; and it is surprising that this should be the only instance in which we find the name of so consummate a master. The pedestal is three feet high, and the work of a modern. Some connoisseurs, from the statue's leaning a little forward, have imagined, that it was intended to be placed on some elevation. Their inference is, however, uncertain; and, probably, the artist intended, by this attitude, to express the modesty with which Venus endeavours to hide, and, as it were, withdraw herself from the eyes of the spectator. The right knee advances a little forward; the left hand is placed before the *pudenda*, and the right across her breasts, but neither touch the body.

This statue is, to appearance at least, less than the life, which is another objection against its being intended to be placed on an elevated situation. The head is placed in a position a little inclining to the left shoulder; and, in the charms of her countenance, the bloom of youth, innocence, beauty, and modesty, seem to contend with each other. She is represented as neither corpulent nor lean, and the flesh is so admirably executed, as to induce the beholder to think it is really soft, and would yield to the touch. The polish of the marble has, indeed, in this particular, greatly assisted the skill of the artist; it was at first of a pure white, but has, by time, contracted a yellowish tinct; which has not yet, however, much impaired its beauty, the marble appearing almost transparent in the rays of the sun. The hair is at present brown, possibly from the remains of the gilding, often used

by

by the ancients. The attitude in which the Venus de Medicis appears, has been given to other antique ſtatues, and even to an image of that goddeſs on a medal of Fauſtina: but it ſhould not be inferred from hence that the poſture was borrowed from this ſtatue as an original, and even in theſe ages eſteemed a maſter-piece of ſculpture; for it ſeems more natural to think that this was the common attitude in which Venus was repreſented.

Though the Venus of Medicis has been the admiration of all ages, and reſorted to by the moſt curious perſons, yet it has not totally eſcaped cenſure. The head is by moſt connoiſſeurs conſidered as too ſmall in proportion to the reſt of the body, particularly the hips; ſome cenſure the noſe as too large; and poſſibly the furrow along the vertebræ of the back is ſomething too deep; eſpecially as the object repreſents a ſoft plump female, and both the bend of the arms, and inclination of the body, jointly conſpire to leſſen the depth of this furrow, if not totally to obliterate it. The fingers are remarkably long, and all, except the little finger of the left hand, deſtitute of joints; but this ſhould not affect the reputation of the artiſt, as it is ſufficiently evident, that the hands had not received his laſt touches. The ſame obſervation might be extended to the dolphin, on which ſome boys are riding, at the ſide of the ſtatue; were we not convinced that it was the common practice of the ancients to execute the capital parts in the moſt maſterly manner, but not to beſtow any great attention on the concomitant ornaments. I ſhall conclude this ſhort criticiſm on the celebrated Venus of Medicis, with the following obſervation made by ſome able connoiſſeurs, namely, that, if the different parts of this famous ſtatue be examined ſeparately, as the head, noſe, &c. and compared with the like parts of others, it would not be impoſſible to find ſimilar parts equal, if not ſuperior to them: but, if the delicacy of the ſhape, the attitude, and ſymmetry of the

whole

whole, be considered as one assemblage of beauties, it cannot be paralleled in the whole world. This beautiful statue is placed between two others of the same goddess, both which would be admired by spectators in any other place; but here all their beauties are eclipsed by those of the Venus de Medicis.

On the left side of the entrance, is a piece of mosaic work, representing an owl surrounded with many other birds. It is composed of several thousands of precious stones, and at the bottom the artist's name, Marcellus Provenzalis a Cento F. 1615. There are also in the Tribuna several pieces of the modern Florentine work, performed by Pietre Commesse; and, among the rest, a pearl-fishery, on a ground of lapis lazuli, is truly admirable. Here is also an octangular table, consisting entirely of agate, chalcedony, lapis lazuli, topaz, rubies, and other oriental gems, representing birds, fruits, leaves, and flowers; valued at a hundred thousand scudi (about 21,250 pounds sterling) thirty persons have been employed above fifteen years on this single piece.

They have removed the famous diamond from the Tribuna to the duke's private cabinet, but a piece of yellowish glass exactly of the same dimensions is deposited in its room. Tavernier tells us that the original weighs an hundred and forty carats and a half, and was the largest in Europe, before Mr. Pitt brought his diamond from the East Indies. The Florentine diamond is of a yellowish water, and is said to have been purchased by the grand duke, of a jesuit, for seventy-five thousand scudi (about 18,750 l. sterling.) The father had, however, no reason to complain of his profit, having bought it for a single paolo (about 7 d. sterling) on the Piazza di Navona, it being there offered as a piece of crystal.

Several large basons of rock crystal, and vases of lapis lazuli, agate, cornelian, jasper, &c. some of them set in gold, and adorned with jewels of immense value,

lue, are alſo depoſited in a particular cloſet of the Tribuna.

They alſo ſhew here a moſt ſuperb ſtudiola or cabinet, decorated with fourteen elegant pillars, the ſhafts being of lapis lazuli, and the pedeſtals and capitals of ſolid gold, adorned with pearls and turquoiſe ſtones. Between the pillars are baſſo-relievos in gold, and the heads of the nails, ſuppoſed to faſten the ſeveral pieces of the cabinet together, are topazes, emeralds, ſapphires, rubies, cryſolites, pearls, and other gems. In the center of the top of this curious piece is a pearl, nearly as large as a walnut, and poſſibly not inferior to any thing of the kind in Europe. But the aqua marina exceeds the pearl in magnitude. It has alſo a topaz, large enough to make a ſnuff-box of the middling ſize, and a granate about the ſame magnitude with the pearl. The pieces depoſited in this grand cabinet are of a proportional value, conſiſting principally of intaglios and cammei, or gems cut in relievo; but the inſide of it is never ſhewn, but by the grand duke's permiſſion, as the ſmallneſs of the pieces render them very ſubject to be loſt. They are equally ſtrict with regard to the medals placed in ten neſts of drawers in the ſides of the Tribuna. Seven of theſe are filled with ancient, and the other three with modern medals.

But to give ſome idea of the gems, &c. The antique intaglios repreſenting the heads of emperors and empreſſes amount to eighty. The antique heads of kings and heroes amount to twenty-two. Beſide theſe, there are about fourteen intaglios repreſenting perſons maſked, twenty-eight philoſophers and poets, and near a hundred heathen deities *en creux*, all antique pieces. After the gems of heathen gods, follow mythological, hiſtorical, and other intaglios, about a thouſand in number.

Here are likewiſe great numbers of modern intaglios ſet in rings, and only twenty-eight antique pieces. Among the latter is an *annulus memoriæ*, or mourning ring, that merits obſervation. In the laſt place are the baſſo-relievos, on precious ſtones; but here modern artiſts, when compared with the ancients, appear to great diſadvantage. The number of modern pieces is only a hundred and twenty; whereas that of the ancients amounts to five hundred. All theſe gems, the whole number of which amounts to three thouſand, are kept in the ſuperb cabinet already deſcribed; and which, together with its contents, is valued at ſix hundred thouſand ſcudi, about 127,000 l. ſterling.

With regard to the number of old coins, they reckon, at preſent, three hundred and twelve medallions, among which are forty five of ſilver. Thoſe who are deſirous of attaining a thorough knowlege of all the curioſities depoſited here muſt often repeat their viſits. There is no difficulty of gaining admittance into the large gallery of ſtatues, a ſmall gratuity to the porter being all that is required.

The *armoria ſecreta*, or private armoury, belonging to the great duke, into which one goes from the large gallery, muſt by no means be omitted. Here are depoſited the armours of the princes of the houſe of Medicis, who, for military exploits, did not, however, make a very extraordinary figure in hiſtory, if we except Lorenzo de Medicis, and prince Matthias, brother to the great duke Ferdinand II. who gained great experience during a thirty years war, and perpetuated his memory by a ſtandard taken from the duke of Weymar.

Beſide theſe, here are ſeveral pieces of Perſian and Turkiſh armour, together with bridles, a quiver, and a maſk that had belonged to a Turkiſh ſultana, found in a ſhip taken by the galleys of Florence. The maſk is intirely plain, but the quiver is adorned with ſmall chryſolites and turquoiſe ſtones. A ſuit of old Roman armour is alſo depoſited here; a ſword of Charlemagne; two piſtols, together with a ſword and ſtilletto in the ſame ſcabbard; a terzetto or piſtolet, with a gold barrel, being a preſent from the emperor Leopold

pold to Cosmo III. a long fusee, with a gold barrel, weighing nineteen pounds; a piece consisting of four pistols joined together, which may be concealed in one's hat, invented by Antonio de Medicis; several small models of all kinds of cannon; two Turkish horse-tails; a saddle that belonged to king John Sobieski; a bridle of prince Radzivil, set with turquoises; an iron casket, which the keeper of the armoury pretends was Hannibal's helmet, from its being found in the Thrasimene lake, and the work, with the characters on it, being Arabic; some shields said to have been painted by Raphael Urbino; another representing the storming of a city, by Julio Romano; and another, upon which a Medusa's head is painted, by Leonardo da Vinci; the dress of a West Indian king, composed of red feathers; a thong, cut out of a single buffalo's hide, two hundred and ten ells in length, with other things of the like nature. On the wall of one of the chambers hangs a grey horse's mane of an unusual size, presented by Charles, duke of Lorrain, to the great duke, Cosmo III. Some say it was twenty feet, and others, fourteen ells long: but I cannot help thinking that both exceed the truth; for I took the liberty of pulling out several hairs, but none exceeded an ell in length.

A few years ago lord G—— e drove a set of grey horses at London, the manes of which almost reached the ground. About this time the English government, apprehensive of a rebellion, thought it adviseable for the public safety to deprive all Roman catholics of their horses, as is usual on such occasions. Upon which lord G—— e abjured the popish religion, but could not escape the severe raillery of his friends, as this change seemed rather from the love he bore to his horses, than from any real conviction of error. The queen, some time after, rallying him upon that account, asked him, why he had not prevailed on his lady to follow his example? To whom lord G—— e made this blunt return: "As for "women, madam, it is no matter what religion they "are of."

The great duke usually resides in the Palezzo de Pitti, so called from the family of that name, who formerly owned it. Its front, from the rustic work, and rough unhewn stones of which it is composed, makes no very striking appearance; but toward the court and the gardens the architecture is pretty elegant. A great defect in the court is its extream smallness in proportion to the length and height of the edifice. On the right hand, as one enters this palace, lies a large magnet, which, according to Spon, lifts five thousand pounds; but, since that, its virtue has been something impaired by fire. Some of the Swiss guards here, upon seeing any travellers approach, run immediately to rub their halberts on the loadstone, and then hold these out with a bunch of keys hanging at them magnetically. Their view in this is to get a little money, but that both here and at the Palazzo Vecchio they should beg, and, without the least shame, keep importuning strangers for a few pence, seems not at all consistent with the dignity and magnificence of their master.

In a grotto belonging to the court-yard of the Palazzo Petti stands a porphyry statue of Moses, bigger than the life; and not a great way from it, in a corner, to the left hand, is a basso-relievo, representing a mule which had been serviceable in carrying, on a sledge, all the materials employed in building this edifice. Pliny, in his Natural History, lib. viii. c. 44. informs us, that the Athenians ordered a mule, which had been very useful to them in the building of the temple, should be maintained all the rest of its life at the public expence, and it is said to have lived 80 years.

From the chambers of the upper story and the Mansarde or garrets with flatted roofs, there is a charming prospect all over the city; the palace standing on a small eminence, which on the side next the gardens is so considerable, that parterres have been raised

raiſed in lines parallel to the ſecond and third ſtories. The great duke's library is but in an indifferent order, though it abounds with books; and its late librarian, the celebrated Antonio Magliabecchi, who died on the 4th of July 1714, did it a great deal of honour.

The jeſuits and he mutually hated each other; and, in particular, he was much diſguſted at the character they gave of him, *Eſt doctor inter bibliothecarios, ſed bibliothecarius inter doctores.* "He is learned among librarians, but a mere librarian among the learned." His own library was no better than a hog's-ſtye, the books lying moſtly on the ground, and in confuſed heaps; but by the help of an extraordinary memory, he could readily find out the volumes that treated on any ſubject ſtarted in converſation. The books he often read in were very much daubed with ſnuff, which he took to exceſs. Eggs being his principal food, ſuch books as ſerved him inſtead of a table were ſmeared all over with the yolks. By the length of his nails, which he never cut, he might have become a very good harper. He never changed his linen, ſo that he kept a ſhirt on as long as it would hang together; and from his living in this beaſtly manner, and ſeldom waſhing himſelf, it is not at all ſurpriſing, that ſuch an offenſive ſtench was emitted from him as muſt diſguſt moſt people. Were we to make out a catalogue of learned men who lived in a ſordid ſlovenly manner, Magliabecchi would undoubtedly be intitled to the firſt place; but in his train would appear many illuſtrious names belonging to the republic of letters. The muſes of Parnaſſus cannot be ladies of a very delicate taſte to be ſo familiar with ſuch forbidding creatures!

From the Palazzo de Pitti, the great duke can come through a covered paſſage to the gallery of curioſities and the Palazzo Vecchio; in the laſt of which, through little private windows, he can hear and ſee what paſſes in the ſeveral courts of juſtice, without being obſerved by any one. The aforeſaid paſſage is ſix hundred paces long, ſix in breadth, and eight in height. On its walls are large pictures, repreſenting the tranſactions of the emperor Charles V. Philip II. king of Spain, Henry IV. king of France, and the great duke Ferdinand II. It is pity this gallery is not in a ſtraight line, for by forming ſeveral turnings and angles its beauty is greatly impaired.

On one ſide of the garden is the duke's menagerie, where are ſome oſtriches, pelicans, Chineſe geeſe, pheaſants, parrots, Egyptian hens, and Corſican deer, very ſmall-ſized; here alſo is kept a kind of outlandiſh crane, called Kurki, which hops or dances, as it were, to a certain tune. The lions, tygers, panthers, buffalos, lynxes, bears, and the like wild beaſts, are kept in another part of the city, not far from St. Mark's-ſquare, in a particular building, called Seraglio de Lioni. Each beaſt has before its den a long open piece of ground to walk and air itſelf in. Some years ago a tygreſs whelped here, but ſhe eat up her young as ſoon as ſhe had brought them forth. The incloſure for hunting theſe wild beaſts is extremely well contrived; and, after this ſport is over, in order to drive the beaſts to their dens, they uſe a particular method, namely, a hollow machine repreſenting a dragon, containing ſeveral perſons with lighted torches, the fire of which blazing through its open jaws and eyes, ſtrikes ſuch a terror into the wild beaſts, that they quiver every limb, and are glad to run to any place of ſhelter.

Near the Seraglio de Lioni is the duke's phyſic garden, or Giardino de Semplici, on which Coſmo I. expended large ſums: and from this garden's having the moſt curious and rare plants growing in it, the Academicia di Botanica, inſtituted at Florence, hold their uſual meetings here. Adjoining to this garden are the ſtables for the manege or riding-ſchool of the ducal family; the career is ſeventy-three common paces in length, and here is ſhewn a horſe who

goes

goes it over in five leaps. The riding with lances is practised by learners against a moveable wooden statue, which, if the lance properly hit the shield in the center, stands still; but, if the thrust be wrong made, the image whirls round, and with its arm gives the rider a sound box on the ear.

Without the city the great duke has two fine seats, called Poggio, or Villa Imperiale, and Pratolino: the former stands only an Italian mile from the city; and on this side the Porta Romana is a charming avenue leading to it. Before the villa is a spacious amphitheatre with cypress-hedges and a stone balustrade: at its entrance, on one side, you see a large marble statue of Atlas with the globe on his shoulder, and, on the other, Jupiter, of the like materials and size, with a thunderbolt in his hand. The outside of the building has no striking appearance, but, within, the apartments are commodious.

The number of churches in Florence is reckoned to be above a hundred and fifty, beside seventy-eight convents and twenty-two hospitals. In such a multitude of religious buildings, especially in a country like this, many of them must, on account of the various curiosities they contain, deserve the notice of a curious traveller.

Among the relics in the cathedral is shewn one of the nails with which Christ was fastened to the cross; a piece of the cross itself; a thorn from our Saviour's crown; and a thumb of John the Baptist, with some of his ashes; a piece of St. Andrew's arm, of Aaron's rod, and Moses's staff; notwithstanding the canons of the church of St. John Lateran at Rome maintain that they have the last intire.

To give a particular account of every chapel, though none of them are destitute of fine paintings and sculpture, would be endless. The marquis de Feroni's chapel is particularly remarkable for its statues; and the Pazzi chapel, at present called Bandinelli's, for marble sculptures of that artist; particularly a group representing the dead body of Chriſt, ſupported by God the Father.

In St. Laurence church, on the left wall, near the main entrance, is a marble monument, decorated with beautiful bronze foliage, by Andrea Verrochio, for Peter and John de Medicis, ſons to the great duke Coſmo. The former died in the Spaniſh ſervice, but the latter was honoured with a cardinal's hat, though he died in the nineteenth year of his age. The circumſtances of his death gave the greateſt affliction to his whole family. He was, it ſeems, one day hunting with his brother Garſias, and happened to have ſome difference with him; upon which, Garſias, being of a malicious diſpoſition, watched an opportunity of meeting his eldeſt brother, and ſtabbed him with a dagger. Garſias, after committing the fact, returned to his companions without ſhewing the leaſt diſcompoſure in his countenance or behaviour. But, prince John's horſe returning without his rider, the company was alarmed, and by following the track found the dead body lying on the ground. When this unfortunate news firſt reached the ears of Coſmo, he ordered that the affair ſhould be kept ſecret, and reported that his ſon died ſuddenly of an apoplexy, as he was hunting. In the mean time he cauſed the body to be carried into an apartment of the palace, and immediately ſent for Garſias, from whoſe malignant and depraved temper he ſuſpected the true cauſe of this unhappy affair. Garſias, at firſt, boldly denied the charge, and even with ſome mixture of reſentment; but, on his being ſhewn the body of his murdered brother, which immediately began to bleed afreſh, he confeſſed the fact, at the ſame time throwing himſelf at his father's feet. Coſmo, after admoniſhing his ſon to call upon the Almighty for mercy, added, "You ought to think it the greateſt happi-"neſs to loſe that life, of which you are now unwor-"thy, by the hand of him from whom you at firſt re-"ceived it." After uttering theſe words, he took, from Garſias's

Garſias's ſide, the dagger which had been the fatal inſtrument of his unnatural revenge, and plunged it into the heart of his ſon, who immediately ſunk down on the dead body of his brother, and expired. This event happened in the year 1562, Garſias being only fifteen years of age. Very few perſons were privy to the whole affair, it being given out that the two brothers died of an infectious diſtemper which then raged in Florence. And, the better to conceal this melancholy tranſaction, they were both honoured with a pompous funeral, and Garſias had a public oration ſpoken in honour of him; but whether his remains are interred in the ſame grave with thoſe of his brother, I never could learn with certainty. The tragical end of theſe princes ſo affected the ducheſs Eleanora, their mother, a lady of excellent ſenſe, that in a few days after ſhe expired. Coſmo had at that time three other ſons living.

Behind the high altar and choir of St. Lorenzo's church, is the entrance into a new chapel, deſigned as a burying-place for the great dukes of Tuſcany, the foundation of which was laid in the year 1604. At firſt, three hundred perſons were conſtantly employed, but afterward the number was reduced to ſixty; notwithſtanding which, eighteen thouſand ſcudi of 4550l. ſterling are annually expended in this work. It is not yet more than half finiſhed; and we have ſeen the whole ducal family extinct, long before the pompous place for the reception of their remains is compleated. This, however, is certain, that, when it is finiſhed, not a chapel in the whole world can be compared with it for elegance It is of an octangular form.

The library of St. Marks is a grand hall, divided by two rows of pillars into three galleries. From this library is a moſt delightful proſpect toward the mountain, on which ſtood the ancient city of Fieſole, and where the ruins of it are ſtill viſible.

Florence is commonly ſtiled La Bella, or the fair, poſſibly from the cleanlineſs of its ſtreets, and the

goodneſs

goodneſs of the pavements, conſiſting moſtly of broad free-ſtone, called Pietre Forti. But the palaces are neither equal in number or grandeur to thoſe of Turin, Genoa, or Rome. The ſtreets are alſo, in general, crooked and narrow; the latter is particularly obſervable in the Corſo, ſaid to be two Italian miles in length; and even ſome are ſo remarkably narrow, that no carriage can paſs through them.

A traveller, who intends to viſit the other parts of Italy, need not ſpend his time here in viewing private palaces. The elegant appearance of this city is greatly leſſened by the paper-windows, common in every part of it; but, with regard to ſtatues, paintings, and monuments, few can be compared to it. Among them the moſt remarkable is the large and beautiful column of the Doric order, erected in the ſquare, before the church of St. Trinita; it is of a greyiſh colour, and formed out of a ſingle piece of granate: on the top of it is a porphyry ſtatue of Juſtice, with her ſcales, and a regal mantle of bronze, done by Romolo del Dadda. Coſmo I. erected it in the year 1564; becauſe, as ſome pretend, he here received advice of the ſurrender of the city of Sienna. The granate column is ſaid to have been diſcovered at Rome in the baths of Antonius, and preſented by pope Pius IV. to Coſmo. No fault can be found with the workmanſhip of the ſtatue, but many except to her ſituation, as the proper place of Juſtice is tribunals and courts of judicature: others are not pleaſed with her lofty and diſtant ſituation, being, as it were, inacceſſible to poor mortals. Others, again, ſatyrically remark that the ſtatue reaches out its hand, as deſirous of receiving ſomething, in order to make the ſcale incline to his ſide who fees the largeſt. And, laſtly, ſome think it ſtrange that Juſtice ſhould turn her back upon the palace Degli Uffizii, where the courts of judicature are held.

The Mercato Nuovo, or New Market-place, is properly the exchange of Florence; for here the principal

cipal merchants, many of whom are of noble families, meet, toward noon, to transact business; trade being here, as well as at Genoa, considered as not the least derogatory from nobility: and hence several families here live in the greatest affluence and reputation; whereas, in other places, particularly Germany, many families of rank, for a whole century together, remain in indigence and obscurity, meerly on account of their poverty; and are excluded, not only from the higher ecclesiastical benefices and canonries (of which there are very few among the Protestants) but likewise from the principal employments of the state. These misfortunes chiefly flow from their bigotry to their rank and nobility, and being more solicitous in their marriages about a long race of ancestors, and the antiquity of a family. than a handsome fortune. The Venetian nobility also trade in secret; whereas those of Florence do it openly, and even by retail; not thinking they in the least injure their titles by standing in their shops, or measuring out a yard of any sort of stuff to a customer. Hence the Florentines are admired for their œconomy; while, on the other hand, the Milanese are branded with the character of the most profuse and lavish of mortals, minding nothing but gaiety in their dress, magnificence in their entertainments, and splendid furniture. Even the ducal family of Florence owe to commerce that grandeur, which they have now supported above two centuries. Cosmo de Medicis, who died in 1465, had upward of twenty warehouses in the chief trading cities of the known world, and was so very fortunate, that, during the course of fifty-four years, he never suffered any considerable loss by the bankruptcy of other merchants.

[Dr. Smollet gives us the following remarks on the manners and dispositions of the Florentines.

'There is a considerable number of fashionable people at Florence, and many of them in good circumstances. They affect a gaiety in their dress,

equipage

equipage, and converſation; but ſtand very much on their punctilio with ſtrangers: and will not, without great reluctance, admit into their aſſemblies any lady of another country, whoſe nobleſſe is not aſcertained by a title. This reſerve is in ſome meaſure excuſable among a people, who are extremely ignorant of foreign cuſtoms, and who know that in their own country, every perſon, even the moſt inſignificant, who has any pretenſions to family, either inherits, or aſſumes, the title of *principe*, *conte*, or *marcheſe*.

With all their pride, however, the nobles of Florence are humble enough to enter into partnerſhip with ſhopkeepers, and even to ſell wine by retail. It is an undoubted fact, that in every palace or great houſe in this city, there is a little window fronting the ſtreet, provided with a iron knocker, and over it hangs an empty flaſk, by way of ſign-poſt. Thither you ſend your ſervant to buy a bottle of wine. He knocks at the little wicket, which is opened immediately by a domeſtic, who ſupplies him with what he wants, and receives the money like the waiter of any other cabaret. It is pretty extraordinary that it ſhould not be deemed a diſparagement in a nobleman to ſell half a pound of figs, a piece of ribbon or tape, or to take money for a flaſk of ſour wine; and yet be counted infamous to match his daughter in the family of a perſon who has diſtinguiſhed himſelf in any one of the learned profeſſions.

Though Florence be tolerably populous, there ſeems to be very little trade of any kind in it; but the inhabitants flatter themſelves with the proſpect of reaping great advantage from the reſidence of one of the arch-dukes, for whoſe reception they are now repairing the palace of Pitti. I know not what the revenues of Tuſcany may amount to ſince the ſucceſſion of the princes of Lorrain; but, under the laſt dukes of the Medici family, they were ſaid to produce two millions of crowns, equal to five hundred

thou-

thousand pounds sterling. These arose from a very heavy tax upon land and houses, the portions of maidens, and suits at law, beside the duties upon traffic, a severe gabelle upon the necessaries of life, and a toll upon every eatable entered into this capital. If we may believe Leti, the grand duke was then able to raise and maintain an army of forty thousand infantry, and three thousand horse; with twelve gallies, two galeasses, and twenty ships of war. I question if Tuscany can maintain, at present, above one half of such an armament. He that now commands the emperor's navy, consisting of a few frigates, is an Englishman, called Acton, who was heretofore captain of a ship in our East India company's service. He has lately embraced the catholic religion, and been created admiral of Tuscany.

There is a tolerable opera in Florence for the entertainment of the best company, though they do not seem very attentive to the music. Italy is certainly the native country of this art; and yet, I do not find the people in general, either more musically inclined, or better provided with ears than their neighbours. Here is also a wretched troop of comedians for the burgeois, and lower class of people: but what seems most to suit the taste of all ranks, is the exhibition of church pageantry. I had occasion to see a procession, where all the noblesse of the city attended in their coaches, which filled the whole length of the great street, called the Corso. It was the anniversary of a charitable institution in favour of poor maidens, a certain number of whom are portioned every year. About two hundred of these virgins walked in procession, two and two together, cloathed in violet-coloured wide gowns, with white veils on their heads, and made a very classical appearance. They were preceded and followed by an irregular mob of penitents, in sackcloth, with lighted tapers, and monks carrying crucifixes, bawling and bellowing the litanies: but the great object was a figure of

the

the Virgin Mary, as big as the life, ſtanding within a gilt frame, dreſſed in a gold ſtuff, with a large hoop, a great quantity of falſe jewels, her face painted and patched, and her hair frizzled and curled in the very extremity of the faſhion. Very little regard had been paid to the image of our Saviour on the croſs; but when his lady-mother appeared on the ſhoulders of three or four luſty friars, the whole populace fell upon their knees in the dirt. This extraordinary veneration paid to the Virgin, muſt have been derived originally from the French, who pique themſelves on their gallantry to the fair ſex.

Amidſt all the ſcenery of the Roman Catholic religion, I have never yet ſeen any of the ſpectators affected at heart, or diſcover the leaſt ſigns of fanaticiſm. The very diſciplinants, who ſcourge themſelves in the holy-week, are generally peaſants, or parties hired for the purpoſe. Thoſe of the confrairies, who have an ambition to diſtinguiſh themſelves on ſuch occaſions, take care to ſecure their backs from the ſmart, by means of ſecret armour, either women's boddice, or quilted jackets. The confrairies are fraternities of devotees, who inliſt themſelves under the banners of particular ſaints. On days of proceſſion they appear in a body dreſſed as penitents, and maſked, and diſtinguiſhed by croſſes on their habits. There is ſcarce an individual, whether noble or plebeian, who does not belong to one of theſe aſſociations, which may be compared to the Free-maſons, Gregoreans, and Antigallicans of England.

Juſt without one of the gates of Florence, there is a triumphal arch erected on occaſion of the late emperor's making his public entry, when he ſucceeded to the dukedom of Tuſcany; and here in the ſummer evenings, the quality reſort to take the air in their coaches. Every carriage ſtops, and forms a little ſeparate converſazione. The ladies ſit within, and the ciciſbei ſtand on the foot-boards, on each ſide of the coach, entertaining them with their diſcourſe."——

Mr. Sharpe likewiſe furniſhes us with many judicious miſcellaneous obſervations on Florence and its inhabitants, which will greatly illuſtrate the preceding deſcriptions.

——' In our way to Florence, ſays Mr. Sharpe, we paſſed through Sienna, the town which gave name to the celebrated Seneſino; as I had always heard he finiſhed his days very comfortably in his native place, and had built a beautiful palace with the thouſands he had acquired in England, one of my firſt enquiries was after his hiſtory and his houſe, which we viſited with a deſign to take only a view of its outſide; but the eagerneſs with which I ſurveyed it, and the appearance of foreigners, ſoon brought the lady of the houſe to the window; and her politeneſs, together with a good-natured officious forwardneſs in the ſervant who attended me, produced an invitation in leſs than half a minute. She proved to be the wife of Seneſino's eldeſt nephew, and principal heir; a very fine, beautiful, and affable woman; and was more rejoiced to ſee us than you can readily imagine, from the grateful ſenſe ſhe entertained of the favours her uncle had received at the hands of the Engliſh nation. The houſe is really handſome, but not ſo gaudy and expenſive as to reflect on the modeſty of the owner: ſome of the rooms are furniſhed entirely with Engliſh furniture, an indication he had ſome prejudices in favour of England, as the freight and carriage muſt have been expenſive. It ſtands in a kind of forebury, the moſt pleaſant ſpot of ground in the city, and very gay, becauſe it is the promenade. Seneſino gave his eldeſt nephew about ten thouſand pounds, and to three or four other nephews, and their ſons, two thouſand five hundred pounds each, a conſiderable fortune at Sienna, but not an enormous one.

It

It is impossible for any man, a little aquainted in history, not to bestow a sigh on this once celebrated city and republic, which, when it flourished, small as it was, by the renown of its arms and its arts, made no despicable figure in Europe; and, in those days, three or four hundred years since, contained within its walls ninety or one hundred thousand inhabitants, where now, there are, at most, twelve or fourteen thousand. A plague greatly depopulated it; but the loss of its liberty proved the incurable wound, which has continued to drain and waste its strength.——The cathedral is a very curious Gothic structure; the Siennese call it a fine one, and believe, if it were at Rome, it would stand in honour next to St. Peter's; but I question whether it be not more whimsical than fine: to the best of my memory, the minster at York, though consisting of stone and white walls only, is a more beautiful design; but this building, both on the inside and out, is entirely marble; and, what renders it so remarkable, is, that some blocks are white, and others black; there is a larger portion of the building white, but the black is in a very considerable quantity: this variegation, upon the first sight, strikes; but I question whether, upon the whole, it will stand the test of criticism.

The river Arno runs through Florence, dividing it as the Thames does London from Southwark. This stream, which, like most others in Italy, is turbid, has found, however, many panegyrical writers, though it has two very bad properties for a river; that is, a propensity to overflow its banks after heavy showers, and to be almost dry at other times. I saw an inscription on the walls of a house, about ten feet from the ground, signifying, that, in the year 1557, the river overflowed the city to the height of that inscription; there was likewise another in 1761, to the height of two feet in the streets. These inundations

undations happen very often, and, though not to the degree I have deſcribed, yet ſufficiently to cauſe much deſolation. A ſhort hiſtory of the rivers, or rather torrents of Italy, their frequent emptineſs, and their frequent overflowings, would give a man the higheſt reliſh for Sir John Denham's few panegyrical lines on our Thames.

I ſaunter now and then, in the ſuburbs, amongſt the poor, and not without finding matter of contemplation. I am very well informed, that a woman here, though ſhe have no children and family to take care of, and employ her time with the utmoſt diligence, cannot earn above two-pence halfpenny a day by ſpinning, the uſual occupation of the poor: yet, compare either their habitations, or their children, with thoſe of the inhabitants of the ſkirts of London, and you will bluſh for the miſery and diſſoluteneſs of our country-folks. It would be wonderful, however, that the poor could ſubſiſt on ſuch ſmall wages, if we did not know, that mere bread alone, in ſufficiency, is their principal object of expence. They talk much here of their preſent wretchedneſs, the laſt year having neither produced corn or wine equal to their home conſumption; and, what is worſe, their manufactures have decayed ſo much, that the induſtrious cannot always find work: they ſay, that, a few years ſince, they exported vaſt quantities of wrought ſilks to England; now they ſend few or none: nay, that the Engliſh have gained ſo much upon them, in the art of weaving, that they find a profit in importing Engliſh ſilk manufactures, particularly ſilk ſtockings, by reaſon of their durableneſs. A man ſhould come abroad, either to raiſe his opinion of his country, or his countrymen. I was much pleaſed, the other day, to hear an Engliſhman, who has lived abroad above thirty years, burſt into an unfeigned exclamation, upon being ſhewn one of the newly invented cork-ſcrews, " Well,

 ſaid

ſaid he, theſe Engliſhmen are the moſt ingenious creatures in the world!"

I have almoſt inſenſibly quitted my ſubject in relation to the poor; but I intended to make a reflection, that, when the populace do not give themſelves up to ſpirituous liquors, they make ſome ſhift to ſcramble through life tolerably well, as may be ſeen at Florence. I am aware that the richeſt cities will always ſwarm, for that very reaſon, with the indigent poor, ſo long as men are men; for, ſince many will be idle, they will conſequently be, in proportion, more wretched, as the means of ſubſiſtence is expenſive; and neceſſaries will grow dearer as riches multiply: nevertheleſs, as brown bread is ſtill cheaper in England than elſewhere, I cannot but impute it to pride and idleneſs, that the greater part of our poor, in and about London, are ever in want. The lower people in Italy ſpend more than you would believe in wine; but neither their abilities, nor the example of their betters, lead them into drunkenneſs: they have a great notion it is wholeſome, and they give it to their children at the breaſt.

I am much pleaſed with the contrivance uſed in the great hoſpital here, to avoid bugs: It is no other than a plain bedſtead of iron, made ſo ſimple, that there is not a crevice where a bug can conceal itſelf. Attempts of this kind have been made in England, but they have proved ineffectual; becauſe they have faſtened ticking to the frame, with oilet-holes, and cording, which afforded ſome harbour to theſe animals. In this hoſpital they only lay acroſs the frame about four or five boards, a little longer than the width of the frame, and about a foot broad, upon which they lay the bedding; theſe are moveable, and if neceſſary, may be bruſhed when the bed is made, as eaſily, and in as ſhort a time as a man bruſhes his hat. In the hoſpitals at London, bugs are frequently a greater evil to the patient, than the malady

malady for which he seeks an hospital; and, could I have interest enough with the governors, to bring about an imitation of this frame, I should be exceedingly rejoiced in the comfort it will afford to so many thousands of miserable wretches, that are tormented by this nauseous vermin.

There is but one theatre open at Florence, just at this juncture, and there is seldom more than one at a time, except in the season of the Carnival; when the rage of frequenting spectacles is such in Italy, that, in this small city, the people fill six or seven houses every night; but, in short, as if it were an act of devotion, every body makes a point of going; whereas, in France, the madness of a Carnival is, in a manner, unknown. There are, however, at Florence, but three considerable theatres, one very large, and two of about the dimension of that in Drury-lane. The large one is dedicated to the serious opera, the other two to comedy and burlettas. Upon a calculation, I find, that though the extent of the house now open, be equal to that of Drury-lane, it does not contain near the number of people, from the nature of its form, there being no galleries, but consisting meerly of boxes and pit. The comedy they exhibit here is very low indeed, by no means exceeding what is called in England a droll, and what would be very tiresome to an Englishman, but for the pleasure there is in novelty. To give you some idea of the small progress of the drama through all Italy, I need only repeat, that I have never yet seen there one play, consisting of five acts; and that the joy it affords arises from mistaking one word for another, blunders, indelicate jokes, &c. At Paris, Harlequin is allowed some freedoms, which, I believe, would hardly be suffered in a London theatre, (however a Frenchman may value himself on the elegance of their taste) but then the Parisians have the resource of another theatre, where both tragedy and comedy may be said to flourish almost to perfection; whereas

Harlequin, and the other Italian characters of Punch, Don Fastidio, Pantaloon, &c. are, in a manner, the only characters you see on the stages of this country. The Harlequin of this theatre is very popular, and, what you will be surprized at, very rich, though the salary paid both to him and his wife be but seventy-five pounds a year sterling; but, to solve the riddle, you must know that the Harlequin is a tradesman, and perhaps may have as much merit in that department, as in his black face and party-coloured suit; however it be, he is a great favourite, and his shop is much frequented: I have been his customer for no other reason, in preference, but the singularity of the tradesman, not that of the goods. Mr. Addison and Sir William Temple, I believe, have both spoken, with great applause, of the Dutch theatres, because the company of comedians was said to be composed of artificers, who, after their day's labour, recreated themselves, and the public, with their dramatic exhibitions, not making the profession as in other kingdoms, an idle calling: but, with submission to such great men, I should imagine, were the practice general, it would spoil both the tradesman and the actor; and these sober comedians would frequently become bankrupts. We have much more pleasure at their burletta operas than at their comedies, though they have not, in their company, any singer or actor of very distinguishable talents; but, upon the whole, it does very well, and passes off the evening pleasantly. The church keeps a strict hand over the subjects of Tuscany, as well as the other states of Italy. On the page of the opera-book, where, in England, the argument is usually printed off, you have here, in capital letters a *Protesta*. This protest is a declaration, that, though the writer of the drama has made use of the words God, gods, deities, &c. he means no offence to the church; but that, in conformity to the mythology of the ancients, he he has been obliged to introduce those fables, and those phrases.

I never trouble you with descriptions of churches and palaces, but, rather, with the customs and manners of the people I visit; yet I cannot forbear mentioning the ducal palace at Florence, which has, by far, the most noble range of rooms I ever beheld: I should not, however, have thought this circumstance worth a paragraph in my letter, but for this particular, that it was built by one Pitti a private man, before the establishment of the Medici family, into whose hands it immediately fell: yet, in spite of their great reputation and magnificence, through a long course of years, it still retains the name of its first owner, and is called the Pitti palace to this hour. I own to you, I look with admiration on this monument of Tuscan taste and grandeur, and cannot but reflect, with astonishment, at the low ebb of commerce, and the fine arts, in other states of Europe, when they flourished with so much vigour in this duchy. The gardens are esteemed fine by the Italians, but, in the eyes of an Englishman, they are execrable; undoubtedly our taste of gardening is infinitely more elegant than that of the Italians; beside, as they cannot have neither green grass, or fine gravel, they want some of the proper materials to render a garden perfectly beautiful: but, what is unpardonable and absurd, amongst a thousand other defects in their laying out a garden, is their contrivance to calculate them for winter, when no body walks, and not for summer, when gardens are agreeable. This absurdity is, the prodigious number of large trees, all of the ever-green kind, with which their gardens abound; it is true, they afford a shade, but of so dismal a hue as is hardly to be imagined, and, at the times they want shade, trees of a beautiful verdure would be stocked with leaves. If they adapt their gardens to the winter, they almost as ridiculously build their houses for the summer only, notwithſtanding the rigour of the winter in this mountainous country. It is hardly thirty years ago, that, except kitchen-chimnies, there were ſcarcely any, not only in Naples, but even in the northern latitude of Venice. Antiquity renders every cuſtom venerable, and almoſt ſacred; but you would wonder to ſee how prejudiced the Italians are againſt the introduction of chimnies; they have an idea they muſt be unwholſome, ſo little do they underſtand the nature of a ventilator, and that a thorough draught muſt purify the air we breathe. It happened that my chimney at Naples took fire, being ill built, and having never been ſwept ſince it was erected (about three or four years ſince) this accident ſo alarmed the landlord, that he demurred whether he ſhould not turn a gentleman, who lodged over my head, out of his apartments, becauſe he refuſed to pull down his chimney on this occaſion. The gentleman is, certainly, one of the beſt tenants in Naples, and the landlord's intereſt prevailed over his frights and prejudices at laſt; but he lives in a ſtate of unhappineſs, that his houſe ſhould be proſtituted to the vile uſe of chimnies.———

The environs of Florence are delightful; the hills round the town, at the diſtance of two or three miles, form an amphitheatre, where a thouſand country houſes, built of white ſtone, beautify the proſpect. The fields, as indeed the whole face of Tuſcany, are, in a manner, covered with olive-trees; but the olive-tree does not anſwer the character I had conceived of it: the Royal Pſalmiſt, and ſome of the ſacred writers, ſpeak with rapture of the green olive-tree, ſo that I expected a beautiful green; and I confeſs to you, I was wretchedly diſappointed, to find its hue reſemble that of our hedges, when they are covered with duſt. The olive-tree may, poſſibly delight in the barren diſtrict of Judæa; but, undoubtedly, will diſguſt a man accuſtomed to Engliſh verdure.

Madam

Madam Minorbetti, a woman of diftinction, has, through the means of ———, fhewn great civilities to my daughters; I mention her name for having given occafion to one of the moft ridiculous events that has fallen within my knowlege, and which will put to fhame fome of the Greek etymologies we are entertained with in the pofthumous works of dean Swift. You may remember, he afferts, for the honour of Great Britain, that many of thofe names which we fuppofe to be originally Greek, are really derived from the Britifh language, and, by corruption, have attained the Greek idiom. For example; he fays, " that *Andromache* is a corruption of the Scotch name Andrew Mackey; *Archimedes*, of Hark ye Maids, &c &c." It feems, that a relation of madam Minorbetti, in the agonies of death, was defirous to have a famous relic in this city, no lefs than an arm of our archbifhop Becket, brought to his bedfide; from a perfuafion he fhould be reftored to health, by its miraculous influence. The monks, in whofe poffeffion the arm is, rejected the petition, and pleaded the impoffibility of carrying it beyond the precincts of the convent; the relations, on the other hand, urged, that they were defcended from the family of the Beckets, and therefore, that fuch a ufage might be difpenfed with: the argument was admitted to be good, and the monks demanded only a proof of the confanguinity, which was demonftrated in the following manner:——" A bifhop, faid they, in England, is always called *milor*, (my lord) which eafily, in Italian, is corrupted into *minor*; then Becket as eafily degenerates into *Betti*; fo that *Milorbecket* naturally becomes *Minor-betti*." This notable argument was deemed fo valid, that the relic was brought out of the convent to the fick man.——Do not doubt the truth of the fact, becaufe of its ludicroufnefs; you may depend on every circumftance of the ftory.

 At

At all the houses of the nobles in Florence, you see an empty flask hanging out, to denote they sell wine by retail; this custom shocks an Englishman, as a practice very derogatory from their dignity; and he cannot but speak of it with surprize. A Florentine coolly and sensibly answers, " Sir, your duke of ——, by the interposition of a steward, sells a tree for ten shillings; our noble, by his porter at the door, sells ten shillings worth of wine; but our noble appears no more in the sale of the wine, than your duke of ——, in the sale of his tree; different countries have their different modes."—— The truth is, that, through all Italy, great part of the rent for estates is paid in kind, which, joined with a certain exemption from the imposts on wine, granted to the nobles in Florence, has led them, I believe, into this seeming littleness.

I was, the other night, at a most elegant concert, given by the Lucchese envoy, at his own palace. The fashion, upon this occasion, is to calculate the number of people the rooms will hold, and to invite accordingly; but ladies only are invited. It is computed, that cards sent to twenty-five or twenty-six ladies, will bring near fourscore gentlemen; and the number at this assembly answered to that calculation. The great disproportion betwixt the number of ladies at the Italian converzationi, and the London routs, is very striking to an Englishman; but the phænomenon admits of an easy solution. No single ladies, as I have told you before, visit in Italy; all who are seen in the world are married women. If a gentleman here has three sons and three daughters, two of the daughters are most probably in a convent, whilst all the three sons, at least two of them, have nothing else to do than to frequent the spectacles and converzationi.

The palace of the Lucchese envoy is very large; so are the palaces of all the nobles in Florence; indeed,

deed, they are of ſuch an extent, that uſually one floor only is occupied at the ſame time. During the winter, they inhabit the upper apartments; and, during the ſummer, they reſide all together on the ground floor; a moſt agreeable piece of luxury in the northern climate of Italy, which is ſo extremely hot, and ſo extremely cold in the two ſeaſons. Houſe-rent at Florence is ſtill cheaper than at Venice.

In Florence, the generality of ladies have each of them three ciceſbeos; the firſt is the ciceſbeo of dignity; the ſecond is the ciceſbeo who picks up the glove, gives the fan, and pulls off, or puts on the cloak, &c. the third ciceſbeo is, by the wags, deemed the ſubſtantial ciceſbeo, or lover.——God knows how theſe matters go; for, in public, the ladies behave with ſo much modeſty and decorum, that I ſhould be tempted to treat ſome of theſe reports as mere detraction, were not the truth of them ſo notorious: in fact, the univerſality of the vice has, in a manner, diveſted it of the appearance of vice: with us, a woman who is publicly criminal, uſually becomes profligate and abandoned; here, almoſt every woman, of however virtuous a diſpoſition, falls into the general cuſtom, and is equally criminal with the woman of looſe principles; ſo that the diſtinction of good and bad, I mean chaſte and diſſolute, is hardly known in Italy. In a word, it is the mode, the etiquette, the bon ton of the fine people; and now wives and ciceſbeos hardly give more ſcandal than wives and huſbands; excite as little animadverſions when together; and, indeed, excluſive of gallantry, lead as innocent and ſober lives.'——]

Florence is ſaid to be decorated with ſeventeen ſquares, or market-places; ſeven fountains, ſix columns, two pyramids, and about a hundred and ſixty public ſtatues. Coſmo I. aſſigned the Jews a particular quarter, or Ghetto; a part of the city formerly noted for infamous houſes and places of proſtitution. We are informed by an inſcription over the

the entrance into this ſtreet, that it was thought more adviſeable to let the Jews remain in a quarter by themſelves, but in the neighbourhood of the Chriſtians, that they might, by the good example of the latter, be induced to ſubmit to the eaſy yoke of Chriſtianity, than expel them intirely.

Florence is ſaid to contain about nine thouſand houſes and ſeventy thouſand ſouls. Its greateſt trade is in woollen and ſilk manufactures. It has been obſerved, that few people in Florence are remarkable for the quickneſs of their ſight; and hence the *Florentini ciechi*, or blind Florentines, has paſſed into a proverbial jeſt. This misfortune ſome attribute to the damp and foggy air of the city; but if this be admitted, it will follow, that moſt of the inhabitants of Mantua, Venice, Leyden, Amſterdam, and other places, would have little or no uſe of their eyes. Beſide, the ſea-coaſts only are ſubject to ſuch moiſt exhalations; whereas Florence is ſituated on a riſing ground, and in a dry part of the country. And it ſhould be remembered, that to the purity, fineneſs, and ſalubrity of the air, the Florentines themſelves attribute the quickneſs and ſagacity of their countrymen, who have made ſo many great improvements in all the branches of ſcience. A famous ſociety of learned men, for the improvement of the Tuſcan language, who ſtile themſelves *Academia della Cruſca*, has been ſome years eſtabliſhed here. Probably this uncommon name, which ſignifies the Bran Academy, was choſen from their propoſing to reject, as Bran, all Italian words that are not elegant Tuſcan. But, notwithſtanding all their care, the Florentines have ſomething of a guttural pronunciation, and conſequently write Italian better than they ſpeak it. They are univerſally admired for their quickneſs in repartees, and their graceful manner in telling a ſtory. But they are ſo infatuated with theſe petty accompliſhments, that they are eternally talking, and never loſe an opportunity of telling a tale. Every lo-

ver

ver of virtue would be pleafed, if this were the only failing that could be laid to their charge: but this is fo far from being the cafe, that they have been branded to a proverb, even by the reft of the Italians, for that abominable vice which brought down the divine vengeance upon Sodom and Gommorah. Should this be really the cafe, it would not be at all furprifing, that a nation fo lafcivious as the Florentines are fhould have weak eyes; it being inconteftable, that immoderate venery is highly detrimental to the fight.

The country, in the neighbourhood of Florence, is indeed extremely delightful, from the gradual afcent of little hills beautifully cultivated. Toward Pifa it forms itfelf into a fpacious plain. Near the city of Florence is found a fpecies of white marble, which fplits almoft like flate, and after polifhing, the variegations of its yellow and brown veins reprefent, in an elegant manner, trees, landfcapes, and ruins of old walls and caftles. The principal parts of thefe paintings owe their origin to a corrofive fluid, which, infinuating itfelf into the minute pores of the ftone, leaves, in time, the traces of fuch figures, which, by a fmall affiftance from imagination, form a refemblance to the works of nature or art. The figures on this marble are not meerly traced on the furface of the ftone, but penetrated the fourth or fixth part of an inch into its fubftance, fo that they are not eafily obliterated by fire, like the Dendrites of Pappenheim, and other places.

A paved road, called Via Caffia, made by the ancient Romans, extended from Florence to Sienna, and from thence to Rome. There are ftill fome confiderable remains of this way, though it is not fo well kept in repair as the Via Appia, which leads from Rome to Naples. Sienna is four poft ftages or thirty-two Italian miles diftant from Florence. The many hills in the road, which is paved all the way, render travelling uneafy; nor is the country fo pleafant as that

that between Pisa and Florence. The prospects, however, are often beautiful, from the many vineyards and olive plantations.

The city of Sienna stands upon three eminences, which consequently make the streets very uneven; but, at the same time, this situation renders the prospects more agreeable, and increases the salubrity of the air. The inhabitants are polite and of a lively disposition, the women beautiful, and under less restraint than in other parts of Italy; for which reason, it is imagined, that the Italian language is spoken at Sienna in its greatest perfection and purity. Charles V. founded an academy here, and granted many privileges to the German students. This academy is at present in a declining state, and the number of German scholars does not exceed ten or twelve. The city itself is far from being populous, seventeen thousand inhabitants being the most that it contains. With regard to the buildings, the Piccolomini palace, and that belonging to the marquis di Londadari, seem to be the best; all the rest are but meanly built; though the city, on account of the great numbers of towers erected on private houses, and which had their rise from the intestine feuds between the parties of the Guelphs and Gibellines, makes an elegant appearance at a distance.

The Siennese still flatter themselves with enjoying a kind of liberty in the choice of their senate, composed of nine persons called Eccelsi, the president of which is stiled Capitaneo del Popolo. But this is only a delusive appearance, the senate itself being under such restrictions to the great duke of Florence, that no measures of consequence can be transacted without his permission.

Among the ecclesiastical buildings, the cathedral is the principal, both its out and inside being incrusted with white and black marble, in alternate rows.

In the two vessels for holy water, at the entrance of the church, are two marble fish, so exquisitely per-

performed, that they appear to ſwim in them. Here are, alſo, ſeveral fine marble ſtatues of Popes, who were natives of Sienna. Mabillon tells us, that formerly the buſt of pope Joan was alſo among them, with this inſcription under it, Joannes VIII. *Fœmina de Anglia.* "John VIII. an Engliſhwoman;" but it has been long ſince taken away. The ſame author ſays, it was altered to pope Zachary; but Baronius affirms, that it was abſolutely broken to pieces and deſtroyed.

Among the reliques of the cathedral, are the right arm of John the Baptiſt, and the ſword with which Peter cut off the ear of Malchus. The latter cannot, indeed, properly, be called a relique, and the ſacriſtan himſelf aſſured us, that no veneration is paid to it, but conſidered only as a curious antique; it is, however, carefully preſerved, and the three principal perſons of Sienna have each a key to it. The hilt is of white ivory, and the blade two ſpans and an half in length, reſembling a large knife. In the Dominican church is the head of St. Catharine of Sienna; one of her countrymen, after her death at Rome, having ſevered it from the body, and brought it to Sienna, where it is kept with the higheſt veneration, and only exhibited to view twice a year. The Dominicans here pretend to have in their poſſeſſion the wedding-ring which our Saviour gave her at the ſolemnization of their nuptials, which, they profanely ſay, were performed with the utmoſt magnificence, king David aſſiſting and playing on the harp. The houſe in which ſhe reſided at Sienna with her parents, is now an oratory; and her private chamber a chapel, decorated in the moſt profuſe manner with ſtucco-work, ſculpture, painting, and gilding. Here they ſhew the window, through which they pretend Chriſt often uſed to come and viſit her. The ſtory of the five ſtigmata, or marks, impreſſed on her by our Saviour, is too well known to need repetition; and with ſuch ridiculous ſtories ſeveral books, pub-

liſhed

lished with the knowledge and approbation of the superior clergy of the Romish church, have been filled.

The hilly situation of the city has occasioned a bridge to be built across a street near the Dominican church; but this structure is of no remarkable height, nor are any buildings under it like that in the city of Genoa.

Sienna embraced the opportunity of the German interregnum to recover its liberty; but its repose was very inconsiderable, from the intestine commotions among its principal families, particularly those of Malatesta and Petruzzi. In 1554, the emperor Charles V. entirely reduced the city under his dominion, and by his abdication afterward in 1556, it devolved to his son Philip II. king of Spain, who ceded it to Cosmo I. duke of Florence, in consideration of a large sum of money, and a promise that he would not assist the French. Some maritime places were however excepted, as Piombino, Orbitello, Telamone, Porto Hercole, Porto St. Stefano, and Porto Longono, together with the island of Elva, which district was called Stato degli Presidii, from the Spaniards keeping garrisons in these places.

In travelling from Sienna to Radicofani, during the two first stages, or till you arrive at Buonconvento, the country is remarkably fertile, and affords the most inchanting prospect; being regularly planted with rows of trees, and covered with vines and olives. But after you have passed this part, the face of the country is less agreeable, its appearance being somewhat more rough and barren. Buonconvento is famous in history, as the place where Henry VII. was poisoned in receiving the sacrament from Bernardo di Montepolitiano, a Dominican monk, in 1313. But the death of the emperor Henry VII. is not the only instance in which priests have abused the sacrament for the accomplishing their revenge. Hieronymo Savina, abbot of St. Maria di Misericordia, was convicted

convicted of the ſame deteſtable crime at Venice. Careus affirms, that pope Adrian VI. was, at the inſtigation of the cardinals, taken off by a poiſoned hoſt. And the ſame villainous action was committed by biſhop Arnefaſt, at Aarhus, in the year 1259, upon Chriſtopher I. king of Denmark, as appears from Hojer's hiſtory of Denmark.

Ten Italian miles from Viterbo toward Rome, at a diſtance from the high road, is the palace of Caprarola, belonging to the duke of Parma. It was built by cardinal Alexander Farneſe, in the ſixteenth century, under the direction of the celebrated architect Giacomo Barocci da Vignola. The ſtructure on the outſide is of a pentagonal form, reſembling a citadel; but the inner court, which is decorated with galleries, is perfectly circular; and yet all the apartments are ſquare and well proportioned. The whole art conſiſts in the different thickneſs of the party-walls. The city of Rome, though thirty Italian miles diſtant, may be ſeen from the top of this palace. The magnificent ſtair-caſe and whiſpering-hall in this palace are particularly admired. In the latter, four perſons ſtanding cloſe to the wall, and over againſt each other, may converſe, while a fifth, ſtanding in the center, will be intirely ignorant of what is ſaid. Upon ſtamping with the foot in the middle of the floor, thoſe without hear a noiſe like the report of a piſtol.

The diſtance between Ronciglioni and Monte Roſi, a well built place, is ſeven Italian miles; and that between Monte Roſi and Baccano the ſame. All the country between Ronciglioni and Storta is mountainous, and the roads very bad. Agriculture is here totally neglected, ſo that the land is over-run with a kind of long heath: had the country been under any other prince, than the ſucceſſor of St. Peter, it would doubtleſs have been long ſince cultivated, as it does not want for water, and might be uſed to advantage in breeding of cattle. But the inhabitants are rendered ſlothful by oppreſſion, well knowing, that the more they acquire by their induſtry, the more they will be expoſed to exactions, till they ſink at laſt under the preſſure of poverty. Near Baccano are ſome ſulphur mines, which produce a conſiderable profit to the papal treaſury.

The rivulet Cremera iſſues from the Lago di Baccano, and after croſſing the road, falls into the Tiber, about three miles from hence. At preſent it is called La Varca; and famous in ancient hiſtory for the ſurpriſe and ſlaughter of the Fabii by the Vejentes.

Nine Italian miles to the northward of Rome, Sixtus V. cauſed a large wood to be deſtroyed, in order to deprive the robbers of a place of retreat, and at the ſame time to open a free paſſage for the north wind to the country about Rome: and accordingly, the air in that city is rendered much more healthy; and alſo, the noxious effects of the ſouth in a great meaſure prevented. For the ſame reaſon, the woods lying to the ſouthward of Rome are not ſuffered to be cut down, becauſe they defend the city and adjacent country from the effects of the Sirocco, or ſouth-eaſt wind, which, being loaded with exhalations, ariſing from moraſſes and ſtagnating water, would otherwiſe prove very prejudicial to the health of the inhabitants.

END of the FOURTH VOLUME.

www.ingramcontent.com/pod-product-compliance
Lightning Source LLC
Chambersburg PA
CBHW022105300426
44117CB00007B/598

* 9 7 8 3 7 4 4 7 9 4 1 7 6 *